Articles Describing Archives and Manuscript Collections in the United States

Articles Describing Archives and Manuscript Collections in the United States

An Annotated Bibliography

Compiled by
Donald L. DeWitt

Bibliographies and Indexes in Library and Information Science,
Number 11

GREENWOOD PRESS
Westport, Connecticut • London

Library of Congress Cataloging-in-Publication Data

DeWitt, Donald L., 1938–
    Articles describing archives and manuscript collections in the
  United States : an annotated bibliography / compiled by Donald L.
  DeWitt.
        p. cm.—(Bibliographies and indexes in library and
  information science, ISSN 0742–6879 ; no. 11)
      Includes bibliographical references and index.
      ISBN 0–313–29598–0 (alk. paper)
        1. Archives—United States—Bibliography. 2. Manuscripts—United
  States—Collections—Bibliography. 3. Libraries—United States—
  Special collections—Manuscripts—Bibliography. 4. United States—
  History—Sources—Bibliography. 5. United States—History—
  Manuscripts—Bibliography. I. Title. II. Series.
  CD3022.A2D478   1997
  016.973—dc21   96–37042

British Library Cataloguing in Publication Data is available.

Library of Congress Catalog Card Number: 96–37042
ISBN: 0–313–29598–0
ISSN: 0742–6879

First published in 1997

Greenwood Press, 88 Post Road West, Westport, CT 06881
An imprint of Greenwood Publishing Group, Inc.

Printed in the United States of America

The paper used in this book complies with the
Permanent Paper Standard issued by the National
Information Standards Organization (Z39.48–1984).

10 9 8 7 6 5 4 3 2 1

Contents

Contents

Introduction

This bibliography is intended as a companion volume to *Guides to Archives and Manuscript Collections in the United States: An Annotated Bibliography* published by Greenwood Press in 1994. My original intent was to include journal articles in *Guides to Archives and Manuscript Collections*, but space limitations prevented their use. It was obvious, though, that there were enough articles for another bibliography, and that many of these articles could be useful to researchers.

Articles describing manuscript collections, archives, or special collections of unpublished sources constitute a subgenre of historical literature. For decades, the bibliographical article has been a traditional way to publicize and improve access to unique collections of unpublished resources that are potentially valuable to researchers. While these articles embrace several academic disciplines, they are the most useful to researchers using the historical method. The authors of these articles sought to inform readers about the existence of specific collections and to analyze collections of papers or records in a way that might help researchers formulate reference questions or make a decision to personally visit an archive. The purpose of this bibliography is to further assist researchers in locating and evaluating primary sources pertinent to their research by bringing together articles describing unpublished resources into a single volume.

Many of the articles cited may be found in other guides, bibliographies, or directories published in traditional print or electronic formats. The value of this bibliography, however, lies in the time saved from consulting one source as opposed to several. The annotations in this bibliography may also help researchers decide the usefulness of titles that appear to be of marginal interest. Also, for those planning to write bibliographical essays, knowing of and reviewing what has already been done is a preliminary step. Hopefully, this bibliography may make that process easier and quicker as well.

The articles cited date from the 1890s to the mid-1990s and describe photograph collections, oral history and sound recording collections, motion pictures, radio and television programs, selected art works, machine readable records, and traditional textual materials. They fall into several categories. There are articles that describe material by identifying record series, inclusive dates, volume, and informational content of manuscript collections and record groups. Others relate the administrative background of record groups, the history of record-creating agencies or organizations, and the provenance of manuscript collections. Some are narrower in scope as they describe only specific record series or a specific manuscript type such as diaries, literary manuscripts, or letters. Another typical category is the article that serves as a directory to repositories holding similar records or manuscript collections. Closely allied to directory articles are those that describe holdings of repositories or special collections in general terms. Yet another type analyzes the informational content and research value of record series, manuscripts, or other unpublished resources. Finally, there are collection inventories listing materials at the folder, box, or collection levels, and calendars with their descriptions of individual documents, manuscripts, or letters.

A few categories of articles were excluded. They included articles describing single documents; those reproducing complete or edited texts of documents; descriptions of exhibitions incorporating documents; and photographic essays reproducing selected photographs instead of describing the collection. Also excluded were newsletter articles, accessioning notes, and acquisition reports. An occasional exception was made for photo essays, exhibition descriptions, and acquisition reports if the article seemed especially informative about a collection or about the type of materials described.

The bibliography is organized topically under thirteen broad headings and forty-six subheadings. Entries appear under each subheading alphabetically by author surname. Every citation includes an entry number, author's name, full title, journal title, volume number, quarter and year of publication, page numbers, and, with a few exceptions, an annotation. If the date of publication does not include an issue number or quarter of issue, the serial may be an annual or a rare instance where a publisher did not identify issues sequentially. The annotations are intended either to clarify or expand upon information conveyed by titles; identify the people and events documented by the papers or records described; or identify the types of materials in a collection and the information they contain. A few citations are unannotated because the journal was not available for review or could not be obtained before the publication deadline.

Key words in an article's title most frequently determined the placement of a citation under a specific heading. At times, placement became arbitrary when an article commented on multiple topics and could be placed under more than one heading. In those instances, the author's principal theme became the deciding factor. Articles having secondary themes, subjects, or categories of materials are brought together in the index under the appropriate entries.

The index is keyed to citation entry numbers. It integrates authors of articles with the names of people, subjects, and repositories appearing in both article titles and annotations. Most of the topical subheadings in the Table of Contents also appear in the index to identify those articles that might appear under more than one heading.

While I encountered no other bibliography devoted solely to articles describing archives and manuscript collections, many standard reference works include some of the citations in this bibliography. Among those consulted and found especially useful were the National Historical Publications and Records Commission's *Directory of Archives and Manuscript Repositories in the United States*, 2nd edition, Phoenix: 1988; Philip Hamer's *A Guide to Archives and Manuscripts in the United States*, New Haven: 1961; Frank B. Evans' *Modern Archives and Manuscripts: A Select Bibliography*, Chicago: 1975; Patricia Andrews' *Writings on Archives, Historical Manuscripts, and Current Records: 1979-1982*, Washington, D.C.: 1985; the Modern Language Association's *American Literary Manuscripts: A Checklist of Holdings in Academic, Historical, and Public Libraries, Museums, and Author's Homes in the United States*, 2nd edition, Athens: 1977; Ray Allen Billington's "Guides to American History Manuscript Collections in Libraries of the United States," *Mississippi Valley Historical Review* (December 1951); Edmund L. Binsfeld's "Church Archives in the United States and Canada: A Bibliography," *American Archivist* (July 1958); *Library Literature*, New York: 1933- ; and *America: History and Life*, Santa Barbara: 1964- . The quarterly bibliographies appearing in the *American Archivist* also provided many entries as did the footnotes and bibliographies in published guides and directories.

In closing I want to acknowledge the work of Shirley Clark, administrative assistant at the Western History Collections. Mrs. Clark's skill and knowledge of word processing saved a great deal of time and effort during the compilation of this bibliography. Her contribution to this bibliography was substantial and greatly appreciated.

Articles Describing Archives and Manuscript Collections in the United States

General Collections

Archives and Manuscripts

1. Akeroyd, Richard and Russell Benedict. "A Directory of Ephemera Collections in a National Underground Network." *Wilson Library Bulletin* 48 (November 1973): 236-254.

   The collections reviewed are at the Universities of Nevada-Reno; California-Berkeley; Virginia; Kansas; Iowa; New York; Buffalo; and Connecticut; and at the Hoover Institute, Stanford; North Las Vegas Library; Tamiment Library; Tulane University; and Washington University-St. Louis.

2. Ames, Herman V. "Report of the Public Archives Commission." *Annual Report of the American Historical Association for the Year 1903* 1 (1904): 407-664.

   Public records and manuscript holdings in the archives of Colorado, Georgia, Mississippi, New Jersey, Rhode Island, and Virginia are included in this report. The Georgia, New Jersey, Rhode Island, and Virginia reviews are the most informative.

3. Brown, Clayton. "Rural Electrification: Sources for the South and West." *Government Publications Review* 7A (March/April 1980): 139-143.

   The author cites several manuscript collections relating to the REA in state archives, public libraries, and university special collections, and provides a review of REA records in the U.S. National Archives.

4. Brown, Richard Maxwell. "The Archives of Violence." *American Archivist* 41 (October 1978): 431-443.

   The author reviews archives he has used that hold collections and record groups with information on violence in the U.S. He cites some specific record series and collections.

5. Brubaker, Robert L. "Manuscript Collections." *Library Trends* 13 (October 1964): 226-253.

   A broad overview of manuscript collections, mostly in state and local historical societies and university libraries. Description is limited to the size and scope of collections cited.

6. Bruce, William J. "The San Francisco UNCIO Documents." *American Archivist* 9 (January 1946): 6-16.

    Bruce describes the records created as a result of the United Nations Conference on International Organization in San Francisco, California, between April 25 and June 26, 1945.

7. Carl-Mitchell, Charlotte. "Medieval and Renaissance Manuscripts at the HRHRC." *Library Chronicle of the University of Texas at Austin* New Series 35 (1986): 89-105.

    The author reviews pre-1700 manuscripts held by the Humanities Research Center. These holdings include codices, legal documents, and fragments or parts of manuscripts.

8. Carl-Mitchell, Charlotte and Karen Gould. "A List of HRHRC Medieval and Renaissance Manuscripts." *Library Chronicle of the University of Texas at Austin* New Series 35 (1986): 107-113.

    Each entry includes the Humanities Research Center's I.D. number, author, title or description, place of origin, language, date, size, collection in which held, physical characteristics, and a cross-reference to Seymour de Ricci's three-volume census.

9. Claus, Robert. "The United Nations Archives." *American Archivist* 10 (April 1947): 129-132.

    A short article that describes four record groups. They include the records of the U.N. Preparatory Commission 1945-46; the Princeton Mission 1940-46; the San Francisco Conference 1945; and record copies of U.N. official documents.

10. Clement, Richard W. "Resources for Scholars: Medieval Manuscripts in Two Illinois Libraries." *Library Quarterly* 57 (January 1987): 61-80.

    The two libraries are the Regenstein Library at the University of Chicago and the main library, University of Illinois, Urbana-Champaign. Specific collections at each are described in general terms, usually noting volume and types of manuscripts in each.

11. Constantine, Richard W., and Arthur C. Detmers. "The Papers of Julius W. Pratt, 1905-1972: A Descriptive Inventory." *Niagara Frontier* 22 (Summer 1975): 39-44.

12. Dodds, Harold W. "The Garrett Collection of Manuscripts." *Princeton University Library Chronicle* 3 (June 1942): 113-115.

    This is a brief introduction to the Robert Garrett Collection of Islamic, Greek, Persian, Indic, and European manuscripts relating to the sciences and the arts. The entire issue is devoted to this collection which includes the following articles:

1. Egbert, Donald D. "The Western European Manuscripts." 123-130.

2. Friend, Albert M. "The Greek Manuscripts." 131-135.

3. Hitti, Philip K. "The Arabic and Islamic Manuscripts." 116-122.

4. Johnson, Allan C. "The Papyri." 141-144.

5. Poleman, Horace I. "The Indic Manuscripts." 145-148.

6. Wilson, J. Christy. "The Persian and Indo-Persian Miniatures." 136-139.

13. Dougall, Richardson. "The Archives and Documents of the Preparatory Commission of the United Nations." *American Archivist* 10 (January 1947): 25-34.
   The records described in this article document the early arrangements for the first sessions of the U.N.'s General Assembly, Security Council, and Economic and Social Council, Trusteeship Council, and the establishment of the Secretariat.

14. Erlandsson, Alf. "Archives of the United Nations." *Archivaria* 7 (Winter 1978): 5-15.
   Erlandsson reviews the administrative history of the U.N. and identifies its component agencies and the record groups that document its function. This article would be useful for those planning research in U.N. records.

15. Fleming, John V. "Medieval Manuscripts in the Taylor Library." *Princeton University Library Chronicle* 38 (Winter/Spring 1977): 107-119.
   Fleming describes the ten 14th-century manuscript books in the Taylor Collection which, he notes, represent the major English authors and literary styles of the late middle ages.

16. Fleming, John V. "The Old English Manuscripts in the Scheide Library." *Princeton University Library Chronicle* 37 (Winter 1976): 126-138.
   Fleming describes the contents and literary values of two rare pre-Norman Conquest manuscripts at Princeton, the will of Æthelgifu and the Blickling Homilies.

17. Hammack, David C. "Private Organizations, Public Purposes: Nonprofits and Their Archives." *Journal of American History* 76 (June 1989): 181-191.
   The author cites several large collections of records of private foundations, charities, and social service agencies as valuable resources for historians. He also identifies repositories holding these records.

18. Herzstein, Robert E. "The Recently Opened United Nations War Crimes Archives: A Researcher's Comment." *American Archivist* 52 (Spring 1989): 208-213.

    This article briefly describes U.N. archives' holdings which include minutes and other meeting records of the War Crimes Commission and its committees, lists of war criminals and suspects, and records of trials of both Japanese and German nationals.

19. Holland, William L. "Source Materials on the Institute of Pacific Relations: Bibliographical Note." *Pacific Affairs* 58 (Spring 1985): 91-97.

    The author identifies U.S. and foreign repositories holding the institute's records. He cites record series titles, volume, and inclusive dates. Holland also identifies published materials documenting the institute's history.

20. Jameson, John Franklin. "The Colonial Assemblies and Their Legislative Journals." *Annual Report of the American Historical Association for the Year 1897* (1898): 403-453.

    A checklist of the journals with inclusive dates, number of volumes, their location at the time, and notes of journals that are missing. Canadian assemblies are included.

21. Jameson, John Franklin. "Report of the Historical Manuscripts Commission of the American Historical Association." *Annual Report of the American Historical Association for the Year 1896* 1 (1897): 467-512.

    Appended to the report (pages 483-512) is a bibliography of printed guides to records and manuscript collections in federal and state archives and state historical societies.

22. Jameson, John Franklin. "Third Annual Report of the Historical Manuscripts Commission." *Annual Report of the American Historical Association for the Year 1898* (1899): 567-745.

    The report contains three appendices that are useful: a state-by-state list of historical manuscripts in libraries and archives; a "Calendar of the Letters of John C. Calhoun;" and an indexed "Guide to the Items Relating to American History in the Reports of the English Historical Manuscripts Commission and Their Appendixes."

23. "The Annie Burr Jennings Collection and the Banks Papers." *Yale University Library Gazette* 14 (April 1940): 53-58.

    This collection contains Aaron Burr and George Washington correspondence, letters from English literary personalities, and the letters and papers (1763-1819) of botanist Sir Joseph Banks.

24. Knox, Bernard M. W. "The Ziskind Collection of Greek Manuscripts." *Yale University Library Gazette* 32 (October 1957): 39-56.

Knox describes sixty-one, 11th- to 18th-century manuscripts of philosophical, military, and scientific writings; Biblical texts; and some church records. A descriptive checklist of titles, dates, physical description, and content notes concludes the article.

25. MacDonald, William. "Report of the Public Archives Commission." *Annual Report of the American Historical Association for the Year 1900* 2 (1901): 5-297.

Volume two describes public records and manuscript collections in Connecticut, Indiana, Iowa, Massachusetts, Michigan, Nebraska, New York, North Carolina, Pennsylvania, and Wisconsin. The New York section is the most thorough. The report includes an index.

26. MacDonald, William. "Report of the Public Archives Commission." *Annual Report of the American Historical Association for the Year 1902* 1 (1903): 331-364.

This report includes descriptions of Oregon records and the Bexar Archives held by the University of Texas, Austin. The Oregon report lists record series and inclusive dates while the Bexar records are described in narrative fashion.

27. MacPhail, Ian and Laurence C. Witten, II. "The Mellon Collection of Alchemy and the Occult." *Yale University Library Gazette* 41 (July 1966): 1-15.

Part one of this article describes printed materials, part two, the manuscripts in the collection. The manuscripts include writings on alchemy, astronomy, astrology, and medicine, dating from the 13th to the 20th century.

28. Marston, Thomas E. "The Collection of Henry Fletcher." *Yale University Library Gazette* 29 (July 1954): 9-12.

Fletcher collected Biblical and medieval manuscripts. This article describes some of the key items in his collection now at Yale.

29. Middleton, Arthur P., and Douglass Adair. "The Mystery of the Horn Papers." *William and Mary Quarterly* 3rd Series 4 (October 1947): 409-445.

A history of the investigation into the authenticity of the diaries and related documents of Jacob and Christopher Horn, assembled and published by W. F. Horn in 1945. The papers were declared fakes.

30. Miller, James E. "La conduite de la guerre economique aux U.S.A.: Organisation, sources et bibliographie." *Cashiers d'histoire de la seconde guerre mondiale* 4 (1976): 203-220.

31. Simmons, Jerold. "The County Courthouse as an Archives: Local Government Sources for the History of the Central Plains." *Government Publications Review* 8A (November/December 1981): 485-497.
     Simmons reviews the typical offices of county government and discusses the types of records found in each, along with their research value.

32. Thwaites, Reuben G. "Fifth Annual Report of the Historical Manuscripts Commission." *Annual Report of the American Historical Association for the Year 1900* 1 (1901): 587-623.
     The report lists newly found correspondence of Andrew Jackson and a supplement to manuscript holdings reported in the third annual report. Appendix two is a calendar of Adm. George Cranfield Berkeley's "North American Papers."

33. Watt, D. C. "U.S. Documentary Resources for the Study of British Foreign Policy, 1919-1959." *International Affairs* 38 (January 1962): 63-72.
     Watt cites manuscript collections of U.S. statesmen and presidents in the Library of Congress, presidential libraries, the National Archives, and colleges and universities. He includes comments on the research values of each.

Maps, Oral Histories, and Photographs

34. Adams, Thomas R. "A List of Eighteenth-Century Manuscript Maps of New England Yearly Meetings." *Quaker History* 52 (Spring 1963): 6-9.

35. Bauner, Ruth. "The Dewey School Photographs." *ICarbS* 4 (Summer/Fall 1978): 25-40.

36. Beliman, James. "The University of Iowa Oral History Project." *Books at Iowa* 27 (November 1977): 21-29.
     Beliman provides the background for an oral history of the University of Iowa. The article concludes with a review of fourteen subject areas covered in the history and a checklist of informants.

37. Brown, Lloyd A. "Manuscript Maps in the William L. Clements Library." *American Neptune* 1 (April 1941): 141-148.
     Brown identifies key maps among the 550 then in the library. They date from 1755 to 1800 and focus on British possessions in North America and the West Indies.

38. "Check List of Maps and Atlases Relating to the City of New York in the New York Public Library." *Bulletin of the New York Public Library* 5

(February 1901): 60-73.
    The list is presented chronologically beginning with 1610 and ending with 1900. Entries include title, publisher and type of printing, scale, and size.

39. "Check List of Maps Relating to the City of Brooklyn and to Kings County." *Bulletin of the New York Public Library* 6 (March 1903): 84-88.
    The list is presented chronologically beginning with 1750 and ending with 1898. Entries include title, publisher and type of printing, scale, and size.

40. Ciampoli, Judith. "Images as Chronicle: The Pictorial History Collections." *Gateway Heritage* 1 (Summer 1980): 28-33.
    This article reviews the prominent photograph collections held by the Missouri Historical Society in St. Louis. The photographs document the development of St. Louis, its society, and the American West.

41. Cox, Richard J. "Trouble on the Chain Gang: City Surveying, Maps, and the Absence of Urban Planning in Baltimore, 1730-1823, with a Checklist of Maps of the Periods." *Maryland Historical Magazine* 81 (Spring 1986): 8-49.
    Mostly a historical essay on city planning, but the checklist includes 401 maps of the Baltimore area. Each entry includes map title, source of map, date, and location of the map. There is also an index to the checklist.

42. Daniell, Jere R. "The Dartmouth College Oral History Project." *Dartmouth College Library Bulletin* 25 (April 1985): 107-109.
    Daniell provides a checklist of Dartmouth presidents, trustees, administrative officers and staff, and faculty who have interviews on file in the archives.

43. Day, James M., and Ann B. Dunlap. "The Map Collection of the Texas State Archives." *Southwestern Historical Quarterly* 65 (January 1962): 399-439; (April 1962): 539-574; and 66 (July 1962): 103-132; and (October 1962): 271-303.
    The authors list the maps in chronological order and include titles, cartographers/publishers, scale, size, and, in some cases, comments on the maps features. This series was published as a monograph in 1964.

44. Deller, Howard and J. B. Harley. "The World by Lake Michigan." *Map Collector* 50 (Spring 1990): 2-9.
    The authors provide an overview of the American Geographical Society map collection in the Golda Meir Library at the University of Wisconsin, Milwaukee. They cite many key maps in the collection.

45. Dexter, Lorraine. "American Collections of Stereoscopic Photographs." *Eye to Eye* 5 (June 1954): 3-23.

46. Dicker, Laverne Mau. "Watkins' Photographs in the California Historical Society Library." *California History* 57 (Fall 1978): 266-267.

    While this entire issue is devoted to Carleton E. Watkins' photography, this short article lists the holdings of his photographs. There are three groups included: stereographs, non-stereo views, and albums and oversize prints.

47. Dixon, Ford. "Texas History in Maps: An Archival and Historical Examination of the James Perry Bryan Map Collection." *Texana* 5 (Summer 1967): 99-116; and (Fall 1967): 238-267.

    At the time Dixon wrote this article, James Bryan still owned the collection. The first part reviews Texas cartography and the history of the collection. The second part is an annotated list of 122 maps dated from 1513 to 1887.

48. Fern, Alan and Milton Kaplan. "John Plumbe, Jr., and the First Architectural Photographs of the Nation's Capitol." *Quarterly Journal of the Library of Congress* 31 (January 1974): 3-20.

    Plumbe was one of the country's early daguerreotypists. This article describes a small collection of his work dating back to the 1840s. It concludes with a checklist of seventy-nine of his daguerreotypes of individuals, buildings, and monuments.

49. Ferris, Ruth. "The D.C. Humphreys Collection of Glass Negatives." *Missouri Historical Society Bulletin* 17 (October 1960): 57-60.

    Humphreys was a member of a U.S. Army Corps of Engineers team surveying the Missouri River in the 1880s. The photographs are scenes of upper Missouri River area landmarks; St. Louis, Missouri; steamboats; and Indians. The article cites 167 images.

50. Fox, Arthur B. "Notes on the Map Collection in the Historical Society of Western Pennsylvania Archives." *Pittsburgh History* 74 (Spring 1991): 29-31.

    Fox gives an overview of more than 550 maps. He divides them into maps of Pittsburgh; Allegheny County; Western Pennsylvania; Pennsylvania; the U.S.; and specialized maps.

51. Frederick, Richard. "Photographer Asahel Curtis: Chronicler of the Northwest." *American West* 17 (November/December 1980): 26-40.

    Frederick includes useful information about the topical content of the Curtis Collection at the Washington State Historical Society. Asahel Curtis was Edward S. Curtis' brother.

52. "The Fritz Henle Collection at the Harry Ransom Humanities Research Center." *Library Chronicle of the University of Texas at Austin* New Series

48 (1989): 87-108.

This article describes the photograph collection of Fritz Henle. The photos represent Henle's work worldwide and include 1,000-plus images of Asia; the Middle East; Europe; southern Europe; Mexico, the U.S.; and the Caribbean countries.

53. Garvin, Carney E. S. "Bonfils and the Early Photography of the Near East." *Harvard Library Bulletin* 26 (October 1978): 442-470.

Garvin describes a long-forgotten photograph collection of 28,000 images of the Levant discovered in the attic of Harvard's Semitic Museum. The article concludes with comments on Félix Bonfils' photographic skills.

54. Grimes, Jack. "Owen Wister: Photographer." *Texas Libraries* 31 (Fall (1969): 130-133.

Grimes calls attention to a collection of fifty-four Texas-related photographs in the Archives Division of the Texas State Library that Wister took.

55. Hafsted, Margaret R. "The Society's Map Collection." *Wisconsin Magazine of History* 52 (Spring 1969): 223-238.

A general description of the origin and development of the State Historical Society of Wisconsin's large and comprehensive map collection.

56. Hébert, John R. "Maps by Ephraim George Squier, Journalist, Scholar, and Diplomat." *Quarterly Journal of the Library of Congress* 29 (January 1972): 2-13.

Squier served as a U.S. diplomat to Latin America and is also known as an amateur archeologist. This article describes a collection of thirty-eight maps of Central America and Peru. A checklist offering a bibliographic description of each concludes the article.

57. Hobart, George S. "The Matson Collection: A Half Century of Photography of the Middle East." *Quarterly Journal of the Library of Congress* 30 (January 1973): 19-43.

This article describes the highlights of a 20,000-image collection of photographs of Palestine and the Middle East taken by Eric Matson. The photographs date from the 1890s to 1946.

58. Hollowak, Thomas L. "Maryland Maps in the Peabody Collection." *Maryland Historical Magazine* 87 (Spring 1992): 72-87.

This is a checklist beginning with Baltimore maps, followed by maps of Maryland state and counties; military maps; transportation maps; and maps of bodies of water.

59. Hoover, Catherine and Robert Sawchuck. "From the Place We Hear

About: A Descriptive Checklist of Pictorial Lithographs and Letter Sheets in the CHS Collection. *California Historical Quarterly* 56 (Winter 1977/1978): 346-367.

The authors divide the holdings into nine groups: letter sheets, urban views, sites of interest, portraits, the gold rush and mining, cartoons and political satire, events and celebrations, architecture, and scenery and natural wonders.

60. Humphreys, Hubert. "Oral History Research in Louisiana: An Overview." *Louisiana History* 20 (Fall 1979): 353-371.

While not describing oral history collections, this article identifies the major oral history projects in Louisiana and the institutions that hold the interviews.

61. Ireland, Florence. "The Northeast Archives of Folklore and Oral History: A Brief Description and Catalog of its Holdings 1958-1972." *Northeast Folklore* 13 (1972): 1-86.

Ireland cites 744 collections. See, however, Edward Ives' article below for a more current listing of this archive's holdings.

62. Ives, Edward D. "The Northeast Archives of Folklore and Oral History: A Catalog of the First 1800 Accessions." *Northeast Folklore* 24/25 (1983/ 1984): 5-236.

This is an update of Florence Ireland's catalog that appeared in volume 13 (1972) of *Northeast Folklore*. The entries in Ives' catalog include collection title, date and location of interview, length of transcript, and subjects treated in the interview.

63. Jehs, Randall W. "A Survey of Oral History Collections in Indiana." *Indiana Magazine of History* 68 (December 1972): 315-337.

The author lists oral history interviews held by several Indiana institutions alphabetically by informant's surname. Entries include a synopsis of the interview, the dates covered in the interview, and length of the transcript.

64. Jillson, Willard R. "Early Kentucky Maps (1673-1825)." *Register of the Kentucky Historical Society* 47 (October 1949): 265-293; and 48 (January 1950): 32-52.

Jillson provides titles; cartographers' names; places of publication, if published; dates; and extensive annotations. The annotations include, at least, the name of one repository holding the map.

65. Johnson, Carol. "Texas and Houston, 1836-1846: Maps in the Houston Public Library's Collection." *Houston Review* 14 (No. 3 1992): 175-192.

The author cites specific maps held by the library, mostly by the names of publishers or cartographers. Description includes the distinguishing features of each map.

66. Kantor, J.R.K. "From the University of California Archives--Muybridge Views of Berkeley in 1874." *California History* 57 (Winter 1978/1979): 376-381.

   The collection described is one of stereographic views taken in 1874 by Eadweard Muybridge of the then new University of California at Berkeley campus. The photos are in the Bancroft Library.

67. Kennedy, Martha. "The California Historical Society's Collection of Daguerreotypes." *California History* 60 (Winter 1981/1982): 370-375.

   Kennedy reports that the society has more than 100 daguerreotypes in its photograph collection and reviews some of the better examples.

68. Kilgo, Dolores. "The Robyn Collection of Langenheim Calotypes." *Gateway Heritage* 6 (Fall 1985): 28-37.

   Eduard Robyn assembled this collection of 152 salted-paper prints made from calotypes. Most of the prints are of city views and landmarks of Philadelphia. The collection is in the Missouri Historical Society, St. Louis.

69. Kurutz, Gary F. "Courtesy of Title Insurance and Trust Company--The Historical Collection at CHS' Los Angeles History Center." *California History* 57 (Summer 1978): 186-194.

   Kurutz describes the Title Insurance and Trust Company photo collection of 18,650 prints and 13,500 negatives of Los Angeles and surrounding area for the period 1860-1930s. Most of the photos were taken by C. C. Pierce.

70. Kurutz, Gary F. "The Image of the Golden State: The Photograph Collection of the California State Library." *Journal of the West* 26 (April 1987): 68-74.

   The author cites many collection titles in this overview of the library's photographs. He notes the collection's geographical strengths are the Sacramento Valley and the San Francisco Bay areas and the "mother lode" counties of California.

71. Kurutz, Gary F. "Pictorial Resources: The Henry E. Huntington Library's California and American West Collection." *California Historical Quarterly* 54 (Summer 1975): 175-182.

   The article provides good coverage of the library's photograph collections with lesser attention given to prints, sketches, and watercolors.

72. Kurutz, Gary F. "Portrait of the Golden State--The California State

Library's Photography Collection." *California History* 60 (Fall 1981): 290-295.

Kurutz reports there are about 50,000 photographs in the state library. He reviews the prominent collections noting the subject content and time period of the photographs.

73. Lage, Ann. "Voices from the Past: The Sierra Club's Oral History Program." *California History* 71 (Summer 1992): 239-253.

The narrative is about the program and potential research uses of the interviews. The article concludes with a checklist of interviews conducted and held by the Regional Oral History Office, UC-Berkeley.

74. Lewis, William D. "Catalogue of the Maps in the Christopher Ward Collection at the University of Delaware." *Delaware Notes* 22 (1949): 67-88.

Lewis describes seventy-one maps of North America, the U.S., New England, and Delaware, dating from 1709 to 1941. Entries include cartographer or publisher, the presence of color, size, scale, and insets.

75. Lowing, Robert. "Airplanes, Automobiles, and Commercial Photography: The Darmstaetter Collection." *Journal of the Lancaster County Historical Society* 93 (Winter 1991): 30-45.

76. Martin, Robert S. "Treasures of the Cartographic History Library at the University of Texas at Arlington." *Map Collector* 25 (December 1983): 14-20.

Martin notes that the collecting focus at UT-Arlington is the American Southwest. He provides a thorough overview of the holdings while citing many key maps.

77. Martínez, Oscar J. "Chicano Oral History: Status and Prospects." *Aztlán* 9 (Spring/Summer 1978): 119-132.

An appendix to the article lists institutions with Chicano oral histories. Entries include project name, institutions, number of interviews, topics covered, geographical areas of interviews, and related access information.

78. Mason, Glenn. "The Libby Collection of Spokane, Washington." *Journal of the West* 28 (January 1989): 59-65.

Mason gives an overview of the collection of 150,000 negatives taken by professional photographers Charles A. Libby and his son Charles Jr. The images document the Spokane area from 1900 to 1980.

79. McComb, David G. "The Oral History of Colorado Project." *Colorado Magazine* 53 (Spring 1976): 185-199.

Most of the article is about the project. It concludes, however, with a checklist noting the length and focus of 116 interviews.

80. McKeen, Ona Lee. "Erwin Evans Smith: Cowboy Photographer."
    Quarterly Journal of Current Acquisitions 9 (May 1952): 133-136.
    McKeen describes the Library of Congress' Smith Collection of 1,800
    cowboy and ranching photographs. From 1905 to 1915, Smith photo-
    graphed the cowboy at work on ranches in the eastern New Mexico and
    Texas panhandle areas.

81. Morrow, Delores J. "Dakota Resources: The Haynes Photograph Collection
    at the Montana Historical Society." *South Dakota History* 12 (Spring 1982):
    65-73.
    F. Jay Haynes is known for his photographs of the Northern Pacific
    Railroad and Yellowstone National Park. This collection of more than
    20,000 images dates from 1876 to the 1960s and documents the park, the
    route of the Northern Pacific, and Haynes' travels.

82. Odgers, Charlotte H. "Federal Government Maps Relating to Pacific
    Northwest History." *Pacific Northwest Quarterly* 38 (July 1947): 261-272.
    A compilation of published maps arranged topically under headings such
    as Indian affairs, military departments and roads, federal surveys,
    railroads, postal routes, and states.

83. O'Kain, Dennis. "Documenting the Deep South: William E. Wilson,
    Photographer." *Georgia Review* 33 (Fall 1979): 662-680.
    Wilson's photographs are of Afro-American sharecroppers, the cotton
    industry, transportation, and other aspects of Southern life in the 1880s and
    1890s. A collection of 750 of his glass plates are in three Georgia archives
    cited in the article.

84. "Oral History Symposium." *Wilson Library Bulletin* 40 (March 1966): 599-
    633.
    This special issue of the *Wilson Library Bulletin* contains articles
    describing oral history projects. Each article provides project background,
    identifies many informants, and comments on the scope and content of the
    recordings. Included are:

    1. Allen, Richard B. "New Orleans Jazz Archive at Tulane." 619-623.

    2. Colman, Gould P. "Oral History at Cornell." 624-623.

    3. Kielman, Chester V. "The Texas Oil Industry Project." 616-618.

    4. Pogue, Forrest C. "The George C. Marshall Oral History Project."
       607-615.

85. Otto, Kathryn. "Dakota Resources: Insurance Maps at the South Dakota
    Historical Resource Center." *South Dakota History* 10 (Fall 1980): 334-
    339.
    The maps include 89 South Dakota towns from the Sanborn Map
    Company and 369 from the lesser-known Fire Underwriters Insurance
    Company of Minneapolis, Minnesota.

86. Pattison, William D. "Collector's Choice: The Photographs of A. J.
    Russell." *American West* 6 (May 1969): 20-23.
    Pattison describes a collection of 200 Russell glass plates which are part
    of the Stephen Sedgwick Collection held by the American Geographical
    Society. Russell is known for his photographs documenting the building
    of the Union Pacific Railroad.

87. "Paul Briol Negatives and Contact Prints." *Queen City Heritage* 47 (Fall,
    1989): 90-95.
    This is a checklist of topics and personalities represented in the Briol
    photograph collection. The number of prints for each subject is also stated.

88. Petterchak, Janice. "The Guy Mathis Collection." *Journal of the Illinois
    State Historical Society* 71 (November 1978): 288-298.
    Mathis was a photographer and automobile dealer. About 1,600 of his
    photographs documenting the Springfield, Illinois, area are in the society
    archives. Photographs of houses and buildings are a strength of the
    collection.

89. "Photographs and Photography in the Archives of American Art." *Archives
    of American Art Journal* 12 (No. 3 1972): 1-18.
    This article reviews the archives' photograph collections and its
    manuscript collections and oral histories documenting the work and careers
    of photographers.

90. Pollack, Jack H. "Tantalizing Glimpses of World's Biggest Stereographic
    Collection at University of California, Riverside." *Smithsonian* 9 (February
    1979): 88-95.
    Pollack provides an overview of the nearly 500,000-image Keystone-Mast
    Collection of stereo cards and glass negatives at the University of
    California-Riverside. Scenes of Czarist Russia are among its strengths.

91. Prater, Leland J. "Historical Forest Service Photo Collection." *Journal of
    Forest History* 18 (April 1974): 28-31.
    The author calls attention to the U.S. Forest Service's significant
    photograph collection. The article contains little description, but does
    include some information on how to access the collection.

92. Reichman, Jessica. "The Far-Mar-Co Collection: Photo Documentation of Rural America." *Journal of the West* 26 (April 1987): 63-67.

    Photographs in this collection are of Kansas and Nebraska places and people associated with the member cooperatives of the parent co-op, Far-Mar-Co. The collection is at Kansas State University.

93. Reynolds, G. Marshall. "From the Archives: Visual Reflections of California History: The Holt-Atherton Photo Collection." *Pacific Historian* 24 (Fall 1980): 252-255.

    Reynolds cites the titles of major collections in the archives and concludes with a list of thirty-seven subjects represented. The Holt-Atherton Photo Collection contains about 40,000 images.

94. Ristow, Walter W. "The Hauslab-Liechtenstein Map Collection." *Quarterly Journal of the Library of Congress* 35 (April 1978): 108-138.

    There are 3,600 maps in this collection assembled by Franz von Hauslab of Austria and subsequently purchased by Prince Johann II von Liechtenstein. The article relates the provenance of the collection and comments on some of the better maps.

95. Ristow, Walter W. "United States Fire Insurance and Underwriters Maps 1852-1968." *Quarterly Journal of the Library of Congress* 25 (July 1968): 194-218.

    A historical essay on the development of fire insurance maps in the U.S. with comments on the Library of Congress collection of these maps.

96. Rogers, Kim Lacy. "Oral History and the History of the Civil Rights Movement." *Journal of American History* 75 (September 1988): 567-576.

    While much of the article is about background and technique, the last four pages are devoted to repositories holding civil rights oral history collections and interviews of individuals who played a major role in the movement.

97. Salvaneschi, Lenore M. "The Rickels Photograph Collection at the State Historical Society of Iowa." *Annals of Iowa* 48 (Winter/Spring 1987): 450-455.

    Gerdjanssen Rickels was a Lutheran minister and amateur photographer. His collection of photographs document rural Iowa society from the 1920s through the 1940s. The article implies that the historical society also holds Rickels' diaries.

98. Saxon, Gerald D. "The Cartographic History Library of the University of Texas at Arlington." *Meridian* 6 (1991): 23-28.

    Saxon gives a brief background of the library, explains its collection policies, and provides an overview of its holdings.

99. Schwoerke, John. "The Peary Photographs." *Dartmouth College Library Bulletin* 26 (April 1986): 82-84.

This article calls attention to, and describes in general terms, a collection of 500 photographs taken by Robert E. Peary on his arctic expeditions.

100. Scotford, Anne H. "Photographic Records Now in Baker." *Dartmouth Library College Bulletin* 26 (November 1985): 44-47.

The author reviews an official college photograph collection begun in 1937. It contains over 100,000 photographs of college-related activities and personalities.

101. Sharp, Jay W. "A Collection of Printed Maps of Texas, 1835-1951, in the Eugene C. Barker Texas History Center." *Southwestern History Quarterly* 64 (July 1960): 96-123.

The article describes 131 maps. Each entry includes title, cartographer/publisher, date of publication, the repository catalog number, and comments on the map's features.

102. Sharp, Jay W. "The Maps of the Stephen F. Austin Collection in the Eugene C. Barker Texas History Center." *Southwestern History Quarterly* 64 (January 1961): 388-397.

These maps, of what is now Texas, date from 1822 to 1829. Entries include title, cartographer/publisher, date of publication, and comments on the map's features. The article describes thirty-six maps.

103. Smith, Murphy D. "Of Certain Manuscript Maps." *Manuscripts* 43 (Summer 1991): 215-231.

Smith reviews some of the key maps found in the American Philosophical Society's manuscript collections.

104. Smith-Baranzini, Marlene. "The CHS Southern California Historical Collection: New Location and New Opportunities for Historical Research." *California History* 70 (Winter 1991/1992): 397-405.

The author devotes most of the article to the society's photograph collections. The narrative is followed by a checklist of the photograph collections at the Regional History Center on the USC campus in Los Angeles.

105. Sneddeker, Duane R., Glen E. Holt, and Glenn S. Hensley. "The Block Brothers Photograph Collection: Treasure House on Grandel." *Gateway Heritage* 5 (Fall 1984): 12-35.

This article describes the huge collection of glass plate negatives, over 200,000, taken by Louis and Ephraim Block, documenting many levels of St. Louis society and the development of the city from 1910 through the 1930s.

106. Southall, Thomas. "The Photography Collection of the Helen Foresman Spencer Museum of Art." *Kansas Quarterly* 11 (Fall 1979): 77-84.
     This 1,000-image collection represents photography as art as opposed to a collection developed for topical or subject content. Significant groups of photos are described and the article ends with a list of twenty-one representative images.

107. Stephenson, Richard W. "The Henry Harrisse Collection of Publications, Papers, and Maps Pertaining to the Early Exploration of America." *Terrae Incognitae* 16 (1984): 37-55.
     The author reviews the content of the collection. While mostly published materials, it does include some 17th-century manuscript maps and hand copies of other rare maps.

108. Stephenson, Richard W. "Maps from the Peter Force Collection." *Quarterly Journal of the Library of Congress* 30 (July 1973): 183-204.
     The author reports there are over 750 maps in the collection that range from the 17th to the mid-19th century. Most are of North America and focus on the French and Indian War, the Revolutionary War, and the city of Washington, D.C.

109. "A Survey of Picture Collections Relating to Individual States." *Eye to Eye* 2 (September 1953): 36-40; and 3 (December 1953): 1-8.

110. Swem, Earl G. "Maps Relating to Virginia in the Virginia State Library and Other Departments of the Commonwealth with the 17th and 18th Century Atlas-Maps in the Library of Congress." *Bulletin of the Virginia State Library* 7 (April/July 1914): 41-263.
     Swem cites 2,036 maps in this article. He includes both manuscript and published maps. They appear chronologically beginning with 1590 and ending with 1914. Entries include titles, topographers, scale, and a note about color.

111. Tracy, Lorna. "Echoes in a Bottle." *Books at Iowa* 8 (April 1968): 24-29.
     Tracy gives an overview of the sound recording collection at the University of Iowa. In 1968, it included 2,200 recordings on several topics, but emphasized poetry and drama.

112. Turner, Decherd. "Photography at the Humanities Research Center." *Library Chronicle of the University of Texas at Austin* New Series 19 (1982): 16-18.
     This entire issue is devoted to photography and this article serves as an introduction to a series of articles describing photograph collections at the center. Each contains biographical information about the photographer, relates the provenance of the collection, states the types of photographs

and related materials that make up the collection, and cites specific images or groups of images as examples of the photographer's work. The articles are:

1. Colson, James B. "Stieglitz, Strand, and Straight Photography." 103-123.

   The photographer featured in this article is Alfred Stieglitz.

2. McCauley, Elizabeth Anne. "The Photographic Adventure of Maxine Du Camp." 19-51.

3. Powers, Mary C. "W.D. Smithers: Photographer-Journalist of the Southwest." 125-147.

4. Prescott, Gertrude Mae. "Public and Private Vision: The Photography of John Benjamin Dancer." 53-77.

5. Pyle, David. "The Ethnographic Photography of W. D. Smithers." 149-165.

6. Vertrees, Alan. "The Picture Making of Henry Peach Robinson." 79-101.

113. Turner, Terry J. "Gildersleeve Photographs Re-create Vanishing Era." *Texas Libraries* 32 (Fall 1970): 161-165.

   Turner calls attention to a collection of Waco, Texas, photographs taken by Fred Gildersleeve. The photos date from the 1900s to the 1950s.

114. Van Ravenswaay, Charles. "The Missouri Historical Society's Photographic Collection." *Eye to Eye* 2 (September 1953): 8-15.

115. Wagner, Ellen D. "Colorado Collection Includes Jackson Photos of Texas." *Texas Libraries* 38 (Spring 1976): 22-26.

   Wagner calls attention to William Henry Jackson photographs of Galveston, and El Paso, Texas, in the Jackson Collection at the State Historical Society of Colorado.

116. Whitehouse, Anne. "Recording the Past: Columbia's Oral History Collection." *Maryland History* 13 (Fall/Winter 1982): 47-52.

   This article provides a broad overview of the collection's scope and content. Few individual recordings or interviews are discussed.

Business Collections

General

117. Barber, Edwin and Virginia P. Barber. "A Description of the Old Harper and Brothers Publishing Records Recently Come to Light." *Bulletin of Bibliography and Magazine Notes* 25 (September/December 1966): 1-6; and (January/April 1967): 29-34.

    A two-part article in which the authors describe the contents of four record series in some detail. The series described are Harper's general catalog, contract files, memorandum files, and priority files. The records date from 1817 to 1918.

118. Barck, Dorothy C. "New York Historical Society." *Bulletin of the Business Historical Society* 8 (January 1934): 1-5.

    Barck provides a general overview of the society's business-related records, manuscript collections, and published holdings. She cites some specific collection titles and strengths.

119. Barrett, Mildred A., and J. Lawrence McConville. "The Amador Collection at New Mexico State University. *Password* 17 (Winter 1972): 196-198.

    Martín Amador was a 19th-century businessman in Las Cruces, New Mexico. Most of his collection consists of newspapers and serial publications, but it also contains records from his freighting and livery business and family correspondence.

120. Bemis, Samuel. "Papers of David Curtis DeForest and J.W. DeForest." *Yale University Library Gazette* 14 (April 1940): 62-63.

    This article focuses on the diaries and correspondence of David C. DeForest, a Connecticut trader operating in Buenos Aires. Bemis notes that the collection is especially rich in details about the independence period in the Rio de la Plata region.

121. Boles, Nancy G. "The Fowler and Oliver Papers." *Maryland Historical Magazine* 67 (Winter 1972): 438-440.

    David Fowler and Robert Oliver were Maryland businessmen and active in state politics. The Oliver family papers document the period of the 1830s to the 1860s and the Fowler family collection the 1830s to the 1950s. Boles cites record series titles in both collections.

122. Bolino, August C. "The Vatican Film Library at Saint Louis University." *Business History Review* 31 (Winter 1957): 425-436.

The article describes business-related records and manuscripts micro-filmed in the Vatican Library. Bolino reviews documents relating to merchants; commercial law; banks and finance; trade in the Americas and Europe; and the finding aids to the collection.

123. Bridner, Elwood L., Jr. "The Robert Oliver Manuscript Collection." *Maryland Historian* 15 (Spring/Summer 1984): 27-37.

Robert Oliver was a Baltimore merchant. His papers and business records date from 1785 to 1833 and document his financial success. The papers include personal and business correspondence, financial journals and ledgers, and daybooks.

124. "The Business Papers of a Great Roman Family." *Bulletin of the Business Historical Society* 3 (September 1929): 1-9.

This article describes records created and kept by the Italian Barberini and Sciarra-Colonna banking families. The records date from 1618 to 1816 and are in Harvard's Baker Library.

125. Christman, Webster M. "The Papers of Stephen Girard: Their Preparation and Historical Interest." *Proceedings of the American Philosophical Society* 110 (December 1966): 383-385.

This article briefly describes the scope and research value of Girard's papers. It also notes that the papers are arranged topically with several topical divisions cited. Girard was a Philadelphia merchant and banker who founded Girard College.

126. Crew, Spencer R., and John A. Fleckner. "Archival Sources for Business History at the National Museum of American History." *Business History Review* 60 (Autumn 1986): 474-486.

Among the collections described are the Parke-Davis Company records; George H. Clark Radioana papers; Allen B. DuMont papers; the Leo M. Baekeland papers; the extensive N.W. Ayer Advertising Collection; the Singer Industrial Design Collection; and others.

127. David, Charles W. "Longwood Library." *Papers of the Bibliographic Society of America* 51 (Third quarter 1967): 183-202.

Longwood was the name of the DuPont estate and the DuPont private library at the estate. The first part of the article describes published materials, and the second half, the personal papers and records of the

DuPont de Nemours family.

128. Dean, Warren. "Sources for the Study of Latin American Economic History: The Records of North American Private Business Enterprises." *Latin American Research Review* 3 (Summer 1968): 79-86.

   This article lists thirty-seven U.S. and Canadian corporations doing business in Latin America and which indicated their records would be open to research. Entries include addresses, volume, type of records, and countries in which they do business.

129. Delaney, Robert and Duane Smith. "Coal, Power, and Cross Ties: A Research Note on Transmississippi Americana." *Manuscripts* 28 (Spring 1976): 149-151.

   This short article calls attention to, and describes the records of the Porter Fuel Company; the Western Colorado Power Company; and the Rio Grande Southern Railroad held by the Center for Southwestern Studies, Fort Lewis College, Durango, Colorado.

130. Dunn, James T. "The Manuscript Collections in the New York State Historical Association Library: Business Account Books." *New York History* 35 (April 1954): 227-235.

   This checklist is arranged alphabetically by business proprietors' surname with entries including type and place of business, record series titles, inclusive dates, volume, and content notes.

131. Field, Alston G. "The Collection of Business Records in Western Pennsylvania." *Bulletin of the Business Historical Society* 8 (June 1934): 57-63.

   Field reviews the business-related collections in the Western Pennsylvania Historical Society at Pittsburgh. He cites several specific collections while noting significant record series and inclusive dates.

132. Fishbein, Meyer H. "Business History Resources in the National Archives." *Business History Review* 38 (Summer 1964): 232-257.

   A lengthy review in which the author cites record groups and key record series that relate to business and commerce. He also comments on the research value of the records and provides inclusive dates in many instances.

133. Garrison, Curtis W. "Economic Materials in the Pennsylvania Archives and Other Repositories." *Bulletin of the Business Historical Society* 8 (December 1934): 97-101.

   Mostly a report of business-related materials in the state archives, but Garrison cites collections in other Pennsylvania historical societies and museums too.

134. Grant, Roger H. "The James J. Hill Papers: An Untapped Source for the Study of Iowa History." *Annals of Iowa* 46 (Summer 1982): 373-376.

    The author notes that most of the Iowa-related materials are in the "Iowa Properties" section and document the development of railroads and the coal mining industry in Iowa for the years 1885-1901. The papers are in the St. Paul, Minnesota, public library.

135. Gras, Norman S. B. "An Early Sedentary Merchant in the Middle West." *Bulletin of the Business Historical Society* 18 (February 1944): 1-8.

    The merchant is Henry Shaw whose papers include real estate records, personal and business correspondence, and financial records from his business activities in early 19th-century St. Louis, Missouri. The records are in Harvard's Baker Library.

136. Gregory, Owen. "The Chicago Board of Trade's Archives." *Agricultural History* 56 (January 1982): 326-327.

    This brief article calls attention to a microfilm set of the board's records which include correspondence of the directors, officers, and committees; market price statistical records; and trading records, all dating from 1859.

137. Haight, Gordon S. "The John William DeForest Collection." *Yale University Library Gazette* 14 (January 1940): 41-46.

    This collection contains the correspondence and business papers (1770s-1830s) of John Hancock DeForest, a cotton merchant from Seymour, Connecticut, and the literary manuscripts and letters of his son, John William DeForest.

138. Hall, John Philip. "Shoemaking in the Post-Revolutionary Period: The Business Records of Three Cordwainers of Reading, Massachusetts." *Bulletin of the Business Historical Society* 25 (September 1951): 169-187.

    Hall describes, in considerable detail, shoemaker account records held by the Reading Antiquarian Society. Much data from the records are reproduced and analyzed.

139. Hancock, Harold B. "Materials for Company History in the National Archives." *American Archivist* 29 (January 1966): 23-32.

    The author reviews U.S. Army and Navy records, the records of the Treasury, the State Department, the Patent Office, the Coast Survey, and those of the House of Representatives for information relating to companies doing business with the federal government.

140. Hanna, Archibald, Jr. "The William W. Miller Papers." *Yale University Library Gazette* 28 (July 1953): 24-26.

    Miller was an early settler in Washington Territory, active in territorial politics, a successful businessman, and a general of volunteers during the

Yakima Indian wars. His papers include business and military papers and personal correspondence.

141. Hedges, James B. "The Brown Papers: The Record of a Rhode Island Business Family." *Proceedings of the American Antiquarian Society* 53 (April 1941): 21-36
    The collection is held by the John Carter Brown Library and contains materials dating from 1726 to 1913 that relate to privateering, trade with the West Indies and Great Britian, whaling, and trade along the eastern U.S. seaboard.

142. Hendricks, William O. "The Collection of the M. H. Sherman Foundation, Inc." *Manuscripts* 21 (Fall 1969): 286-289.
    This is obviously a forerunner of the following article. Of the two, the one in *California History* is the more informative.

143. Hendricks, William O. "The Sherman Library." *California History* 59 (Winter 1980/1981): 352-375.
    This library is named after Moses Hazeltine Sherman, a California businessman and real estate developer. The keystone of the collection is Sherman's personal papers which are briefly described. The papers of his associates are also in the library.

144. Hidy, Muriel E. "The George Peabody Papers." *Bulletin of the Business Historical Society* 12 (February 1938): 1-6.
    This collection includes correspondence and financial records of Peabody's business interests and investments for the period 1830-1857. The Essex Institute in Salem, Massachusetts, holds the collection.

145. Humphreys, Glenn E. "Printing, Publishing, and Ancillary Trades: A Checklist of Manuscript and Archival Holdings in the Edward C. Kemble Collections on Western Printing & Publishing, California Historical Society Library, San Francisco." *California History* 66 (March 1987): 55-67.
    Humphreys provides a brief introduction to the collections followed by guide-like entries in alphabetical order by collection title and including record series titles, volume, inclusive dates, and detailed content notes.

146. Hussey, Miriam. "Business Manuscripts in the Library of the Historical Society of Pennsylvania." *Bulletin of the Business Historical Society* 10 (June 1936): 48-51.
    Hussey cites collection titles, record series, and inclusive dates, along with brief comments on the topical strengths of the collections.

147. Johansen, Dorothy O. "The Simeon G. Reed Collection of Letters and

Private Papers." *Pacific Northwest Quarterly* 27 (January 1936): 54-65.
Reed was a pioneer Oregon businessman involved in agriculture, railroads and ocean transportation, lumbering, and mining. His papers, held by Reed College, Portland, Oregon, include over fifty volumes of letterbooks dating from the 1860s to 1908.

148. Johnson, Bruce. "The Kemble Collections." *California History* 60 (Summer 1981): 188-193.
The Kemble Collections are mostly published materials about the history of printing and publishing in the American West. They include, however, the archives of Taylor & Taylor, a printing firm in San Francisco. The materials are in the California Historical Society.

149. Kunstling, Frances W. "The John Sumner Russwurm Papers: A Bibliographical Note." *Tennessee Historical Quarterly* 32 (Fall 1973): 285-289.
Russwurm was a 19th-century Tennessee farmer, merchant, and state politician. His papers (1786-1914) held by the Tennessee State Library and Archives include family and political correspondence, biographical and genealogical data, financial records, and legal documents.

150. Kwedar, Melina F., James R. Allen, and John A. Patterson. "Illinois General Store Manuscripts, 1825-1845: A Bibliography." *Illinois Libraries* 62 (April 1980): 303-309.
This article contains a checklist of eighty-nine collections of Illinois retail store records. Entries include collection titles, volume, inclusive dates, location of stores, location of records, and content notes.

151. Lemke, W. J. "The Papers of Samuel Evans of Ozark." *The Arkansas Historical Quarterly* 13 (Autumn 1954): 278-300.
Evans was a retail store owner and postmaster in Ozark, Arkansas. The materials described include correspondence and financial records from his business and postal records of the Ozark post office.

152. Loehr, Rodney C. "Business History Material in the Minnesota Historical Society." *Bulletin of the Business Historical Society* 14 (April 1940): 21-28.
Loehr uses a topical approach to describe the society's holdings. He cites specific collections relating to retail merchandising, the fur trade, lumbering, hotels, agriculture, transportation, labor, and others.

153. Long, Elfrieda. "The Columbia Conserve Company Papers." *Indiana University Bookman* 2 (November 1957): 18-25.
This company was an employee-owned and -managed cannery in Indianapolis, Indiana, from 1903 to the 1950s. Its records include corporate minutes; correspondence; finance; advertising; sales; and

company publications. The records are at Indiana University.

154. Lovett, Robert W. "Business Manuscripts in Baker Library, Harvard Graduate School of Business Administration." *Business History Review* 34 (Autumn 1960): 345-351.

    This article provides an overview of business manuscript collections. While general in nature, it cites many specific collections.

155. Lovett, Robert W. "Business Manuscripts in Baker Library: The Pierson Collection: Life in an Early Company Town." *Bulletin of the Business Historical Society* 27 (December 1953): 260-263.

    The Pierson Company was an iron dealer and manufactured nails and screws in Ramapo, New York. The records date from 1795 to 1865.

156. Lovett, Robert W. "The Heard Collection and Its Story." *Business History Review* 35 (Winter 1961): 567-573.

    Lovett writes about a huge accumulation of records documenting the Heard family's business activities in the 19th-century China trade. He traces the collection's provenance and comments on its research values.

157. Lovett, Robert W. "Publisher and Advertiser Extraordinary: The E. C. Allen Collection." *Bulletin of the Business Historical Society* 24 (December 1950): 210-215.

    The E. C. Allen Company was a mail-order firm and magazine publisher in Augusta, Maine. Lovett cites record series titles and comments on the research potential of this huge collection.

158. Lovett, Robert W. "Storekeeping in a Maine Seacoast Town: Records of the W. G. Sargent Company." *Bulletin of the Business Historical Society* 27 (June 1953): 121-123.

    A brief review of the record series in this collection along with comments on their research values. The records date from 1834 to 1904.

159. Lovett, Robert W. "Manuscripts at Baker Library, Harvard Business School, Broaden Economic History." *Manuscripts* 11 (Spring 1959): 30-34, 38, 52.

    A general article about the collection policies at the library, but also mentioning some of the key collections held with comments on their scope and content.

160. Marshall, Jeffrey D. "Vilas Family Papers, 1794-1925." *Vermont History* 62 (Winter 1994): 42-44.

    This collection contains mostly correspondence and legal records documenting the family business and social life in pre-Civil War Vermont and New York.

161. Matthews, Linda M. "The Archives of the Coca-Cola Company. Preserving 'the Real Thing.'" *Georgia Archive* 1 (Spring 1973): 12-20.

Matthews describes three record groups: company art and memorabilia; advertising and promotional records; and employee reminiscences.

162. Mazuzan, George T. "The Challenge of Nuclear Power Development Records." *American Archivist* 44 (Summer 1981): 229-235.

Mazuzan identifies some key federal record series and where they may be found and comments on records created by General Electric, Westinghouse, and Betchel and nuclear-related organizations such as the Atomic Industrial Forum and Edison Electric Institute.

163. McCabe, James M. "Early Ledgers and Account Books: A Source for Local Vermont History." *Vermont History* 37 (Winter 1969): 5-12.

McCabe cites titles of some collections containing financial records, but he devotes most of the article to describing the types of information that are typically found in these records.

164. McCann, Helen. "The Business Papers of Emerson Cole." *Bulletin of the Business Historical Society* 14 (December 1940): 81-86.

These are the records of lumber, real estate, and savings and loan businesses in Minnesota and the upper midwest during the 1880s-1890s. The records are in the Minnesota Historical Society.

165. McClurkin, A. J. "Summary of the Bank of North America Records." *Pennsylvania Magazine of History and Biography* 64 (January 1940): 88-96.

The author comments on the research significance of the minute and letterbooks; journals and memorandum books; reports on the state of the bank; general ledgers; clerks daily records; stock records; and legal, real estate and miscellaneous records.

166. Means, Carroll A. "Leffingwell Papers." *Yale University Library Gazette* 29 (July 1954): 13-20.

This article describes a collection of more than 1,000 letters written by Christopher Leffingwell of Norwich, Connecticut. The letters are dated 1764-1810 and are descriptive of the family's paper business and his participation in the American Revolution.

167. Nash, Michael. "Business History at the Hagley Museum and Library." *Business History Review* 60 (Spring 1986): 104-120.

Nash reviews key collections which include an extensive photograph collection; the DuPont family papers; records of DuPont de Nemours & Company; the Philadelphia Quartz Company; Sperry-UNIVAC; Bethlehem Steel; National Industrial Conference Board; and others.

168. Nute, Grace L. "Calendar of the American Fur Company's Papers." *Annual Report of the American Historical Association for the Year 1944* 2 (1945): 1-982; and 3 (1945): 983-1951.

All of volumes two and three are devoted to this calendar. It lists correspondence, memoranda, shipping records, and financial records relating to the company's costs, profits, and policies for the period 1832 to 1847.

169. Nute, Grace Lee. "The Papers of the American Fur Company: A Brief Estimate of Their Significance." *American Historical Review* 32 (April 1927): 519-538.

Nute reviews the history of the company and how the different record series in the collection document the changes that it underwent from the 1830s to 1847. This article is reproduced in part one of the calender, see entry 168 above.

170. "Original Manuscripts of the Medici." *Bulletin of the Business Historical Society* 1 (November 1927): 1-6.

A description of original account books and correspondence of the Medici family dating from 1377 to 1597. The records are in Baker Library, Harvard University.

171. Paltsits, Victor H. "Business Records of Brown Brothers & Co., New York - 1825-1880." *Bulletin of the New York Public Library* 40 (June 1936): 495-498.

The Browns were early merchants, foreign exchange specialists, and bankers in Baltimore, Philadelphia, and New York. This article reviews the firm's history and closes with a checklist of record series, inclusive dates, and volume.

172. Pike, Charles B. "Chicago Historical Society." *Bulletin of the Business Historical Society* 8 (May 1934): 37-41.

This article reviews, in general terms, the society's business-related records, manuscript collections, and published materials. Several specific collections are cited.

173. Porter, Patrick G. "Source Material for Economic History: Records of the Bureau of Corporations." *Prologue* 2 (Spring 1970): 31-33.

Porter relates the background and function of the bureau, notes that its records span the years 1903-1914, and reviews the type of information found in its records and their research value.

174. Price, Thomas E. "Manuscript Sources for Nineteenth-Century Banks and Banking in Louisiana and the Lower Mississippi Valley in the Louisiana State University Libraries." *Louisiana History* 29 (Winter 1988): 65-75.

Price cites collection titles, record series, inclusive dates, volume, and content notes to describe bank records and manuscript collections of bankers.

175. Quenzel, Carrol H. "West Virginia University Collection of Historical Manuscripts." *Bulletin of the Business Historical Society* 8 (March 1934): 21-23.
    Quenzel describes a few of the university's stronger business-related collections in the areas of railroads, coal and oil field development, and family businesses.

176. Rau, Louise. "Dutilh Papers." *Bulletin of the Business Historical Society* 13 (November 1939): 73-74.
    Rau calls attention to the existence and research potential of a large collection of world-wide, business-related, correspondence of the Dutilh family. The letters dating from 1755 to 1874 are in the Burton Historical Collection, Detroit Public Library.

177. Rau, Louise. "The Robert Sanders Papers." *Bulletin of the Business Historical Society* 12 (April 1938): 28-30.
    Robert Sanders was an 18th-century Detroit merchant. Rau evaluates a collection of his correspondence in the Burton Historical Collection, Detroit Public Library. The letters date from 1804 to 1810.

178. Reeves, Dorothea. "Come All for the Cure-All: Patent Medicines, Nineteenth Century Bonanza." *Harvard Library Bulletin* 15 (July 1967): 253-272.
    The article describes the large patent medicine collection of handbills, trade cards, and advertising leaflets and brochures in the Manuscript Division of Harvard's Baker Library.

179. Reynolds, Regina and Mary Elizabeth Ruwell. "Fire Insurance Records: A Versatile Resource." *American Archivist* 38 (January 1975): 15-21.
    The authors describe several record series such as blotters, policies, surveys, and proofs of loss, and comment on their usefulness for research. The records of the Insurance Company of North America are cited as examples.

180. Saretzky, Gary D. "Oral History in American Business Archives." *American Archivist* 44 (Fall 1981): 353-355.
    Saretzky identifies specific business archives that have conducted oral history projects and, consequently, have oral histories as part of their archival holdings.

181. Seager, Robert, II. The Samuel S. Wood Papers." *Yale University Library*

Gazette 34 (April 1960): 166-177.

Wood was an American merchant in Nicaragua during the 1850s. His papers, mostly correspondence, document the turbulent political conditions of that period, including the activities of William Walker.

182. Sellers, Charles C. "Sellers Papers in the Peale-Sellers Collection." *Proceedings of the American Philosophical Society* 95 (June 1951): 262-265.

The papers of the Sellers family include correspondence, diaries, land surveys, maps, legal documents, and patents for inventions. They document life in Philadelphia and the family's business interests from the 1700s to 1900.

183. Skemer, Don C. "German Emigre Publishers in New York: The Archives of the Frederick Ungar Publishing Company." *Publishing History* 31 (1992): 77-84.

The author calls attention to the Ungar Publishing Company's records at the State University of New York--Albany. Most of the article is devoted to Ungar's publishing career in the U.S.

184. Smith, Alice. "Business Manuscripts in the Possession of the State Historical Society of Wisconsin." *Business History Review* 37 (Autumn 1963): 270-277.

The author cites collection titles under subject headings such as the fur trade, forestry, small businesses, agriculture, real estate, transportation, banking, public utilities, manufacturing, and the McCormick Collection.

185. Smith, Murphy D. "The Stephen Girard Papers." *Manuscripts* 29 (Winter 1977): 14-22.

Girard was one of the most successful U.S. bankers and businessmen of the 19th century. This article describes his papers of which a 650-roll microfilm set is in the American Philosophical Society library.

186. Stephens, Robert O. "The Oral History of Texas Oil Pioneers." *Library Chronicle of the University of Texas* 7 (Fall 1961): 35-39.

The author reports on the progress of the collection of more than 200 recordings and notes the existence of interview typescripts and the type of information found within them.

187. Thayer, Theodore. "The Pemberton Papers." *Pennsylvania Magazine of History and Biography* 67 (July 1943): 280-286.

This Quaker family collection contains business account books, legal documents, genealogical data, correspondence, and land records dating from 1641 to the 1880s.

188. Turner, Morris K. "The Baynton, Wharton, and Morgan Manuscripts."
     Mississippi Valley Historical Review 9 (December 1922): 236-241.
     The records described in this article are those of the Philadelphia trading
     and land speculation firm of Baynton, Wharton, and Morgan for the period
     1754-1776. Financial records and correspondence predominate.

189. Vail, R. W. G. "The American Antiquarian Society." *Bulletin of the
     Business Historical Society* 7 (December 1933): 1-5.
     Vail provides a general overview of the society's business-related
     records, manuscript collections, and published holdings.

190. Williams, Richmond D. "The Eleutherian Mills Historical Library."
     Manuscripts 14 (Spring 1962): 38-41.
     The Longwood Collection of DuPont family correspondence, 1780-1954;
     the Henry Francis DuPont Winterthur Collection, 1588-1926; and the E.I.
     DuPont de Nemours & Co., business records form the nucleus of the
     manuscript holdings of the library.

191. Wing, John D. "Mills Olcott and His Papers in the Dartmouth Archives."
     Dartmouth College Library Bulletin 22 (April 1982): 76-83.
     Olcott was an 18th- and 19th-century banker and businessman. His
     papers and records document the development of locks and canals on the
     Connecticut River and banking and business in the Connecticut River
     valley.

192. Withington, Mary. "The Nathaniel and Thomas Shaw Papers." *Yale
     University Library Gazette* 1 (April 1927): 47-52.
     The Shaws were New London, Connecticut, merchants engaged in the
     West Indies trade. Their papers include account books, ledgers, corre-
     spondence, and other business records, mostly dating from the period of
     the American Revolution.

193. Zabrosky, Frank A. "The Archives of Industrial Society at the University
     of Pittsburgh." *Records Management Quarterly* 3 (April 1969): 8-11.
     While mostly about management concepts, the author does review the
     holdings of the archives which contains manuscript collections, organiza-
     tional records, business records, and some public records. Collection titles
     or record groups are listed for each category.

Agriculture and Forestry

194. "Agricultural Records in the Baker Library." *Bulletin of the Business
     Historical Society* 9 (June 1935): 60-63.
     A checklist of twenty-six collections dating from 1762 to 1917. The

brief citations include record series titles, inclusive dates, volume, and content notes.

195. Berner, Richard C. "Source Materials for Pacific Northwest History: The Port Blakely Mill Company Records." *Pacific Northwest Quarterly* 49 (April 1958): 82-83.
    The Port Blakely Mill supplied lumber nationally and to South America, Asia, and Great Britain. Its records, dating 1876 to 1923, are at the University of Washington. Berner cites record series and comments on the research value of the materials.

196. Berner, Richard C. "Sources for Research in Forest History: The University of Washington Manuscripts Collection." *Business History Review* 35 (Autumn 1961): 420-425.
    Berner describes ten collections of records from milling and lumber companies. His description includes historical background of the companies, record series titles, inclusive dates, volume statements, and content notes.

197. Bowers, Douglas E., and Douglas Helms. eds. "History of Agriculture and the Environment." *Agricultural History* 66 (Spring 1992): 1-361.
    The entire issue is devoted to a single theme and includes four essays on records relating to agriculture and the environment. They are:

    1. Adams, Margaret O. "Electronic Records and the Environment." 339-344.

    2. Cunliffe, William H. "Special Media Records Relating to the Environment." 345-350.

    3. Lowell, Waverly B. "Documenting the Environment: Records in the Regional Archives." 351-360.

    4. Rush, James A., Jr. "War of Attrition: Textual Records Relating to the Environment in the National Archives--Arizona, a Case Study." 331-338.

198. Campbell, Ann Morgan. "Reaping the Records: Research Opportunities in Regional Archives Branches." *Agricultural History* 49 (January 1975): 100-104.
    Campbell reviews federal records that relate to agriculture in the American West. She includes records of the Farm Security Administration, General Land Office; Bureaus of Indian Affairs, Reclamation, and Agricultural Economics; and the federal courts.

199. Colley, Charles C. "Keeping the Records in Arizona." *Agricultural History* 49 (January 1975): 92-94.

     This article locates and identifies agriculture-related records at the University of Arizona; Arizona State University; Northern Arizona University; the Arizona Historical Society; and the Arizona State Archives. Description is limited to collection titles.

200. Davis, Charles. "Extension Service Records in Alabama." *American Archivist* 4 (October 1941): 275-280.

     Davis reviews the location of agriculture extension service records in Alabama and comments on the more important record series. He concluded that extension service records were important for understanding agricultural education and the history of Alabama.

201. Edwards, Everett E. "Agricultural Records: Their Nature and Value for Research." *Agricultural History* 13 (January 1939): 1-12.

     The article reviews the types of agricultural records available, analyzes their value to historians, and cites representative collections and their locations.

202. Frame, Robert M., III. "Mills, Machines, and Millers: Minnesota Sources for Flour-Milling Research." *Minnesota History* 46 (Winter 1978): 152-162.

     Much of this article is devoted to the history of milling in Minnesota and to the location of existing mills. Frame does mention, however, several manuscript collections relating to milling.

203. Friedel, Janice N. "The Henry Field Collection at the State Historical Society of Iowa." *Annals of Iowa* 48 (Summer/Fall 1986): 304-313.

     Henry Field was known for the seed business he founded and his pioneering use of radio advertising. Friedel describes the business records of the Henry Field Seed Company, Field family papers, and records relating to radio, especially station KFNF.

204. Haffner, Gerald O. "Amos Lemmon's Farm Journal, 1902-1937." *Indiana Magazine of History* 83 (September 1987): 267-277.

     Haffner describes the contents of three journals and their value to research. The records are held by the archives at Indiana University Southeast, New Albany, Indiana.

205. Homsher, Lola M. "Archives of the Wyoming Stock Growers' Association." *Mississippi Valley Historical Review* 33 (September 1946): 279-288.

     These records date from 1873 to 1923 and include the association's minutes; correspondence; stock inspectors records; and membership and financial records. Homsher provides content notes for each record series and identifies other related collections.

206. Honhart, Frederick L. "Sources of Forest History: The Hackley & Hume Papers." *Journal of Forest History* 23 (July 1979): 136-143.

Charles H. Hackley and Thomas Hume operated a lumber business in Michigan. Their papers date from 1870 to 1946 and include letterbooks, legal documents, financial records, maps, and photographs.

207. Kahn, Herman. "Records in the National Archives Relating to the Range Cattle Industry, 1865-1895." *Agricultural History* 20 (July 1946): 187-190.

There are nineteen record groups cited in this article. The author briefly describes the scope and content of each and notes record series of value.

208. Kellar, Lucile. "The McCormick Collection." *Autograph Collectors' Journal* 4 (Spring 1952): 40-43.

The article describes the papers of Cyrus Hall McCormick and the records of his farm implement business held by the Wisconsin State Historical Society. Kellar notes McCormick's other business interests and lists several related collections at the society.

209. Kulsrud, Carl J. "The Archival Records of the Agricultural Adjustment Program." *Agricultural History* 22 (July 1948): 197-204.

This article describes the first accession by the U.S. National Archives of 400 feet of records dating 1933-1935 from this New Deal agency. The description includes background on the agency's purpose and information on the content of the records.

210. Kunitz, Don. "The Higgins Library: A Source for the Study of Agricultural History." *Agricultural History* 49 (January 1975): 89-91.

Mostly books, serials, and equipment catalogs, but the author notes that the library also has a collection of agriculture-related photographs.

211. Larson, Olaf F., and Thomas B. Jones. "The Unpublished Data from Roosevelt's Commission on Country Life." *Agricultural History* 50 (October 1976): 583-599.

The unpublished data refers to the commission's circular letters soliciting information on country life and the summary reports of this data. Cornell University holds these records.

212. Lee, Guy A. "The General Records of the United States Department of Agriculture in the National Archives." *Agricultural History* 19 (October 1945): 242-249.

A useful article describing record groups and sub-groups of federal records within the Department of Agriculture. The author lists key record series along with inclusive dates, subjects documented, and background information where appropriate.

213. Lennes, Greg. "International Harvester Archives." *Illinois Libraries* 63
     (April 1981): 289-291.
         Lennes devotes most of this article to the establishment and organization
     of the archives. However, it contains some general information that might
     be useful for those planning research in this agricultural business archives.

214. Loehr, Rodney C. "Farmers' Diaries: Their Interest and Value as
     Historical Sources." *Agricultural History* 12 (October 1938): 313-325.
         The author analyzes the type of information found in farmers' diaries
     and cites several examples located in the Minnesota Historical Society, St.
     Paul.

215. Maxwell, Robert S. "Forest History Collections at Stephen F. Austin."
     Texas Libraries 40 (Summer 1978): 88-94.
         Description of forest-related collections includes collection title,
     inclusive dates, record series titles, volume, and comments on research
     values.

216. McCormick Historical Association. "The McCormick Historical Associa-
     tion." *Bulletin of the Business Historical Association* 10 (November 1936):
     76-78.
         A brief review of the business records and manuscripts in the associa-
     tion's library in Chicago, Illinois. The materials relate to the McCormick
     family and its business interests, and to farm machinery.

217. McDonald, Michael J. "Tennessee Valley Authority Records." *Agricultural
     History* 58 (April 1984): 127-137.
         After giving an adminstrative history of the agency, the author
     identifies, locates, and describes TVA records relating to family removal,
     land purchases, demonstration farms, and soil erosion.

218. Overfield, Richard A. "State Agricultural Experiment Stations and the
     Development of the West, 1887-1920: A Look at the Sources." *Govern-
     ment Publications Review* 8A (November/December 1981): 468-472.
         Overfield provides several examples of state and federal records
     documenting the scientific role of agriculture experiment stations in the
     western U.S.

219. Palmer, Arelene. "The Lloyd Papers." *Maryland Historical Magazine* 65
     (Winter 1970): 430-432.
         Most of these papers document the lives of eight different Edward
     Lloyds of Talbot County, Maryland. Dating from the 1740s through the
     19th century, the collection is a rich source for Maryland's agricultural

history and Lloyd family genealogy.

220. Parker, William N. "New Sources for Rural History." *Agricultural History* 58 (April 1984): 105-138.

    There are five short essays within this article that describe and comment upon farm account books; probate and land records; rural social surveys; the records of the Tennessee Valley Authority; and land ownership maps.

221. Pinkett, Harold T. "Archival Product of a Century of Federal Assistance to Agriculture." *American Historical Review* 69 (April 1964): 689-706.

    Pinkett reviews the types of federal records in the U.S. National Archives that relate to agriculture. His description of the records is in general terms, but useful for understanding the types of activities the records document.

222. Pinkett, Harold T. "Early Records of the U.S. Department of Agriculture." *American Archivist* 25 (October 1962): 407-416.

    Pinkett identifies extant records, including some in manuscript collections, and accounts for many record series that have been destroyed.

223. Pinkett, Harold T. "Federal Archives and Western Agriculture." *Agricultural History* 49 (January 1975): 95-99.

    A general description that focuses more on agricultural topics documented by federal records than on the records themselves.

224. Pinkett, Harold T. "Forest Service Records as Research Material." *Forest History* 13 (January 1970): 19-29.

    Pinkett notes the types of forestry-related records available. These include the papers of chief and associate foresters, and the records of forest research and conservation programs, land use in national forests, and forest conferences.

225. Pinkett, Harold T. "Records of the First Century of Interest of the United States Government in Plant Industries." *Agricultural History* 29 (January 1955): 38-45.

    Pinkett identifies sub-groups and record series in the National Archives that document the history of federal interest in crop development in the U.S. His description includes the background of the records, their informational content, and their research values.

226. Pinkett, Harold T. "Records of Research Units of the United States Forest Service in the National Archives." *Journal of Forestry* 45 (April 1947): 272-275.

    Pinkett reviews the types of forestry research records found in the U.S. Forest Service's research compilation files; Forest Products Laboratory project files; the Sen. Royal S. Copeland Report; and forest taxation records. These records date from 1897 to 1937.

227. Pinkett, Harold T. "Sources of American Forest and Conservation History." *Journal of Forest History* 25 (October 1981): 210-212.
     Pinkett identifies forestry-related record groups and manuscript collections in federal and state archives, university libraries, historical societies, and business archives. He cites collection and record series titles and inclusive dates.

228. Shelley, Fred. "The Papers of Moreton Frewen." *Quarterly Journal of Current Acquisitions* 6 (August 1949): 15-20.
     While Shelly makes occasional reference to the papers, much of this essay is biographical in content. Moreton Frewen was an Englishman who spent several years ranching in Wyoming in the 1880s. The papers include records of the Powder River Cattle Company.

229. Steck, Larry and Francis Blouin. "Hannah Lay and Company: Sampling the Records of a Century of Lumbering in Michigan." *American Archivist* 39 (January 1976): 15-20.
     A review of record series retained from the records of a Michigan lumber and mercantile company. The records date from the 1880s to the 1930s.

230. Stegh, Leslie J. "Deere & Company Archives and Records Services." *Illinois Libraries* 63 (March 1981): 276-279.
     This article relates the history of this farm implement company archives and the services it offers. Description is limited to key record series titles.

231. Swem, Earl G. "A List of Manuscripts Relating to the History of Agriculture in Virginia ... Now in the Virginia State Library." *Bulletin of the Virginia State Library* 6 (January 1913): 5-20.
     There are 133 manuscripts cited in the list. They date from 1749 to 1879. Entries include author, type of document, length, and content note. The article concludes with an index to the checklist.

232. Viccars, Marion. "... Conducted Himself as a Peaceful Citizen." *Manuscripts* 26 (Fall 1974): 283-287.
     The University of West Florida holds the papers of Gerhard Rolfs, a German who came to western Florida as Germany's consul to protect the interests of the German-American Lumber Company. His papers document his activities from 1901 to the 1930s.

233. Wright, Almon R. "World War Food Controls and Archival Sources for Their Study." *Agricultural History* 15 (April 1941): 72-73.

The article is mostly an adminstrative history of the Food Administration, the Grain Corporation, and the Sugar Equalization Board, followed by brief descriptions of key sub-groups and record series created by these agencies.

Manufacturing

234. Barker, Ellen Lee. "G. Krug & Son, Makers of Artistic Wrought Iron Work." *Maryland Historical Quarterly* 64 (Winter 1969): 420-421.
    The Maryland Historical Society has a collection of more than 100 volumes of letterbooks, financial records, and drawings from this Baltimore company. The records date from the 1840s.

235. Bining, Arthur C. "The Margaret C. Buckingham Collection and Other Business Records." *Pennsylvanian Magazine of History and Biography* 68 (April 1944): 189-193.
    The Buckingham Collection contains 450 business account books from a number of 18th- and 19th-century Pennsylvania iron works. This article also cites many other iron works collections among the Historical Society of Pennsylvania holdings.

236. Buchanan, John. "The Western Electric Historical Library." *American Archivist* 29 (January, 1966): 55-59.
    A review of the types of records held by the library that document the company's history from the 1870s forward.

237. Doster, James F. "The Shelby Iron Works Collection in the University of Alabama Library." *Bulletin of the Business Historical Society* 26 (December 1952): 214-217.
    The author gives a brief company history and calls attention to the research values of the collection. He cites record series titles and dates.

238. Edwards, Nina L. "The Stevens Mill Records: Triumph Over Chaos." *American Archivist* 26 (January 1963): 59-62.
    There are nearly 1,000 feet of records dating 1811-1919 in this collection held by the Merrimack Valley Textile Museum, North Andover, Massachusetts. The article concludes with a checklist of record series and inclusive dates.

239. Freudenberger, Herman. "Records of the Bohemian Iron Industry, 1694-1875: The Basis for a Comprehensive Study of Modern Factories." *Business History Review* 43 (Autumn 1969): 381-384.
    The author describes a collection of Bohemian iron works records microfilmed in Czechoslovakian archives. The records date from 1694 to

1875. The microfilm is in Harvard's Baker Library.

240. Lyman, Susan E. "The Albany Glass Works and Some of the Records."
New York Historical Society Quarterly Bulletin 26 (July 1942): 55-61.
    This is mostly a history of the company with passing comments on
extant company records at the historical society. The records date from
the 1780s to 1804 with minutes of stockholders' meetings, correspondence
files, and financial records identified as the key series.

241. Marks, Bayly Ellen. "Iron Manufacturing in Maryland, a Look at
Surviving Records." *Maryland Historical Magazine* 64 (Fall 1969): 297-
299.
    Marks reviews collections of 18th- and 19th-century records of the
Principio Company; the North Hampton Furnace; Franklinville Forge; the
Ashland Iron Company; the Muirkirk Iron Company; the Deer Creek Iron
Company; and George's Creek Coal and Iron Company.

242. Overman, William D. "The Firestone Archives and Library." *American
Archivist* 16 (October 1953): 305-309.
    Overman provides a history of the archives, which includes a brief
description of Harvey S. Firestone's papers and records. The author notes
that the archives holds "an unbroken line of top management records from
1900 to the present [1953]."

243. Schwoerke, John. "The Papers from Dewey Mills." *Dartmouth College
Library Bulletin* 28 (November 1987): 33-40.
    This article describes a collection of 19th-century business records and
papers from companies begun by A. G. Dewey. Schwoerke cites the
companies represented and the extant record series.

244. Truman, Dorothy. "The Museum of American Textile History: Archival
Sources for Business History." *Business History Review* 60 (Winter 1986):
641-650.
    The museum holds the 19th- and 20th-century records of the Nathaniel
Stevens family woolen business; the Essex Company; the Davis & Furber
Machine Company; the Whiten Machine Works; and papers of several
manufacturers associations.

Maritime Industries

245. Corning, Howard. "The Essex Institute of Salem." *Bulletin of the Business
Historical Society* 7 (October 1933): 1-5.
    This article reviews, in general terms, the institute's maritime-related
records, manuscript collections, and published materials. Some specific

collections and special strengths are cited.

246. Griffin, Katherine H. "Ships' Logs in the Collections of the Massachusetts Historical Society." *Proceedings of the Massachusetts Historical Society* 105 (1993): 96-123.
    Griffin identifies the types of information found in these logs and lists the society's holdings alphabetically by ship's name. Entries include dates of log; ship's master or log keeper; destination; and port of departure.

247. Griffin, Katherine H., and Peter Drummey. "Manuscripts on the American China Trade at the Massachusetts Historical Society." *Proceedings of the Massachusetts Historical Society* 100 (1988): 128-139.
    The authors cite collection and record series titles with inclusive dates under the headings of early voyages; merchants and trading houses; ship captains; and other Americans in China.

248. Lovett, Robert W. "Maritime Manuscripts in Baker Library." *American Neptune* 13 (April 1953): 118-124.
    Lovett cites collection titles, record series, and inclusive dates for collections at Harvard documenting maritime-related occupations and businesses.

249. Medina, Isagani. "American Logbooks and Journals in Salem, Massachusetts on the Philippines, 1796-1894." *Asian Studies* 11 (April, 1973): 177-198.
    Part one lists the Essex Institute's holdings of logbooks and journals for 179 ships on pages 180-187; part two lists the holdings of the Peabody Museum for 81 ships on pages 187-191.

250. Olsberg, R. Nicholas. "Ship Registers in the South Carolina Archives." *South Carolina Historical Magazine* 74 (October 1973): 189-299.
    The author provides an introduction about ship registers that identifies the types of information found in them and their historical value. Entries include vessel type, name, size, and masters' and owners' names. Entries are also indexed.

251. Parmi, Erika S. "Arctic Logbooks in the Stefansson Collection." *Dartmouth College Library Bulletin* 27 (April 1987): 54-64; and 28 (April 1988): 54-74.
    Parmi describes the contents of twenty-two logs of trading and whaling ships on voyages to the arctic seas, especially to Baffin Island, between 1877 and 1925.

252. Rowland, Buford and Gerald B. Snedeker. "The United States Court of Claims and French Spoliation Records." *Bulletin of the Business Historical*

Society 18 (April 1944): 20-27.

The authors describe selected claims while noting that these records are a rich source for the writing of U.S. maritime history for the period 1792-1801. The claim files are federal records in the U.S. National Archives.

253. Schultz, Charles R. "Manuscript Collections of the Marine Historical Association, Inc." *American Neptune* 25 (April 1965): 99-111.

The author cites collection titles, record series, and inclusive dates of maritime-related collections, many of which are also business-related such as records of shipbuilding firms, working vessels, marine salvage companies, and merchants or traders.

254. "The Shipping Papers of James Hunnewell." *Bulletin of the Business Historical Society* 8 (June 1934): 63-68.

The papers document the beginning of Hunnewell's shipping business in Hawaii during the 1820s and his, later, worldwide shipping business headquartered in Boston. The papers are in Harvard's Baker Library.

255. Tanner, Earl C. "The Providence Federal Customhouse Papers as a Source of Maritime History Since 1790." *New England Quarterly* 26 (March 1953): 88-100.

Most of this article comments on the research values of customhouse records. It concludes, however, with checklists of the Providence, Rhode Island, customhouse records in the National Archives and the Rhode Island Historical Society and State Archives.

Organized Labor

256. Bonfield, Lynn A. "To the Source: Archival Collections for California Labor History." *California History* 66 (December 1987): 286-299.

A review of labor-related holdings at Wayne State University; the Bancroft Library; San Francisco State University; Southern California Library for Social Studies and Research; the Anne Rand Library; and the Urban History Center, California State University--Northridge.

257. Brennan, John A., and Cassandra M. Volpe. "Sources for Studying Labor at the Western Historical Collections of the University of Colorado, Boulder." *Labor's Heritage* 1 (January 1989): 68-74.

The authors cite records of the Western Federation of Miners; the Oil, Chemical, and Atomic Workers International Union; the United Brotherhood of Carpenters and Joiners; and union photographs as being representative of the university's holdings.

258. Cannon, M. Hamlin and Herbert Fine. "Repository of Labor Records."

American Federationist 50 (July 1943): 29-30.

The authors review labor-related records in the U.S. National Archives. They cite record groups along with specific record series and inclusive dates.

259. Cooper, Sarah. "Labor History Resources at the Southern California Library for Social Studies and Research." *Southwest Economy and Society* 6 (January 1984): 47-53.

Cooper reviews the book and pamphlet collection; motion picture films; union records; and manuscript collections. Description is limited mostly to collection titles with some comment on research potentials.

260. Crane, Maurice A. "Labor History Materials in the G. Robert Vincent Voice Library, Michigan State University." *Labor History* 26 (Spring 1985): 288-290.

Crane offers a brief overview of labor-related sound recordings. He calls attention to the nine-part "Labor History Cassette" series; speeches of U.S. and foreign labor leaders; and recordings of labor-related music.

261. East, Dennis. "Social Welfare Case Records: Valuable or Valueless for Working Class History." *Labor History* 17 (Summer 1976): 416-421.

East uses the records of Associated Charities of Detroit held by the labor archives at Wayne State University to provide many examples of the types of information found in case files.

262. Filippelli, Ronald L. "Labor Manuscripts in the Pennsylvania State University Library." *Labor History* 13 (Winter 1972): 79-88.

Penn State is the official repository for the United Steelworkers of America and the Pennsylvania AFL-CIO. Filippelli cites record series titles, inclusive dates, volume, and content notes for these two collections and for many smaller collections.

263. Fishbein, Meyer H. "Labor History Resources in the National Archives." *Labor History* 8 (Fall 1967): 330-351.

Fishbein cites record groups and record series titles under headings of federal judicial and law enforcement; military; housing and construction; labor; agricultural; economic control agencies; and the Department of the Interior.

264. Fones-Wolf, Ken. "Labor History Sources at the West Virginia and Regional History Collection, West Virginia University." *Labor's Heritage* 3 (July 1991): 62-65.

The author cites many extensive union archives and labor-related manuscript collections. His description of specific collections includes volume, inclusive dates, and record series titles, along with the research values of the collection.

265. Gamble, Robert A., and George N. Green. "The Texas Labor Archives."
     Texas Library Journal 45 (Winter 1969): 212-213, 234.
     Gamble reviews the archives background and cites some of its key
     collections by title.

266. Gates, Francis. "Labor Resources in the University of California
     Libraries." *Labor History* 1 (Spring 1960): 196-205.
     Gates reviews both published and unpublished sources. He lists selected
     manuscript collections by title and includes volume, inclusive dates, and
     content notes. Oral histories are mentioned by informants' names.

267. Gracy, David B., II. "A History and Reminiscence: Archives for Labor
     in the United States." *Archivaria* 4 (Summer 1977): 151-165.
     Gracy reviews the institutions that have collected labor and union
     records in the U.S. While mentioning some key collections, his emphasis
     is on the institutions and not their record holdings.

268. Ham, F. Gerald. "Labor Manuscripts in the State Historical Society of
     Wisconsin." *Labor History* 7 (Fall 1966): 313-342.
     The article begins with a general description of the society's labor
     resources and concludes with a checklist of collections of organizational
     records and personal papers. Entries include record series titles, volume,
     inclusive dates, and content notes.

269. Heffron, Paul T. "Manuscript Sources in the Library of Congress for a
     Study of Labor History." *Labor History* 10 (Fall 1969): 630-638.
     The article is divided into three parts: organizational records, personal
     papers, and presidential papers. Description is limited to collection titles,
     inclusive dates, and comments on research values of a few key collections.

270. Huth, Geoffrey A. "Labor Archives in the University at Albany, State
     University of New York." *Labor History* 32 (Winter 1991): 130-135.
     Huth cites collection and record series titles and inclusive dates of labor-
     related collections. These include records of union and trade guilds;
     public employee unions; and labor councils.

271. Johnpoll, Bernard K. "Manuscript Sources in American Radicalism."
     Labor History 14 (Winter 1973): 92-97.
     Johnpoll lists eighteen libraries that, in his opinion, have the richest
     labor-related manuscript resources. He cites titles and inclusive dates of
     key collections held by each repository and notes their research potentials.

272. Leab, Daniel J., ed. *Labor History* 23 (Fall 1982): 485-581.

A substantial portion of the Fall, 1982 issue of *Labor History* is devoted to articles describing labor-related holdings at specific archives and manuscript repositories. Description of holdings follows a similar format that generally includes collection titles, record series titles, inclusive dates, and content notes. Article titles and authors are:

1. Boccaccio, Mary. "Labor Resources at the University of Maryland at College Park." 498-501.

2. Dinwiddie, Robert and Leslie Hough. "The Southern Labor Archives." 502-512.

3. East, Dennis. "Labor History Resources in the Ohio Historical Society." 513-515.

4. Filippelli, Ronald L., and Alice Hoffman. "Labor Sources at Penn State University." 516-519.

5. Fones-Wolf, Ken. "Sources for the Study of Labor History in the Urban Archives, Temple University." 520-525.

6. Gamble, Robert A., and George Green. "Labor Archives at the University of Texas at Arlington." 526-527.

7. Lazar, Robert E. "The International Ladies' Garment Workers' Union." 528-533.

8. Mason, Philip P. "The Archives of Labor and Urban Affairs, Walter P. Reuther Library, Wayne State University." 534-545.

9. Miller, Harold L. "Labor Records at the State Historical Society of Wisconsin." 546-552.

10. Strassberg, Richard. "Labor History Resources in the Martin P. Catherwood Library of the New York State School of Labor and Industrial Relations at Cornell University." 553-561.

11. Swanson, Dorothy. "Tamiment Institute/Ben Josephson Library and Robert F. Wagner Labor Archives." 562-567.

12. Vecoli, Rudolph J. "Labor Related Collections in the Immigration History Research Center." 568-574.

13. Weber, Edward C. "The Labadie Collection in the University of Michigan Library." 575-581.

273. Leab, Daniel J. *Labor History* 31 (Winter/Spring 1990): 7-226.

This special issue of *Labor History* focuses on labor-related archives and manuscript collections in the U.S. The individual articles describe repository holdings and special collections in general terms by noting collection strengths and citing collection and record series titles, inclusive dates, volume, and the research potential of collections. Article titles and authors are:

1. Ashyk, Dan and Wendy S. Greenwood. "Labor History Resources at the Ohio Historical Society." 133-138.

2. Becker, Ronald L. "Labor History Resources at the Rutgers University Libraries." 67-70.

3. Bernhardt, Debra E. "Labor History Resources at New York University. The Robert F. Wagner Labor Archives." 54-58.

4. Bonfield, Lynn A., and Leon J. Sompolinsky. "The Labor Archives and Research Center at San Francisco State University." 219-226.

5. Brown, Lauren. "Labor Union History and Archives: The University of Maryland at College Park Libraries." 113-116.

6. Cooper, Eileen M. "Labor Archives at Indiana University of Pennsylvania." 77-80.

7. Cooper, Sarah. "Sources on Labor History at the Southern California Library for Social Studies and Research." 208-212.

8. Danky, James P., and Harold L. Miller. "Sources for the Study of the Labor Movement at the State Historical Society of Wisconsin." 176-184.

9. Dinwiddie, Robert and Leslie S. Hough. "The Southern Labor Archives." 124-132.

10. Fones-Wolf, Ken. "Labor History Sources at the University of Massachusetts at Amherst." 31-38.

11. Gottlieb, Peter and Diana L. Shenk. "Historical Collections & Labor Archives, Penn State University." 81-85.

12. Green, George N. "The Texas Labor Archives." 202-207.

13. Haynes, John E. "Labor History Sources in the Manuscript Division of the Library of Congress." 89-97.

14. Jimerson, Randall C. "The Connecticut Labor Archives." 39-43.

15. Lages, J. David and Neal Moore. "The Ozarks Labor Union Archives at Southwestern Missouri State University." 163-167.

16. Lewis, Tab. "Labor History Sources in the National Archives." 96-104.

17. Lichtenstein, Nelson. "Labor and Social History Records at the Catholic University of America." 105-108.

18. McColloch, Mark. "The UE/Labor Archives, University of Pittsburgh." 86-88.
    UE is an abbreviation for United Electrical, Radio, and Machine Workers of America.

19. Marshall, Robert G. "The Urban Archives Center at California State University, Northridge." 213-218.

20. Mason, Philip P. "Labor Archives and Collections in the United States." 10-15.

21. Mason, Philip P. "The Archives of Labor and Urban Affairs, Walter P. Reuther Library, Wayne State University." 145-154.

22. Montgomery, Bruce P. "The Joseph A. Beirne Memorial Archives." 109-112.

23. Moseley, Eva. "Labor Holdings at the Schlesinger Library, Radcliffe College." 16-24.

24. Rocha, Guy Louis. "Labor Resources at the Nevada State Library and Archives." 197-201.

25. Schacht, John N. "Labor History Resources in the University of Iowa Libraries, the State Historical Society of Iowa/Iowa City, and the Herbert Hoover Presidential Library." 168-175.

26. Sheridan, Clare M. "Labor Material in the Collections of the Museum of American Textile History." 25-30.

27. Strassberg, Richard. "Sources on Labor History in the Martin P. Catherwood Library." 59-66.

28. Swanson, Dorothy. "Labor History Resources at New York University: The Tamiment Institute/Ben Josephson Library." 48-54.

29. Vancil, David E., Robert L. Carter and Charles D. King. "The Debs Collection at Indiana State University." 139-144.

30. Vogel, Katharine. "The George Meany Memorial Archives." 117-123.

31. Volpe, Cassandra M. "Labor Collections in the Western History Collections at the University of Colorado, Boulder." 192-196.

32. Weber, Edward C. "The Labadie Collection in the University of Michigan Library." 155-162.

33. Weinberg, David M. "Labor Collections at the Urban Archives Center, Temple University Libraries." 71-76.

34. Witkowski, Mary K. "Sources for Business and Labor History in the Bridgeport Public Library." 44-47.

35. Wurl, Joel. "The Immigration History Research Center as a Source for Labor History Research." 185-191.

274. Lewinson, Paul and Morris Rieger. "Labor Union Records in the United States." *American Archivist* 25 (January 1962): 39-57.
     The significant portion of this article is survey data on pages 46-57. There is a checklist of labor unions with statistics on their record holdings. The locations of labor records are often mentioned in the notes.

275. Lovett, Robert W. "Labor History Materials in the Harvard University Library." *Labor History* 4 (Fall 1963): 273-279.
     A narrative review of holdings in which Lovett cites collection titles, volume, and inclusive dates and includes comments on a collection's research value and special strengths.

276. Lovett, Robert W. "The Thompson Products Collection." *Bulletin of the Business Historical Society* 23 (December 1949): 191-195.
     This collection documents Thompson Product's relations with labor unions and the federal government for the period 1933-1948.

277. Mason, Philip P. "Labor History Archives at Wayne State University." *Labor History* 5 (Winter 1964): 67-75.
     Mason relates the collection policy of the archives, notes the types of records it holds, including oral histories, and describes several representative collections by mentioning collection titles, volume, key record series, and research values.

278. Mason, Philip P. "Wayne State University: The Archives of Labor and

Urban Affairs." *Archivaria* 4 (Summer 1977): 137-150.

While mostly a review of the archives' development and collection policy, Mason does cite some key collections to illustrate the scope and content of the holdings.

279. Miller, J. G. "Labor Resources in the Cornell University Library." *Labor History* 1 (Fall 1960): 319-326.

Miller lists personal papers, organizational records, and court cases in the Labor-Management Documentation Center of the library. Entries include collection and record series titles, volume, inclusive dates, and content summaries.

280. Motley, Archie. "Labor History Manuscripts in the Chicago Historical Society." *Labor History* 32 (Spring 1991): 290-294.

Motley cites collection and record series titles and inclusive dates of labor-related collections. They include union records and the personal papers of union leaders and of attorneys representing them.

281. Nelson, Steve. "Performing Arts Collections at the Robert F. Wagner Labor Archives." *Performing Arts Resources* 10 (1985): 17-21.

This archive holds the records of Actors' Equity Association; American Guild of Variety Artists; the American Federation of Musicians; and other performing arts union records.

282. Onsi, Patricia W. "Labor History Resources of the University of Illinois." *Labor History* 7 (Spring 1966): 209-215.

Onsi cites both published and unpublished materials. Her description of records and manuscripts includes collection titles, record series titles, dates, and content notes.

283. Parnes, Brenda and Debra Bernhardt. "Labor Archives Roundtable of the Society of American Archivists: A Directory and Concise Guide to Holdings." *Labor History* 33 (Fall 1992): 538-562.

Entries for this directory to repositories with labor-related holdings appear alphabetically by state beginning with California and include volume, inclusive dates, a scope and content summary, and access information.

284. Petterchak, Janice A. "Resources for the Study of Labor History at the Illinois State Historical Library." *Labor's Heritage* 3 (October 1991): 50-55.

Petterchak cites specific labor-related collections with inclusive dates, volume, and record series titles. She also comments on the library's extensive collection of labor-related photographs.

285. Ray, Joyce. "Documenting Workers and Health: Federal Sources."
     Labor's Heritage 3 (April 1991): 66-77.

286. Rosswurm, Steve. "Sources for the Study of Labor History at the Chicago
     Historical Society." *Labor's Heritage* 2 (January 1990): 64-75.

287. Rosswurm, Steve and Toni Gilpin. "The FBI and the Farm Equipment
     Workers: FBI Surveillance Records as a Source for CIO Union History."
     Labor History 27 (Fall 1986): 485-505.
        The authors explain the FBI surveillance system, identify record series
     and the types of information they contain, and comment on the records'
     research values.

288. Scanlan, Eleanor H. "The Labadie Collection." *Labor History* 6 (Fall
     1965): 244-248.
        Charles Joseph Labadie was a labor leader and anarchist. Scanlan briefly
     describes his papers at the University of Michigan. They include corre-
     spondence and periodical literature documenting the labor movement in the
     Detroit area, 1880-1920.

289. Schwartz, Stephen. "Holdings on the 1934 West Coast Maritime Strike in
     the San Francisco Headquarters Archives, Sailors' Union of the Pacific:
     A Descriptive Summary." *Labor History* 27 (Summer 1986): 427-430.
        Among the records Schwartz identifies are minutes; correspondence; and
     strike files. His description includes correspondents' names, inclusive
     dates, content notes, and comments on missing records.

290. Shaughnessy, D. F. "Labor in the Oral History Collection of Columbia
     University." *Labor History* 1 (Spring 1960): 177-195.
        After commenting on the worth of oral history as a historical source, the
     author concludes with a checklist of twenty-seven labor-related oral
     histories. Entries include informants' occupation, date and length of
     transcript, and content notes.

291. Skeels, Jack W. "Oral History Project on the Development of Unionism
     in the Automobile Industry." *Labor History* 5 (Spring 1964): 209-212.
        The article calls attention to this project and its value as a historical
     source. While not listing interviews, it cites the types of interviews done
     and the topics covered.

292. White, Earl Bruce. "A Note on the Archives of the Western Federation of
     Miners and International Union of Mine, Mill & Smelter Workers." *Labor
     History* 17 (Fall 1976): 613-617.
        White calls attention to the University of Colorado's holdings of 1,000
     linear feet of minutes; financial and court records; and published materials

from this miners' union. He also provides a description of the fifty-one roll microfilm set of these records.

293. Zieger, Robert H. "The CIO: A Bibliographic Update and Archival Guide." *Labor History* 31 (Fall 1990): 413-440.

The second part of Zieger's article locates and describes holdings of CIO records throughout the U.S. He cites record series, volume, and contents of major collections under state headings.

294. Zieger, Robert H. "Labor and the State in Modern America: The Archival Trail." *Journal of American History* 75 (June 1988): 184-196.

This article reviews federal records relating to labor relations and the records of labor unions. It closes by noting Communist influences in the labor movement and citing repositories holding materials relating to Communism and other left-wing parties.

Transportation

295. Aiken, M. Chalon. "Illinois & Michigan Canal Records." *Illinois Libraries* 25 (October 1943): 340-341.

A brief article reviewing the provenance and record series of this canal project. Dating from 1836 to 1933, the records include financial ledgers, administrative and survey records, and maps.

296. Corbett, William P. "Resources for Modern Highway Development: Oklahoma as a Case Study." *Government Publications Review* 8A (November/December 1981): 473-483.

The author reviews the usefulness of federal records such as reports of the postmaster general, U.S. Army post returns, and the territorial papers of Oklahoma, along with many published state and federal document series.

297. Davis, Robert S., Jr. "Records of the Western & Atlantic Railroad and Related Historical Resources in Georgia." *Railroad History* 158 (Spring 1988): 151-155.

Davis reports on the informational content of key record series and concludes with an inventory of subgroups, record series titles, volume, and inclusive dates.

298. Edmunds, Henry E. "The Ford Motor Company Archives." *American Archivist* 15 (April 1952): 99-104.

In his review of the archives, Edmunds refers to about 4,000 linear feet of records in two record groups, Henry Ford's personal papers, and the records of the company.

299. Ellis, Mary B. "The Hale Family Papers." *Quarterly Journal of Current Acquisitions* 12 (May 1955): 106-111.

     This collection contains the papers of Nathan Hale, railroad builder and nephew of the Revolutionary War hero of the same name, and of his brothers-in-law Alexander and Edward Everett. The article focuses on the correspondence of both Hale and the Everetts.

300. Hofsommer, Don L. "Of Buffs and Professionals: Iowa's Expanded Transportation Archives." *Books at Iowa* 48 (April 1988): 29-32.

     This article reports on the railroad collection of John P. Vander Maas which includes photographs of locomotives and rolling stock, timetables, train orders, tickets, passes, and other railroad ephemera.

301. Kolbet, Richard M. "The Levi O. Leonard Railroad Collection." *Books at Iowa* 8 (April 1968): 3-10.

     Leonard spent the majority of his life studying the development of the Union Pacific and Rock Island Railroads and collecting their records. The nucleus of this collection at the University of Iowa is the papers of Union Pacific vice president Thomas C. Durant.

302. Koplowitz, Bradford. "The Rock Island Line is a Mighty Good Line -- for Research." *Chronicles of Oklahoma* 66 (Summer 1988): 206-215.

     A description of the five record groups making up the Rock Island Collection at the University of Oklahoma's Western History Collections. Koplowitz concludes the article by listing the volume and inclusive dates for each record series.

303. Lacy, Harriet S. "Inventory, the Abbott-Downing Company Records, 1813-1945." *Historical New Hampshire* 20 (Autumn 1965): 39-46.

     The records are located in the New Hampshire Historical Society. The Abbott-Downing Company made Concord coaches and wagons.

304. Luckett, Perry D., and Jennings R. Mace. "USAF Academy Research Materials on American Flight, 1903-1927 from the Gimble Collection." *Journal of American Culture* 7 (Spring/Summer 1984): 104-107.

     While mostly published materials, the Gimble Collection does contain letters by Otto Chanute, Samuel P. Langley, the Wrights, Cyrus Adler, and WWI aviator A. E. Parr, plus early aviation prints and photographs.

305. McFarland, Marvin W. "Three Aeronautical Collections." *Quarterly Journal of Current Acquisitions* 13 (November 1955): 1-11.

     McFarland describes the papers of Igor I. Sikorsky and Lt.Gen. Elwood R. Quesada along with the records of the Daniel Guggenheim Fund for the Promotion of Aeronautics. McFarland focuses his description mostly upon the collections' correspondence files.

306. McFarland, Marvin W., and Arthur Renstrom. "The Papers of Wilbur and Orville Wright." *Quarterly Journal of Current Acquisitions* 7 (August 1950): 22-34.

    The Wrights' papers include correspondence, 1881-1948; diaries and notebooks, 1901-1920; business and legal papers, 1894-1930; miscellaneous papers, 1900-1948; and photographs and published materials. The authors provide descriptions under each of these categories.

307. Meinig, Donald W. "Research in Railroad Archives." *Pacific Northwest Quarterly* 47 (January 1956): 20-22.

    The author used railroad records in the corporate archives of the Northern Pacific Railroad in St. Paul, Minnesota, and the Union Pacific Railroad in Omaha, Nebraska. He provides a description of the types of records found in both archives.

308. Neils, Allan E. "A New Collection: The Burlington Northern." *Oregon Historical Quarterly* 74 (March 1973): 79-82.

    Neils reviews a collection of Burlington Northern Railroad records at the Oregon Historical Society. He notes that they are mostly records of a subsidary line, the Spokane, Portland, and Seattle Railway Company, for the period 1898-1970.

309. Nolan, Patrick B. "The Wright Brothers Collection." *Aerospace Historian* 31 (Winter 1984): 272-276.

    A brief overview of the collection at Wright State University. It contains 1,500 photographs, a library of early aviation books and journals, the Wrights' business and legal records, and the diaries of Milton Wright, Orville's and Wilbur's father.

310. Post, Robert C. "Manuscript Sources for Railroad History." *Railroad History* 137 (Fall 1977): 38-63.

    Post's article is a mini-guide listing 500 collections relating to railroads. Entries include collection title, record series titles, inclusive dates, volume, and content notes. It is also indexed.

311. "Reading Railroad Collection." *Business History Review* 35 (Autumn 1961): 426-427.

    The article calls attention to Reading Railroad records at the Historical Society of Pennsylvania. It lists many record series and inclusive dates.

312. Schiff, Judith A. "The Life and Letters of Charles A. Lindbergh: A Commemorative View." *Yale University Library Gazette* 51 (April 1977): 173-189.

    This article is mostly biographical. It focuses on Lindbergh's correspondence with several excerpts showing the progress of his career.

313. Schuster, Richard. "Railroad Collections at the New Hampshire Historical Society." *Historical New Hampshire* 45 (Fall 1990): 235-252.

314. Sheppard, Milton. "The Lammot DuPont Aeronautical Collection of Aircraft Negatives." *American Aviation Historical Society Journal* 24 (Summer 1979): 90-98.
    The article lists images by manufacturer and then by aircraft make and model and angles of view. The collection is held by Eleutherian Mills Historical Library.

315. Stoll, C. W. "The Arthur E. Hopkins River Collection and Its Significance." *Filson Club History Quarterly* 20 (October 1946): 291-301.
    Much of the Hopkins Collection is published books about steamboating, but it also contains photographs, scrapbooks, manuscripts, and unpublished papers regarding river travel.

316. Streeter, Jean Douglas. "Charles A. Lindbergh's Papers: Aviation History Spiced with Hero Worship." *Gateway Heritage* 4 (Winter 1983/1984): 30-37.
    The short narrative of this article notes that the Lindbergh papers at the Missouri Historical Society cover the period 1927-1942 and relate to his trans-Atlantic flight; his work with the Rockefeller Institute; and his stand on U.S. neutrality in WWII.

317. Streeter, Jean Douglas. "The Charles A. Lindbergh Photograph Collection." *Gateway Heritage* 7 (Winter 1986/1987): 34-41.
    Streeter comments on the 3,800-image Lindbergh photograph collection at the Missouri Historical Society in St. Louis.

Ethnic Minorities and Women

General

318. Anderson, R. Joseph. "Building a Multi-Ethnic Collection: The Research Library of the Balch Institute for Ethnic Studies." *Ethnic Forum* 5 (Fall 1985): 7-19.

    In describing the institute's archival holdings, the author identifies ethnic groups represented, cites collection titles, inclusive dates, volume, record series, and comments on the contents and research values of collections.

319. Grabowski, John J. "Ethnic Collections of the Western Reserve Historical Society." *Illinois Libraries* 57 (March 1975): 171-174.

    Grabowski reviews the types of materials in the society relating to ethnic groups including manuscript collections, newspapers, photographs, and records of local government agencies and private social service organizations.

320. Grabowski, John J. "Ethnicity in Perspective. The Collections of the Western Reserve Historical Society." *Ethnic Forum* 1 (September 1981): 29-30.

321. Harding, Bruce C. "Sources for Ethnic Studies in the Region 5 Archives." *Illinois Libraries* 57 (March 1975): 184-185.

    Description in this article is limited to three record series, U.S. courts case files; U.S. court records on immigration and naturalization; and U.S. census records on microfilm. The Region 5 Archives Branch is in Chicago, Illinois.

322. Hoffman, Abraham. "A Note on the Field Research Interviews of Paul S. Taylor for Mexican Labor in the United States Monographs." *Pacific Historian* 20 (Summer 1976): 123-131.

    This article reviews and lists fifteen categories of Taylor's field interviews now held by the Bancroft Library. The entries appear by category of informant or geographical location and indicate the number of interviews in each group.

323. Howerton, Joseph B. "The Resources of the National Archives for North-Central States Ethnic Research." *Illinois Libraries* 57 (March 1975): 174-184.

     Record cited by Howerton include those of the Bureau of Customs; Immigration & Naturalization Service; U.S. Conciliation Service; Bureau of Labor Statistics; Public Housing Administration; Work Projects Administration; and the War Relocation Authority. The author concludes the article by identifying access problems and citing restrictions on several record series.

324. Kreneck, Thomas H. "Documenting a Mexican American Community: The Houston Example." *American Archivist* 48 (Summer 1985): 272-285.

     The author describes efforts of the Houston [Texas] Public Library's Metropolitan Research Center to develop a Mexican-American collection. He mentions many of the key manuscript collections acquired and areas of Mexican-American history and culture that they document.

325. Maciuszko, Jerzy J. "Ethnic Libraries in the Greater Cleveland Area." *Ethnic Forum* 9 (No. 1 1989): 52-64.

     The author identifies ethnic groups represented and provides a brief overview of each library's holdings.

326. Nealand, Daniel. "Chinese American Historical Studies: A Summary of Resources at the National Archives-Pacific Sierra Region." *Chinese America: History and Perspectives* (1991): 121-134.

     Nealand offers a checklist of record groups containing information on Chinese in the U.S. In most instances, he also cites record series and inclusive dates. Some entries have content notes and he includes micro-filmed records.

327. Peters, Gayle, Jonathan Goldstein, and Merlin Kirk. "Historical Documents Relating to Asian-Americans and to East Asia in the Atlanta Regional Archives Branch." *West Georgia College Studies in the Social Sciences* 22 (June 1983): 3-12.

328. Potter, Constance. "St. Albans Passenger Arrival Records." *Prologue* 22 (Spring 1990): 90-93.

     These records document immigrants arriving in the U.S. from Canada. Potter explains the types of information found in the records and how to use them.

329. Worden, Robert L. "Chinese Immigration Files at the National Archives." *Annals of the Chinese Historical Society of the Pacific Northwest* (1983): 56-67.

Afro-Americans

330. Abbott, Craig S., and Kay Van Mol. "The Willard Motley Papers at Northern Illinois University." *Resources for American Literary Study* 7 (Spring 1977): 3-26.

    This Afro-American author's collection includes thirty-one feet of diaries, correspondence, photographs, sound recordings, manuscripts of his writings, and published materials. Abbott and Van Mol provide detailed descriptions of each record series in the collection.

331. Alexander, Lee G. "Expanding Sources for Black Research at Atlanta University." *Georgia Archive* 7 (Spring 1979): 16-21.

    The author cites many collections in the Trevor Arnett Library. Description is limited to collection titles with occasional scope and content notes and comments on research values.

332. Biddle, Stanton F. "The Schomburg Center for Research in Black Culture: Documenting the Black Experience." *Bulletin of the New York Public Library* 76 (1972): 21-35.

    The author provides an overview of this rich resource that contains clipping files; sound recordings; manuscript collections; motion pictures; archives; and photographs.

333. Billington, Monroe. "Black Slavery in Indian Territory: The Ex-Slave Narratives." *Chronicles of Oklahoma* 60 (Spring 1982): 56-65.

    An analysis of data in interviews of former slaves gathered by the WPA's Federal Writers Project in the 1930s. Most the narratives are in the Library of Congress, but the article also cites those in the Oklahoma Historical Society.

334. Boles, Nancy G. "Black History Collections." *Maryland Historical Magazine* 66 (Spring 1971): 72-78.

    Boles cites manuscript collections in the Maryland Historical Society by collection title and content notes under the headings plantation accounts; slaves and slavery; Africa and colonization; abolitionists; freedmen; the Civil War; and post-Civil War.

335. Bontemps, Arna. "The James Weldon Johnson Memorial Collection of Negro Arts and Letters." *Yale University Library Gazette* 18 (October 1943): 19-26.

    This is an overview of a collection assembled by Carl Van Vechten. Its purpose was to portray Afro-American life in the 20th century through books and unpublished materials. Bontemps mentions some manuscripts and photographs in the collection, but not in detail.

336. Botkin, B. A. "The Slave as His Own Interpreter." *Quarterly Journal of Current Acquisitions* 2 (July 1944): 37-46.
    This article relates the provenance of the photographs and typescript interviews of former slaves accumulated by the WPA's Federal Writers Project in the late 1930s. The article includes several excerpts of interviews.

337. Clayton, Minnie H. "A Survey of Archival Holdings Relating to the Black Experience in the Civil Rights Movement." *Georgia Archive* 7 (Spring 1979): 22-35.
    Clayton identifies repositories and cites specific collections in Georgia and other states. Description is limited to collection titles with some comments about scope and content.

338. Cox, Dwayne. "Records of Louisville's State University: A Case Study in Afro-American History." *Library Review* 34 (1984): 23-30.

339. Crouch, Barry A. "Hidden Sources of Black History: The Texas Freedmen's Bureau Records as a Case Study." *Southwestern Historical Quarterly* 83 (January 1980): 211-226.
    Crouch concentrates on the types of information that may and may not be found in the bureau's records while also commenting on their research values.

340. Davis, Lenwood G. "Sources for History of Blacks in Oregon." *Oregon Historical Quarterly* 73 (September 1972): 197-211.
    Davis cites mostly published materials, but does identify some manuscript collection titles and record groups relating to Afro-Americans.

341. Frazier, E. Franklin. "The Booker T. Washington Papers." *Quarterly Journal of Current Acquisitions* 2 (February 1945): 23-31.
    Frazier describes the papers under headings of Tuskegee Institute materials; family correspondence; speeches and writings; National Negro Business League materials; and correspondence with various people and organizations.

342. Goggin, Jacqueline. "Carter G. Woodson and the Collection of Source Materials for Afro-American History." *American Archivist* 48 (Summer 1985): 261-271.
    While explaining Woodson's collecting role at the Library of Congress, Goggin also briefly describes the Woodson Collection of Negro Papers which includes the papers of Whitfield McKinlay, Benjamin Tucker Tanner, John T. Clark, and Carter G. Woodson.

343. Greene, Lorenzo J. "Negro Manuscripts Collections in Libraries." *Negro*

History Bulletin 30 (March 1967): 20-21; and (October 1967): 14-15.

These articles cite collections at the University of Michigan, Columbia University, Atlanta University, the Huntington Library, Wilberforce University, and several public libraries in the northeastern U.S.

344. Hoyt, William D., Jr. "The Papers of the Maryland State Colonization Society." *Maryland Historical Magazine* 32 (September 1937): 247-271.

Aside from a short introduction, this article is an inventory of the Colonization Society's records. Hoyt lists record series titles with inclusive dates under fifteen record groups.

345. Johnson, Clifton H. "Some Archival Sources on Negro History in Tennessee." *Tennessee Historical Quarterly* 28 (Winter 1969): 397-416.

Johnson uses an institutional approach to cite collection titles and provide content information on record groups and manuscript collections in Tennessee archives and manuscript repositories.

346. Johnson, Clifton H. "Some Archival Sources of Negro History in Tennessee." *Tennessee Librarian* 22 (Winter 1970): 80-94.

Johnson describes archives and manuscript collections in the Tennessee State Library and Archives; Library of the Methodist Publishing House; Disciples of Christ Historical Society; and at several universities of which Fisk has the largest collection.

347. Joyce, Donald Franklin, ed. "Resources for Scholars: Four Major Collections of Afro-Americana. Part I: Two Public Library Collections. Part II: Two University Library Collections" *Library Quarterly* 58 (January 1988): 66-82; and (April 1988): 143-163.

The public library collections described are the Vivian G. Harsh Collection for Afro-American History and Literature in the Chicago Public Library and the Schomburg Center for Research in Black Culture in the New York Public Library. The university collections are the Moorland-Spingarn Research Center at Howard University and Fisk University's special collections. All four essays in this series describe unpublished materials along with book holdings.

348. Klinkowitz, Jerome, James Giles, and John T. O'Brien. "The Willard Motley Papers at the University of Wisconsin." *Resources for American Literary Study* 2 (Autumn, 1972): 218-273.

Willard Motley was an Afro-American novelist. Klinkowitz provides a checklist of Motley correspondence from 1951 to 1965, reviews of his works, clipping files, notebooks, and story lines. The article concludes with an index.

349. Lachatanere, Diana. "Blacks in California: An Annotated Guide to the

Manuscript Sources in the CHS Library." *California History* 57 (Fall 1978): 271-276.

The author describes twenty-six collections with each entry including collection title, inclusive dates, volume, type of materials, and content summary.

350. Lindsey, Arnett G. "Manuscript Materials Bearing on the Negro in America." *Journal of Negro History* 27 (January 1942): 94-101.

The author briefly describes Afro-American-related manuscript collections at the Southern Historical Collection, University of North Carolina; Duke University; the Historical Society of Pennsylvania; the Library of Congress; and Berea College.

351. Malval, Fritz J. "The Archives of Hampton Institute, Hampton, Virginia." *Journal of the Afro-American Historical and Genealogical Society* 3 (No. 1 1982): 14-17.

352. McConnell, Roland C. "Importance of Records in the National Archives on the History of the Negro." *Journal of Negro History* 34 (April 1949): 135-152.

A review of record groups containing records relating to Afro-Americans. The author notes record series and inclusive dates while commenting on the type of information found in each record group and its research value.

353. McConnell, Roland C. "A Small College and the Archival Record." *Journal of Negro Education* 32 (Winter 1963): 84-86.

This article describes Emmett J. Scott's correspondence files (1916-1951) from his service as secretary to Booker T. Washington, an assistant secretary of war, a university official, and service on several boards and commissions relating to Afro-Americans.

354. McDonough, John J. "Manuscript Resources for the Study of Negro Life and History." *Quarterly Journal of the Library of Congress* 26 (July 1969): 126-148.

McDonough describes several significant Afro-America-related collections including the papers of the NAACP; the papers of Arthur Spingarn; records of the National Urban League; the Carter G. Woodson papers; records of the American Colonization Society; and many others.

355. Mock, James R. "The National Archives with Respect to the Records of the Negro." *Journal of Negro History* 23 (January 1938): 49-56.

Mock reviews record groups containing materials relating to Afro-Americans. He relates the purpose of the record-creating agencies, cites specific record series titles, and comments on the types of information found in each and their research value.

356. Pinkett, Harold T. "Recent Federal Archives as Sources for Negro History." *Negro History Bulletin* 30 (December 1967): 14-17.
     Pinkett suggests records created during the 1930s and especially Roosevelt's New Deal agencies. Specifically, he mentions the records of the Civilian Conservation Corps, National Recovery Administration, Department of Agriculture, WPA Federal Theatre Project, Public Housing Administration, and the Department of Labor.

357. Raboteau, Albert J., and others. "Retelling Carter Woodson's Story: Archival Sources for Afro-American Church History." *Journal of American History* 77 (June 1990): 183-199.
     The authors identify and locate significant Afro-American church-related records and manuscript collections. Description, which is in narrative format, includes repository names, collection and record series titles, volume, inclusive dates, and research values.

358. Roff, Sandra. "Researching the History of Blacks in New York State: Resources Available at the New York Historical Society." *Afro-Americans in New York Life and History* 9 (No. 1 1985): 43-49.

359. Rogers, Ben. "Black Texas Baptist Church Records." *Journal of the Afro-American Historical and Genealogical Society* 3 (No. 2 1982): 65-66.

360. Scally, Sister Anthony. "The Carter Woodson Letters in the Library of Congress." *Negro History Bulletin* 38 (June/July 1975): 419-421.
     The author calls attention to the collection of papers Woodson assembled during his editorship of the *Journal of Negro History*. Description is limited to citing examples from the collection's correspondence. The letters date from 1916 to 1927.

361. Scherer, Lester B., and Susan M. Eltscher. "Afro-American Baptists: A Guide to Materials in the American Baptist Historical Society." *American Baptist Quarterly* 4 (No. 3 1985): 282-299.

362. Schneider, Gilbert D. "Daniel Emmett's Negro Sermons and Hymns: An Inventory." *Ohio History* 85 (Winter 1976): 67-83.
     Daniel Emmett was a musician, performer, and composer, perhaps, best known for writing "Dixie." This article reviews Emmett's papers and especially the forty Afro-American dialect sermons among them. The Ohio Historical Society holds the collection.

363. Sims-Wood, Janet. "Researching Black Women's History: Resources and Archives at the Moorland-Spingarn Research Center." *Ethnic Forum* 7

(No. 1 1987): 38-47.

The author lists collections of manuscripts, records, photographs, oral histories, music, and the Alpha Kappa Alpha sorority archives. Description is limited to collection titles and content notes.

364. Storey, Moorfield, Jr. "The May Papers." *More Books* 19 (May 1944): 171-175.

Storey describes correspondence to and from the Rev. Samuel May, a Unitarian minister and principal figure in the Massachusetts Anti-Slavery Society. His correspondence reflects the anti-slavery movement in Massachusetts from the 1840s to the 1860s.

365. Weisman, Kay. "Black History Resources at the Ohio Historical Society." *Journal of the Afro-American Historical and Genealogical Society* 2 (No. 2 1981): 47-52.

366. White, Deborah G. "Mining the Forgotten: Manuscript Sources for Black Women's History." *Journal of American History* 74 (June 1987): 237-242.

White identifies collections and organizational records and the repositories holding them.

367. Wilkinson, Norman B. "Papers of the Pennsylvania Society for Promoting the Abolition of Slavery." *Pennsylvania Magazine of History and Biography* 68 (July 1944): 286-290.

The records of the society include indenture and manumission certificates; minutes; membership lists; correspondence; and reports dating from the 1780s to the 1860s.

368. Williams, Joan B. "Some Special Collections in the Fisk University Library." *Tennessee Librarian* 16 (Winter 1964): 47-52.

Williams reports on Afro-American-related manuscript collections including the Robert E. Pike, John M. Langston, James Carroll Napier, Jean Toomer, Charles S. Johnson, Scott Joplin, Robert Ezra Park, and Charles W. Chesnutt Collections, and the American Missionary Association records.

369. Wynne, Frances H. "Records Pertaining to Blacks in North Carolina." *Journal of the Afro-American Historical and Genealogical Society* 8 (No. 1 1987): 14-26.

370. Zangrando, Robert L. "Manuscript Sources for 20th-Century Civil Rights Research." *Journal of American History* 74 (June 1987): 243-251.

Zangrando identifies repositories holding manuscript collections and organization records. He also cites many collection titles, occasionally with inclusive dates.

American Indians

371. Alden, John Richard. "The Eighteenth Century Cherokee Archives."
American Archivist 5 (October 1942): 240-244.
The archive was captured by an American military force in 1781. Many
of the records ultimately became a part of the papers of the Continental
Congress. A checklist of the records concludes the article.

372. Anderson, Charles A. "Index of American Indian Correspondence."
Presbyterian Historical Society Journal 31 (March 1953): 63-70.
This index is to more than 14,000 letters from Presbyterian missionaries
to North American Indian tribes written between 1833 and 1893. The
index is by tribe and also by principal correspondents or authors of the
letters.

373. Ballenger, T. L. "The Andrew Nave Letters: New Cherokee Source
Material at Northeastern State College." *Chronicles of Oklahoma* 30
(Spring 1952): 2-5.
This article describes a small cache of correspondence and business
records of a Cherokee Indian family of Park Hill, Indian Territory. The
materials date from the 1830s to the 1860s and include letters from John
Ross.

374. Bischoff, W. N. "The Yakima Indian War, 1855-1856: A Problem in
Research." *Pacific Northwest Quarterly* 41 (April 1950): 162-169.
A portion of this article locates thirty manuscript collections relating to
the Yakima Indian War. Specific collections are cited by title with
statements about their contents and value to the topic.

375. Borst, John C. "Dakota Resources: The John R. Brennan Family Papers
at the South Dakota Historical Resource Center." *South Dakota History* 14
(Spring 1984): 68-72.
Brennan was one of the founders of Rapid City, South Dakota, a
businessman, and Indian agent at the Pine Ridge Reservation. His papers
reflect his career and especially, his work as Indian agent from 1901 to
1917.

376. Burns, Robert J. "Pere Joset's Account of the Indian War of 1858."
Pacific Northwest Quarterly 38 (October 1947): 285-314.
Beginning on page 307 of this article is a "Descriptive Calendar of the
Joset Papers" held by Gonzaga University in Spokane, Washington. The
calendar provides document titles, dates, length, and content statements.

377. "Catalogue of Microfilmed Publications of the Archives and Manuscripts
Division, Oklahoma Historical Society." *Chronicles of Oklahoma* 60

(Spring 1982): 74-87; (Summer 1982): 218-231; (Fall 1982): 348-359; and
(Winter 1982): 473-480.

A four-part catalogue, published in consecutive issues of the *Chronicles*,
listing by tribe, the microfilmed records and manuscripts of the OHS's
Indian Archives Division. The lists include record series titles, inclusive
dates, and number of rolls.

378. Crampton, C. Gregory. "The Archives of the Duke Projects in American
Indian Oral History." in *Indian-White Relations: A Persistent Paradox*,
edited by Jane F. Smith and Robert M. Kvasnicka. Washington, D.C.:
Howard University Press, 1976. 119-128.

Crampton writes in general terms about the seven Doris Duke-funded
projects at the Universities of Arizona, Florida, Illinois, New Mexico,
Oklahoma, South Dakota, and Utah. Two accompanying tables list the
addresses of the institutions holding these collections and the Indian tribes
represented in them.

379. Day, Gordon M. "The Dartmouth Algonkian Collection." *Dartmouth
College Library Bulletin* 5 (May 1962): 41-43.

Day calls attention to an extensive oral history collection of interviews
with St. Francis Indians, descendants of an Algonquin group. The
collection is rich in linguistic and ethnological data.

380. Debo, Angie. "Major Indian Record Collections in Oklahoma." in *Indian-
White Relations: A Persistent Paradox* edited by Jane F. Smith and Robert
B. Kvasnicka. Washington, D.C.: Howard University Press, 1976. 112-
118.

Debo discusses several of the more comprehensive collections at the
University of Oklahoma, the Oklahoma Historical Society, and the
Gilcrease Institute. Records of the Five Civilized Tribes at these three
institutions are highlighted.

381. Ellis, Richard N. "The Duke Indian Oral History Collection at the
University of New Mexico." *New Mexico Historical Review* 48 (July
1973): 259-263.

Ellis describes the subject contents of the interviews in general terms.
He notes that Indians in Alaska, California, Montana, Washington, and
Canada are represented, but most of the 982 interviews are with Navajos
and Indians of the New Mexican pueblos.

382. Fenton, William N. "Calendar of Manuscript Materials Relating to the
History of the Six Nations, or Iroquois Indians, in Depositories Outside of
Philadelphia, 1750-1850." *Proceedings of the American Philosophical
Society* 97 (October 1953): 578-595.

The article lists the repositories, names the collections and the inclusive dates of each, and notes the availability of the collections on microfilm. Fenton describes several collections in some detail.

383. Fenton, William N. "Iroquois Studies at the Mid-Century." *Proceedings of the American Philosophical Society* 95 (June 1951): 296-310.
  Fenton describes the primary sources available in northeastern U.S. repositories on the six nations of the Iroquois. He cites collection titles, comments on the scope and content of each, and mentions many specific documents within key collections.

384. Freeman, John F. "Manuscript Sources on Latin American Indians in the Library of the American Philosophical Society." *Proceedings of the American Philosophical Society* 106 (December 1962): 530-540.
  The article reviews the society's acquisitions of collections relating to Latin American Indians and concludes with guide-like entries for fifty-four collections. Entries include collection titles, record series, volume, inclusive dates, and content notes.

385. Foreman, Grant. "A Survey of Tribal Records in the Archives of the United States Government in Oklahoma." *Chronicles of Oklahoma* 11 (March 1933): 625-634.
  Foreman lists the record series that were found among the records collected by the Commission to the Five Civilized Tribes. The Oklahoma Historical Society accessioned many of these records as part of its Indian Archives Division.

386. Gibson, Arrell M. "Sources for Research on the American Indian." *Ethnohistory* 7 (Spring 1960): 121-136.
  Gibson cites record groups held by the National Archives and collection titles in manuscript repositories, historical societies, and college and university special collections nationwide. Description of collections cited is brief.

387. Gormly, Mary. "Spanish Documentary Material Pertaining to the Northwest Coast Indians." *Davidson Journal of Anthropology* 1 (Summer 1955): 21-41.

388. Hoopes, Alban W. "Preliminary Report Upon the Correspondence of the Indian Rights Association in the Welsh Collection." *Pennsylvanian Magazine of History and Biography* 67 (October 1943): 382-389.
  This article describes the personal papers of Herbert Welsh, founder of the Indian Rights Association, along with the association's organizational records. Hoopes reports that the correspondence files and field reports are the most significant record series.

389. Hoxie, Frederick E. "The View from Eagle Butte: National Archives Field Branches and the Writing of American Indian History." *Journal of American History* 76 (June 1989): 172-180.

The author reviews the types of records relating to American Indians held in National Archives branches while discussing their research values and their deficiencies.

390. Hruneni, George A., Jr. "A Touch of Western Americana in the Archives of the Catholic University of America." *Manuscripts* 27 (Spring 1975): 95-101.

Hruneni highlights the papers of E.W.J. Lindesmith, a U.S. Army chaplain and missionary to the Crow Indians; Col. Jehiel Brooks, Indian agent to the Caddo Indians; and a "Special Document" series relating to the Yankton Sioux Indians.

391. Jones, William K. "General Guide to Documents on the Five Civilized Tribes in the University of Oklahoma Library Division of Manuscripts." *Ethnohistory* 14 (Winter/Spring 1967): 47-76.

There are three divisions to this guide: maps, microfilmed records, and manuscript collections. The entries include collection title, inclusive dates, and content notes.

392. Jordan, Julia A. "Oklahoma's Oral History Collection: New Source for Indian History." *Chronicles of Oklahoma* 49 (Summer 1971): 150-172.

Jordan describes the Indian oral history project at the University of Oklahoma which became known as the Doris Duke Indian Oral History Collection. The project was one of seven sponsored by the Duke Foundation.

393. Kelly, Lawrence C. "Indian Records in the Oklahoma Historical Society Archives." *Chronicles of Oklahoma* 54 (Summer 1976): 227-244.

A history of how a substantial body of Indian-related records were transferred from agency storage to the Oklahoma Historical Society. The article concludes by citing the volume, tribes, and general type of records transferred. Entries 377 and 385 describe these records in more detail.

394. Koplowitz, Bradford. "The Doris Duke Indian Oral History Projects." *Popular Culture in Libraries* (No. 3 1993): 23-38.

Koplowitz identifies the tribes represented and reviews the scope and content of each of the seven Duke-sponsored oral history projects. The Universities of Arizona, Florida, Illinois, New Mexico, Oklahoma, South Dakota, and Utah participated.

395. Litton, Gaston. "Enrollment Records of the Eastern Band of Cherokee Indians." *North Carolina Historical Review* 17 (July 1940): 199-231.

Litton explains the background, length, and contents of Cherokee Indian censuses known as the Henderson; Mullay; Siler; Chapman; Swetland; Hester; Churchill; and Guion Miller Rolls.

396. Litton, Gaston. "The Resources of the National Archives for the Study of the American Indian." *Ethnohistory* 2 (Summer 1955): 191-208.

While offering some useful information on several record groups relating to Indians, this article contains mostly information about the National Archives and archivists.

397. Logsdon, Guy. "Indian Studies Resources at the University of Tulsa." *Chronicles of Oklahoma* 55 (Spring 1977): 64-77.

The Alice Robertson and the John W. Sleppey Collections form the nucleus of Indian-related materials at the University of Tulsa. Logsdon cites both published and manuscript materials.

398. Masterson, James R. "The Records of the Washington Superintendency of Indian Affairs, 1853-1874." *Pacific Northwest Quarterly* 37 (January 1946): 31-57.

This article is a guide to the microfilm set of records from the superintendency. It includes an administrative history of the superintendency, a list of agency employees, and a roll list of the microfilm with record series titles and inclusive dates.

399. Ortiz, Alfonso. "A Uniquely American Legacy." *Princeton University Library Chronicle* 30 (Spring 1969): 147-157.

This article describes a Princeton University collection of sound recordings of Pueblo Indian songs, myths and folktales, prayers, and speeches.

400. Palmquist, Peter E. "The Roberts Collection of California Indian Photographs: A Brief Review." *Journal of California and Great Basin Anthropology* 5 (Summer/Winter 1983): 3-32.

Palmquist calls attention to a collection of 536 photographs taken by Crescent City, California, resident Ruth F. Roberts. The photos, dating from WWI through the 1950s, are mostly of Jurok Indians.

401. Pilling, James C. "Catalogue of Linguistic Manuscripts in the Library of the Bureau of Ethnology." *Bureau of Ethnology First Annual Report* (1881): 553-577.

This is an alphabetical presentation by author with entries including manuscript title, length, place at which the data was gathered, and occasional bibliographical notes. Most of the manuscripts relate to North American Indian languages.

402. Randle, Martha C. "The Waugh Collection of Iroquois Folktales."
     Proceedings of the American Philosophical Society 97 (October 1953):
     611-633.
     Frederick W. Waugh was an ethnologist at the National Museum of
     Canada. His papers, held by the society, consists of 157 Iroquois Indian
     stories and folktales collected between 1911-1918. The article lists each
     tale and analyzes many in detail.

403. Rodabaugh, James H. "American Indian Ethnohistorical Materials in
     Ohio." *Ethnohistory* 8 (Summer 1961): 242-255.
     Only the last one-third of this article discusses manuscripts and archives
     where the author cites collection titles and comments on research values
     of holdings at the Ohio Historical Society, the Western Reserve Historical
     Society, and the Ohio Historical and Philosophical Society.

404. Rogers, Virginia. "The Indians and the Métis: Genealogical Sources on
     Minnesota's Earliest Settlers." *Minnesota History* 46 (Fall 1979): 172-178.
     Rogers reviews manuscript collections and several record series titles
     that are useful for Indian-related research. She also explains how the
     records may be useful to historical research.

405. Ryan, Carmelita S. "The Written Record and the American Indian: The
     Archives of the United States." *Western Historical Quarterly* 6 (April
     1975): 163-173.
     Valuable for its description of Bureau of Indian Affairs records, (RG
     75), and explanation of some of the bureau's functions. Ryan also
     describes Indian-related records of the Departments of War, State, and the
     Interior; U.S. Court of Claims; General Accounting Office; General Land
     Office; and the Bureau of Reclamation.

406. Scherer, Joanna C. "Repository Sources of Northwest Coast Indian
     Photographs." *Arctic Anthropology* 27 (No. 2 1990): 40-50.

407. Schusky, Mary Sue and Ernest L. Schusky. "A Center of Primary Sources
     for Plains Indian History." *Plains Anthropologist* 15 (May 1970): 104-108.
     This article gives an overview of federal records in the federal records
     centers at Kansas City, Missouri; Fort Worth, Texas; Denver, Colorado;
     and Seattle, Washington.

408. Smith, Murphy D. "The Indian and the American Philosophical Society
     Library." *Manuscripts* 23 (Summer 1971): 202-205.
     Smith describes the holdings in general terms, citing Thomas Jefferson's
     gift of the Lewis and Clark papers; the collecting activities of Peter
     DuPonceau, and the acquisition of the Franz Boas papers as examples of
     Indian-related collections.

409. Snyderman, George S. "The Manuscript Collections of the Philadelphia Yearly Meeting of Friends Pertaining to the American Indian." *Proceedings of the American Philosophical Society* 102 (December 1958): 613-620.

    A detailed review of the records of the Philadelphia yearly meetings. Snyderman cites record series and inclusive dates and comments on the records' research values, especially as they relate to Seneca Indians. He also notes series available on microfilm.

410. Snyderman, George S. "A Preliminary Survey of American Indian Manuscripts in Repositories of the Philadelphia Area." *Proceedings of the American Philosophical Society* 97 (October 1953): 596-610.

    Snyderman reviews the manuscript holdings of the Chester County Historical Society; Quaker Historical Society; Haverford College; Historical Society of Pennsylvania; Swarthmore College; Library Company of Phildadelphia; and the American Philosophical Society.

411. Strickland, Rennard. "The Price of a Free Man: Resources for the Study of Indian Law, History, and Policy at the University of Tulsa." *University of Tulsa Law Journal* 15 (Summer 1980): 720-732.

    Strickland reviews manuscript collections, federal records, sound recordings, and published documents. Description is limited to collection and record series titles.

412. Swadesh, Frances L. "Analysis of Records of the Southern Ute Agency, 1877 through 1952, National Archives RG 75, in the Federal Records Center, Denver, Colorado." In *Ethnohistorical Bibliography of the Ute Indians of Colorado*, by Omer C. Stewart. Boulder: University of Colorado Press, 1971. 61-71.

    After a brief analysis, Swadesh lists the contents of sixty-three boxes of Bureau of Indian Affairs records. The listing includes record series titles, inclusive dates, and content notes.

413. Turcheneske, John A., Jr. "The Southwest in La Follette Land: The Carlos Montezuma Papers." *Manuscripts* 25 (Summer 1973): 202-207.

    In addition to describing the Montezuma papers held by the Wisconsin State Historical Society, Turcheneske cites several other collections relating to the southwestern U.S. and Indians.

414. Wallace, Anthony F. "The Frank G. Speck Collection." *Proceedings of the American Philosophical Society* 95 (June 1951): 286-289.

    Speck was an ethnographer whose papers document Eastern Woodlands Indian cultures. The papers include fieldnotes, manuscripts, correspondence, drawings, and photographs.

415. Wallace, Paul A. "They Knew the Indian: The Men Who Wrote the Moravian Records." *Proceedings of the American Philosophical Society* 95 (June 1951): 290-295.

   The article reviews the writings and papers of Moravian missionaries, especially those of John Heckewelder, which include journals, diaries, linguistic notes, and correspondence, all relating to American Indians and dating from 1742 to the 1830s.

416. Wehrkamp, Tim. "Manuscript Sources in Sioux Indian History at the Historical Resource Center." *South Dakota History* 8 (Spring 1978): 143-156.

   The author provides collection titles, inclusive dates, volume, record series titles, and content notes for forty-four Indian-related collections.

417. Yarmolinsky, Avrahm. "Aleutian Manuscript Collection." *Bulletin of the New York Public Library* 48 (August 1944): 671-680.

   Yarmolinsky describes a collection of eighty manuscripts compiled in the field by Russian ethnographer Waldemar Jochelson in 1909-1910. The field notes are mostly stories and songs of Aleut Indians.

418. Yarmolinsky, Avrahm. "Kamchadal and Asiatic Eskimo Manuscript Collections." *Bulletin of the New York Public Library* 51 (November 1947): 659-667.

   This article describes two collections. The first is a series of Kamchadal stories recorded by Waldemar Jochelson in 1910. The second contains field notes about Yuits collected by Waldemar Borogas in 1901.

Europeans

419. Corrsin, Stephen. "Polish Archival and Manuscript Sources for the Study of the Migrations to America." *East European Quarterly* 17 (Fall 1983): 299-309.

   The author visited Poland in search of materials documenting Polish migration to the U.S. In this article, he reviews collections of correspondence, private archives, Polish governmental records, church records, and published materials.

420. Csillag, András. "The Edmund Vasváry Collection." *Hungarian Studies* 1 (No. 1 1985): 123-130.

421. Hansen, Thorvald. "Danish Immigrant Materials: The Archives at Grand View College." *Annals of Iowa* 45 (Spring 1980): 313-318.

   Among the materials described are church records, especially those of the Lutheran Church; locally published newspapers; personal papers and narratives; and photographs. Grand View College is in Des Moines, Iowa.

422. Jaroszynska, Anna D. "The American Committee for Resettlement of Polish Displaced Persons (1948-1968) in the Manuscript Collection of the Immigration History Research Center." *Polish American Studies* 44 (Spring 1987): 67-74.

The committee helped displaced Poles find jobs and housing. Among its records are minutes, reports, and published materials.

423. Johnson, Timothy J. "Swedish-American Genealogy and the Archives of North Park College." *Illinois Libraries* 74 (November 1992): 446-448.

Johnson describes records gathered by the Evangelical Covenant Church and the Swedish-American Archives of Greater Chicago and lists available finding aids for these collections.

424. Nilsson, B.O. "A Survey of Swedish-American Museum and Archival Collections." *Swedish Pioneer Historical Quarterly* 27 (July 1976): 189-203.

425. Nir, Roman. "The Central Archives of Polonia." *Ethnic Forum* 14 (No. 2 1994): 70-78.

Instead of describing individual collections, Nir comments on the types of Polish-related materials that may be found at this archives in Orchard Lake, Michigan.

426. Olson, Nils W. "Source Materials on Emigration in the United States National Archives with Particular Emphasis on Swedish Emigration to the United States." *Swedish Pioneer Historical Quarterly* 12 (January 1961): 17-34.

Olson identifies passenger lists, U.S. census records, military service records, land warrant applications and land entry records, and merchant seamen certificates as being useful. He provides comments on the types of information found in each record series.

427. Tedebrand, Lars-Göran. "Sources for the History of Swedish Emigration." In *From Sweden to America: A History of the Migration*, edited by Harald Runblom and Hans Norman. Minneapolis: University of Minnesota Press, 1976. 76-93.

The author reviews the types of records available for documenting immigration to the U.S.; the time periods for which these records exist; where they may be found; and their usefulness.

428. Westerberg, Kermit B. "Genealogical Research and Resources at the Swenson Swedish Immigration Research Center." *Illinois Libraries* 74

(November 1992): 443-446.

Church records, Swedish immigration records, and Swedish-American benevolent society records are the primary record groups discussed in this article.

429. Westerberg, Kermit B. "Swedish Roots: Collections of Swedish-Americana and the Swenson Swedish Immigration Research Center at Augustana College, Rock Island, Illinois." *Illinois Libraries* 66 (April 1984): 171-173.

An overview of the center's holdings, most of which seem to be microfilmed records of Swedish churches, ministers, and benevolent organizations, along with the papers of the college's presidents.

430. Westerberg, Kermit B. "Swenson Swedish Immigration Research Center." *Illinois Libraries* 69 (October 1987): 601-606.

The author outlines the history and services of the center and describes its manuscript, photograph, map, and microform holdings. He cites collection titles, inclusive dates, and provides occasional content notes.

431. Westerberg, Wesley M. "The Swedish Pioneer Archives." *Illinois Libraries* 63 (April 1981): 296-298.

Only about one-third of this article describes archival holdings and that description is limited to collection titles.

432. Wurl, Joel. "Research Opportunities in the Immigration History Research Center's Polish American Collection." *Polish American Studies* 45 (Autumn 1988): 61-70.

Jews

433. Dubester, Henry J. "Resources on American Jewish History at the Library of Congress." *Publications of the American Jewish Historical Society* 47 (June 1958): 179-185.

The author cites titles of specific manuscript collections containing materials relating to Jewish involvement in politics, banking and industry, philanthropy, music, and the entertainment fields. He also calls attention to the library's photo holdings.

434. Dubow, Sylvan M. "The Jewish Historical Society of Greater Washington: Its Archival Program." *American Archivist* 30 (October 1967): 575-580.

This article contains a checklist of five major record groups and selected record series held by the society.

435. Kramer, William M., and Norton B. Stern. "A Guide to California Jewish

History." *Western States Jewish History* 24 (July 1992): 377-383; and 25 (July 1993): 369-376.

The authors list repositories holding Jewish archival and published resources with no description of individual collections.

436. Macleod, Celeste L. "The Western Jewish History Center." *American Jewish Historical Quarterly* 63 (December 1968): 271-277.

Macleod relates the history and mission of the center and provides an overview of its holdings which include published materials and manuscript and photograph collections.

437. Marcus, Jacob R. "The American Jewish Archives." *American Archivist* 23 (January 1960): 57-61.

The archives, located on the Cincinnati campus of the Hebrew Union College-Jewish Institute of Religion, collects material relating to American Jewry. This article is a review of the archives background with mention of its major holdings.

438. Mendelsohn, John. "The Holocaust: Records in the National Archives on the Nazi Persecution of the Jews." *Prologue* 16 (Spring 1984): 23-39.

The author notes eleven record groups in the National Archives that contain records relating to Jews. Most are captured German records and the records of the Nuremberg trials.

439. Mendelsohn, John. "The Holocaust: Rescue and Relief--Documentation in the National Archives." *Annals of the American Academy of Political and Social Sciences* 450 (July 1980): 237-249.

In this article, Mendelsohn cites records of the War Refugee Board; the Nuremberg trials; the Office of Military Government for Germany; the Evian les Bains Conference; the Rublee-Schacht negotiations; and the Bermuda Conference.

440. Meyer, Isidore S. "The American Jewish Historical Society." *Journal of Jewish Bibliography* 4 (January/April 1943): 6-24.

Meyer provides a history of the society and an overview of its holdings, including books, newspapers, serials, and manuscripts. Description of manuscripts is limited to collection and record series titles.

441. Nemoy, Leon. "Hebrew and Kindred Manuscripts in the Yale University Library." *Journal of Jewish Bibliography* 1 (July 1939): 107-110; and 3 (January/April 1941): 44-47.

The author calls attention to significant, but little known Jewish manuscripts at Yale, primarily from the Alexander and George Kohut Collection. He lists individual manuscripts by category with entries including title, date, language, and content notes.

442. Profitt, Kevin. "The American Jewish Archives: Documenting and Preserving the American Jewish Experience." *Ethnic Forum* 5 (Fall 1985): 20-29.

    The first one-half of the article relates the archive's history. Profitt offers an overview of its holdings in the second part, but cites only a few collection titles.

443. Reingold, Nathan. "Resources on American Jewish History in the National Archives." *Publications of the American Jewish Historical Society* 47 (June 1958): 186-194.

    Reingold cites record groups and gives specific examples of the types of information that might be found in each. Description is limited to the record group level with only occasional mention of record series.

444. Rhodes, Irwin S. "Early Legal Records of Jews of Lancaster County, Pennsylvania." *American Jewish Archives* 12 (April 1960): 96-108.

    This is a register of Lancaster County deeds, wills, and miscellaneous legal records involving Jews. The records date from the 1740s to 1902.

445. Spungen, Norma. "The Chicago Jewish Archives." *Illinois Libraries* 74 (November 1992): 466-467.

    An overview of records and manuscript collections relating to Jews in the Chicago area. Description is limited to collection titles.

Women

446. Adams, Margaret O. "Electronic Records at the National Archives: Resources for Women's Studies." *NWSA Journal* 2 (Spring 1990): 269-272.

    Adams reviews record groups that contain materials by or about women or women's issues. She describes records of the Office of the Secretary of Defense; National Institute of Health; Social Security Administration; Commission on Civil Rights; and Merit Protection Board.

447. Carter, Christie. "Sources of Women's History at the Vermont State Archives." *Vermont History* 59 (Winter 1991): 30-48.

448. Chaff, Sandra L. "Archives and Special Collections on Women in Medicine at the Medical College of Pennsylvania." *Medical Library Association Bulletin* 66 (January 1978): 55-57.

    The college's archival holdings include records of the college; records of Northwestern University Woman's Medical School; oral histories; Philadelphia-area hospital records; photographs; and manuscript collections, all dating from the 1850s to the 1960s.

449. Chepesiuk, Ron. "The Winthrop College Archives and Special Collections: Selected Resources for the Study of Women's History." *South Carolina Historical Magazine* 82 (April 1981): 143-172.

    A guide to selected holdings follows a short introduction to the collection. Entries include collection titles, record series titles, volume, inclusive dates, and content notes.

450. Donovan, Lynn Bonfield. "Library Resources: CHS Collection on the History of Women in California." *California Historical Quarterly* 52 (Spring 1973): 81-84.

    The breviety of this article limits its usefulness. It, however, does list collection titles of women-related collections held by the California Historical Society Library.

451. Eaton, Dorothy S. "Some Letters of Abigail Adams." *Quarterly Journal of Current Acquisitions* 4 (August 1947): 3-6.

    This article draws attention to, and analyzes, 112 letters written by Adams to her sister and her niece and nephew between 1784 and 1818. The letters are part of the Shaw family papers in the Library of Congress.

452. Fisken, Patricia B. "Alternate Definitions of Reality: Sources of the Female Perspective." *Dartmouth College Library Bulletin* 20 (April 1980): 98-105.

    The author provides a checklist of women-related collections at Dartmouth. Entries include collection and record series titles and inclusive dates.

453. Gould, Lewis L. "Modern First Ladies: An Institutional Perspective." *Prologue* 19 (Summer 1987): 71-84.

    Gould introduces a special issue on the contributions of presidents' wives to the political and cultural life of the country. Six essays on the papers of presidents' wives follow:

    1. Mayer, Dale C. "Not One to Stay at Home: The Papers of Lou Henry Hoover." 85-93.

    2. Rohrer, Karen M. "'If There Was Anything You Forgot to Ask...': The Papers of Betty Ford." 143-152.

    3. Seeber, Frances M. "'I Want You to Write to Me': The Papers of Anna Eleanor Roosevelt." 95-105.

    4. Smith, Nancy K. "A Journey of the Heart: The Papers of Lady Bird Johnson." 127-134.

5. Teasley, Martin M. "Ike Was Her Career: The Papers of Mamie Doud Eisenhower." 107-115.

6. Watson, Mary Ann. "An Enduring Fascination: The Papers of Jacqueline Kennedy." 117-125.

454. Hill, Robert W. "The Schwimmer-Lloyd Collection." *Bulletin of the New York Public Library* 47 (May 1943): 307-309.

This collection contains original records, pamphlets and other published materials, and ephemera relating to feminist causes, both national and international, dating from 1904 into the 1920s. Description is limited to mention of record series and dates.

455. Holbert, Sue E. "Women's History Resources at the Minnesota Historical Society." *Minnesota History* 52 (Fall 1990): 112-118.

This is an essay reviewing holdings of museum collections; audio-visual materials; archives and manuscripts; and published materials. Description of archives and manuscripts is limited to collection titles.

456. Hummel, Arthur W. "The Journal of Harriet Low." *Quarterly Journal of Current Acquisitions* 2 (January/June 1945): 45-60.

Hummel describes the nine-volume diary of Harriet Low which records her impressions and experiences in Macao, and Canton, China, during the years 1829-1834.

457. Huth, Mary B. "Records of Women's Organizations in the Department of Rare Books and Special Collections." *University of Rochester Library Bulletin* 41 (1989-1990): 52-57.

Huth lists and describes thirteen collections. Entries include collection titles, volume, inclusive dates, record series titles, and content notes.

458. James, Janet W. "History and Women at Harvard: The Schlesinger Library." *Harvard Library Bulletin* 16 (October 1968): 385-399.

James provides an overview of the library and cites key women's collections held. She limits description to collection titles and inclusive dates.

459. Jones, Clifton H. "Manuscript Sources in Women's History at the Historical Resource Center." *South Dakota History* 7 (Winter 1976): 57-65.

This article provides guide-like entries for forty collections. Entries include collection title, inclusive dates, volume, record series titles, and content notes.

460. Kenney, Anne R. "The Papers of International Women's Year, 1977."

American Archivist 42 (July 1979): 345-347.

This article identifies National Women's Conference records in federal repositories, and the locations of International Women's Year records created by state committees.

461. Miller, Edwin H. "A Calendar of the Letters of Sophia Peabody Hawthorne." *Studies in the American Renaissance* (1986) 199-281.

The calendar lists 1,464 letters written between 1822-1871. Entries include dates, places of origin, correspondents' names, locations, and publication information. The list is indexed to correspondents.

462. Moseley, Eva. "Women in Archives: Documenting the History of Women in America." *American Archivist* 36 (April 1973): 215-222.

The article is limited to identifying archives and manuscript repositories with substantial holdings of women's papers and records.

463. Nolen, Anita Lonnes. "The Feminine Presence: Women's Papers in the Manuscript Division." *Quarterly Journal of the Library of Congress* 32 (October 1975): 348-365.

Nolen provides an overview of the library's holdings by citing collection titles and inclusive dates while commenting on the research potential of collections documenting women's involvement in politics, social reform, career fields, performing arts, and literature.

464. Otto, Kathryn. "Dakota Resources: The Jane Breeden Papers at the South Dakota Historical Resource Center." *South Dakota History* 10 (Summer 1980): 241-244.

Jane Breeden was a Pierre, South Dakota, club woman, temperance worker, and advocate for women's suffrage. Her papers, dating from 1888 to 1932, include materials relating to suffrage, personal and social life, temperance, and anti-German propaganda.

465. Plumb, Milton M. "Records of the National Women's Trade Union League of America." *Quarterly Journal of Current Acquisitions* 8 (August 1951): 9-16.

These records document the league's work to promote the welfare of women workers at the national level and include minutes of national conventions and international congresses and correspondence files, all dating from 1903-1950.

466. Requardt, Cynthia H. "Women's Deeds in Women's Words: Manuscripts in the Maryland Historical Society." *Maryland Historical Magazine* 73 (Summer 1978): 186-204.

Requardt lists women's collections under the headings of artists; authors; education; housekeeping; marriage; motherhood; travel; organizations; and war work.   Entries include collection and record series titles, dates, volume, and content notes.

467. Schmidt, Cheryl. "Manuscript Collections: The Papers of Amelia Jenks Bloomer and Dexter Bloomer." *Annals of Iowa* 45 (Fall 1979): 135-146.
     Amelia Bloomer is known for her temperance work and her advocacy of women's rights. Her husband, Dexter, was an educator. The article locates and describes the Bloomers' papers in six repositories in Iowa and New York state.

468. Schultz, Constance B. "Daughters of Liberty: The History of Women in the Revolutionary War Pension Records." *Prologue* 16 (Fall 1984): 139-153.
     A report on how these pension records are of value in writing women's history. Useful, but for a broader overview of these records see entries 541 and 595.

469. Scott-Elliot, A. H., and Elspeth Yeo. "Calligraphic Manuscripts of Esther Inglis (1571-1624): A Catalogue." *Papers of the Bibliographical Society of America* 84 (March 1990): 11-85.
     Inglis was a 16th-century copyist of exceptional ability. This catalogue lists fifty-five of her manuscripts in eighteen U.S. and European libraries, along with those known to be in private collections.

470. Simmons, Nancy C. "A Calendar of the Letters of Mary Moody Emerson." *Studies in the American Renaissance* (1993): 1-42.
     Mary Emerson was Ralph Waldo Emerson's aunt. This calendar lists over 900 her letters to Emerson family members between 1793-1862. Entries include date, place of origin, correspondent's name, and location of the original letter.

471. Sklar, Kathryn Kish. "Organized Womanhood: Archival Sources on Women and Progressive Reform." *Journal of American History* 75 (June 1988): 176-183.
     While general in nature, the article does cite many prominent women reformers' manuscript collections and records of women's groups and organizations while commenting on their respective research values.

472. Smith, Nancy Kegan. "Private Reflections on a Public Life: The Papers of Lady Bird Johnson at the LBJ Library." *Presidential Studies Quarterly* 20 (Fall 1990): 737-744.
     Smith identifies several record series titles in Mrs. Johnson's papers that provide insights into her private life.

473. Smith, Nancy Kegan. "Women and the White House: A Look at Women's

Papers in the Johnson Library." *Prologue* 18 (Summer 1986): 123-129.

Smith describes Lady Bird Johnson's social files. She notes that the files are especially rich in information about the welfare of children, conservation, and education, three of Mrs. Johnson's main interests. She also comments on the papers of Liz Carpenter.

474. Stamper, Anita M., and Mary Edna Lohrenz. "Manuscript Sources for 'Mississippi Homespun: Nineteen-Century Textiles and the Women Who Made Them.'" *Journal of Mississippi History* 53 (August 1991): 185-217.

The article describes six women's diaries that document the making of clothing in the 19th-century South. The diaries are in the Mississippi Department of Archives and History, Jackson.

475. Sung, Carolyn Hoover. "Catharine Mitchill's Letters from Washington, 1806-1812." *Quarterly Journal of the Library of Congress* 34 (July 1977): 171-189.

Catharine Mitchill was the wife of Sen. Samuel L. Mitchill of New York. This article describes a small collection of her letters to her sister, Margaretta A. Miller, which are significant because of their women's perspective on politics in Washington, D.C.

476. Ten Houten, Elizabeth S. "Some Collections of Special Use for Women's History Resources in the U.S." *American Association of University Women Journal* 67 (April 1974): 35-36.

A checklist of repositories holding manuscript collections, records, and oral histories relating to women. With a few exceptions, description is at the repository level.

477. Wagner, Sally R. "Dakota Resources: The Pioneer Daughters Collection of the South Dakota Federation of Women's Clubs." *South Dakota History* 19 (Spring 1989): 95-109.

This is a collection of nearly 6,000 unpublished biographies of women pioneers in South Dakota and throughout the West. The collection is in the South Dakota State Historical Society, Pierre.

478. Wilson, Joan Hoff and Lynn Bonfield Donovan. "Women's History: A Listing of West Coast Archival and Manuscript Sources." *California Historical Quarterly* 55 (Spring 1976): 74-83.; and (Summer 1976): 170-185.

A two-part series listing forty-one repositories in California, Oregon, Washington, and British Columbia. Each institution lists its women-related collections along with dates and volume.

479. "Women's Studies Archives in Northwest Ohio." *Northwest Ohio Quarterly* 56 (Fall 1984): 105-112.

This article lists women-related manuscript collections at Bowling Green State University, pages 105-110, and at the University of Toledo's Ward M. Canaday Center, pages 111-112.

480. Young, Louise M. "The Records of the League of Women Voters." *Quarterly Journal of Current Acquisitions* 8 (February 1951): 3-11.

This group of records dates from 1920 to 1944 and includes minutes of boards, conventions, and committees; correspondence; reports; circular letters; and legislation program files. Young also writes about research uses for the records.

Federal Archives

General

481. Allen, Andrew H. "Historical Archives of the Department of State." *Annual Report of the American Historical Association for the Year 1894* 1 (1895): 281-298.

    The records and papers described in this article are those of the Continental Congress, George Washington, James Madison, Thomas Jefferson, Alexander Hamilton, James Monroe, and Benjamin Franklin.

482. Cain, Robert H. "Policy and Administrative Records of the Veterans Administration." *American Archivist* 25 (October 1962): 455-466.

    The author explains and briefly analyzes the categories of regulatory, interpretative, intelligence, promotional, and informational records created by the Veterans Administration. The article is useful to those planning research in V.A. records.

483. Casari, Robert B. "A Bibliography of Federal World War I Aviation Agencies and Their Records, 1917-1921." *American Aviation Historical Society Journal* 10 (Spring 1965): 62-63.

484. Collier, Clyde M. "The Archivist and Weather Records." *American Archivist* 26 (October 1963): 477-485.

    This article identifies, in general terms, some of the weather-related records held at the National Weather Records Center in Asheville, North Carolina.

485. Daniels, Maygene. "District of Columbia Building Permits." *American Archivist* 38 (January 1975): 23-30.

    Daniels notes that building permits offer information for documenting development of urban areas and explains how they can be used. The District of Columbia permits used as examples are in the National Archives, Record Group 351.

486. Dewing, C. E. "The Wheeler Survey Records: A Study in Archival Anomaly." *American Archivist* 27 (April 1964): 219-227.

The author notes a major acquisition of the records from Lt. George M. Wheeler's geographical survey west of the 100th meridian in the 1870s. He identifies other repositories holding Wheeler Survey records, and discusses the dispersal of the records from the 1880s to the 1960s.

487. Dickson, Maxey R. "Sources for South Carolina History in the Nation's Capital." *Proceedings of South Carolina Historical Association* (1942): 50-54.

Dickson limits description to collection titles in the Library of Congress and record groups and record series titles, with inclusive dates, in the National Archives.

488. Evans, Luther H. "Texana in the Nation's Capital." *Southwest Historical Quarterly* 50 (October 1946): 220-235.

Most of this article reviews published materials held by the Library of Congress. The last five pages, however, cite records and manuscript collections at the Library of Congress and the National Archives from the Spanish colonial period to WWI.

489. Ferrand, Max. "The Records of the Federal Convention." *American Historical Review* 13 (October 1907): 44-65.

Ferrand reviews the personal notes taken by delegates to the federal convention held at Philadelphia in 1787 at which the U.S. constitution was drafted. He assesses each extant group of notes for their objectivity and informational value.

490. Friedenwald, Herbert. "The Journals and Papers of the Continental Congress." *Annual Report of the American Historical Association for the Year 1896* 1 (1897): 85-135.

The author reports on the journals, letterbooks, reports, Articles of Confederation, correspondence, and related papers. The article concludes with a checklist of the journals.

491. Gumm, Clark L. "The Foundation of Land Records." *Our Public Lands* 7 (October 1957): 4-5, 12-14.

While this article does not describe a body of records, it does identify and explain some of the basic land records and how public lands were surveyed. It may be useful for those researching federal land records.

492. Harrison, Robert W. "Public Land Records of the Federal Government." *Mississippi Valley Historical Review* 41 (September 1954): 277-288.

Harrison provides a very useful survey on the types, informational content, and research values of public land records. The record series reviewed are survey plates and field notes; tract books; land entry files; register's returns; and patents.

493. Jameson, John R. "The National Park System in the United States: An Overview with a Survey of Selected Government Documents and Archival Materials." *Government Publications Review* 7A (March/April 1980): 145-158.

Jameson provides a brief history of the park system, cites numerous published federal sources, and concludes with a review of federal records relating to national parks.

494. Kinney, Gregory. "Federal Land Records in State Repositories: The Experience in the Old Northwest." *American Archivist* 52 (Spring 1989): 152-164.

Kinney locates and reviews federal land records held by state archives in Ohio, Indiana, Illinois, and Minnesota, and accounts for the destruction of these records in Michigan and Wisconsin.

495. Lathrop, Barnes F. "History from the Census Returns." *Southwestern Historical Quarterly* 51 (April 1948): 293-312.

The author describes the schedules of the U.S. census from 1790 through 1880 and comments on their research values.

496. Meek, W. Frank. "Federal Land Office Records." *University of Colorado Law Review* 43 (November 1971): 177-197.

A useful article for those researching federal land records. Meek identifies record series and discusses the type of information found in each. This article was reprinted in *Public Land and Resources Law Digest* 9 (Fall, 1972).

497. Morison, Samuel E. "The Customhouse Records in Massachusetts as a Source of History." *Proceedings of the Massachusetts Historical Society* 54 (1920/1921): 324-331.

Morison identifies the types of information found in these records and reports on the records in Massachusetts' eleven customs districts.

498. Morris, Richard B. "The Federal Archives of New York City: Opportunities for Historical Research." *American Historical Review* 42 (January 1937): 256-272.

Morris reviews the records of federal courts; customs offices; public health agencies; the immigration service; the military services; federal employment services; and several agencies related to the U.S. economy.

499. Reingold, Nathan. "U.S. Patent Office Records as Sources for the History of Invention and Technological Property." *Technology and Culture* 1 (Spring 1960): 156-167.

Reingold describes record series created by the Patent Office and discusses the types of information they contain and their research value.

These records date from the 1790s into the 20th century.

500. Rowe, Judith S. "Administrative Records as a Source of Federal Statistics." *Government Publications Review* 10 (September/October 1983): 455-458.

     Rowe cites record series titles from several federal agencies which she considers useful as statistical sources.

501. Strobridge, Truman R. "Archives of the Supervising Architect, Treasury Department." *Journal of the Society of Architectural Historians* 20 (December 1961): 198-199.

     These records date from 1853 to 1939 and include architectural drawings, both interior and exterior; correspondence files; and photographs, all documenting the acquisition of building sites and construction and maintenance of government buildings.

502. Thomas, Earl J. "From Old Records to New." *Our Public Lands* 7 (October 1957): 6-7, 15.

     This article describes record series found among federal land records. It would be useful for those researching land records.

503. Wright, Almon R. "Records of the Food Administration: New Field for Research." *Public Opinion Quarterly* 3 (April 1939): 278-284.

     In this article Wright identifies Food Administration record series that could be used to interpret public opinion during WWI.

Library of Congress

504. Alcock, N. W. "English Archives at the Library of Congress." *Archives: The Journal of the British Records Association* 16 (April 1984): 273-277.

505. Andreassen, John C. L. "Archives in the Library of Congress." *American Archivist* 12 (January 1949): 20-26.

     This article notes and describes four basic types of archives in the Library of Congress: 1). the library's administrative records; 2). federal records relating to the legislative branch of government; 3). fugitive records donated or purchased by the library; and 4). organizational records such as businesses, churches, or associations.

506. Burr, Nelson R. "Sources for the Study of American Church History in the Library of Congress." *Church History* 22 (September 1953): 227-238.

     Burr reviews some of the larger collections such as the records of the Society for the Propagation of the Gospel. He also reviews copies of ecclesiastical records from European archives and cites manuscript collections of church leaders.

507. Cole, John Y. "Studying the Library of Congress: Resources and Research Opportunities." *Libraries & Culture* 24 (Summer 1989): 357-366.

The article reviews materials documenting the history of the Library of Congress. Included are manuscript collections of its librarians; official records; sound recordings and oral histories; and architectural drawings and photographs of its buildings.

508. Eaton, Dorothy S., and Vincent L. Eaton. "Manuscripts Relating to Early America." *Quarterly Journal of Current Acquisitions* 8 (November 1950): 17-28.

The Eatons review the library's collection of pre-1801, U.S. manuscripts. They include the Peter Force Collections and the papers of the Continental Congress, George Washington, Benjamin Franklin, Thomas Jefferson, James Madison, and Alexander Hamilton.

509. Eaton, Vincent L. "The American Academy of Arts and Letters Collection." *Quarterly Journal of Current Acquisitions* 10 (August 1953): 190-193.

In this article, Eaton calls attention to this collection of 400 letters written by leading 19th-century American and British authors, politicians, artists, and men and women of science. Description is limited, mostly to names of correspondents.

510. Friedenwald, Herbert. "Historical Manuscripts in the Library of Congress." *Annual Report of the American Historical Association for the Year 1898* 1 (1899): 37-45.

A brief overview of collection titles, inclusive dates, and subjects treated. Most relate to the colonial period with others ranging from the early- to the mid-19th century.

511. Garrison, Curtis W. "List of Manuscript Collections in the Library of Congress to July, 1931." *Annual Report of the American Historical Association for the Year 1930* 1 (1931): 123-249.

A checklist of collections in alphabetical order under six broad, historical periods of the U.S. Included are collection titles, record series titles, inclusive dates, and volume statements. The guide was published separately in 1932.

512. Jenkins, William S. "Records of the States of the United States." *Quarterly Journal of Current Acquisitions* 6 (May 1949): 3-7.

Jenkins was the director of the Library of Congress project to film the records of selected state legislatures. In this article, he describes the groups of microfilmed records and the type of records within each group.

513. Jenkins, William S. "Records of the States: Supplementary Microfilms."
     Quarterly Journal of Current Acquisitions 13 (November 1955): 12-16.

     Among the supplemental microfilmed records are those of selected local
     governments, records of the governments of American Indian tribes,
     records of proposed states and provisional governments, and records of
     mining districts.

514. LeGear, Clara E. "The Hotchkiss Map Collection." *Quarterly Journal of
     Current Acquisitions* 6 (November 1948): 16-20.

     Jedediah Hotchkiss was a topographical engineer in the Confederate
     army. Among his papers are 600 maps dated 1861-1865, of which over
     one-half are manuscript maps. LeGear reviews Hotchkiss's career and
     comments on some of the better maps.

515. LeGear, Clara E. "Maps of Early America." *Quarterly Journal of Current
     Acquisitions* 8 (November 1950): 44-53.

     LeGear reviews the Library of Congress maps dating from the 16th
     century through the 18th century. She cites the titles of several collections
     containing manuscript maps of what is now the U.S., along with individual
     map titles.

516. Mathews, Thomas. "Documentación sobre Puerto Rico en la Biblioteca del
     Congreso." *Historia* 6 (October 1956): 89-142.

     This article reviews manuscripts, published materials, maps, and
     photographs. Mathews cites collection and record series titles and
     analyzes their research potential. The article concludes with an extensive
     checklist of sources.

517. McDonough, John J. "Kentuckiana in the Manuscript Division, Library of
     Congress." *Filson Club Historical Quarterly* 62 (July 1988): 356-379.

     McDonough reviews the contents of several collections that relate to the
     history of Kentucky. He mentions the collection title of each, the types of
     material found within, the inclusive dates, and its special strengths.

518. Mearns, David C. "A Fog-Laden Panorama of LC's Collections. Parts I
     and II." *Library Journal* 90 (April 1, 1965): 1600-1007; and (April 15,
     1965): 1834-1840.

     Mearns provides an overview of the types of materials found in the
     Library of Congress. He includes newspapers; maps; photographs and
     motion pictures; music; prints; rare books; and manuscripts. While
     description is general, he mentions many key collections.

519. Powell, C. Percy. "List of Manuscript Collections Received in the Library
     of Congress, July, 1931 to July, 1938." *Annual Report of the American
     Historical Association for the Year 1937* 1 (1939): 113-145.

A continuation of a previous list published in the 1930 *Annual Report*. Entries are grouped under six chronological periods with citations alphabetical by collection title and including record series titles, inclusive dates, and volume. Indexed.

520. Selim, George Dimitri. "Arabic Calligraphy in the Library of Congress." *Quarterly Journal of the Library of Congress* 36 (Spring 1979): 140-178.

The Library of Congress has a collection of seventy manuscripts as examples of Arabic calligraphy styles. This article illustrates several outstanding manuscripts representing thirteen styles.

521. Sioussat, St. George L. "The John Cleves Short Collection of Papers of the Short, Harrison, Symmes, and Allied Families, Library of Congress." *Quarterly Journal of Acquisitions* 2 (July 1944): 76-85.

These papers relate the personal, business, and political affairs of the Short family from the late 18th- to the mid 19th-centuries. The collection includes many letters to and from William Henry Harrison, John Cleves Short's father-in-law.

522. Sweetland, James H. "Federal Sources for the Study of Collective Communities." *Government Publications Review* 7A (March/April 1980): 129-138.

While mostly a review of published federal documents, the author does cite some manuscript material in the Library of Congress.

523. Vanderbilt, Paul. "The Arnold Genthe Collection." *Quarterly Journal of Current Acquisitions* 8 (May 1951): 13-18.

Genthe was an early 20th-century photographer of America's famous and social elite. This 20,000-print collection includes New York City portraits, San Francisco and Chinatown scenes, Isadora Duncan and her dance troupe, and images from his many foreign travels.

524. Webb, Willard. "The Hotchkiss Papers: An Additional Note." *Quarterly Journal of Current Acquisitions* 7 (November 1949): 23-24.

Webb cites record series titles of papers in the Jedediah Hotchkiss Collection. They include pre-Civil War diaries and extensive correspondence from the Civil War period. The article also identifies related materials in other repositories.

National Archives

525. Alagoa, E. J. "Preliminary Inventory of the Records of the United States Diplomatic and Consular Posts in West Africa, 1865-1935." *Historical Society of Nigeria Journal* 2 (December 1960): 78-104.

An administrative history precedes the inventory. Record series, inclusive dates, volume, and content notes appear under each U.S. legation in Liberia, Senegal, Sierra Leone, Gold Coast, Gambia, and Nigeria.

526. Basu, Purnendu. "Materials in the National Archives Relating to India." *Indian Archives* 5 (January/June 1951): 42-53.
    The author reviews record groups and record series in the U.S. National Archives documenting economic and commercial relations; agriculture; trade and tariffs; immigration; and military affairs.

527. Bethel, Elizabeth. "Early Records of the War Department General Staff in National Archives." *American Archivist* 8 (October 1945): 241-247.
    The records described in this article date from the creation of the War Department General Staff in 1901 through 1919. Bethel comments specifically on three major sub-groups: General Staff records, Army War College records, and Board of Ordnance and Fortification records.

528. Bhagat, Sheela. "Materials on India in the Dwight D. Eisenhower Library." *Indian Archives* 23 (January/December 1974): 47-60.
    The author provides a checklist of papers by record group with annotated folder titles. The annotations identify subjects treated or correspondents' names and inclusive dates.

529. Blanton, DeAnne and Jennifer D. Heaps. "The Home Front: Letters Received." *Prologue* 23 (Fall 1991): 289-294.
    The authors review the topical content of civilian letters written to federal officials and agencies during WWII and explain how to locate these letters in the National Archives.

530. Bunce, Peter W. "Genealogical Resources in the National Archives -- Chicago Branch." *Illinois Libraries* 68 (April 1986): 259-261.
    Bunce cites record groups, with inclusive dates, that contain rich materials for genealogists. Most appear to be microfilmed records.

531. Bunce, Peter W., Kenneth W. Shanks, and David S. Weber. "Of Trials, Tribes, and Topographers: Holdings of the Chicago Regional Branch of the National Archives." *Illinois Libraries* 63 (April 1981): 283-286.
    Records of the U.S. courts; Bureau of Indian Affairs; Corps of Engineers; and U.S. censuses are the principal record groups that the authors describe. They mention, with less detail, records of other federal agencies and the branch's microfilm holdings.

532. Burdick, Charles B. "Foreign Military Records of World War I in the National Archives." *Prologue* 7 (Winter 1975): 213-220.
    A historical report on a project to copy German, French, and British

records. It says very little about the records copied.

533. Burger, Barbara L. "American Images: Photographs and Posters in the Still Picture Branch." *Prologue* 22 (Winter 1990): 353-368.

   In this overview, Burger relates the types of materials found in the branch and the photographers and subjects represented.

534. Butler, Stuart L., and Graeme McCluggage. "Taking Measure of America: Records in the Cartographic and Architectural Branch." *Prologue* 23 (Spring 1991): 41-57.

   A thorough review of categories of maps found in the branch which includes military surveys and explorations; military campaign and battle maps; Indian-related maps; international boundaries; public land surveys; roads and railroads; agricultural and forestry maps; waterways and shipyards; federal buildings; and many others.

535. Calkin, Homer L. "The United States Government and the Irish: A Bibliographical Study of Research Materials in the U.S. National Archives." *Irish Historical Studies* 9 (March 1954): 28-52.

   At the record group level, Calkin describes the records of the Departments of State, the Treasury, and Justice; the Immigration and Naturalization Service; the Public Health Service; U.S. courts; Bureau of Census, and other agencies. The footnotes contain record series titles, with volume, and inclusive dates.

536. Carrera Stampa, Manuel. "Mapas y planos relativos a México en The National Archives of the United States of America (1776-1849)." *Revista Ibero-americana* 12 (Febrero 1947): 153-198.

   Following a short introduction, the author lists 178 maps of Mexico. They depict Mexico's coasts; interior states, districts, and towns; battle sites of the Mexican War; and international boundaries with the U.S.

537. Carter, Kent. "Oklahoma History: In Texas? The Fort Worth Branch of the National Archives." *Chronicles of Oklahoma* 64 (Spring 1986): 85-95.

   Carter describes federal records relating to Oklahoma. Records of U.S. courts and attorneys, Bureau of Indian Affairs, Corps of Engineers, Southwestern Power Administration, Bureau of Public Roads, and the Federal Power Commission are a few of those mentioned.

538. Carter, Kent. "Wantabees & Outalucks: Searching for Indian Ancestors in Federal Records." *Chronicles of Oklahoma* 66 (Spring 1988): 94-104.

   In this article, Carter describes federal records in the Fort Worth Branch of the National Archives that are useful for documenting one's Indian heritage. He emphasizes microfilmed records.

539. Cobb, Josephine. "The Still Picture Program at the National Archives."
     Special Libraries 45 (September 1954): 269-273.
     Cobb cites several federal agencies and several series of photos that, in
     a limited manner, represent the richness of the National Archives Still
     Picture Branch.

540. Connor, R. W. D. "The National Archives and Pennsylvania History."
     Pennsylvania History 7 (April 1940): 63-78.
     A review of federal records relating to Pennsylvania by the archivist of
     the U.S.   Connor cites federal agencies and record series along with
     examples of how they might serve researchers.

541. Crackel, Theodore J. "Revolutionary War Pension Records and Patterns
     of American Mobility, 1780-1830." *Prologue* 16 (Fall 1984): 155-167.
     A review of how pension records in the U.S. National Archives' RG 15
     might be useful in writing social history.

542. Crowe, David M., Jr. "The Holocaust: Documents in the National
     Archives of the United States." *American Jewish History* 70 (March 1981):
     362-378.
     Crowe describes civilian records and military records separately.   He
     cites record groups, record series, and inclusive dates while commenting
     on the content and research values of these records.

543. Danovitch, Sylvia E. "The Past Recaptured? The Photographic Record of
     the Internment of Japanese-Americans." *Prologue* 12 (Summer 1980): 91-
     103
     A description of 12,500 photographs among the records of the War
     Relocation Authority in the U.S. National Archives.   The photos are
     divided into five groups: preevacuation; evacuation; assembly center;
     relocation camps; and resettlement from the camps.

544. Darter, Lewis J., Jr. "Federal Archives Relating to Matthew Fontaine
     Maury." *American Neptune* 1 (April 1941): 149-158.
     Maury is known for his charting of winds and ocean currents.   Darter
     identifies correspondence, logs, and charts in the National Archives that
     document his work at the Naval Observatory between 1840-1860.

545. Dewberry, Suzanne J. "San Diego: Historical Resources of the Federal
     Government in the National Archives Pacific Southwest Region." *Journal
     of San Diego History* 38 (No. 2 1992): 112-128.

546. Drewry, Elizabeth B. "Material in the National Archives Relating to
     Florida." *Florida Historical Quarterly* 23 (October 1944): 97-115.
     Drewry gives a thorough review of the record groups that have Florida-

related records in them. She notes that the Departments of State and War, the General Land Office, U.S. Senate, and Freedman's Bureau, offer the most possibilities.

547. Duerksen, Jacob A., and John F. Schmidt. "Passenger Ship Lists in the National Archives." *Mennonite Quarterly Review* 42 (July 1968): 219-224.

The authors have prepared a guide to these lists by keying vessel names and ports of departure to numbered microfilm reels containing records of the named vessels. Added data is the date of arrival in the U.S. and the number of Mennonites on board.

548. Everly, Elaine C. "Marriage Register of Freedmen." *Prologue* 5 (Fall 1973): 150-154.

The author reviews the background of these federal records and explains the variation in records created in different states. She notes that the records are a rich source for information about Afro-American families immediately following the Civil War.

549. Franklin, W. Neil. "Materials in the National Archives Relating to Vermont." *Vermont History* 27 (July 1959): 240-255.

Franklin reviews federal records by agency name. He cites specific record series and inclusive dates and comments on the research value of each.

550. Gondos, Victor and Dorothy Gondos. "Materials in the National Archives Relating to Alexandria, Virginia." *Virginia Magazine of History and Biography* 57 (October 1949): 421-432.

The authors cite record groups and record series with a focus on the colonial and early national periods of Virginia's history.

551. Gorham, Alan. "Federal Court Records Pertaining to Vermont: Sources for Study." *Vermont History* 36 (Summer 1968): 142-143.

The author calls attention to holdings of U.S. civil, criminal, and bankruptcy case files; civil and criminal dockets; and related records at the Waltham, Massachusetts, Federal Records Center.

552. Gustafson, Milton O. "State Department Records in the National Archives: A Profile." *Prologue* 2 (Winter 1970): 175-180.

The author explains the department's filing system, identifies key record series, and comments on their research values.

553. Guthrie, Chester L. "The United States Grain Corporation Records in the National Archives." *Agricultural History* 12 (October 1938): 347-354.

Guthrie reviews the agency's background, describes the scope and volume of the records, and cites the record series he considers most valuable for historical research.

554. Harding, Bruce C. "Regional Archives Branch--Chicago." *Illinois Libraries* 57 (March 1975): 186-192.
 Harding lists records of the U.S courts; Coast Guard; Weather Bureau; Bureau of Customs; IRS; U.S. Navy; Bureau of Indian Affairs; U.S. Attorneys; and the private papers of Judge William J. Campbell. The article also lists microfilm of federal records held by the Chicago branch.

555. Harrison, John P. "The Archives of United States Diplomatic and Consular Posts in Latin America." *Hispanic American Historical Review* 33 (February 1953): 168-183.
 Harrison reviews the extant U.S. diplomatic and consular records from Latin America, describes the key record series, and comments on their research values.

556. Hawkins, Mary Ann. "Searching for the South: Resources for Southern History in the National Archives--Atlanta Branch." *Proceedings and Papers of the Georgia Association of Historians 9* (1988): 76-89.

557. Heard, John P. "Resource for Historians: Records of the Bureau of Land Management in California and Nevada." *Forest History* 12 (July 1968): 20-26.
 Heard identifies five of the bureau's record series including land entry records; contest and investigative files; administrative and correspondence files; tract books and plats; and miscellaneous records. He includes volume and inclusive dates for each series.

558. Heaps, Jennifer D. "World War II Prisoner-of-War Records." *Prologue* 23 (Fall 1991): 324-328.
 Heaps notes that most of the POW records are in RG 389, Records of the Office of the Provost General. She reviews the types of information they contain and cites other record groups that also contain POW records.

559. Holdcamper, Forrest R. "Registers, Enrollments, and Licenses in the National Archives. *American Neptune* 1 (July 1941): 275-294.
 This article explains the creation and purpose of these records and concludes with a list of each series in the archives. The list is presented by seaports within a state with the inclusive dates of the series.

560. Holmes, Oliver W. "Indian-Related Records in the National Archives and Their Use: Observations over a Third of a Century." In *Indian-White Relations: A Persistent Paradox*, edited by Jane F. Smith and Robert M. Kvasnicka. Washington, D.C.: Howard University Press, 1976. 13-32.
 The essay briefly reviews the records of the Bureau of Indian Affairs,

Secretary of the Interior, General Land Office, Geological Survey, Bureau of Reclamation, National Park Service, Office of Territories, Department of War, and the Department of Justice.

561. Holmes, Oliver W. "Territorial Government and the Records of Its Administration." In *The Frontier Re-Examined. Papers Presented at a Conference Sponsored by Southern Illinois University, Edwardsville, November 11-12, 1965*, edited by John F. McDermott. Urbana: University of Illinois Press, 1967. 97-109.

A very general treatment in which Holmes suggests some research opportunites using territorial records and notes that there are two basic groups of territorial records, those of federal agencies operating in a territory, and those of the territorial government itself.

562. Jackson, W. Turrentine. "Dakota Territorial Papers in the Department of the Interior Archives." *North Dakota Historical Quarterly* 11 (July 1944): 209-220.

Jackson describes mostly records created within the Department of the Interior. He first cites record series titles and then reviews each territorial governor's administration chronologically by noting its key events and the record series that describe them.

563. Jackson, W. Turrentine. "Materials for Western History in the Department of the Interior Archives." *Mississippi Valley Historical Review* 35 (June 1948): 61-76.

The author cites federal agencies and record series titles and notes the research values of each. While using a record group approach, Jackson, regrettably, did not cite the National Archives record group numbers.

564. Jackson, W. Turrentine. "Territorial Papers in the Department of Interior Archives, 1873-1890: Washington, Idaho, and Montana." *Pacific Northwest Quarterly* 35 (October 1944): 323-341.

Jackson notes specific subgroups of records for each territory, along with a description of useful record series for each governor of the territories cited. Also included are brief descriptions of records relating to territorial prisons.

565. Jackson, W. Turrentine. "Territorial Papers of Wyoming in the National Archives." *Annals of Wyoming* 16 (January 1944): 45-55.

Jackson lists groups of papers in the Departments of State and the Interior that relate to the administrations of Wyoming's governors from 1869-1889. He also notes that the Interior records include those of Wyoming's territorial prison from 1870 to 1890.

566. Joerg, W. L. G. "Archival Maps as Illustrated by Those in the National

Archives." *American Archivist* 4 (July 1941): 188-193.

A brief discussion of maps as records followed by comments of the different types of maps found in the National Archives. Maps from the Office of the Chief of Engineers, the Department of State, the Senate, and the Office of Indian Affairs are mentioned.

567. Kahn, Herman. "World War II and Its Background: Research Materials at the Franklin D. Roosevelt Library and Policies Concerning Their Use." *American Archivist* 17 (April 1954): 149-162.

A review of Franklin D. Roosevelt's papers as they regard WWII, along with discussion of the papers of other leaders such as Harry Hopkins, Henry Morgenthau Jr., John G. Winant, Charles W. Taussig, Herbert C. Pell, and Elbert D. Thomas.

568. Kepley, David R. "Congressional Records in the Archives." *Prologue* 19 (Spring 1987): 23-33.

The author comments on the records of the U.S. House and Senate; joint committees of congress; operating records of the Government Printing Office; the Temporary National Economic Committee; and congressional appointed commissions.

569. Larson, Sarah. "Records of the Southern Claims Commission." *Prologue* 12 (Winter 1980): 207-218.

The commission heard Southern claims for supplies furnished to, or appropriated by, Union forces during the Civil War. Larson puts the records in historical perspective explaining why and how they were created and how they might be used for research.

570. Larson, Sarah. "The War of 1812 Papers: State Department Records for Genealogy and Local History." *Prologue* 13 (Summer 1981): 115-126.

While intended for genealogists, this article gives a useful synopsis for each of the seven rolls of microfilm that make up this small block of records in the U.S. National Archives' RG 57.

571. Lokke, Carl L. "The Food Administration Papers for the State of Virginia in the National Archives." *Virginia Magazine of History and Biography* 50 (July 1942): 220-226.

Lokke devotes most of this article to a history of the agency's work in Virginia. He concludes by citing record series titles and volume of records held by the archives with comments on their research value.

572. Lounsbury, Ralph G. "Early Texas and the National Archives." *Southwestern Historical Quarterly* 46 (January 1943): 203-213.

A general description of record groups in the National Archives relating to Texas. The author concentrates on the records of the U.S. Senate, the

Department of State, and the U.S. Army.

573. Lounsbury, Ralph G. "Materials in the National Archives for the History of New Mexico before 1848." *New Mexico Historical Review* 21 (July 1946): 247-256.

    The author cites specific documents and groups of records from the Department of State, the Department of War, the U.S. Senate, and the Department of the Treasury.

574. Luomala, Katharine. "Research and the Records of the War Relocation Authority." *Applied Anthropology* 7 (Winter 1948): 23-32.

    After a review of the WRA's functions, the author describes the agency's records at the series level. The records are held by the U.S. National Archives. The WRA administered the relocation camps for Japanese living in the U.S. during WWII.

575. "Materials in the National Archives Relating to the Scandinavian Countries." *Norwegian-American Studies and Records* 13 (1943): 163-170.

    This article cites records of U.S. Consuls and the Departments of State and the Treasury; agricultural agencies; WWI agencies; economic and trade agencies; and the armed forces. Record groups and record series titles are not identified in this review.

576. Maxwell, Richard S. "Louisiana and Its History: A Discussion of Sources in the National Archives." *Louisiana History* 13 (Spring 1972): 169-180.

    Maxwell cites record series titles with inclusive dates under the headings of legislative, judicial, and diplomatic records; social and economic records; modern and old military records; cartographic and audio-visual records; and presidential records.

577. McCain, William D. "The Papers of the Food Administration for Missouri, 1917-1919, in the National Archives." *Missouri Historical Review* 32 (October 1937): 56-61.

    McCain provides a history of the agency's state work, lists its administrative divisions, and cites extant record series titles and volume of records for each division.

578. McConnell, Roland C. "Records in the National Archives Pertaining to the History of North Carolina." *North Carolina Historical Review* 25 (July 1948): 318-340.

    This is an overview of federal records from the colonial period through the New Deal. McConnell's description is at the record group level using agency names instead of record group numbers. He does include record series titles and inclusive dates.

579. McReynolds, R. Michael. "Legacy of Justice: Legal Records in the National Archives." *Prologue* 16 (Winter 1984): 261-269.
     Described are U.S. Supreme Court records, Department of Justice records, FBI records, and U.S. District Court records. The author also comments on how the records might be used.

580. Meany, Edmond S., Jr. "Food Administration Papers for Washington, Oregon, and Idaho Deposited in the National Archives." *Pacific Northwest Quarterly* 28 (October 1937): 373-382.
     Meany reviews the agency's work in the Pacific Northwest, identifies key record series, and comments on the research value of each.

581. Morris, Robert C. "The Government's Lawyers: United States Attorneys Records in the National Archives." *Prologue* 22 (Winter 1990): 388-395.
     Morris explains that these records are mostly case files in National Archives field branches. He reviews the record series represented and the types of cases tried in U.S. courts. Several well-known cases are cited as examples.

582. Novick, David. "Research Opportunities in the War Production Board Records." *American Economics Review* 37 (May 1974): 690-699.
     The author provides a history of the agency, reviews the record series it produced, and comments on those he believed most valuable for economic research. He identifies the policy documentation files and plant data integration files as especially useful.

583. Oberly, James W. "Military Bounty Land Warrants of the Mexican War." *Prologue* 14 (Spring 1982): 25-34.
     An analysis of land warrants issued by the federal government after the war with Mexico. The author tells why the records were created, how to use them, and comments on related records in the National Archives.

584. Owens, James K. "Federal Court Records of New Hampshire." *Historical New Hampshire* 25 (Fall 1970): 37-49.
     Owens calls attention to the court records held by the National Archives' regional branch in Waltham, Massachusetts. He reviews the basic types of court records and the time periods they cover.

585. Palmer, Charlotte. "Conservation and the Camera." *Prologue* 3 (Winter 1971): 183-196.
     An essay on the photographic records produced between 1895-1910 by the U.S. Forest Service at the order of Gifford Pinchot. The photos are held by the U.S. National Archives Audiovisual Division. They mostly document the Forest Service's programs.

586. Phillips, Dennis H. "The Deanship Records of the Tangier Diplomatic Corps and the Conseil Sanitaire". *Prologue* 5 (Fall 1973): 167-169.

These records reflect the administrative work of an international council in the municipal affairs of Tangier, Morocco, from the 1890s to 1926. The records are in the U.S. National Archives.

587. Pinkett, Harold T. "Records in the National Archives Relating to the Social Purposes and Results of the Operations of the Civilian Conservation Corps." *Social Service Review* 22 (March 1948): 46-53.

Pinkett reviews the functions of the CCC such as employment, job training, health care, safety, and character development and then describes CCC record series that document these activities.

588. Pinkett, Harold T. "Records in the National Archives as Sources for Research in the Social Sciences." *Social Studies* 43 (April 1952): 147-151.

Pinkett cites federal agencies and record series titles that are rich in social science data and comments on the research values of selected records.

589. Pinkett, Harold T. "Records of a Historic Trust for Conservation." *Prologue* 8 (Summer 1976): 77-84.

Pinkett comments on records relating to conservation in the National Archives. He cites those of the Civilian Conservation Corps, the Work Projects Administration, the Bureau of Reclamation, and the Tennessee Valley Authority.

590. Pomrenze, Seymour J. "Materiales relativos a Cuba en los archivos nacionales de los Estados Unidos." *Revista Bimestre Cubana* 62 (julio/diciembre 1948): 5-22.

Pomrenze uses a chronological approach to identify records relating to Cuba. His first time period is pre-1895; second is 1895-1902; and post-1902. He cites record groups, record series, and inclusive dates, and offers comments on research values.

591. Rapport, Leonard. "The Interstate Commerce Commission Formal Case Files: A Source for Local History." *Prologue* 15 (Winter 1983): 229-242.

These case files include affidavits, depositions, and testimony of witnesses; correspondence; plaintiff and defendant briefs; and decisions of commissioners, mostly regarding complaints against railroads. The article includes suggestions for using the records.

592. Reeves, Charles R. "Exploring the Coast: Use of Records at the National Archives--Southeast Region for Researching Coastal Georgia." *Proceedings and Papers of the Georgia Association of Historians* 10 (1989): 65-70.

593. Reeves, Charles R. "The Wider World: Resources for National and International History at the National Archives--Atlanta Branch." *Proceedings and Papers of the Georgia Association of Historians* 9 (1988): 90-99.

594. Reingold, Nathan. "The National Archives and the History of Science in America." *Isis* 46 (March 1955): 22-28.
      Reingold reviews the records of federal agencies engaged in scientific research or having a scientific mission. While he names some personalities, the article mostly identifies the types of research done by agencies and the time period of the records.

595. Resch, John P. "The Continentals of Peterborough, New Hampshire: Pension Records as a Source for Local History." *Prologue* 16 (Fall 1984): 169-183.
      Resch describes record series in the National Archives' RG 15 that are useful in writing local and social history.

596. Rhoads, James B. "The Taming of the West: Military Archives as a Source for the Social History of the Trans-Mississippi Region to 1900." In *People of the Plains and Mountains: Essays in the History of the West, Dedicated to Everett Dick,* edited by Ray Allan Billington. Westport, Conn.: Greenwood Press, 1973. 175-203.
      Rhoads cites records in the National Archives that document five basic military activities in the West: exploration and surveys; campaigns and battles; garrison duty; relations with Indians; and relations with white settlers.

597. Rieger, Morris. "Preliminary Report on Materials in the National Archives Relating to Africa." *African Studies Bulletin* 2 (April 1959): 1-13.
      Rieger provides scope and content notes for record groups relating to Africa along with citations for finding aids to each of the record groups mentioned.

598. Robinson, William W. "Land Grant Records that Survived a Great Fire: An Inventory of Early California Historical Material Transferred to the National Archives." *Southern California Quarterly* 26 (March 1944): 28-44.

599. Roland, Alex. "The National Advisory Committee for Aeronautics." *Prologue* 10 (Summer 1978): 69-81.
      This articles describes the records of the committee from 1915 to the 1950s. Roland cites specific record series and comments on the research value of the records. The records are in the U.S. National Archives.

600. Schultz, Constance B. "Revolutionary War Pension Applications: A Neglected Source for Social and Family History." *Prologue* 15 (Summer 1983): 103-114.

The author notes that data supplied by pension applicants is a rich source for social history. She provides the legislative background for federal pensions and describes the types of records found in the files held by the U.S. National Archives.

601. Shaughnessy, Charles A., Margaret O. Adams, and Elizabeth L. Hill. "Vietnam Records in the National Archives." *Prologue* 23 (Spring 1991): 69-85.

The authors review and describe photographic, electronic, and textual records, both military and civilian.

602. Stark, Marie C. "Materials for Research in the Files of International Claims Commissions." *American Neptune* 3 (January 1943): 48-54.

Stark notes there were records from ninety-six claims commissions in the U.S. National Archives. He identifies record series that are especially useful for historical research.

603. Strong, Dennis F. "Sources for Pacific Northwest History: The Federal Records Center in Seattle." *Pacific Northwest Quarterly* 49 (January 1958): 19-20.

Strong reviews federal records available at the National Archives' regional archives in Seattle. He cites the agencies that offer the greatest volume of records and comments on their research value.

604. Swerczek, Ronald E. "Records Relating to India in the Archives of the United States." *Indian Archives* 32 (1983): 15-26.

The author uses a record group approach to identify India-related records. This article is more general in nature than the one by Basu cited in entry 526 above.

605. Swierenga, Robert P. "List Upon List: The Ship Passenger Records and Immigration Research." *Journal of American Ethnic History* 10 (Spring 1991): 42-53.

The author comments extensively on the research values of these records, notes those that have been published, discusses the types of information they contain, and offers tips on use.

606. Thaler, Katherine W. "The Fort Worth Federal Records Center." *Texas Libraries* 39 (Summer 1977): 76-83.

The author provides an overview of the center's services and holdings while mentioning specific federal record groups and microfilm publications held by the center's archives branch.

607. Tutorow, Norman E. "Library Resources: Potpourri of Graphic Materials in the Los Angeles Federal Records Center." *California Historical Quarterly* 52 (Winter 1973): 366-370.

   Tutorow reviews the best sources for photographs in the records center. He includes the U.S. Navy, the Bureau of Public Roads, the Forest Service, and the Reconstruction Finance Corporation, along with several southwestern water reclamation projects.

608. Tutorow, Norman E. "Source Materials for Historical Research in the Los Angeles Federal Records Center." *Southern California Quarterly* 53 (December 1971): 333-344.

   A thorough review of the center's holdings of records of the federal courts; Departments of Justice, the Interior and the Treasury; the Forest Service; Customs Service; military services; and others. The center is particularly rich in Indian-related records.

609. Tutorow, Norman E., and Arthur R. Abel. "Western and Territorial Research Opportunities in Trans-Mississippi Federal Records Centers." *Pacific Historical Review* 40 (November 1971): 501-518.

   The authors provide an overview of federal records in six western federal record centers. Description includes record series titles, volume, and inclusive dates with comments on the research values of records of each federal agency that the authors cite.

610. Van Dereedt, Angie S. "Do We Have Any Records Relating to French Spoliation Claims?" *Prologue* 23 (Spring 1991): 92-97.

   The author reviews and describes records from the Department of Justice (RGs 123 and 205); Department of State (RGs 57, 59, 84); the Legislative Branch (RGs 46 and 233); and others, all relating to spoliation claims.

611. White, Gerald T. "Government Archives Afield: The Federal Records Centers and the Historian." *Journal of American History* 55 (March 1969): 833-842.

   White reviews record groups common to most all federal record centers such as U.S. court records; Bureau of Indian Affairs and Bureau of Land Management records; and Bureau of Customs records. He also cites some record groups unique to specific centers.

612. Wilson, Allison. "The Center for Polar Archives, Washington, D.C." *Polar Record* 16 (January 1973): 541-552.

   The U.S. National Archives administers this center which serves as repository for polar-related materials. The article describes the center's collections of personal papers and federal records relating to polar explorations.

613. Wilson, Don W. "Federal Court Records in the Regional Archives System." *Prologue* 21 (Fall 1989): 176-177.

Wilson introduces a series of articles that review and describe U.S. court records in the National Archives field branches. The individual articles focus on different types of court records for which a specific branch has special strengths, and on ways the records may be used. The articles are:

1. Burton, Shirley and Kellee Green. "Defining Disloyalty: Treason, Espionage, and Sedition Prosecutions, 1861-1946." 215-221.

2. Chambers, Susan. "Western Natural Resources: Documenting the Struggle for Control." 239-245.

3. Corriston, Mark A. "Discovering Frontier History Through Territorial Court Records." 223-229.

4. Lothyan, Phillip E. "A Question of Citizenship." 267-273.

5. Lowell, Waverly B. "Where Have All the Flowers Gone? Early Environmental Litigation." 247-255.

6. Morris, Robert C. "From Piracy to Censorship: The Admiralty Experience." 187-195.

7. Nixon, Dianne S. "Hollywood's Immigrants: Naturalizing the Makers of America's Dream Machine." 257-265.

8. Owens, James K. "Documenting Regional Business History: The Bankruptcy Acts of 1800 and 1841." 179-185.

9. Plowman, Robert J. "An Untapped Source: Civil War Prize Case Files, 1861-65." 197-205.

10. Rust, Barbara. "The Right to Vote: The Enforcement Acts and Southern Courts." 231-237.

11. Watkins, Beverly. "'To Surrender All His Estate:' The 1867 Bankruptcy Act." 207-213.

614. Wood, Richard G. "Research Materials in the National Archives Pertaining to Pennsylvania." *Pennsylvania Magazine of History and Biography* 69 (April 1945): 89-102.

Wood cites military records from the American Revolution to WWI; land records; records of the Continental Congress; customs records;

immigration records; and many others. He identifies the materials by the
federal agency source and by record series.

615. Wright, Almon R. "Archival Sources for the Study of War-Time Relations
     of Latin America with the United States, 1917-1920: Illustrations of Their
     Use." *Inter-American Bibliographical Review* 1 (Spring 1941): 23-35.
         This article is about U.S. Food Administration records. Wright
     identifies record series that relate to sugar, coffee, and sisal and comments
     on U.S. trade with Cuba, Brazil, and Mexico for these materials.

616. Wright, Almon R. "Food and Society: War Time Archives of the United
     States Food Administration." *American Scholar* 7 (Spring 1938): 243-246.
         The author notes that the records of the U.S. Food Administration were
     the first to be made available by the then new National Archives. He
     recounts some of the agency's functions and notes areas in which the
     records might be of use to scholars.

617. Wright, Almon R. "Sources for Ohio World War History in the Papers of
     the Food Administration in the National Archives." *Ohio Archaeological
     and Historical Quarterly* 47 (October 1938): 355-362.
         Wright cites record series titles among these records and analyzes their
     research value to historians. The scope of the article is limited to the
     agency's work in Ohio.

618. Younkin, C. George. "The Role of the Regional Archives." *Louisiana
     History* 13 (Summer 1972): 311-319.
         Younkin provides an overview of federal records in the National
     Archives regional branch at Fort Worth, Texas. The article ends with a
     checklist of U.S. court, Navy, Customs Service, and agricultural records.

Fine Arts Collections

General

619. Balkansky, Arlene. "Through the Electronic Looking Glass: Television Programs in the Library of Congress." *Quarterly Journal of the Library of Congress* 37 (Summer/Fall 1980): 458-475.

    The author reports on the origins of the library's collection and reviews some of the popular and historically significant programs that are documented by these holdings. The article closes with a checklist of selected programs held by the Library of Congress.

620. Bensman, Marvin R. "Obtaining Old Radio Programs: A List of Sources for Research and Teaching." *Journal of Popular Culture* 12 (Fall 1978): 360-367.

    The article does not describe programs or broadcasts, but does cite sources and repositories holding collections of radio programs. Among the citations are associations, colleges and universities, special libraries, and museums.

621. Brylawski, Samuel. "Armed Forces Radio Service: The Invisible Highway Abroad." *Quarterly Journal of the Library of Congress* 37 (Summer/Fall 1980): 441-457.

    The first part of this article traces the history of the AFRS and its development during WWII. The article closes with a general description of the Library of Congress' collection of about 170,000 AFRS recordings and a checklist of selected AFRS programs.

622. Brylawski, Samuel. "Cartoons for the Record: The Jack Knapp Collection." *Quarterly Journal of the Library of Congress* 38 (Summer 1981): 180-195.

    Knapp founded Decca Records in 1934. He also collected cartoons about the recording industry and this collection of seventy-five examples is in the Library of Congress. While heavily illustrated, this article is mostly biographical in content.

623. Crain, William H. "The Hoblitzelle Theatre Arts Library, University of

Texas at Austin." *Special Collections* 1 (Fall 1981): 53-64.

Crain mentions several key collections. They include the Messmore Kendal Collection with its Harry Houdini material, the Norman Bel Geddes Collection, the John Gassner Collection, the G. C. Howard Collection, and others.

624. Fletcher, James E., and W. Worth McDougald. "The Peabody Collection at the University of Georgia." *Performing Arts Resources* 2 (1975): 31-40.

The authors describe a body of performing arts materials submitted and accumulated in the course of accepting nominations for Peabody Awards. The materials include scripts, press clippings, reviews, correspondence, and sound and video recordings.

625. Gerdts, Abigail Booth. "Newly Discovered Records of the New York Gallery of the Fine Arts." *Archives of American Art Journal* 21 (No. 4 1981): 2-9.

Gerdts reviews the contents of a set of minutes kept by the gallery's Board of Trustees and Executive Committee for the period 1844-1858.

626. Godfrey, Donald. "History Held as a Microphone." *Film and History* 3 (February 1973): 13-16.

This article calls attention to a collection of CBS newscasts dating from September, 1939 through May, 1945 broadcast from KIRO, a Seattle, Washington, radio station. The newscasts represent nearly complete coverage of WWII in the European Theater.

627. Gustafson, R. Eric. "The San Francisco Archives for the Performing Arts." *Performing Arts Resources* 6 (1980): 106-109.

The author provides an overview of the archives and concludes the article with a list of arts-related materials including manuscript collections, sound recordings, photographs, ephemera, and published items.

628. Henderson, George. "Fine Arts Archives Collections at Dallas Public Library." *Texas Libraries* 39 (Winter 1977): 151-160.

Henderson reviews the types of materials held including symphony orchestra performance programs; scrapbooks; music manuscripts; photographs; correspondence; costume designs; and collections of performers' personal papers.

629. Ingerman, Elizabeth A. "The Joseph Downs Manuscript and Microfilm Library." *Winterthur Portfolio* 1 (1964): 150-159.

This article calls attention to a collection of manuscripts, photographs, and drawings documenting the decorative arts and, especially, furniture and cabinet making.

630. Miller, J. Wesley. "The Madison People's Poster and Propaganda Collection." *Resources for American Literary Study* 7 (Autumn 1977): 158-161.
    This is a collection of ephemera including posters, handbills, signs, cartoons, radical newspapers, etc., collected during the late 1960s and early 1970s. The materials housed at the University of Wisconsin document the street people culture of that period.

631. Nelson, Richard A. "Sources for Archival Research on Film and Television Propaganda in the United States." *Film History* 3 (No. 4 1989): 333-340.
    This is a review of repositories holding propaganda-related records and manuscript collections. Nelson cites specific collections and provides scope and content notes for the repositories.

632. Ostrom, Nicki N. "The Gordon Craig-Isadora Duncan Collection: A Register." *Bulletin of the New York Public Library* 76 (1972): 181-198.
    This is a collection of Duncan's papers accumulated by Edward Gordon Craig between 1901-1957. The collection contains drawings; sketchbooks and notebooks; correspondence; programs; photographs; and ephemera. The register includes an index.

633. Ostrom, Nicki N. "The Papers of Gabriel Astruc (1864-1938): A Register." *Bulletin of the New York Public Library* 75 (October 1971): 357-370.
    Astruc was a French publisher and theatre director. His papers, in the Dance Collection of the New Public Library, date from 1906 to 1914 and relate to Russian ballet in western Europe. Ostrom prepared the register at the folder level and included an index.

634. Perry, Ted. ed. *Performing Arts Resources* 1 (1974): 1-218.
    This is the first volume of an annual serial that frequently contains articles about research materials relating to the performing arts. Perry devoted much of this issue to sources. It contains sixteen essays locating and describing key performing arts collections in the U.S. The articles are:

    1. Browne, Ray B., and William Schurk. "The Popular Culture Library and Audio Center." 74-78.

    2. Correll, Laraine. "The Belknap Collection for the Performing Arts: University of Florida Libraries." 56-65.

    3. Hunter, Frederick J. "Theatre and Drama Research Sources at the University of Texas at Austin." 43-47.

4. Johnson, Kay. "The Wisconsin Center for Theatre Research." 66-73.

5. Krivatsy, Nati H., and Laetitia Yeandle. "Theatrical Holdings of the Folger Shakespeare Library." 48-55.

6. Kuiper, John B. "The Motion Picture Section of the Library of Congress." 88-92.

7. Lichty, Lawrence W. "Sources for Research and Teaching in Radio and Television History." 218-231.

8. Pilkington, James P. "Vanderbilt Television News Archive." 213-217.

9. Powers, James. "The Film History Program of the Center for Advanced Film Studies of the American Film Institute." 79-87.

10. Rachow, Louis A. "Performing Arts Research Collections in New York City." 1-16.

11. Schlosser, Anne G. "Film/Broadcasting Resources in the Los Angeles Area." 17-32.

12. Wharton, Betty. "The Chamberlain and Lyman Brown Theatrical Agency Collection." 93-98.

13. Witham, Barry B. "An Index to 'Mirror Interviews.'" 153-155.

14. Woods, Alan. "A Survey of the Ohio State University Theatre Research Institute." 33-42.

15. Wortis, Avi. "The R. H. Burnside Collection of the New York Public Library." 99-146.

16. Zucker, Phyllis. "The American Film Institute Catalog Project." 147-152.

635. Sanborn, Herbert J. "The Cleland Papers." *Quarterly Journal of Current Acquisitions* 20 (June 1963): 163-169.
Thomas Maitland Cleland is known as a printer and illustrator. His papers in the Library of Congress include correspondence, drawings, designs, and corrected proofs of books. The article reviews some of the key items in the collection.

636. Shaw, Renata V. "Nineteenth Century Tobacco Label Art." *Quarterly Journal of the Library of Congress* 28 (April 1971): 76-102.

A profusely illustrated article describing a collection of tobacco labels in the Prints and Photographs Division of the Library of Congress. The article traces the development of the art used from the 1840s to the 1890s.

637. Swank, Cynthia G. "Performing Arts on Madison Avenue." *Performing Arts Resources* 10 (1985): 23-25.
Swank describes the archives of the J.W. Thompson Company. The Thompson Company did many of the commercials on radio and T.V. and its archives contain the scripts of more than 200 radio and T.V. shows, some dating back to the 1930s.

638. Taylor, Robert N., and Helen Parr Taylor. "The Eric Gill Collection of the Humanities Research Center: A Catalogue." *Library Chronicle of the University of Texas at Austin* New Series 18 (1982): 9-193.
This entire issue is devoted to the catalog of Gill's books and papers. Gill is known for his work in the book-arts field. His collection, dating from the 1890s to 1940, includes art work, books, and his correspondence and manuscripts.

639. Wentink, Andrew M. "The Ruth Page Collection: An Introduction and Guide to Manuscript Materials through 1970." *Bulletin of Research in the Humanities* 83 (Spring 1980): 67-162.
Ruth Page was an American dancer and choreographer. Her papers in the New York Public Library contain costume and set designs; motion pictures; photographs; scrapbooks and clippings; manuscripts; music scores; correspondence; and business records. The guide is indexed.

Art

640. "The Archives of American Art Oral History Program: A Preliminary Guide to Tape-Recorded Interviews." *Journal of the Archives of American Art* 8 (January 1968): 1-9; 9 (January 1969): 1-10; 11 (Nos. 1-4 1971): 1-48; and 14 (No. 3 1974): 14-24.
This series of articles describes the archives oral histories relating to art and artists. Entries appear alphabetically by surname of informant and also include interviewers' names, date of interview, content note, and length of transcripts.

641. Bailey, Elizabeth G. "The Cecilia Beaux Papers." *Archives of American Art Journal* 13 (No. 4 1973): 14-19.
Beaux was a well-known American artist of the 1920s. Her papers on microfilm include correspondence, notebooks and diaries, speeches, poetry, reviews of her work, and drafts of her autobiography.

642. Blayac, Alain. "Evelyn Waugh's Drawings." *Library Chronicle of the University of Texas at Austin* New Series 7 (Spring 1974): 43-57.

    This article describes 110 of Waugh's drawings. It concludes with a checklist of each with entries including subject of the drawing, its medium, size, and date, when known.

643. Bond, John. "The Augustus Saint-Gaudens Collection." *Dartmouth College Library Bulletin* 8 (November 1967): 3-9.

    This collection of Saint-Gaudens papers includes business and personal correspondence; Dolley family correspondence; Saint-Gaudens' manuscripts; photographs; and drawings

644. Brubaker, Robert L. "Toward a History of the Art Institute of Chicago: A Survey of Sources." *Chicago History* 8 (Spring 1979): 61-63.

    The last third of this article describes the records of the institute. They include minutes; correspondence files; reports and memoranda; and acquisitions records, all dating from the 1870s to the 1970s.

645. Bry, Doris. "The Stieglitz Archive at Yale University." *Yale University Library Gazette* 25 (April 1951): 123-130.

    The Alfred Stieglitz Archive at Yale includes correspondence files; paintings, drawings, and sketches; clipping files; scrapbooks; an autograph collection; and manuscripts by others than Stieglitz. The article cites many of Stieglitz's correspondents.

646. Chinard, Gilbert. "The American Sketchbooks of Charles-Alexandre Lesueur." *Proceedings of the American Philosophical Society* 93 (May 1949): 114-118.

    Lesueur was a French painter-naturalist whose sketchbooks and papers document an 1816-1837 residence in the U.S. Chinard describes and evaluates the collection from historical and artistic viewpoints.

647. Cohen, Phyliss S. "The Gaston Lachaise Collection." *Yale University Library Gazette* 58 (October 1983): 64-73.

    Lachaise is known as a sculptor. Cohen describes correspondence and manuscripts held by Yale and notes that correspondence to Lachaise and his wife between 1917-1945 make up most of the collection. The library, however, also holds the papers of his sister and mother.

648. Eisler, Colin. "The Egmont Albums: A New Collection of Drawings for Yale." *Yale University Library Gazette* 32 (January 1958): 85-92.

    Eisler calls attention to four volumes containing 541 drawings from the 16th to the mid-18th centuries. He notes that most of the drawings were by 16th- and 17th-century northern European artists.

649. Gee, Kathleen. "A Checklist of D. H. Lawrence Artwork at the HRHRC."
     Library Chronicle of the University of Texas at Austin New Series 34
     (1986): 61-73.
     The checklist cites twenty-three items.   Entries include title, size,
     medium, date, Humanities Research Center catalog number, inscription,
     if any, and descriptive note.

650. Grier, Katherine C. "Cathedrals of Commerce: The Skyscraper Etchings
     of Joseph Pennell." *Library Chronicle of the University of Texas at Austin*
     New Series 17 (1981): 15-29.
     Joseph Pennell was an American artist and illustrator known for his
     architectural drawings.   Grier describes the substantial collection of
     Pennell's work at the University of Texas.

651. Hunter, Margaret Traux. "The Photograph Archive of the Art Reference
     Library." *Huntington Library Quarterly* 24 (February 1961): 175-179.
     This article calls attention to the library's 40,000 reference photographs
     of 18th-century European paintings.   It concludes with a checklist of
     photographed collections.

652. Iben, Icko. "The Literary Estate of Lorado Taft." *American Archivist* 26
     (October 1963): 493-496.
     Iben reviews a collection of letters, manuscripts, and papers of sculptor
     Lorado Taft held by the University of Illinois, Urbana.

653. Kirwin, Liza. "Documenting Contemporary Southern Self-Taught Artists."
     Southern Quarterly 26 (Fall 1987): 57-75.
     The Archives of American Art has acquired audiovisual materials to
     document the work of artists lacking accumulations of personal papers.
     Kirwin reviews some of these collections in this article.

654. Kirwin, Liza. "Visual Thinking: Sketchbooks from the Archives of
     American Art." *Archives of American Art Journal* 27 (No. 1 1987): 21-29.
     Artists whose sketchbooks Kirwin describes include Worthington
     Whittredge, David Smith, David Park, Albert Kahn, John Alexander,
     Fairfield Porter, John Graham, George Tooker, and Reginald Marsh.

655. Leland, Waldo G. "The Lesueur Collection of American Sketches in the
     Museum of Natural History at Havre, Seine-Inférieure." *Mississippi Valley
     Historical Review* 10 (June 1923): 53-78.
     Charles Alexander Lesueur was a French natural history artist who spent
     twenty-one years in the U.S. (1816-1837).   Leland provides an introduc-
     tion to Lesueur's work and concludes the article with a checklist of
     Lesueur's drawings.

656. Lyman, Susan E., and Donald A. Shelley. "Greenwood Family Manu-
scripts and Portraits." *New York Historical Society Quarterly Bulletin* 27
(April 1943): 43-44.
    The manuscripts are mostly 18th-century travel diaries kept by John
Greenwood, an artist; his dentist-cousin also named John Greenwood; and
Isaac Greenwood.

657. Maline, Sarah. "The Arabian Sketches of T. E. Lawrence." *Library
Chronicle of the University of Texas at Austin* New Series 38/39 (1987):
17-39.
    Maline describes a sketchbook and selected photographs among the T.
E. Lawrence papers at the Humanities Research Center. The drawings
and photos illustrate Lawrence's artistic abilities.

658. Mattson, Francis O. "The John Quinn Memorial Collection: An Inventory
and Index." *Bulletin of the New York Public Library* 78 (Winter 1975):
145-230.
    Quinn was a successful attorney, collector of art and English literature,
and the friend of many artists and authors. This is an inventory of his
extensive correspondence.

659. Mayerson, Charlotte L. "The Maurice Sterne Papers." *Yale University
Library Gazette* 45 (October 1970): 73-76.
    The article calls attention to Sterne's papers at Yale which are mostly
correspondence and autobiographical notes. Sterne was a successful
American artist during the 1920s whose work lost favor in subsequent
decades.

660. McCoy, Garnett. "An Archivist's Choice: Ten of the Best." *Archives of
American Art Journal* 19 (No. 2 1979): 2-18.
    The Archives of American Art director describes what he considers to
be the ten best collections of papers in the archives. He provides
biographical information about the people who formed the collections and
describes their papers.

661. McCoy, Garnett. "Archives of American Art." *Manuscripts* 26 (Summer
1974): 176-183.
    McCoy provides a brief history of the archives followed by a review of
its holdings, including oral histories and microfilmed materials. McCoy
notes that the strength of the archives is in the papers of 20th-century
American painters.

662. McCoy, Garnett. "The Archives of American Art." *American Archivist* 30
(July 1967): 443-451.
    An overview of Archives of American Art holdings which includes

mention of significant collections and record series.

663. McCoy, Garnett. "A Preliminary Guide to the Collections of the Archives of American Art." *Journal of the Archives of American Art* 5 (January 1965): 1-20; and 7 (January 1967): 1-20.
      Part one describes 129 manuscript collections. Entries include collection and record series titles, volume, inclusive dates, and content notes. Part two lists another 113 collections. Both parts also include checklists of oral histories.

664. McCoy, Garnett. "The Rockwell Kent Papers." *Archives of American Art Journal* 12 (January 1972): 1-20.
      McCoy focuses this article on the research value of the more than 50,000 letters and documents in the Kent Collection.

665. McCoy, Garnett. "The Walt Kuhn Papers." *Journal of the Archives of American Art* 5 (October 1965): 1-6.
      Kuhn was an American artist. His papers include letters to his father and his wife, notebooks and diaries, and published materials relating to his art. The materials date from 1908 to 1948.

666. Parker, Alice L. "The Whistler Material in the Rosenwald Collection." *Quarterly Journal of Current Acquisitions* 3 (October 1945): 63-66.
      Parker describes six letterbooks containing 100 letters and miscellaneous writings of the artist James A. M. Whistler.

667. Peritore, Laura. "The Cartoon Collections at the State Historical Society." *Missouri Historical Review* 73 (April 1979): 363-377.
      Peritore describes editorial cartoons in the Daniel R. Fitzpatrick, Silvey J. Ray, Peter Mayo, and the Society Collections. Description focuses on the artists, topical content, and number of drawings in a collection.

668. Rothrock, O. J. "Rowlandson Drawings at Princeton: Introduction and Checklist." *Princeton University Library Chronicle* 36 (Winter 1976): 87-110.
      The checklist describes 109 of Thomas Rowlandson's drawings with entries including the drawing's title or subject; its size and medium; and a brief summary of what the drawing represents.

669. Smith, Richard C. "Modern Art and Oral History in the United States: A Revolution Remembered." *Journal of American History* 78 (September 1991): 598-606.
      The value of this article lies in Smith's identification of major collections of art-related oral history collections. He limits description, mostly to types of information found in interviews.

670. Smith, Robert C. "The Archive of Hispanic Culture." *Quarterly Journal of Current Acquisitions* 1 (October 1943): 53-57.

  This archive is a photograph collection in the Library of Congress devoted to the arts in Latin America. The collection contains several thousand photographs of Latin American frescos, paintings, architectural drawings, and historical buildings.

671. Stehle, Raymond L. "Five Sketchbooks of Emanuel Leutze." *Quarterly Journal of the Library of Congress* 21 (April 1964): 81-94.

  Stehle describes a collection of sketchbooks and correspondence by the German-American artist Emanuel Leutze. The sketches date from 1841 and 1859-1861.

672. "The Leo D. Stein Papers." *Yale University Library Gazette* 51 (January 1977): 164-166.

  This article calls attention to Stein's papers at Yale which include his notebooks, manuscripts and correspondence. Leo Stein was an artist and brother of author Gertrude Stein.

673. Stout, Leon J. "Pennsylvania Town Views, 1850-1922: A Union Catalogue." *Western Pennsylvania Historical Magazine* 58 (July 1975): 409-428; (October 1975): 546-571; and 59 (January 1976): 88-103.

  Stout provides a checklist of 324 views in a three-part catalog. Entries include name of town, date, artist, publisher, size, colors used, insets, and locations of known copies.

674. Taylor, Kendall. "The Philip Evergood Papers." *Archives of American Art Journal* 18 (No. 3 1978): 2-19.

  Evergood was an American artist. His papers include correspondence, speeches, writings, sketches, scrapbooks, and published material, all dating from 1927 to 1964.

675. Vail, R.W.G. "The American Sketchbooks of a French Naturalist, 1816-1837." *Proceedings of the American Antiquarian Society* 48 (April 1938): 49-155.

  The sketches are those of Charles Alexander Lesueur. Vail provides historical background about Lesueur and his career and concludes the article with a list of Lesueur's drawings. Entries include geographical locations, subjects sketched, and date, when available.

676. Witthoft, Brucia. "The James D. Smillie Diaries, 1865-1880: Artist Friends." *Archives of American Art Journal* 25 (No. 3 1985): 24-26.

  Smillie was an American painter who recorded his contacts with other artists in forty-five diaries. Witthoft concludes this article with a list of artists mentioned in Smillie's diaries.

677. Zigrosser, Carl. "The Medallic Sketches of Augustin Dupré in American Collections." *Proceedings of the American Philosophical Society* 101 (December 1957): 535-550.

Zigrosser describes Dupré's sketches in the society and the Boston Public Library and writes about the artist's work and his relationship with Thomas Jefferson and Benjamin Franklin.

Drama, Theatre, Motion Pictures

678. Allison, William. "The Penn State Archives of American Theatre Lighting Including Century Lighting and Century Strand Control System Drawings: 1950-70." *Performing Arts Resources* 10 (1985): 40-47.

Allison reports that the collection contains drawings; photographs and graphic art; research and development files; sound recordings of interviews with lighting designers; and lighting systems and equipment.

679. Balio, Tino. "Wisconsin Center for Film and Theatre Research." *Special Collections* 1 (Fall 1981): 65-74.

This center is on the campus of the University of Wisconsin at Madison, but the article notes the materials described are in the state historical society. The author uses a media approach to describe film, theatre, television, and graphic materials.

680. Barnouw, Erik. "The Sintzenich Diaries." *Quarterly Journal of the Library of Congress* 37 (Summer/Fall 1980): 310-331.

Arthur H. C. Sintzenich was a motion picture cameraman. His collection in the Library of Congress consists of sixty-one diaries dating from 1913 in which he documents his work and provides many insights into the early motion picture industry.

681. Bourne, Tom. "Hollywood in Beverly Hills: The Academy of Motion Pictures Library." *Wilson Library Bulletin* 55 (January 1981): 342-346.

This library holds two million MGM movie still pictures; manuscript collections of people associated with the motion picture industry; scripts; and records of film companies. Description is limited to collection titles.

682. Brokaw, John W. "Wilson Barrett's Papers: A Theatrical Legacy." *Library Chronicle of the University of Texas at Austin* New Series 7 (Spring 1974): 11-20.

Barrett was a 19th-century English playwright-actor. His papers at the Humanities Research Center date from the 1870s to his death in 1904 and include financial and legal records and his personal and business correspondence.

683. Burner, Alma J. "A Chapter of the London Stage: The Clement Scott Papers." *University of Rochester Library Bulletin* 27 (Winter 1973/1974): 71-75.

    Scott was a 19th-century English theatrr critic. His papers include correspondence; manuscripts of his poetry; newspaper clippings; and photographs. The article focuses on his correspondence dating from the 1880s to the 1890s.

684. Cain, Melissa and Michael Mullen. "Design by Motley: A Theatre and Costume Arts Collection." *Performing Arts Resources* 8 (1983): 14-21.

    The authors call attention to a large collection of costume and set design drawings from the English designing firm of Motley. The materials are at the University of Illinois, Urbana.

685. Correll, Laraine. "Federal Theatre Project Records at George Mason University." *Performing Arts Resources* 6 (1980): 1-77.

    These records include administrative correspondence; publicity files; financial records; reports; play readers' reports; audience surveys; production records; photographs; costume and set design materials; radio scripts; and other record series.

686. Corwin, Betty L. "Theatre on Film and Tape." *Performing Arts Resources* 3 (1976): 41-60.

    Corwin relates how this collection came to be and concludes the article with a list of stage productions, special events, and videotaped dialogues. Entries include titles, names of performers, dates, and content notes.

687. Crawford, Dorothy. "The Crawford Theatre Collection." *Yale University Library Gazette* 41 (January 1967): 131-135.

    This collection focuses on modern drama and contains programs; photographs; biofiles on actors and actresses; scenes of plays and motion pictures; data files on theatres; and an extensive file of play reviews.

688. Doherty, Katherine M. "Playbills in the Massachusetts Historical Society of Amateur Theatricals, 1775-1921: A Preliminary Checklist." *Proceedings of the Massachusetts Historical Society* 91 (1979): 101-211.

    There are 211 entries in this checklist. Playbills are listed chronologically with most falling in the 19th century. Entries include theatre or theatrical group, date, text of playbill, size, and cast, if listed. The checklist is indexed.

689. Eaton, Walter P. "The Eugene O'Neill Collection." *Yale University Library Gazette* 18 (July 1943): 5-8.

    Eaton describes the drafts and related papers of O'Neill's plays *Strange Interlude, Mourning Becomes Electra, Lazarus Laughed, The Great God*

Brown, Marco Millions, Dynamo, and *Days Without End.*

690. Freedley, George. "The 26 Principal Theatre Collections in American Libraries and Museums." *Bulletin of the New York Public Library* 62 (July 1958): 319-329.
    This is a directory arranged alphabetically by state and with scope and content notes for each repository entry.

691. Gassner, John. "The Theatre Guild Collection at Yale." *Yale University Library Gazette* 32 (April 1958): 113-121.
    This collection includes 200 volumes of play scripts; 96 technical plats and ground plans; musical scores; records of the guild's productions; reviews of its plays; the guild's financial records; play reports by guild readers; and radio and T.V. scripts.

692. Gibson, Rebecca Campbell and Judith Van Sant. "Another Chance for a Swell Scene: The Filmscripts of Darryl Zanuck." *Indiana University Bookman* 15 (October 1983): 36-81.
    A narrative description of Zanuck's personal copies of scripts to films he produced. The collection is in Indiana University's Lilly Library. A checklist of the filmscripts concludes the article.

693. Gibson, Rebecca Campbell and Judith Van Sant. "The John Ford Collection." *Indiana University Bookman* 15 (October 1983): 20-35.
    This article comments on selected documents in the Ford Collection in the Lilly Library. It concludes with a listing of Ford films represented in the collection, along with the record series associated with each.

694. Gibson, Rebecca Campbell and Judith Van Sant. "After the Invasion from Mars: Orson Welles and RKO." *Indiana University Bookman* 15 (October 1983): 3-19.
    A narrative description of papers directly related to several films Welles directed between 1939-1942. The article concludes with a list of films and the record series associated with each.

695. Gutiérrez-Witt, Laura. "Archives of the Carlos Villalongín Dramatic Company." *Library Chronicle of the University of Texas at Austin* New Series 10 (1978): 76-80.
    This collection, in the Nettie Lee Benson Latin American Collection, contains 247 play scripts, 15 playbills, and 33 photographs of actors. Many of the play scripts contain annotations and set design notes.

696. Hoffman, Judi. "The Norman O. Dawn Collection of Cinematic Special Effects." *Library Chronicle of the University of Texas at Austin* 20 (Number 3 1990): 97-118.

Dawn is known for his pioneer work with motion picture special effects. This collection consists of 164 cards illustrating more than 230 special effects he developed. The article illustrates and discusses several examples of his work.

697. Howe, Ellen V., and R. Russell Malone. "The Dublin Gate Theatre at Northwestern University Library." *Performing Arts Resources* 10 (1985): 34-39.

   The Dublin Gate Theatre records date from 1928 to 1979 and include scripts; music; photographs; lighting and set designs; costume sketches; correspondence; and other miscellaneous papers.

698. Hunter, Frederick J. "Drama and Theatre Arts Resources at TxU." *Library Chronicle of the University of Texas* 7 (Spring 1964): 55-59.

   Description is at the collection level as Hunter cites the titles of key collections and notes the types of materials found in each.

699. Jensen, Mary Ann. "The William Seymour Theatre Collection, Princeton University Library." *Special Collections* 1 (Fall 1981): 41-51.

   A history of the Seymour Collection which includes the papers of William Seymour, the McCaddon Collection of circus-related materials, Albert M. Friend Collection of 18th-century theatre drawings, and the musical material in the Tams-Witmark Archives.

700. Jensen, Mary Ann. "The William Seymour Theatre Collection: A Curator's View." *Princeton University Library Chronicle* 48 (Autumn 1986): 7-20.

   This is a history of the collection's development, including a review of its holdings. Jensen cites titles of other theatre-related archives and manuscript collections that make up the Seymour Collection.

701. "The Joseph Norton Ireland Collection." *Yale University Library Gazette* 41 (July 1966): 25-27.

   Ireland was a historian of the 19th-century theatre in New York. The collection contains many of his manuscripts including those of his publications and his notes on theatre performances he attended between 1826 and 1888.

702. Kaiser, Barbara J. "Resources in the Wisconsin Center for Theatre Research." *American Archivist* 30 (July 1967): 483-492.

   Kaiser's description includes the papers of Harry and Roy Aitken, The Playwrights' Company, Kermit Bloomgarden, Richard Myers, Herman Shumlin, Moss Hart, Gore Vidal, and several others. The papers are in the Wisconsin State Historical Society's manuscript library.

703. Malkin, Audree. "Twentieth Century Fox Corporate Archives at the UCLA Theatre Arts Library." *Performing Arts Resources* 10 (1985): 1-9.

Malkin reviews 20th Century Fox movie and T.V. scripts; movie and T.V. still photos; legal records; call sheets; and synopsis files. Description includes many film titles and inclusive dates.

704. McCown, Robert A. "Records of the Redpath Chautauqua." *Books at Iowa* 19 (November 1973): 8-23.

Much of this article is devoted to the history of the Redpath Chautauqua and Keith Vawter's involvement with it. It concludes with a description of the company's records, including talent contracts, Vawter's correspondence, business correspondence, route books, photographs, financial records, and printed materials.

705. Millie, Elena and Andrea Wyatt. "Tomorrow Night, East Lynne! American Drama as Reflected in the Theatre Poster Collection at the Library of Congress." *Quarterly Journal of the Library of Congress* 37 (Winter 1980): 114-151.

This profusely illustrated article presents the development of theatre art in the U.S. The illustrations are representative of the library's extensive theatre poster collections.

706. Myers, Paul. "The New York Public Library: The Billy Rose Theatre Collection." *Special Collections* 1 (Fall 1981): 23-28.

Myers describes David Belasco's papers, Robinson Locke's scrapbook collection and George Beck's collection of promptbooks and scripts of 18th- and 19th-century plays. He concludes with graphic resources relating to the theatre, movies, radio, and T.V.

707. Nece, Bernice M. "The Kirsten Flagstad Memorial Collection." *American Archivist* 30 (July 1967): 477-482.

Nece discusses and analyzes some of the richer record series in the Kirsten Flagstad Collection held by the California Historical Society. The author describes the collection as one of the larger theatre collections in California.

708. Nemchek, Lee R. "The Pasadena Playhouse Collection." *Performing Arts Resources* 10 (1985): 26-33.

The Playhouse Collection includes financial records; box office records; playbills; scrapbooks; scripts; drama school records; correspondence; and more than 5,000 photographs of performers and productions dating back to 1900.

709. O'Grady, Gerald. "Resources for the Oral History of the Independent American Film at Media Study/Buffalo, New York." *Performing Arts*

Resources 3 (1976): 24-31.

The author tells why and how these interviews were accumulated. The article ends with a checklist of people interviewed, names of interviewers, and the date of the interview.

710. Oggel, L. Terry. "A Short Title Guide to the Edwin Booth Literary Materials at the Players." *Performing Arts Resources* 3 (1976): 98-142.

While much of this collection is published materials, the guide also lists over 3,000 letters to and from Booth; his promptbooks and scrapbooks; financial ledgers; manuscripts by Booth; and legal documents.

711. Perkins, Daniel J. "The American Archives of the Factual Film." *Historical Journal of Film, Radio and Television* 10 (No. 1 1990): 71-80.

Perkins calls attention to this archives located at Iowa State University, Ames, Iowa, and reviews its holdings. The archives holds films produced by U.S. businesses, professional groups, federal agencies, the military services, and other organizations.

712. Pinthus, Kurt. "The World's Largest Theater Library." *Quarterly Journal of Current Acquisitions* 1 (October 1943): 32-39.

Pinthus provides an overview of the holdings in the Library of Congress' theatre collection. While discussing, mostly, published materials, he also notes extensive manuscript collections such as the papers of Charlotte Cushman and the Federal Theatre Project.

713. Rachow, Louis A. "The Players, New York." *Special Collections* 1 (Fall 1981): 29-39.

This article describes collections in the library of the Players Club in New York City that contain manuscript and iconographic materials. He specifically names the Walter Hampton Collection, the Union Square Theatre Collection, the Max Gordon Collection, the Newman Levy Collection, and several others.

714. Renza, Christa R. "The MacKaye Family Papers." *Dartmouth College Library Bulletin* 22 (November 1981): 15-24.

Renza reviews the papers of the family's principal members, dramatists James Steele and Percy MacKaye, and Benton MacKaye, Jesse MacKaye, and Hazel MacKaye.

715. Rosenzweig, Roy and Barbara Melosh. "Government and the Arts: Voices from the New Deal Era." *Journal of American History* 77 (September 1990): 596-608.

The authors discuss the research values and types of information found in over 1,000 art-related interviews in the Archives of American Art and in the Federal Theatre Project at George Mason University.

716. Schmitt, Anthony R. "The Ernest Lehman Collection of the Hoblitzelle Theatre Arts Library." *Library Chronicle of the University of Texas at Austin* New Series 13 (1980): 71-81.

     Lehman is best known as a screenwriter and director of motion pictures. His papers include motion picture scripts, story lines, screenplays, correspondence, and photographs.

717. Sharp, Nicholas A. "The Federal Theatre Project Research Center at George Mason University." *Resources for American Literary Study* 7 (Autumn 1977): 152-157.

     The center's collections include scripts, production photographs and notebooks, research materials for federal theatre productions, and oral histories of those associated with federal theatre projects.

718. Silver, Charles. "Using MOMA." *American Film* 1 (May 1976): 72-73.

     This is an overview of services and holdings of the Film Study Center, Museum of Modern Art. Holdings include 35mm and 16mm motion picture films, manuscript collections, and film still pictures.

719. Smith, David R. "Archives of the Mouse Factory." *Performing Arts Resources* 6 (1980): 94-96.

     Smith gives an overview of the Walt Disney Archives. Besides the correspondence and film production records and scripts, the archives also has extensive publicity files, Disney books, and examples of Disney merchandise.

720. Smith, David R. "Comics and Cels: The Walt Disney Archives." *California Historical Quarterly* 56 (Fall 1977): 270-276.

     Among the records described are films and still photographs, books and comic books, sound recordings, awards, promotional materials, insignia and character merchandise, props and costumes, and employee publications.

721. Spehr, Paul C. "Edison Films in the Library of Congress." *Quarterly Journal of the Library of Congress* 32 (January 1975): 34-50.

     Spehr describes some of Edison's earlier films in the Library of Congress. He concludes the article with a title checklist of Edison films, their copyright date, and the library's holdings.

722. Stoddard, Richard. "The Barrett H. Clark Collection." *Yale University Library Gazette* 45 (January 1971): 93-103.

     Clark was a critic and patron of the theatre in the U.S. His papers include manuscripts of his own writings and those of his proteges, and his correspondence with leading literary and theatre personalities.

723. Swerdlove, Dorothy L. "Research Materials of the Federal Theatre Project in the Theatre Collection of the New York Public Library at Lincoln Center." *Performing Arts Resources* 6 (1980): 78-81.

Among these papers are scripts; correspondence files; speeches; photographs; scrapbooks; financial records; set designs; press releases; and other similar record series.

724. Van Lennep, William. "The Harvard Theatre Collection." *Harvard Library Bulletin* 6 (Autumn 1952): 281-301.

Van Lennep's essay describes the scope and content of what he calls an "unrivaled" collection on the theatre. While much of the collection is published, it also contains manuscripts, music, photographs, correspondence, programs, and playbills.

725. Wead, George. "Introduction." *Library Chronicle of the University of Texas at Austin* New Series 36 (1986): 7-10.

Wead introduces the David O. Selznick Collection held by the Humanities Research Center. Selznick's papers include scripts; correspondence; set designs; business records; and artifacts, all documenting his career in motion pictures.

726. Wheaton, Christopher D., and Richard B. Jewell. "The Cinema Library at the University of Southern California." *Performing Arts Resources* 3 (1976): 61-97.

This is a mini-guide of recorded interviews with people associated with the film industry; recordings of USC film conferences; manuscript collections; and of then unprocessed collections.

727. Wortis, Avi. "The Burnside Mystery: The R. H. Burnside Collection and the New York Public Library." *Bulletin of the New York Public Library* 75 (October 1971): 371-409.

Wortis relates the provenance of a large collection of plays in manuscript and typescript formats accumulated by R. H. Burnside. The article ends with an alphabetical listing of playwrights and titles of their plays represented in the collection.

728. Yeandle, Laetitia and W. R. Streitberger. "The Loseley Collection of Manuscripts at the Folger Shakespeare Library, Washington, D.C." *Shakespeare Quarterly* 38 (Summer 1987): 201-207.

The authors note that the collection is rich in materials documenting 16th- and 17th-century England, especially drama and the theatre. While focusing on the collection's provenance, the article concludes with a list of copied documents and finding aids.

729. Yeck, Joanne. "'Verbal Messages Cause Misunderstanding and Delays

(Please Put Them in Writing)': The Warner Bros. Collection." *Performing Arts Resources* 10 (1985): 10-15.

Yeck explains how the collection at the University of Southern California is organized and notes that it contains story files; research files; legal records; production records; scripts; still photos; correspondence files; and publicity materials.

730. Zvonchenko, Walter. "Theatre Materials in the Library of Congress." *Special Collections* 1 (Fall 1981): 13-22.

Zvonchenko describes materials in the Rare Books Division; the Manuscript Division, including the Federal Theatre Project records and materials; the Music Division; Prints and Photographs Division; the Area Studies Division; and the Microform Reading Room.

Music

731. Albrecht, Otto E. "Musical Treasures in the Morgan Library." *Manuscripts* 25 (Spring 1973): 75-86.

The article mostly describes the impressive Mary Flagler Cary Collection acquired by the library in 1968, which, according to the author, placed the Morgan Library second only to the Library of Congress for music resources.

732. Apel, Willi. "The Collection of Photographic Reproductions at the Isham Memorial Library, Harvard University." *Journal of Renaissance and Baroque Music* 1 (March 1946): 68-73; (June 1946): 144-418; and (December 1946): 235-238.

These reproductions, dating from the 15th century, are of keyboard compositions in European repositories. Entries include composer's name, title of work, place of composition, and content note.

733. Berger, Karol. "The Yale Collection of Historical Sound Recordings." *The Journal of the Association for Recorded Sound Collection* 6 (No. 1 1975): 13-25.

Berger notes that the strength of the collection is its holdings of vocal recordings and of composers performing their own works. The author cites collection titles and many performers whose recordings form part of the archive.

734. Blier, Carol. "Stephen Foster at Pittsburgh: Memorial to His Music." *Wilson Library Bulletin* 61 (January 1987): 25-28.

The Stephen Foster Memorial Collection at the University of Pittsburgh contains the composer's manuscript compositions; arrangements and recordings of his music; letters; photographs; and related artifacts.

735. Boswell, George W. "Kentucky Folksongs in the Tennessee Archives."
     Kentucky Folklore Review 4 (July/September 1958): 115-121.
         Boswell cites the titles of forty-eight folksongs originating in Kentucky.
     He includes the lyrics and tunes to four of them.

736. Brett, Philip and Thurston Dart. "Songs by William Byrd in Manuscripts
     at Harvard." *Harvard Library Bulletin* 14 (Autumn 1960): 343-365.
         The authors describe and analyze, in detail, a series of late 16th-century
     solo songs by the English composer, William Byrd.

737. Campbell, Frank C. "The Musical Scores of George Gershwin." *Quarterly
     Journal of Current Acquisitions* 11 (May 1954): 127-139.
         This article analyzes several Gershwin manuscripts in the Library of
     Congress collection. Campbell notes that all of Gershwin's important
     compositions are represented in the library's holdings.

738. Campbell, Frank C. "Schubert Song Autographs in the Whittall Collec-
     tion." *Quarterly Journal of Current Acquisitions* 6 (August 1949): 3-8.
         The Gertrude Clarke Whittall Foundation Collection in the Library of
     Congress contains manuscript compositions by noted European composers,
     including Austrian composer Franz Schubert. This article describes seven
     of his solo song manuscripts.

739. Campbell, Frank C. "Some Manuscripts of George Gershwin (1898-
     1937)." *Manuscripts* 6 (Fall 1953): 67-75.
         Campbell describes some of the manuscripts of Gershwin's works in the
     Library of Congress. He includes "Rhapsody in Blue," "Concerto in F,"
     "American in Paris," "Second Rhapsody," "Cuban Overture," and "Porgy
     and Bess."

740. Coad, Oral S. "Songs America Used to Sing." *Journal of the Rutgers
     University Library* 31 (June 1968): 33-45.
         Coad describes Rutgers' collection of about 400 different songs popular
     in America between 1850 and 1890. He identifies the dominant themes of
     these songs and cites many titles.

741. Filby, P. William. "Music in the Maryland Historical Society." *Notes* 32
     (March 1976): 503-517.
         While mostly a review of published music, Filby includes a list of music
     manuscripts and records of music clubs and associations.

742. Green, Archie. "A Discography of American Coal Miners' Songs." *Labor
     History* 2 (Winter 1961): 101-115.
         Most of this article analyzes miners' songs and locates collections of this
     musical genre. The article concludes with a checklist of recorded songs

that includes recording artist, recording company, and song titles.

743. Hanna, Archibald, Jr. "The Lindley and Charles Eberstadt Collection of Early American Music." *Yale University Library Gazette* 49 (January 1975): 299-301.
     Hanna calls attention to a collection of sheet music dating from 1830 to 1930 which, he notes, reflects America's social scene for the period.

744. Kaufman, Charles H. "The Hodges and Newland Collections in the Library of Congress: A Preliminary Report." *Current Musicology* 18 (1974): 79-89.
     Edward Hodges and William Newland were 19th-century church musicians. Kaufman reviews the contents of their personal collections which include manuscript materials.

745. Kimball, Robert E. "The Cole Porter Collection at Yale." *Yale University Library Gazette* 44 (July 1969): 8-15.
     The Porter Collection includes manuscripts of his published and unpublished songs; scrapbooks; photographs; recordings of his songs, both commercially and privately recorded; music notebooks; travel journals; and unfinished songs and music.

746. Lawn, Richard. "From Bird to Schoenberg: The Ross Russell Collection." *Library Chronicle of the University of Texas at Austin* New Series 25/26 (1984): 137-147.
     Ross Russell is known as a historian of jazz music and founder of Dial Records. Lawn describes Ross' sound recordings, research files, manuscripts, photographs, correspondence, and publications, most of which relate to jazz in the U.S.

747. Moore, Jerrold N. "The Purpose and Scope of the Historical Sound Recordings Program." *Yale University Library Gazette* 38 (January 1964): 92-110.
     This article provides a thorough review of the performers, composers, and instruments represented in the sound recording collection. It contains recordings of many European artists as well as those from the U.S.

748. Moseley, Caroline. "Music in a Nineteenth-Century Parlor." *Princeton University Library Chronicle* 41 (Spring 1980): 231-242.
     Moseley provides an overview of the more than 3,000 pieces of American sheet music published between the 1820s and 1860s. She divides the collection into different categories of music and cites several titles from each category.

749. O'Meara, Eva J. "The Lowell Mason Papers." *Yale University Library*

Gazette 45 (January 1971): 123-126.

Lowell Mason was a 19th-century educator and sacred music scholar. His papers include his correspondence, personal journals, and diaries.

750. Orledge, Robert. "From a Vision of Death to the Genesis of 'Pénélope': The Gabriel Fauré Manuscript Collection." *Library Chronicle of the University of Texas at Austin* New Series 25/26 (1984): 51-67.

Fauré was a French composer. His collection at the Humanities Research Center includes manuscripts of his compositions and seventy-one of his letters. Orledge describes both the manuscripts and the correspondence series in detail.

751. Paton, Christopher A., and others. "My Huckleberry Friend: The Life and Times of Johnny Mercer." *Manuscripts* 37 (Spring 1985): 89-100.

The authors review the record series in the Mercer papers at Georgia State University. Those mentioned include correspondence; manuscript music and lyrics; theatre scripts; copyright records; contracts; photographs; and published materials.

752. Réti-Forbes, Jean. "The Olin Downes Papers." *Georgia Review* 21 (Summer 1967): 165-171.

Olin Downes was a music critic. Réti-Forbes calls attention to Downes' papers at the University of Georgia, focuses on the correspondence and lectures in them to illustrate their research values, and concludes with a list of principal correspondents.

753. Rutschman, Edward R. "University of Washington: The Microfilm Collection of 17th- and Early 18th-Century Manuscript Opera Scores and Libretti." *Current Musicology* 21 (1976): 11-15.

This article includes a checklist of scores and libretti arranged by composer with titles and location of original manuscripts.

754. Seaton, Douglas. "Important Library Holdings at Forty-One North American Universities." *Current Musicology* 17 (1974): 7-68.

Many of the holdings summaries include extensive manuscript and archival collections. Typical are symphony orchestra archives, compositions, photographs, performance records, scores and parts, personal papers of performers and composers, etc.

755. Shepard, Brooks, Jr. "The Charles E. Ives Collection." *Yale University Library Gazette* 30 (April 1956): 146-149.

Shepard describes a collection of 2,500 pages of music manuscripts by composer Charles Ives.

756. Silet, Charles L. P. "The Letters of Paul Rosenfeld." *Yale University*

Library Gazette 55 (January 1981): 121-127.

Silet calls attention to, and describes the contents of, an accumulation of 454 Rosenfeld letters in Yale's Collection of American Literature. The letters date from 1910 until his death in 1946. Rosenfeld is primarily known as a music critic.

757. Slobin, Mark. "The Music of the Yiddish Theater: Manuscript Sources at YIVO." *YIVO Annual of Jewish Social Studies* 18 (1983): 372-390.

Slobin describes music scores in the Perlmutter Theatre Archive. The article concludes with a container list of the Perlmutter Collection.

758. Spivacke, Harold. "Paganiniana." *Quarterly Journal of Current Acquisitions* 2 (February 1945): 49-67.

Spivacke describes a collection of papers relating to Niccolò Paganini including his journals or diaries; correspondence; posters of his performances; portraits and drawings; financial records; and music manuscripts. The materials date from 1825 to 1838.

759. Tilghman, Wendy B. "Music in Special Collections." *Dartmouth College Library Bulletin* 15 (November 1974): 18-22.

This is a checklist of music manuscripts at Dartmouth presented alphabetically by composer. Entries include type of piece, length, where and when published, and dates.

760. Watanabe, Ruth. "Autograph Scores from the American Composers' Concerts, 1925-1930." *University of Rochester Library Bulletin* 17 (Spring 1962): 58-62.

The author reviews the background of the concerts and presents a checklist of composers represented and the titles of their compositions held by the university's Sibley Music Library.

761. Watanabe, Ruth. "Music Manuscripts of Weldon Hart." *University of Rochester Library Bulletin* 19 (Winter 1964): 27-30.

Watanabe provides a brief review of Hart's career as a composer and concludes the article by listing thirty-five of his compositions and arrangements by title.

762. Watanabe, Ruth. "The Percy Grainger Manuscripts." *University of Rochester Library Bulletin* 19 (Winter 1964): 21-26.

Grainger was a pianist and composer. This article reviews the manuscripts of his compositions at the University of Rochester and locates other libraries holding additional Grainger papers.

763. Waters, Edward N. "New Loeffleriana." *Quarterly Journal of Current Acquisitions* 1 (April 1944): 6-14.

Waters describes a collection of correspondence, maps, posters, photographs, and music manuscripts of composer Charles Martin Loeffler.

764. Winfrey, Dorman H. "The Toscanini Archives." *American Archivist* 30 (July 1967): 465-470.
    An overview of holdings in two archives named after Arturo Toscanini. The first is the Toscanini Memorial Archives in the Performing Arts at Lincoln Center, New York City. The other is the Toscanini Archives in Toscanini's home at Riverdale, New York.

765. Winfrey, Dorman H. "The Toscanini Archives." *Texas Libraries* 29 (Summer 1967): 146-159.
    Winfrey provides an overview of holdings in the Toscanini Memorial Archives at Lincoln Center, New York City, and the Toscanini Archives at Riverdale, New York.

766. Witten, Cora W., and Laurence C. Witten, II. "Early Recordings from the Witten Collection at Yale." *Yale University Library Gazette* 43 (July 1968): 1-12.
    The Wittens call attention to, and describe, the component parts of a major collection of historical sound recordings dating from 1895 to 1940. They name many early performers whose recordings are in the collection.

767. Witten, Laurence C., II. "The Early Zonophone Recordings at Yale." *Yale University Library Gazette* 52 (October 1977): 70-74.
    This article describes a collection of sound recordings dating from 1901 to 1907. They record the work of early 20th-century vocal artists and musicians, along with dramatic readings.

768. Wright, Craig. "Rare Music Manuscripts at Harvard." *Current Musicology* 10 (1970): 25-33.
    Wright reviews many key manuscripts as a sample of what was to appear in a more complete catalog. He cites composers and titles of their work with comments on their significance.

Literary Collections

769. Adams, Hazard. "The William Butler Yeats Collection at Texas." *Library Chronicle of the University of Texas* 6 (Spring 1957): 33-38.

    Adams provides an overview of Yeats-related holdings, both published and unpublished.

770. Adams, Léonie. "The Ledoux Collection of Edwin Arlington Robinson Manuscripts." *Quarterly Journal of Current Acquisitions* 7 (November 1949): 9-13.

    Adams describes manuscripts of Robinson's poetry from his middle and later periods with the earliest manuscript dated 1910, and the latest, 1934. The author notes that this Library of Congress Robinson Collection rivals that of the New York Public Library.

771. Anderson, Frederick. "Twain Papers: A Fount of Biographical Studies." *Manuscripts* 11 (Fall 1959): 14-15.

    A short article that describes the scope of the Mark Twain papers at the library of the University of California, Berkeley.

772. Angell, Joseph W. "The Thomas Mann Collection." *Yale University Library Gazette* 13 (October 1938): 41-45.

    Angell describes mostly published works, but the collection does contain thirty-eight manuscripts of Mann's novels, speeches, essays, and lectures, along with Mann family photographs.

773. Archer, H. Richard. "Literary and Historical Manuscripts in the Clark Memorial Library." *Autograph Collectors' Journal* 3 (January 1951): 7-13.

    Key collections described include the Charles Kessler Collection relating to Montana history; Spanish and Mexican documents; Oscar Wilde papers; musicians papers; Rulers and Statesmen Collection; Brete Harte correspondence; and the Literary Collection.

774. August, Eugene R. "A Checklist of Materials Relating to the Hopkins Family in the State Archives of Hawaii." *Hopkins Quarterly* 6 (Summer 1979): 61-83.

    Most of these papers are to, from, or about Gerard Hopkins' father and uncle, Manely Hopkins and Charles Gordon Hopkins. The article lists 148 documents with an introductory essay placing them in historical context.

775. Avery, Laurence. "The Maxwell Anderson Papers." *Library Chronicle of the University of Texas* 8 (Spring 1965): 21-33.

A review of several types of materials in the Anderson Collection, including the playwright's diaries, correspondence, poems, plays, and other writings.

776. Ayling, Ronald. "A Note on Sean O'Casey's Manuscripts and His Working Methods." *Bulletin of the New York Public Library* 7 (June 1969): 359-367.

O'Casey was an Irish playwright and poet. Ayling reviews O'Casey's manuscripts in the New York Public Library's Berg Collection.

777. Barez, Reva R. "The H. Bacon Collamore Collection of D. H. Lawrence." *Yale University Library Gazette* 34 (July 1959): 16-23.

While mostly a collection of published works by Lawrence, it does contain Lawrence's correspondence, notebooks, and manuscripts of both poetry and prose.

778. Barnes, Warner. "The Browning Collection." *Library Chronicle of the University of Texas* 7 (Summer 1963): 12-13.

The author cites several examples of Elizabeth Browning's and Robert Browning's manuscripts held by the Humanities Research Center. He also notes names of correspondents represented in the Brownings' correspondence files.

779. Bartlett, Phyllis. "George Meredith: Early Manuscript Poems in the Berg Collection." *Bulletin of the New York Public Library* 61 (August 1957): 396-415.

Bartlett lists and describes forty-one poems. Entries include title, length, where published, excerpts, and analytical notes.

780. Bassan, Maurice. "Papers of Julian Hawthorne at Yale." *Yale University Library Gazette* 39 (January 1964): 84-89.

Julian Hawthorne, the son of Nathaniel Hawthorne, was a prolific author in his own right whose papers include his correspondence, notebooks, and his "Indian journal."

781. Bennett, Charles E. "The Letters of Charles Brockden Brown: An Annotated Census." *Resources for American Literary Study* 6 (Autumn 1976): 164-190.

Bennett has located and described 187 of Brown's personal letters in eleven U.S. libraries. Entries include names of correspondents, location, date, a publication note, and a content note.

782. Bowden, Ann. "The T. E. Lawrence Collection at the University of Texas." *Texas Quarterly* 5 (Fall 1962): 54-63.
     Bowden notes that there are 525 of Lawrence's letters in the collection and it is upon this correspondence that she bases this article. She names many of Lawrence's correspondents and provides several insights evident from their exchange of letters.

783. Boyce, George K. "Modern Literary Manuscripts in the Morgan Library." *Publications of the Modern Language Association* 67 (February 1952): 3-36.
     Boyce provides a checklist of literary manuscripts and authors' papers arranged alphabetically by author surname under headings of English, American, French, Italian, and Germanic. Entries include record series, manuscript titles, volume, and dates.

784. Bosha, Francis J. "The John Cheever Manuscript Collection at Brandeis University." *Resources for American Literary Study* 20 (January 1994): 45-53.
     Bosha gives a short introduction to the Cheever papers at Brandeis and notes additional materials in Harvard's Houghton Library. The article concludes with an inventory of items in the seven boxes of Cheever papers at Brandeis.

785. Bowden, Ann. "The Thomas Hardy Collection." *Library Chronicle of the University of Texas* 7 (Summer 1962): 7-14.
     The author reviews Hardy books, manuscripts, correspondence, and drawings in the Humanities Research Center.

786. Bowen, Dorothy and Philip Durham. "Walt Whitman Materials in the Huntington Library." *Huntington Library Quarterly* 19 (November 1955): 81-96.
     This is a checklist of seventy Whitman items. Numbers 1-32 are published works, while 33-70 are poetry and prose manuscripts and letters. Entries include correspondents' names, dates, length of documents, and content notes.

787. Bracker, Jon. "The Christopher Morley Collection." *Library Chronicle of the University of Texas* 7 (Summer 1962): 19-35.
     Bracker reviews Morley manuscripts, correspondence, and published materials in the Humanities Research Center. He cites several specific examples of outstanding manuscript material.

788. Bridgwater, Dorothy W. "The Barlow Manuscripts in the Yale Library." *Yale University Library Gazette* 34 (October 1959): 57-63.
     Joel Barlow served as U.S. minister to France and on other diplomatic

missions. His papers at Yale include correspondence dating from the 1770s to 1823; a manuscript of his epic poem *The Columbiad*; and manuscripts of his other writings.

789. Brinkley, R. Florence. "Some Notes Concerning Coleridge Material at the Huntington Library." *Huntington Library Quarterly* 8 (May 1945): 312-320.

   Mostly a review of published material by or about Samuel Taylor Coleridge, but the essay does include the library's holdings of Coleridge correspondence and literary manuscripts.

790. Broderick, John C. "The Greatest Whitman Collector and the Greatest Whitman Collection." *Quarterly Journal of the Library of Congress* 27 (April 1970): 109-128.

   Broderick relates the provenance of the Walt Whitman papers and describes the Charles E. Feinberg Collection of Whitman's manuscripts, correspondence, and related papers at the Library of Congress.

791. Bump, Jerome. "Catalogue of the Hopkins Collection in the Humanities Research Center of the University of Texas." *Hopkins Quarterly* 5 (Winter 1979): 141-150.

   This article lists Gerard Manley Hopkins' poetry manuscripts and family letters, drawings, photographs, page proofs, and inscribed books. Entries include titles, correspondents' names, place of origin of letters, and size of documents where appropriate.

792. Butterworth, Keen. "A Census of Manuscripts and Typescripts of William Faulkner's Poetry." In *A Faulkner Miscellany,* edited by James B. Meriwether. Jackson: University Press of Mississippi, 1974. 70-97.

   The author lists both published and unpublished poetry with first lines, annotations, and location of the manuscript.

793. Byrd, Cecil K. "Check List of the Melcher Lindsay Collection." *Indiana University Bookman* 5 (December 1960): 64-106.

   This is actually a checklist of Nicholas Vachel Lindsay's writings contained in the Frederic G. Melcher Collection at Indiana University. Many of these items were privately published and carry Lindsay's annotations and illustrations.

794. Byrd, Charles. "The Oliver La Farge Collection." *Library Chronicle of the University of Texas at Austin* New Series 7 (Spring 1974): 81-85.

   The collection contains manuscripts of La Farge's books, short stories, poetry, and anthropological notes; his journals from WWII; correspondence; his sketches; and examples of published works.

795. Cahoon, Herbert. "Herman Melville: A Check List of Books and Manuscripts in the Collections of the New York Public Library." *Bulletin of the New York Public Library* 55 (June 1951): 263-275; and (July 1951): 325-338.

     It is part two of this checklist that describes manuscripts, which are mostly essays and stories. Melville's letters date from 1837 to 1889 with entries identifying correspondents, place of origin, date, and length.

796. Cahoon, Herbert. "Some Manuscripts of Concord Authors in the Pierpont Morgan Library." *Manuscripts* 18 (Fall 1966): 44-50.

     The article reviews some of the authors represented in the Stephen H. Wakeman Collection purchased by the library in 1909. The authors mentioned include Bryant, Emerson, Hawthorne, Holmes, Longfellow, Lowell, Poe, Thoreau, and Whittier.

797. Cameron, Kenneth W. "Inventory of Hawthorne's Manuscripts, Part One." *Emerson Society Quarterly* 29 (4th Quarter 1962): 5-20.

     Cameron lists correspondence, manuscripts, and memorabilia relating to Nathaniel Hawthorne, chronologically under repository headings. Entries provide titles, dates, names of correspondents, and content notes.

798. Cary, Richard. "American Literary Manuscripts in the Colby College Library: A Checklist." *Resources for American Literary Study* 5 (Autumn 1975): 217-240.

     The checklist is alphabetical by author with entries including type of materials, volume, and dates, with some titles for poetry and prose manuscripts.

799. Cary, Richard. "A Willa Cather Collection." *Colby Library Quarterly* 8 (June 1968): 82-95.

     Mostly a checklist of published works, but Colby Library does hold a small collection of Willa Cather letters. They are listed with names of correspondents, length, date, and content notes on pages 94-95 of this article.

800. Cauvin, Jean-Pierre. "Literary Games of Chance: The André Breton Manuscripts." *Library Chronicle of the University of Texas at Austin* New Series 16 (1981): 17-41.

     Breton, a French poet, is known as one of the founders of surrealism. Cauvin describes his literary manuscripts written between 1918 and 1959.

801. Charters, Ann. "Kerouac's Literary Methods and Experiments: The Evidence of the Manuscript Notebooks in the Berg Collection." *Bulletin of Research in the Humanities* 84 (Winter 1981): 431-450.

     The author analyzes manuscript notebooks of author Jack Kerouac that are in the New York Public Library's Berg Collection. The notebooks date from 1956-1959. Charters lists the contents of each at the end of the article.

802. Clark, C. E. Frazer, Jr. "Census of Nathaniel Hawthorne Letters, 1813-1849." In *Nathaniel Hawthorne Journal*, Dayton: National Cash Register Co., 1971. 257-282.
   Clark lists 417 letters with entries including dates, place of origin, correspondents' names, and name of the repository holding the letters.

803. Cline, C. L. "The Letters of George Meredith." *Library Chronicle of the University of Texas* 6 (Spring 1957): 30-32.
   Cline calls attention to a University of Texas collection of 154 letters of this English novelist and poet, which Cline identifies as the richest source of Meredith correspondence in the U.S.

804. Cohen, Joseph. "The Wilfred Owen War Poetry Collection." *Library Chronicle of the University of Texas* 5 (Spring 1955): 24-35.
   Cohen describes a new collection established at the University of Texas which was built around the poetry of Wilfred Owen. The article cites many unpublished manuscripts along with manuscripts microfilmed in other repositories.

805. Colby, Robert A. "'What Fools Authors Be!': The Authors' Syndicate 1890-1920." *Library Chronicle of the University of Texas at Austin* New Series 35 (1986): 61-87.
   The Authors' Syndicate was a literary agency in London, England, founded and run by William Morris Colles. This article describes a collection of 2,000 letters from authors, publishers, and agents dated between 1890 and 1920.

806. Collins, Rowland L. "The Frederick Tennyson Collection." *Indiana University Bookman* 6 (October 1963): 66-89.
   A listing and description of Alfred Tennyson's poetry manuscripts, essays, family correspondence, business records, and photographs at Indiana University.

807. Cook, Martha Emily and Thomas Daniel Young. "Fugitive/Agrarian Materials at Vanderbilt University." *Resources for American Literary Study* 1 (Spring 1971): 113-120.
   This is a checklist, by author, of letters, manuscripts, books, and miscellaneous publications. The entries include author's name, number of items, and inclusive dates.

808. Cooney, Charles. "Sinclair Lewis Manuscripts in the Library of Congress

Manuscript Division: A Preliminary Checklist." *Prospects* 1 (1975): 75-79.

The checklist appears as an appendix to Cooney's article "Walter White and Sinclair Lewis." Cooney lists manuscript collections that contain Lewis correspondence. Entries include volume, dates, names of correspondents, and content statements.

809. Costello, Bonnie. "'Rhinoceros Companions': Letters of Marianne Moore." *Library Chronicle of the University of Texas at Austin* 22 (Nos. 1/2 1992): 53-71.

Costello describes several letters that are representative of those in the Moore Collection at the Humanities Research Center. While dating from the 1920s, most of the correspondence is from the 1940s.

810. Crandell, George W. "'A Good Bad Poet': The Ogden Nash Collection." *Library Chronicle of the University of Texas at Austin* New Series 16 (1981): 63-77.

The Nash Collection includes manuscripts of Nash's writings, correspondence, drawings, photographs, and published materials. Crandell emphasizes Nash's correspondence in this article.

811. Davis, Kenneth W. "Jeanne Williams--Novelist: The Williams Papers in the Southwest Collection, Texas Tech University." *West Texas Historical Association Year Book* 63 (1987): 77-83.

The first part of this article reviews Williams' writing career. Williams' papers consist of correspondence; manuscripts of novels and stories; photographs; story lines; scrapbooks; and published materials.

812. Dawson, Giles E. "The Resources and Policies of the Folger Shakespeare Library." *Library Quarterly* 19 (July 1949): 178-185.

Much of the article describes the library's published holdings, but Dawson also notes that the library has about 5,000 pre-18th-century manuscripts and cites several of these collections by title.

813. DeHamer, Nancy. "Dakota Resources: The Rose Wilder Lane Papers at the Herbert Hoover Presidential Library." *South Dakota History* 14 (Winter 1984): 335-346.

The Lane papers include thirty feet of Lane's correspondence, notes, drafts of articles and books, her diaries, photographs, sound recordings, and published materials that reflect her writing career and interests.

814. Delaney, John. "The Archives of Charles Scribner's Sons." *Princeton University Library Chronicle* 47 (Winter 1985): 137-177.

Delaney offers a lengthy narrative citing examples of materials found among trade lists, promotional materials, royalty accounts, advertising and

inventory records, editors' correspondence, and authors' correspondence.
The materials date from 1875 to 1967.

815. Dickson, Vivienne. "Herman Charles Bosman." *Library Chronicle of the
University of Texas at Austin* New Series 4 (February 1972): 31-37.
Bosman was a South African writer. His papers in the Humanities
Research Center include manuscripts of his poems, novels, and short
stories.

816. Dillard, Henry B. "The Manuscript Poems of Alfred Edward Housman."
Quarterly Journal of Current Acquisitions 5 (February 1948): 7-8.
This short article relates the provenance of this collection and reviews
the Housman manuscripts held by the Library of Congress.

817. Doyle, Joseph. "A Finding List of Manuscript Materials Relating to
George Edward Woodberry." *Papers of the Bibliographic Society of
America* 46 (2nd Quarter 1952): 165-168.
Doyle locates extant Woodberry letters and manuscripts in U.S. libraries
and in private collections.

818. Doyle, N. Ann and Neal B. Houston. "Ernest Hemingway's Letters to
Adriana Ivancich." *Library Chronicle of the University of Texas at Austin*
New Series 30 (1985): 15-37.
The authors describe a separate group of sixty-five letters dating from
April, 1950 to September, 1955 in the Humanities Research Center's
Hemingway Collection.

819. "Edward Albee Manuscript Materials in the HRHRC." *Library Chronicle
of the University of Texas at Austin* 20 (No. 3 1990): 94-95.
This is a checklist describing Albee materials in seven different
collections.

820. "The Edwin Markham Archives and *The Markham Review*." *The Markham
Review* 1 (February 1968): 2-4.
Edwin Markham was a poet and advocate of social reforms. His
papers, at Wagner College, include personal financial records; his poetry
and prose manuscripts; notebooks; correspondence; photographs; and his
published writings and criticism of his writings.

821. Eppard, Philip B., and Alan Seaburg. "American Literary Manuscripts in
the Andover-Harvard Theological Library: A Checklist." *Resources for
American Literary Study* 10 (Autumn 1980): 146-153.
The list is alphabetical by author's surname with inclusive dates and
record series, volume, and availability of related materials.

822. Erdelyi, Gabor and Mary A. Glavin. "John Holmes: A Bibliography of Published and Unpublished Writings in the Special Collections of the Tufts University Library." *Bulletin of the New York Public Library* 73 (June 1969): 375-397.

    The bibliography is in two sections. The first lists published materials, the second, Holmes' unpublished poems; essays, articles, and reviews; plays; stories; correspondence; and autobiographical items.

823. Farmer, David. "The Bibliographical Potential of a 20th Century Literary Agent's Archive: The Pinker Papers." *Library Chronicle of the University of Texas at Austin* New Series 2 (November 1970): 27-35.

    Farmer relates how J. B. Pinker's correspondence with many of the leading literary figures of the 20th century might be useful in determining bibliographic variations of an author's work.

824. Feeney, Joseph J. "The Gerard Manley Hopkins Archive of the Harry Ransom Humanities Research Center." *Library Chronicle of the University of Texas at Austin* New Series 46/47 (1989): 11-39.

    Hopkins was an English poet. The Hopkins Archive contains correspondence, manuscripts, drawings, photographs, and published materials. A checklist on pages 29-39 of this article describes many of these materials.

825. Fennell, Francis. "The Rossetti Collection in the Library of Congress: A Checklist." *Bulletin of Bibliography and Magazine Notes* 30 (July/September 1973): 132-136.

    The checklist cites 244 letters from Dante Gabriel Rossetti to others with citations noting date, correspondents, and brief content summaries, and 40 of Rossetti's manuscript poems.

826. Franklin, Phyllis. "A Handlist of the Robert Herrick Papers at the University of Chicago." *American Literary Realism* 8 (Spring 1975): 109-154.

    Robert W. Herrick is known as a novelist and professor of English. His papers, which are listed in detail in this article, include correspondence, manuscripts of both published and unpublished writings, and clipping files.

827. Fraser, Robert S. "The Rossetti Collection of Janet Camp Troxell: A Survey with Some Sidelights." *Princeton University Library Chronicle* 33 (Spring 1972): 146-176.

    This article describes both published and manuscript material of the Rossetti family. The collection contains over 3,000 manuscript items.

828. Gallup, Donald. "The Ezra Pound Archive at Yale." *Yale University Library Gazette* 60 (April 1986): 161-177.

    This article relates the provenance of the Pound papers. While not descriptive of the papers, it does give a sense of the scope of Yale's Pound Collection.

829. Gallup, Donald. "The Gertrude Stein Collection." *Yale University Library Gazette* 22 (October 1947): 21-32.
    Gallup reviews many of the Stein manuscripts and letters at Yale by title and correspondent. He estimated that Yale held ninety percent of her bibliography in manuscript form.

830. Gallup, Donald. "The Mabel Dodge Luhan Papers." *Yale University Library Gazette* 37 (January 1963): 97-105.
    The Luhan papers include manuscripts of *Intimate Memories* and other unpublished writings, and her correspondence. The article concludes with a checklist of correspondents represented in her letters.

831. Gallup, Donald. "The 'Lost' Manuscripts of T. S. Eliot." *Bulletin of the New York Public Library* 72 (December 1968): 641-652.
    The author relates the provenance of a group of Eliot manuscripts that were in the private collection of John Quinn and describes the manuscript copy of "The Waste Land" and "The Notebook."

832. Gallup, Donald. "New Papers of William Lyon Phelps." *Yale University Library Gazette* 32 (July 1957): 28-29.
    Gallup calls attention to an accretion of more than 300 letters exchanged between Phelps and notable authors, mostly American.

833. Gallup, Donald. "The Paul Leicester Ford Collection." *Yale University Library Gazette* 30 (October 1955): 70-73.
    Ford was a 19th-century American historian and novelist. His papers include his correspondence and manuscripts of his writings.

834. Gallup, Donald. "The William Carlos Williams Collection at Yale." *William Carlos Williams Review* 7 (Spring 1981): 1-8.
    Gallup relates the acquisition of the Williams Collection and notes that it contains 286 manuscripts of Williams' writings and extensive correspondence. He cites the principal correspondents and mentions other Yale collections also containing Williams letters.

835. Gallup, Donald. "The William Carlos Williams Collection at Yale." *Yale University Library Gazette* 56 (October 1981): 50-59.
    While most of the article is devoted to the acquisition of the collection and published materials, Gallup also reviews manuscript material which includes 286 manuscripts of prose and poetry and a significant amount of Williams' incoming correspondence.

836. Gates, Norman T. "The Richard Aldington Collection at Morris Library." *ICarbS* 3 (Summer/Fall 1976): 61-68.

Aldington is an English poet and author. The Morris Library has a collection of more than 1,000 of his letters along with screen plays and manuscripts of his poetry and short stories.

837. Givner, Joan. "'Letters to the Editor:' The Correspondence of Mazo de la Roche and Edward Weeks." *Library Chronicle of the University of Texas at Austin* New Series 40 (1987): 67-87.

According to the author, the exchange of correspondence between Canadian author Mazo de la Roche and Weeks, editor of *Atlantic Monthly*, constitutes the largest block of papers in the Humanities Research Center's Edward Weeks Collection.

838. Goff, Frederick R. "The Hersholt Collection of Anderseniana." *Quarterly Journal of Current Acquisitions* 9 (May 1952): 123-127.

This article describes a collection, published and unpublished, of materials by the Danish author Hans Christian Andersen. Goff devotes most of the article to the published works, but also describes Andersen's correspondence and literary manuscripts.

839. Goff, Frederick R. "The Hersholt Gift of Works of Hugh Walpole and Sinclair Lewis." *Quarterly Journal of Current Acquisitions* 11 (August 1954): 195-198.

This article describes bibliophile Jean Hersholt's gift to the Library of Congress of a collection of books and correspondence by Walpole and Lewis. Most of the article is devoted to the books with occasional reference to the correspondence.

840. Gottesman, Ronald. "Upton Sinclair and the Sinclair Archives." *Manuscripts* 17 (Fall 1965): 11-20.

This articles describes some of the manuscripts in the Upton Sinclair Collection in the Lilly Library at Indiana University, Bloomington.

841. Grant, Rena V. "The Livezey-Whitman Manuscripts." *Walt Whitman Review* 7 (March 1961): 3-14.

This collection is mostly manuscripts of Walt Whitman's published writings along with a few photographs and other memorabilia. The focus of the article is on content analysis of the manuscripts.

842. Greenbaum, Leonard. "The 'Hound and Horn' Archives." *Yale University Library Gazette* 39 (January 1965): 137-146.

The *Hound & Horn* was a "little magazine" that published between 1927 and 1934. This article calls attention to its correspondence files in Yale's Beinecke Library. The letters are primarily between authors and editors.

843. Gribben, Alan. "'The Heart is Insatiable': A Selection from Edith Wharton's Letters to Morton Fullerton, 1907-1915." *Library Chronicle of the University of Texas at Austin* New Series 31 (1985): 7-18.

     Gribben calls attention to the Humanities Research Center's collection of 300 Wharton letters among which are many that clarify her relationship with writer Morton Fullerton.

844. Griffin, Lloyd W. "The John Pendleton Kennedy Manuscripts." *Maryland Historical Magazine* 48 (December 1953): 327-336.

     Kennedy is known primarily as an author, but he also was a soldier, U.S. and state congressman, businessman, and benefactor of the arts and sciences in Baltimore. Griffin describes manuscripts of his writings and his correspondence and journals, all dated 1812-1870.

845. Haight, Gordon S. "The Tinker Collection of George Eliot Manuscripts." *Yale University Library Gazette* 29 (April 1955): 148-150.

     Haigh reviews the Eliot papers collected by Chauncey Tinker. They include her journals, notebooks, letters, and manuscripts.

846. Haight, Gordon S. "The George Eliot and George Henry Lewes Collection." *Yale University Library Gazette* 46 (July 1971): 20-23.

     This short article reviews the extant papers of George Eliot with an emphasis on those at Yale. Among the latter are some of her manuscripts and her journals, diaries, notebooks, and letters.

847. Hairston, Maxine Cousins. "The George Sessions Perry Manuscript Collection." *Library Chronicle of the University of Texas at Austin* New Series 2 (November 1970): 63-71.

     The Perry Collection includes manuscripts of the author's novels, short stories, reviews of his writings, published materials, scrapbooks, and photographs. The author cites some key examples and comments on the collection's research potential.

848. Hale, David G. "Interviews from the Brockport Writers Forum." *Bulletin of Bibliography* 42 (March 1985): 34-41.

     This is a checklist of videotaped interviews with poets, novelists, and literary critics. Entries are alphabetical by surname of writer or critic and include interviewers' names and dates and length of interviews.

849. Hamilton, David M. "The Conrad Potter Aiken Collection at the Henry E. Huntington Library." *Studies in the Literary Imagination* 13 (Fall 1980): 137-142.

     Hamilton describes Aiken's correspondence; photographs; ephemera; poetry and prose manuscripts; and published books. Description includes manuscript titles, correspondents' names, volume and dates of letters, and personalities represented in the photo collection.

850. Hanford, James H. "The Paul Elmer More Papers." *Princeton University Library Chronicle* 22 (Summer 1961): 163-168.

More is known for his writings about Christian philosophy and the classics. His papers at Princeton University include literary manuscripts, correspondence, and notebooks.

851. Hanlin, Frank S. "The Brewer-Leigh Hunt Collection at the State University of Iowa." *Keats-Shelley Journal* 8 (Autumn 1959): 91-94.

Hanlin calls attention to the collection of Leigh Hunt books and manuscripts formed by Luther A. Brewer. It includes a "voluminous" correspondence and over 100 manuscripts. Description is limited to a few manuscript titles and correspondents' names.

852. Harding, Walter and Carl Bode. "Henry David Thoreau: A Check List of His Correspondence." *Bulletin of the New York Public Library* 59 (May 1955): 227-252.

The list is chronological with entries identifying correspondents, place of origin, location of originals, place of publication, if any, and date. Letters in private collections are included.

853. Harris, Margaret. "George Meredith's Notes and Notebooks." *Yale University Library Gazette* 52 (October 1977): 53-65.

Harris lists and describes the contents of twelve notebooks kept by author George Meredith. They are part of the Frank Altschul Meredith Collection at Yale.

854. Hayman, David. "Shadow of His Mind: The Papers of Lucia Joyce." *Library Chronicle of the University of Texas at Austin* New Series 20/21 (1982): 65-79.

Hayman discusses the contents of a group of three biographical manuscripts by Lucia Joyce, James Joyce's daughter.

855. Heiman, Monica. "Maupassant and Others: The Artinian Collection." *Library Chronicle of the University of Texas* 8 (Spring 1968): 56-57.

This short article cites 19th- and 20th-century French writers represented in the Artine Artinian Collection. Description is limited to the types of materials representing each writer.

856. Henderson, Cathy. "Research Opportunities: The Alfred A. Knopf, Inc. Archives." *Library Chronicle of the University of Texas at Austin* 22 (No. 4 1992): 145-161.

This article identifies the record groups and record series in the Knopf Collection and provides content summaries of each. It also calls attention to, and briefly describes, Knopf materials in the New York Public Library, New York City.

857. Henderson, Cathy. "Supplement to Marcella Booth's *A Catalogue of the Louis Zukofsky Manuscript Collection.*" *Library Chronicle of the University of Texas at Austin* New Series 38/39 (1987): 107-181.

Henderson lists Zukofsky materials acquired since 1969 when Booth's catalog was published. This supplement includes literary criticism essays; pamphlets and books; poetry and novel manuscripts; plays; miscellaneous manuscripts; and correspondence.

858. Hendrick, George. "American Literary Manuscripts in Continental Libraries." *Bulletin of Bibliography and Magazine Notes* 25 (May/August 1967): 49-58.

This is a checklist of mostly correspondence to and from U.S. authors in European libraries. The list is alphabetical by author surname with individual letters cited under each. The citations include dates, correspondents, and location.

859. Hendrick, George. "A Checklist of American Literary Manuscripts in Australia, Canada, India, Israel, Japan, and New Zealand." *Bulletin of Bibliography and Magazine Notes* 29 (July/September 1972): 84-86, 92.

Similar in purpose and presentation to Hendrick's 1967 article above, but with less detail in the citations. The citations in this article contain only the author's name and an abbreviation for the repository holding the documents.

860. Hendrickson, Gordon O. "The WPA Writers' Project in Wyoming: History and Collections." *Annals of Wyoming* 49 (Fall 1977): 175-192.

This is a history of the project in Wyoming. The last four pages identify and briefly describe the project's own records and the historical data it collected.

861. Hepburn, William M. "The Charles Major Manuscripts in the Purdue University Libraries." *Indiana Quarterly for Bookmen* 2 (July 1946): 71-81.

Major was an Indiana literary figure. The collection includes his book and article manuscripts, reviews of his work, and materials relating to plays and movies based upon his writing. The article lists and comments on many of the book manuscripts.

862. Hergenhan, Laurie. "The C. Hartley Grattan Manuscript Collection: A Critical Introduction." *Library Chronicle of the University of Texas at Austin* New Series 42/43 (1988): 51-75.

This article reviews Grattan's papers which consist of research notes, correspondence, publishing records, and manuscripts of his writings, all dating from 1924 to 1964 and relating mostly to his writing career and his interest in Australia.

863. Herring, Jack W. "Camberwell to Venice to Waco." *Manuscripts* 26 (Winter 1974): 2-11.

Herring provides an overview of a collection of 700 letters written by the poet Robert Browning and held by Baylor University, Waco, Texas. The letters date from 1837 to the 1880s.

864. Highsmith, James M. "A Description of the Cornell Collection of Eugene O'Neill's Letters to George Jean Nathan." *Modern Drama* 14 (February 1972): 420-425; and 15 (May 1972): 68-88.

The first of this two-article series relates the provenance of these letters and lists all 130 of them. Entries include date, place of origin, and length. The second article analyzes their content.

865. Hoffmann, Lois. "A Catalogue of the Frieda Lawrence Manuscripts in German at the University of Texas." *Library Chronicle of the University of Texas at Austin* New Series 6 (December 1973): 87-105.

After a short introduction explaining the relationship of the correspondents, Hoffmann provides a checklist of 133 letters between Frieda Lawrence Ravagli and her friends and family. Entries include length of letters, dates, correspondents' names, and content notes.

866. Hogan, Charles B. "The Robinson Jeffers Manuscripts at Yale." *Yale University Library Gazette* 29 (October 1954): 81-84.

Hogan comments on seven Jeffers manuscripts. They include those of *Roan Stallion*, *The Woman at Point Sur*, *Cawdor*, *Dear Judas*, *Descent to the Dead*, *Thurso's Landing*, and *Give Your Heart to the Hawks*.

867. Hogan, Charles B. "The Yale Collection of the Manuscripts of John Ruskin." *Yale University Library Gazette* 16 (April 1942): 61-69.

Hogan reviews Ruskin's papers beginning with the bound notebooks of his youth, some 1,600 letters, his travel diaries, and manuscripts of his writings and lectures.

868. Holloway, Mark. "The Norman Douglas Collection at Yale." *Yale University Library Gazette* 50 (July 1975): 1-14.

Douglas manuscript material at Yale includes manuscripts of his writings, correspondence, and diaries. The article focuses on the correspondence and its value to researchers. Douglas was a British novelist and writer of travel books.

869. Holt, Rochelle. "Laurence Housman's Letters to George Galloway, 1903-

1905." *Books at Iowa* 15 (November 1971): 3-10.
   This article describes a collection of eighty-three letters from Laurence
Housman, the brother of A. E. Housman, and also a poet.

870. Holtz, William. "The Rose Wilder Lane Papers." *Annales of Iowa* 47
    (Winter 1985): 646-653.
       The Lane papers consist of correspondence and subject files; materials
    relating to Laura Ingalls Wilder; diaries and notes; and manuscripts. The
    collection is in the Herbert Hoover Library, West Branch, Iowa.

871. Hoyt, William D., Jr. "The Warden Papers." *Maryland Historical
    Magazine* 36 (September 1941): 302-314; and 38 (March 1943): 69-85.
       Hoyt describes the papers of David Baile Warden, 18th-century author
    and man of letters. He names correspondents and comments on the scope
    and content of their correspondence with Warden. Hoyt also notes a
    Warden Collection in the Library of Congress.

872. Hudson, Richard B. "The Altschul Collection of George Meredith
    Seventeen Years Later." *Yale University Library Gazette* 22 (April 1948):
    129-133.
       Hudson reviews notebooks and poetry and prose manuscripts by title that
    have been added to the Frank Altschul Collection since 1931.

873. Hummel, Madeline. "Fifty Unpublished Letters from Joseph Conrad."
    Library Chronicle of the University of Texas as Austin New Series 3 (May
    1971): 53-57.
       Hummel relates the provenance of these letters and concludes the article
    with a checklist that includes place of origin, date, and content note for
    each.

874. Hutton, Muriel. "The George MacDonald Collection." *Yale University
    Library Gazette* 51 (October 1976): 74-85.
       MacDonald was a 19th-century Scottish cleric and poet. Hutton reviews
    the content and correspondents represented in Yale's collection of more
    than 3,000 MacDonald letters.

875. Isaacs, Edith J. R. "Edwin Arlington Robinson: A Descriptive List of the
    Lewis M. Isaacs Collection of Robinsoniana." *Bulletin of the New York
    Public Library* 52 (May 1948): 211-233.
       While mostly a description of published materials, pages 213-223
    describe Robinson's correspondence and poetry, prose, and play manu-
    scripts.

876. Isles, Duncan. "The Lennox Collection." *Harvard Library Bulletin* 18
    (October 1970): 317-344.

The author describes nearly fifty letters to Charlotte Lennox, an 18th-century English novelist. The article gives the collection's provenance, identifies the correspondents, and places the letters in historical context.

877. Johnson, Neil M. "George Sylvester Viereck: Poet and Propagandist." *Books at Iowa* 9 (November 1968): 22-24, 29-36.
Viereck was known as a poet and journalist and for his pro-German sentiments. His papers at the University of Iowa include poetry, correspondence, and legal documents relating to his prosecution and imprisonment in 1943.

878. Jones, Joseph. "From Sydney to Cape Town to Austin: The R. G. Howarth Collection." *Library Chronicle of the University of Texas at Austin* New Series 13 (1980): 65-69.
R. G. Howarth was an Australian literature professor at the University of Cape Town, South Africa. His papers include clipping files, manuscripts, and correspondence with authors and scholars, all regarding Australian and South African literature.

879. Jordan, Heather B. "The Territory of Elizabeth Bowen's Wartime Short Stories." *Library Chronicle of the University of Texas at Austin* New Series 48 (1989): 69-85.
Bowen was an Irish novelist and short story writer. Her papers at the Humanities Research Center include manuscripts of her novels and stories; autobiographical notes; transcripts of interviews; teaching notes; and correspondence.

880. Kafka, Robert M. "Unpublished Manuscripts in the Robinson Jeffers Collection at the HRHRC." *Library Chronicle of the University of Texas at Austin* New Series 40 (1987): 25-45.
Kafka reviews four groups of Jeffers' manuscripts at the Humanities Research Center. The groups are fragments or unfinished poems; suppressed poems; post-1954 poems; and unpublished prose.

881. Kappes, Carolyn and others. "A Calendar of the Correspondence of Henry D. Thoreau." *Studies in the American Renaissance* (1982): 325-399.
The calendar lists 763 letters with entries including dates, places of origin, correspondents' names, publication notes, and location of originals. There is an index to correspondents and repositories.

882. Keane, Robert N. "D. G. Rossetti in Texas." *Library Chronicle of the University of Texas at Austin* New Series 41 (1987): 63-81.
Keane describes the poetry and prose manuscripts and correspondence of English artist-poet Dante Gabriel Rossetti. The Humanities Research Center's Rossetti Collection also contains manuscripts of Rossetti's sister

Christina, and his brother William.

883. Keller, Dean H. "The Albion W. Tourgée Papers." *Manuscripts* 20 (Summer 1968): 50-51.
   Tourgée is best known as a novelist, but also was a keen observer of the post-Civil War South. Keller provides a brief description of Tourgée's personal and literary papers held by the Chautauqua Historical Society in Westfield, New York.

884. Kingsland, Dorothea. "The Ridgely Torrence Collection." *Princeton University Library Chronicle* 15 (Summer 1954): 213-214.
   Kingsland calls attention to the papers of poet Frederic Ridgely Torrence. They include his correspondence, manuscripts of his poetry, photographs, and family-related papers.

885. Kintner, Anne Genung. "James Norman Hall Papers, 1906-1951." *Annals of Iowa* 44 (Spring 1979): 658-668.
   Hall was a writer of adventure stories and poetry. His papers at Grinnell College include correspondence; notebooks; manuscripts of his writings; and photographs. The materials date from 1906 to 1951.

886. Kleinfield, H. L. "A Census of Washington Irving Manuscripts." *Bulletin of the New York Public Library* 68 (January 1964): 13-32.
   The author locates Irving's correspondence, journals and notebooks, literary manuscripts, and miscellaneous papers in twenty-eight repositories in the U.S. Entries include record series titles, inclusive dates, titles, volume, and names of correspondents.

887. Kramer, Victor A. "James Agee Papers at the University of Texas." *Library Chronicle of the University of Texas* 8 (Spring 1966): 33-36.
   Kramer notes that the University of Texas collection contains mostly post-1946 Agee papers. They include manuscripts of novels, screenplays, movie reviews, unpublished poems, and story outlines.

888. Lake, Carleton. "A Catalogue of Books, Manuscripts, and Other Materials Relating to Samuel Beckett in the Collections of the Humanities Research Center." *Library Chronicle of the University of Texas at Austin* New Series 28 (1984): 5-185.
   This entire issue is devoted to the catalog. While this appears to be an exhibit catalog, or derived from one, it is still useful as a guide to holdings because of the large number of manuscript and unpublished items included in it.

889. Lake, Carleton and Linda Ashton. "A Descriptive Catalogue of Photographs, Manuscripts, and other Materials Relating to Henri-Pierre Roché."

Library Chronicle of the University of Texas at Austin 21 (Nos. 1/2 1991):
9-238.

This entire issue is devoted to the Humanities Research Center's
collection of Roché materials. This is an exhibition catalog, but may be
useful in that 392 items are described in detail. The entries are also
indexed.

890. Larabee, Benjamin W., and B. Bernard Cohen. "Hawthorne at the Essex
Institute." *Essex Institute Historical Collections* 94 (July 1958): 297-308.

This is a checklist of letters written by Nathaniel Hawthorne between
1819 and 1863, books in Hawthorne's library, and portraits and photographs of Hawthorne.

891. Lease, Benjamin. "The Joseph Kirkland Papers." *American Literary
Realism* 2 (Spring 1969): 73-75.

Lease calls attention to a small collection of Kirkland's correspondence
and an autobiography in the Newberry Library, Chicago, Illinois.

892. Lewis, Jim G. "The Augustus Thomas Collection at the University of
North Carolina." *Resources for American Literary Study* 4 (Spring 1974):
72-89.

Augustus Thomas was an American playwright. This article lists 234
manuscripts of his plays; letters to and from Thomas; his speeches; essays;
poetry; and published materials.

893. Little, Thomas. "The Thomas Wolfe Collection of William B. Wisdom."
Harvard Library Bulletin 1 (Autumn 1947): 280-287.

Little describes the Harvard College library's holdings of Thomas
Wolfe's literary manuscripts, correspondence, publications, and personal
books. Several of Wolfe's literary manuscripts are described in some
detail.

894. Lohf, Kenneth A. "Treasures for Alma Mater: How Columbia University
Acquired the Papers of Major New York Publishers and Literary Agents."
Manuscripts 29 (Spring 1977): 102-109.

Lohf reviews some key literary collections held by Columbia. He
mentions record series titles, volume, and the names of principal
correspondents represented in selected collections.

895. Ludwig, Richard M. "A Reading of James Gould Cozzens' Manuscripts."
Princeton University Library Chronicle 19 (Autumn 1957): 1-14.

Ludwig reviews Cozzens' literary manuscripts at Princeton with an
emphasis on that of *By Love Possessed*.

896. Lund, Steven P., and Alan M. Cohn. "James Joyce Collections at Morris

Library." *ICarbS* 2 (Winter/Spring 1975): 67-75.

The authors point out that the Joyce Collection at Southern Illinois University was accumulated by Harley K. Croessman and is made up of three components, the Herman Gorman papers; the Georg Goyert papers; and miscellaneous Joyce materials.

897. Mann, David D. "The Pugh Gift of the George Hewitt Myers, Yale 1898, Collection of Robert Louis Stevenson Materials." *Yale University Library Gazette* 64 (April 1990): 167-171.

Among the materials in this collection are twenty-two Stevenson letters dating from 1866; manuscripts of Stevenson's poetry and prose writings; notebooks from Stevenson's youth and those prepared by his mother; and some published materials.

898. Marshall, William J. "Thomas Merton Collection at the University of Kentucky." *Kentucky Review* 7 (Summer 1987): 145-153.

This article is mostly about the acquisition of Merton's papers, but it does mention key record series such as correspondence, manuscripts of Merton's writings; galley proofs; book reviews of his works; and poetry worksheets.

899. Martz, Louis L. "Manuscripts of Wallace Stevens." *Yale University Library Gazette* 54 (October 1979): 51-67.

Martz relates the provenance of Stevens' poetry manuscripts and one of his plays, analyzes their contents, and concludes with a descriptive checklist of manuscripts, letters, and miscellaneous items in the Stevens Collection.

900. Mason, Dorothy E., Elaine Fowler, and Philip Knachel. "The Folger Shakespeare Library in Washington." *Records of the Columbia Historical Society of Washington, D.C.* 69/70 (1971): 346-370.

The authors provide a brief biography of Henry Folger and a history of his collection and the establishment of the library. They include a review of the library's holdings in which they discuss manuscripts, but do not describe them in detail.

901. May, Anne C. "The Kathryn Hulme Collection." *Yale University Library Gazette* 53 (January 1979): 129-134.

Hulme was an American writer known for her description of post-WWII Germany and as the author of *The Nuns Story*. Her papers, mostly post-WWII, include correspondence, manuscripts, and photographs relating to her writings.

902. McAneny, Marguerite L. "Eleven Manuscripts of Eugene O'Neill." *Princeton University Library Chronicle* 4 (February/April 1943): 86-89.

The author describes highlights of manuscript copies of O'Neill's plays *The Straw, Gold, Anna Christie, Emperor Jones, The Hairy Ape, Different, The Fountain, Welded, All God's Chillun Got Wings, The First Man,* and *Desire Under the Elms.*

903. McCusker, Honor and Zoltán Haraszti. "The Correspondence of R. W. Griswold." *More Books* 16 (March 1941): 105-116; (April 1941): 152-156; (May 1941): 190-196; (June 1941): 286-289; 18 (February 1943): 57-68; and (September 1943): 323-333.

This is a checklist of letters and manuscripts in the 1,200-item Griswold Collection held by the Boston Public Library. The items described appear alphabetically by correspondent's surname or author and include length, date, and content note. Rufus Griswold was a poet and editor of *Graham's Magazine* in the 1840s.

904. McCusker, Honor and Zoltán Haraszti. "The Correspondence of R. W. Griswold." *Boston Public Library Quarterly* 1 (July 1949): 62-74; (October 1949): 156-165; 2 (January 1950): 77-84; (April 1950): 172-179; (July 1950): 269-275; (October 1950): 354-368; 3 (January 1951): 61-73; and (April 1951): 146-154.

The authors continue the calendar of Griswold's correspondence begun in 1941 in *More Books*. There were fourteen installments in all.

905. McDonald, W. U. "Eudora Welty Manuscripts: An Annotated Finding List." *Bulletin of Bibliography and Magazine Notes* 24 (September/ December 1963): 44-46; and 31 (July/September 1974): 95-98, 126, 132.

Entries to the this article and the 1974 supplement are divided under published and unpublished works and include titles; places and dates of publication; and the physical characteristics, length, and significant features of the manuscripts.

906. McDowell, Frederick P. W. "The Angus Wilson Collection." *Books at Iowa* 10 (April 1969): 9-23.

McDowell provides representative examples and excerpts from the collection which includes manuscripts and notebooks of British author Angus Wilson's stories and novels.

907. McElrath, Joseph R., Jr. "Interviews with Contemporary Writers: The Brockport Video-Tape Collection." *Resources for American Literary Study* 6 (Spring 1976): 70-78.

This is a checklist of seventy-six interviews with entries including names of authors and interviewers and the dates and length of interviews.

908. McLaren, John. "Iris Milutinovic--Between Two Worlds." *Library Chronicle of the University of Texas at Austin* New Series 42/43 (1988):

143-159.

Milutinovic was an Australian broadcaster and novelist. This article describes her papers in the Humanities Research Center which include manuscripts of her novels and short stories, radio scripts, correspondence, and notebooks.

909. Merrill, Ginette De B. "Two Howells Collections." *Resources for American Literary Study* 11 (Spring 1981): 81-90.

Merrill provides a narrative description of the Howells/Fréchette papers at Alfred University, Alfred, New York, and the Howells, Mead, Noyes, and Dock family papers at the Massachusetts Historical Society.

910. Metzdorf, Robert F. "Southey Manuscripts at Yale." *Yale University Library Gazette* 30 (April 1956): 157-162.

This article describes English poet Robert Southey's letters and manuscripts held by Yale. It concludes by citing other repositories in the U.S. and England also holding Southey papers.

911. Mizener, Arthur. "The F. Scott Fitzgerald Papers." *Princeton University Library Chronicle* 12 (Summer 1951): 190-195.

Mizener describes key literary manuscripts and highlights of Fitzgerald's correspondence.

912. Moldenhauer, Joseph J. "Poe Manuscripts in Austin." *Library Chronicle of the University of Texas at Austin* New Series 3 (May 1971): 83-88.

This is a description of the William H. Koester Collection of Poe materials at the Humanities Research Center. It includes manuscript poems, stories, and essays and correspondence.

913. Morton, Gerald W. "Unpublished Poems in the Edith Sitwell Collection." *Library Chronicle of the University of Texas at Austin* 22 (Nos. 1/2 1992): 31-51.

The Humanities Research Center's collection of Sitwell's papers includes unpublished manuscripts; correspondence; photographs; notebooks; and published materials. This article focuses on unpublished poems in some of her earlier notebooks.

914. Mott, Howard S. "The Walter Beinecke Jr., J. M. Barrie Collection." *Yale University Library Gazette* 39 (April 1965): 163-167.

Mott describes Beinecke's collection of Barrie manuscripts and books and correspondence. The author notes the titles of Barrie's books of which the manuscripts are at Yale, and cites the principal correspondents represented in Barrie's letters.

915. Mudge, Bradford K. "Sara Coleridge: A Portrait from the Papers."

Library Chronicle of the University of Texas at Austin New Series 23 (1983): 15-35.

Sara Coleridge was the daughter of English poet Samuel Taylor Coleridge. Mudge discusses the diaries, commonplace books, essays, and correspondence in the Humanities Research Center's collection of Coleridge family papers that document Sara Coleridge's life.

916. Murray, William M. "A Note on the Iris Murdoch Manuscripts in the University of Iowa Library." *Modern Fiction Studies* 15 (Autumn 1969): 445-448.

Murray describes eight Murdoch manuscripts. They are *Under the Net, The Ball, A Severed Head, An Unofficial Rose, The Unicorn, The Red and Green, The Time of Angels,* and *Bruno's Dream.*

917. Myerson, Joel, Daniel Shealy and Madeleine B. Stern. "A Calendar of the Letters of Louisa May Alcott." *Studies in the American Renaissance* (1988): 361-399.

The authors cite 649 letters written between 1840 and 1888. Entries include date, place of origin, correspondent's name, publication data, length, and location of original. The calendar is indexed to correspondents and repositories.

918. Newberry Library. "Letters and Papers of Henry Kitchell Webster." *Newberry Library Bulletin* 6 (December 1946): 3-14.

Webster was an Illinois novelist. His papers, dating from 1912 to the 1930s, include his correspondence and manuscripts. The article is mostly biographical.

919. Newberry Library. "Letters of a Pioneer Realist." *Newberry Library Bulletin* 3 (December 1945): 3-7.

The pioneer realist was Joseph Kirkland, a Chicago novelist. His papers, mostly dating in the 1880s, include correspondence, a travel diary, biographical materials, and manuscripts.

920. Newberry Library. "The Sherwood Anderson Papers." *Newberry Library Bulletin* 2nd Series 2 (December 1948): 64-70.

Anderson's papers include over 1,000 of his manuscripts and 7,000 letters. The article focuses on the letters and cites many of his correspondents.

921. Newberry Library. "Struggles of a Pioneer Midland Authoress." *Newberry Library Bulletin* 8 (December 1947): 16-21.

This article describes the papers of Illinois author Mary Hartwell Catherwood. The papers include her correspondence and book and short story manuscripts.

922. Nickerson, Edward A. "Freedom, Democracy, and Poetry: What Robinson Jeffers Really Said at the Library of Congress." *Library Chronicle of the University of Texas at Austin* New Series 40 (1987): 47-65.

    Jeffers made a speaking tour of the U.S. in 1941. This article reviews the texts of his speeches in the Jeffers Collection at the Humanities Research Center.

923. Nordloh, David J. "The Howells Collection at Miami." *Old Northwest* 8 (Summer 1982): 189-195.

    While most of this William Dean Howells Collection consists of published materials, it also contains several literary manuscripts and a number of the author's letters.

924. Norman, Dorothy. "The Dorothy Norman Papers." *Yale University Library Gazette* 42 (January 1968): 131-139.

    Norman's papers relate to literature, her promotion of the arts, her own writings, and civil liberties in the U.S. from the 1930s to the 1950s.

925. O'Connor, Margaret Anne. "A Guide to the Letters of Willa Cather." *Resources for American Literary Study* 4 (Autumn 1974): 145-172.

    O'Connor's guide locates 900 Cather letters in libraries throughout the U.S. Entries for collections or individual letters appear alphabetically by name of collection or recipient, with volume and dates included. There is an index to correspondents.

926. Osborn, James M. "The Osborn Collection, 1934-1974." *Yale University Library Gazette* 49 (October 1974): 154-170.

    This article reviews some of James M. Osborn's key purchases of literary and 17th- and 18th-century political manuscripts. It is followed by a catalog by Stephen Parks of 119 items from the collection.

927. Ostrom, John W. "Revised Check List of the Correspondence of Edgar Allan Poe." *Studies in the American Renaissance* (1981): 169-255.

    This list cites 830 Poe letters with entries including location, publication data, correspondent's name, place of origin, and dates. There is also an index and list of prices realized for Poe letters.

928. Paluka, Frank. "American Literary Manuscripts in the University of Iowa Libraries: A Checklist." *Resources for American Literary Study* 3 (Spring 1973): 100-120.

    The list is alphabetical by author's surname. Entries include only types of materials held, volume, inclusive dates, and occasional titles of poetry and prose manuscripts.

929. Paluka, Frank. "English Literary Manuscripts in the University of Iowa

Libraries." *The Library Scene* 1 (Summer 1972): 31-40.

This is a checklist presented alphabetically by author surname. Entries include record series titles, volume, and inclusive dates.

930. Paluka, Frank. "Ruth Suckow: A Calendar of Letters." *Books at Iowa* 1 (October 1964): 34-40; and 2 (April 1965): 31-40.

Suckow wrote novels and short stories with Iowa settings. Her papers include notebooks, manuscripts of her writings; and 200 letters. The calendar begins in 1918 with entries including correspondents' names, dates, length, and content notes.

931. Parks, Stephen. "The Osborn Collection: A Biennial Report." *Yale University Library Gazette* 44 (January 1970): 114-138; 46 (January 1972): 128-152; 48 (January 1974): 145-162; (April 1974): 277-283; 50 (January 1976): 164-187; 52 (January 1978): 103-121; and 54 (January 1980): 114-128.

James Marshall Osborn collected literary manuscripts and 17th- and 18th-century political papers which he gave to Yale over a period of years. This series of articles reviews the periodical accretions to the original Osborn Collection. The April, 1974, article provides an extended description of the collection and its component parts which include English poetry; manuscripts before 1700; 18th-century manuscripts; and music manuscripts.

932. Patrick, David H. "The T. E. Lawrence Collection: Its Historical Uses for the Biographer." *Library Chronicle of the University of Texas at Austin* 20 (No. 3 1990): 17-47.

Patrick notes that the collection includes Lawrence's published and unpublished writings; books from his library; an art collection; photographs; correspondence; clippings; and miscellaneous papers. Patrick emphasizes the letters and miscellaneous papers.

933. Pearson, Norman Holmes. "The Gertrude Stein Collection." *Yale University Library Gazette* 16 (January 1942): 45-47.

This article focuses on Carl Van Vechten's collection of Stein materials which includes 299 typescripts of her writings and 136 photographs of Stein and her associates. Pearson notes that 231 of the typescripts were unpublished writings.

934. Pearson, Norman Holmes. "The John Gould Fletcher Collection." *Yale University Library Gazette* 30 (January 1956): 120-125.

Most of the article is biographical or relating to Fletcher's published work. It concludes, however, by describing the poet's manuscripts and correspondence at Yale.

935. Penberthy, Jenny. "'The Very Variant': Lorine Niedecker's Manuscript Collection." *Library Chronicle of the University of Texas at Austin* 22 (Nos. 1/2 1992): 113-147.

     This article describes a collection of letters Niedecker wrote to Louis Zukofsky and many of her poetry and prose manuscripts. A chronological checklist of her manuscripts closes the article.

936. Peterson, Gerald L. "The Hearst Papers." *Annals of Iowa* 46 (Fall 1982): 459-463.

     This collection contains Charles Hearst's agricultural and political correspondence and the correspondence and manuscripts of his son James Hearst, a poet and writer. The papers are held by the University of Northern Iowa, Cedar Falls, Iowa.

937. Plummer, Linda. "The Steinbeck Collection in the Salinas Public Library, Salinas, California." *Steinbeck Quarterly* 12 (Summer/Fall 1979): 122-123.

     Among the primary sources are manuscripts of Steinbeck's writings, motion picture and televison scripts, movie posters and ephemera, sound recordings, and photographs.

938. Pottle, Frederick A. "The Scott-Croker Correspondence in the Yale University Library." *Yale University Library Gazette* 2 (January 1928): 33-45.

     This article describes an exchange of correspondence between Sir Walter Scott and John Wilson Croker. The letters date from 1810 to 1831.

939. Poyas, Frank B. "C. Hartley Grattan: The Man and the Collection." *Library Chronicle of the University of Texas at Austin* New Series 42/43 (1988): 11-37.

     Grattan was a U.S. writer interested in Australian affairs. The first one-half of this article is biographical, the second one-half describes Grattan's papers in the Humanities Research Center.

940. Pratt, Willis W. "Lord Byron and His Circle: Recent Manuscript Acquisitions." *Library Chronicle of the University of Texas* 5 (Spring 1956): 16-25.

     This article contains a checklist of thirty-two manuscripts and Byron letters added to the Byron Collection at the University of Texas. Entries include correspondents names or manuscript titles, dates, places of origin, and content notes.

941. Preston, Jean F. "Thomas Mann Papers at Princeton." *Princeton University Library Chronicle* 50 (Autumn 1988): 61-66.

     Preston describes the Mann correspondence in the Caroline Newton

Collection. Most of the letters date from 1939 to 1955.

942. Purdy, Richard L. "The Altschul Collection of George Meredith." *Yale University Library Gazette* 6 (July 1931): 11-13.

The author provides a brief overview of the George Meredith books, manuscripts, and correspondence in the Frank Altschul Collection. Purdy cites the titles of the manuscripts and several of the correspondents represented in the letters.

943. Purdy, Richard L. "Journals and Letters of George Eliot." *Yale University Library Gazette* 7 (July 1932): 1-4.

Purdy reviews the contents of Eliot's diaries and letters at Yale. The materials date from 1839 to 1861.

944. Randall, David A. "The J. K. Lilly Collection of Edgar Allan Poe." *Indiana University Bookman* 4 (March 1960): 46-58.

Mostly a checklist of Poe books and articles, but also included are twenty-three Poe letters, of which fifteen are to Sarah H. Whitman; an autograph album; crayon sketches by Poe; and two daguerreotypes.

945. Rannit, Aleksis. "The Archives of Nina Berberova." *Yale University Library Gazette* 38 (January 1964): 81-85.

Berberova was a Russian writer who fled the Bolshevik Revolution. Her papers include correspondence reflecting the society of Russian exiles; manuscripts of her prose and poetry; and photographs.

946. Ratliff, Clare. "A Bloomsbury Friendship: The Correspondence of Mary Hutchinson and Lytton Strachey." *Library Chronicle of the University of Texas at Austin* New Series 48 (1989): 15-51.

Ratliff notes that the Hutchinson Collection is rich in letters from members of the Bloomsbury Group. While naming many of the correspondents, he focuses on 169 letters between Hutchinson and Strachey.

947. Ray, Gordon N. "The Bentley Papers." *Library* 5th series 7 (September 1952): 178-200.

This collection of papers of English publisher Richard Bentley is in the University of Illinois Library, Urbana-Champaign. Ray cites the names of many correspondents, comments on the papers research value, and notes similar papers in private hands.

948. Reed, Doris M. "Letters of Vachel Lindsay in the Lilly Library at Indiana University." *Indiana University Bookman* 5 (December 1960): 21-63.

Several of Lindsay's letters are published in this article. It concludes with a checklist of Lindsay's correspondence.

949. Reeves, John K. "The Literary Manuscripts of W. D. Howells: A
     Descriptive Finding List." *Bulletin of the New York Public Library* 62
     (June 1958): 267-278; (July 1958): 350-363; and 65 (September 1961):
     465-476.
       This three-part list includes manuscripts of books, stories, poems,
     essays, and reviews; correspondence; outlines; diaries; and speeches.
     Entries include titles, correspondents, location of the manuscripts, and
     length and physical descriptions of the documents.

950. Rice, Howard C., Jr. "The Sylvia Beach Collection." *Princeton University
     Library Chronicle* 26 (Autumn 1964): 7-13.
       Sylvia Beach operated the Shakespeare and Company bookstore in Paris,
     France, during the 1920s and 1930s. Her store was the gathering point for
     many writers of the period and her papers contain a wealth of correspon-
     dence with leading literary figures.

951. Roberts, F. W. "The Manuscripts of D. H. Lawrence." *Library Chronicle
     of the University of Texas* 5 (Spring 1955): 36-43.
       This article identifies many Lawrence manuscripts then in private
     collections, especially that of Frieda Lawrence Ravagli.

952. Robinson, Kee. "The Edgar Lee Masters Collection: Sixty Years of
     Literary History." *Library Chronicle of the University of Texas* 8 (Spring
     1968): 42-49.
       Robinson reviews several items in the Masters Collection which includes
     manuscripts of published and unpublished poetry; essays; plays; novels;
     and over 12,000 letters.

953. Roe, Jill. "'Tremenjus Good for What Ails Us': The Correspondence of
     Miles Franklin and C. Hartley Grattan." *Library Chronicle of the
     University of Texas at Austin* New Series 42/43 (1988): 77-101.
       Roe describes the exchange of correspondence between Australian author
     Miles Franklin and Grattan. These letters, in the Grattan Collection, date
     from the 1930s to the 1950s.

954. Rolfe, Franklin P. "The Dickens Letters in the Huntington Library."
     Huntington Library Quarterly 1 (April 1938): 335-363.
       A checklist of 1,350 letters to, from, or about Charles Dickens. Entries
     include correspondents' names, dates, and place of origin.

955. Ryskamp, Charles. "William Cowper and His Circle: A Study of the
     Hannay Collection." *Princeton University Library Chronicle* 24 (Autumn
     1962): 3-26.
       The author describes several of the better items among the correspon-
     dence, diaries, and manuscripts by 18th-century English poet William

Cowper and his friend John Newton. Neilson C. Hannay formed the collection.

956. Sackton, Alexander. "T. S. Eliot at Texas." *Library Chronicle of the University of Texas* 8 (Spring 1967): 22-26.
    Sackton cites titles of key Eliot manuscripts and calls attention to the presence of more than 700 letters in the collection.

957. Sammons, Christa. "Recent Additions to the Hermann Broch Archive." *Yale University Library Gazette* 47 (April 1973): 228-229; and 53 (April 1979): 217-220.
    The Beinecke Library at Yale establishcd the Broch Archive in 1951. It includes the manuscripts, correspondence, and related papers of Hermann Broch, Austrian novelist. These two articles review additional Broch correspondence acquired since 1951.

958. Schaffer, Aaron. "Unpublished Letters of Emile Deschamps." *Library Chronicle of the University of Texas* 4 (Summer 1952): 112-117.
    Deschamps was a 19th-century French poet. This collection of 300 of his letters is in the University of Texas Libraries. The author places the correspondence in its historical context and comments on the general themes found in the letters which date from 1822 to 1860.

959. Schulz, Herbert C. "American Literary Manuscripts in the Huntington Library." *Huntington Library Quarterly* 22 (May 1959): 209-250.
    Schultz presents the library's holdings alphabetically by collection title. Each entry includes record series titles, volume, and inclusive dates.

960. Schulz, Herbert C. "English Literary Manuscripts in the Huntington Library." *Huntington Library Quarterly* 31 (May 1968): 251-302.
    An alphabetical presentation by collection title of the library's English literary manuscripts. Entries include record series titles, volume, and inclusive dates.

961. Scott, Richard W. "Coleridge Manuscripts in the W. Hugh Peal Collection." *Kentucky Review* 11 (Spring 1992): 83-84.
    This is a checklist of fifty-eight items, mostly letters from Samuel Taylor Coleridge. Entries include document type, place of origin, length, date, name of correspondent, and content note.

962. Shannon, Edgar F., and W. H. Bond. "Literary Manuscripts of Alfred Tennyson in the Harvard College Library." *Harvard Library Bulletin* 10 (Spring 1956): 254-276.
    The authors describe Tennyson's notebooks and 317 folders of manuscript pages of poetry and biographical notes. The article concludes

with indexes of titles and first lines of writings in the collection.

963. Sherry, Margaret M. "Uncommon Gentlemen and Outstanding Ladies: The J.A. Symington Collection in Rutgers' Special Collections and Archives." *Journal of the Rutgers University Libraries* 52 (December 1990): 27-52.

     James A. Symington was an English librarian and collector of English literature. Rutgers University acquired his collection in 1947 and Sherry analyzes its components, such as the Thomas J. Wise correspondence, and the Brontë and Swinburne manuscripts.

964. Silet, Charles L. P. "The Upton Sinclair Archives." *Southern California Quarterly* 56 (Winter 1974): 407-414.

     A review of Sinclair's papers in the Lilly Library, Indiana University, which includes his manuscripts of novels and plays, correspondence, printed materials, photographs, and memorabilia.

965. Skemp, Shelia L. "The Judith Sargent Murray Papers." *Journal of Mississippi History* 53 (August 1991): 241-250.

     Murray was a 19th-century Massachusetts novelist and playwright whose papers are in the Mississippi Department of Archives and History. The papers include letterbooks, correspondence, essays, and poetry manuscripts, and her husband's correspondence.

966. Slate, Joseph E. "The Joseph Hergesheimer Collection." *Library Chronicle of the University of Texas* 7 (Fall 1961): 24-31.

     Slate notes that the University of Texas, Austin, holds many of Hergesheimer's novels, plays, and screenplays in manuscript format, along with his correspondence. The author continues by describing selected Hergesheimer manuscripts in detail.

967. Slater, John R. "The Adelaide Crapsey Collection." *University of Rochester Library Bulletin* 16 (Spring 1961): 37-40.

     A brief review of Crapsey's papers which include her poetry in manuscript form, correspondence, and notebooks.

968. Smith, Susan S. "Adelaide Crapsey: Materials for a Bibliographical and Textual Study." *University of Rochester Library Bulletin* 25 (1969/1970): 3-32.

     Crapsey is known for her poetry. This article discusses her life, her poetry, and her papers at the University of Rochester, among which are manuscripts of her poetry, notebooks, and letters.

969. Smith, Warren H. "The Manuscript Collections at the Lewis Walpole Library." *Yale University Library Gazette* 56 (April 1982): 53-60.

     Smith identifies the sources and context of the Walpole Collection. The material includes correspondence, diaries, business records, cookbooks, notebooks and sketchbooks, and genealogical materials, all relating to Horace Walpole and his times.

970. Spann, Marcella. "The Zukofsky Papers." *Library Chronicle of the University of Texas at Austin* New Series 2 (November 1970): 49-59.
Louis Zukofsky is known for his poetry which is well represented in manuscript form along with more than 450 letters and miscellaneous other manuscripts. Spann cites several examples while commenting on how they might be used for research.

971. Stanford, Donald E. "The First Mrs. Eliot." *Library Chronicle of the University of Texas at Austin* New Series 40 (1987): 89-111.
This article identifies correspondence series in several Humanities Research Center collections that serve to clarify the effects T. S. Eliot's marriage to Vivienne Haigh-Wood had on his career.

972. Stark, Lewis M. "Walt Whitman: The Oscar Lion Collection." *Bulletin of the New York Public Library* 58 (May 1954): 218-229; (June 1954): 305-308; (July 1954): 348-359; (August 1954): 397-410; (September 1954): 455-461; and (October 1954): 497-514.
This six-part series describes published and unpublished materials by and about Walt Whitman. Part one is devoted to Walt Whitman's manuscripts and correspondence and manuscripts and correspondence of his associates. Part five includes some Whitman photographs.

973. Steiner, Herbert. "The Harvard Collection of Hugo von Hofmannsthal." *Harvard Library Bulletin* 8 (Winter 1954): 54-64.
Hofmannsthal was an Austrian poet. The collection Steiner describes contains examples of the poet's manuscripts and published works.

974. Stevens, Fran. "The Coleridge Collection: A Sample." *Library Chronicle of the University of Texas at Austin* New Series 1 (March 1970): 33-38.
Stevens reviews the contents of the Hartley Coleridge Collection at the Humanities Research Center. Description is limited to record series titles and volume with some comments on the subject content of the correspondence series.

975. Stoddard, F. G. "The Lord Dunsany Collection." *Library Chronicle of the University of Texas* 8 (Spring 1967): 27-31.
Edward John Plunkett Lord Dunsany was an Irish poet and dramatist. His papers at the University of Texas contain over 850 items, mostly literary manuscripts.

976. Stoddard, F. G. "The Louis MacNeice Collection." *Library Chronicle of*

the University of Texas 8 (Spring 1968): 50-55.
    MacNeice is known primarily as an English poet, but he also wrote radio and television scripts and literary criticism. Stoddard describes some of the materials found in the collection at the University of Texas.

977. Stone, Albert E., Jr. "The Twichell Papers and Mark Twain's *A Tramp Abroad.*" *Yale University Library Gazette* 29 (April 1955): 151-164.
    The Rev. Joseph H. Twichell accompanied Mark Twain on a hiking tour of Europe in 1870. Twichell's papers include Twain's diary of the trip, correspondence between Twain and Twichell, and a ten-volume journal kept by Twichell.

978. Swayze, Walter E. "The Sir William Watson Collection." *Yale University Library Gazette* 27 (October 1952): 71-76.
    This collection contains the English poet's letters, manuscripts of his poems and music he composed, and photographs. The article focuses on the correspondence files.

979. Tate, Allen. "The Elizabeth Madox Roberts Papers." *Quarterly Journal of Current Acquisitions* 1 (October 1943): 29-31.
    Roberts was a novelist and poet. This article briefly describes her papers in the Library of Congress. The papers include drafts and manuscripts of her novels, poems, and short stories, along with correspondence and reminiscences.

980. Taylor, Robert H. "The J. Harlin O'Connell Collection." *Princeton University Library Chronicle* 19 (Spring/Summer 1958): 149-152.
    O'Connell collected manuscripts and books of late-19th-century British writers. This article reviews the correspondence of those represented in his collection.

981. Taylor, Robert N., and others. "Lewis Carroll at Texas. The Warren Weaver Collection and Related Dodgson Materials at the Harry Ransom Humanities Research Center." *Library Chronicle of the University of Texas at Austin* New Series 32/33 (1985): 7-233.
    This entire issue is devoted to Lewis Carroll-related manuscripts, books, and photographs in the Warren Weaver and Charles L. Dodgson Collections. The compilers describe manuscripts on pages 174-184 and photographs on pages 185-213. This catalog includes an index.

982. Teagarden, Lucetta J. "The J. B. Priestley Collection." *Library Chronicle of the University of Texas* 7 (Summer 1963): 27-32.
    John B. Priestley was an English author. The Humanities Research Center holds unpublished manuscripts, manuscripts of published works, playbills and theatre posters, paintings, correspondence, and photographs

in its Priestley Collection.

983. Terrie, Henry. "Caldwell at Dartmouth." *Southern Quarterly* 27 (Spring 1989): 36-41.
      The author reviews Erskine Caldwell's long association with Dartmouth College and provides an overview of the writer's papers there. Description is limited to record series titles and volume.

984. Thornton, Weldon. "Books and Manuscripts by James Joyce." *Library Chronicle of the University of Texas* 7 (Fall 1961): 19-23.
      Thornton describes Joyce correspondence, drawings, photographs, and individual Joyce manuscripts at the Humanities Research Center.

985. Thorp, Willard. "The Ruskin Manuscripts." *Princeton University Library Chronicle* 1 (February 1940): 1-10.
      This collection at Princeton University includes John Ruskin's notes on geology and the natural sciences, his poetry and prose writings, his lectures on Florentine and Greek art, and his notebooks.

986. Tibbetts, Robert. "The Thurber Collection at Ohio State University." *Lost Generation Journal* 3 (Winter 1975): 12-15.
      The James Thurber Collection includes oral histories and recordings of Thurber's stories; his correspondence; manuscripts of his writings; and published materials by and about Thurber. The author reviews some of the better manuscripts in the article.

987. Triesch, Manfred. "The Lillian Hellman Collection." *Library Chronicle of the University of Texas* 8 (Spring 1965): 17-19.
      Triesch describes some of the 210 Hellman notebooks and drafts of her writings held by the Humanities Research Center.

988. Tunis, Mildred C. "The Corey Ford Collection." *Dartmouth College Library Bulletin* 13 (April 1973): 109-121.
      Ford was a professional writer. His papers include manuscripts of his writings; correspondence; scrapbooks; financial records; and photographs.

989. Turner, Decherd. "Robinson Jeffers at Texas." *Library Chronicle of the University of Texas at Austin* New Series 40 (1986): 21-23.
      Turner offers an introduction to the Jeffers Collection at the Humanities Research Center. Jeffers' papers include his diaries; manuscripts; correspondence; royalty records; music lyrics; and photographs.

990. Van der Elst, Marie-Claire. "The Manuscripts of Anaïs Nin at Northwestern." *Mosaic* 11 (Winter 1978): 59-63.
      Nin was a French-born novelist and diarist. Van der Elst lists and

describes manuscripts and drafts of Nin's writings at Northwestern University, Evanston, Illinois. Van der Elst's description focuses on the content of the manuscripts.

991. Vitoux, Pierre. "Aldous Huxley at Texas: A Checklist of Manuscripts." *Library Chronicle of the University of Texas at Austin* New Series 9 (1978): 41-58.
Vitoux divides the checklist into four categories: plays, novels and essays, poems, and other essays and miscellaneous materials. Entries include manuscript titles, places and dates of publication, types of manuscripts, length, and bibliographical notes.

992. Wainwright, Alexander D. "The Morris L. Parrish Collection of Victorian Novelists: A Summary Report and an Introduction." *Princeton University Library Chronicle* 17 (Winter 1956): 59-67.
This is an introductory article for an entire issue of the *Chronicle* devoted to the Parrish Collection. While mostly published materials, the collection does contain some signficant manuscript material of prominent authors. The other articles in the issue are:

1. Ashley, Robert P. "The Wilkie Collins Collection." 81-84.

2. Beinecke, Jr., Walter. "Barrie in the Parrish Collection." 96-98.
An article about Scottish author James Matthew Barrie.

3. Martin, Robert B. "The Reade Collection." 77-80.
This is a collection of materials by Charles Reade, playwright and novelist.

4. Randall, David A. "The Stevenson Collection." 92-95.
The article contains references to a few Robert Louis Stevenson manuscript items.

5. Weaver, Warren. "The Parrish Collection of Carrolliana." 85-91.
An accumulation of Lewis Carroll items.

993. Watson, James G. "Carvel Collins' Faulkner: A Newly Opened Archive." *Library Chronicle of the University of Texas at Austin* 20 (No. 4 1991): 17-35.
Much of the Collins Collection had been closed until the death of Carvel Collins. Watson describes the voluminous correspondence, research notes, photographs, and related Faulkner memorabilia accumulated by Collins, a prominent Faulkner scholar.

994. Welsh, John R. "The Charles Carroll Sims Collection." *South Atlantic*

Bulletin 31 (November 1966): 1-3.

Sims was a 19th-century author and man of letters. His papers include manuscripts of his writings, notebooks, scrapbooks, speeches and lectures, and published materials. Welsh notes the collection is valuable for locating Sims' fugitive writings.

995. West, James L. W., III. "The Mencken-Fitzgerald Papers: An Annotated Checklist." *Princeton University Library Chronicle* 38 (Autumn 1976): 21-35.

West has located and described 113 letters exchanged between H. L. Mencken and F. Scott Fitzgerald or written by or about Mencken and Fitzgerald. Entries include date, length, a publication note, physical characteristics, location, and a content note.

996. Westbrook, Max. "Necessary Performance: The Hemingway Collection at Texas." *Library Chronicle of the University of Texas* 7 (Spring 1964): 27-31.

While mostly a review of published works, the author does describe a few Hemingway manuscripts and letters.

997. Wilentz, Gay. "White Patron and Black Artist: The Correspondence of Fannie Hurst and Zora Neale Hurston." *Library Chronicle of the University of Texas at Austin* New Series 35 (1986): 21-43.

This article describes the manuscript collection of novelist and feminist Fannie Hurst, and especially her correspondence with Afro-American writer Zora Hurston. The collection includes Hurst's manuscripts, correspondence, and published writing.

998. Williams, Stanley T. "The Adrian Van Sinderen Collection of Walt Whitman." *Yale University Library Gazette* 15 (January 1941): 49-53.

Most of the material in this collection is published, but it also contains Whitman letters, his poetry manuscripts, essays, and lectures, along with a few photos.

999. Williams, Stanley T. "The Irving Manuscripts." *Yale University Library Gazette* 1 (January 1927): 35-38.

Williams describes a small collection of Washington Irving's letters and notebooks dating from 1810. The notebooks contain reminiscences of Irving's travels.

1000. Wilson, Althea G. "The James Gates Percival Papers." *Yale University Library Gazette* 28 (October 1953): 77-81.

Percival's papers reflect his varied career as physician, linguist, geologist, and poet. Wilson notes that Percival's poetry manuscripts constitute the largest record series in the collection.

1001. Wing, Donald G. "The Katherine S. Dreier Collection of Oscar Wilde."
Yale University Library Gazette 28 (October 1953): 82-87.
While mostly published materials, the Dreier Collection also contains
some manuscript poems and a number of letters by Wilde.

1002. Woodman, Leonora. "'The Big Old Pagan Vision': The Letters of D. H.
Lawrence to Frederick Carter." *Library Chronicle of the University of
Texas at Austin* New Series 34 (1986): 39-51.
Woodman describes a collection of twenty-nine Lawrence letters to
English mystic and artist Frederick Carter. The letters reveal Lawrence's
interest in Carter's writings and document the origin of Lawrence's last
book, *Apocalypse.*

1003. Woodress, James. "The Tarkington Papers." *Princeton University Library
Chronicle* 16 (Winter 1955): 45-53.
Dating from the 1860s to the 1940s, Booth Tarkington's papers include
manuscripts of his novels, short stories, plays, essays, and miscellaneous
writings; letters; scrapbooks; notebooks; drawings; and photographs.

1004. Woodring, Carl R. "Charles Lamb in the Harvard Library." *Harvard
Library Bulletin* 10 (Autumn 1956): 367-401.
This article is divided into five sections, of which sections four and five
describe Lamb's correspondence and literary manuscripts at Harvard.

1005. Woodward, Robert H. "The Steinbeck Research Center at San Jose State
University: A Descriptive Catalogue." *San Jose Studies* 11 (Winter 1985):
1-128.
This entire issue is a catalog of John Steinbeck materials at San Jose
State. Among the material listed are manuscript film scripts and
screenplays; correspondence files; photographs; scrapbooks; motion
picture films; and sound recordings.

1006. Wynne, Marjorie G. "The Edward Beinecke Collection of Robert Louis
Stevenson." *Yale University Library Gazette* 26 (January 1952): 117-136.
Wynne describes both published and unpublished Stevenson materials
with description of the manuscript materials beginning on page 129.
Stevenson's papers include manuscript poems, notebooks, lecture notes,
sketches, personal notes, and correspondence.

1007. Wynne, Marjorie G. "Robert Louis Stevenson Manuscripts in the Yale
University Library." *Autograph Collectors' Journal* 5 (Winter 1953): 3-8.
This article describes the scope of the manuscript portion of the Edward
Beinecke Collection of Stevenson's work. Wynne notes that correspon-
dence files, manuscripts of published and unpublished works, and
illustrations by Stevenson are well represented.

Military Collections

General

1008. Allen, Lafon. "Lafon Allen Collection of Posters of the World War." *Yale University Library Gazette* 12 (July 1937): 1-16.

Allen reviews representative British, French, Belgian, and German WWI posters and public proclamations that are in his collection at Yale. U.S. posters are included in the collection, but not discussed in this article.

1009. Butow, Robert J. C. "IMTFE: Tokyo Trial Holdings." *Princeton University Library Chronicle* 18 (Autumn 1956): 33-36.

This short article calls attention to a group of papers and official records of the International Military Tribunal for the Far East accumulated by Smith N. Crowe, Jr., a U.S. legal advisor to the proceedings of the tribunal.

1010. Cappon, Lester J. "The Collection of World War I Materials in the States." *American Historical Review* 48 (July 1943): 733-745.

Cappon identifies the states that undertook the collection of WWI-related records. He concludes the article by reviewing the types of records accumulated and the effectiveness of the projects.

1011. Clark, Davis S. "Journals and Orderly Books Kept by Massachusetts Soldiers During the French and Indian Wars." *New England Historical and Genealogical Register* 95 (April 1941): 118-122.

This is a checklist of twenty-six manuscript journals compiled as a supplement to Harriette Forbes guide to New England diaries. The entries appear chronologically (1755-1758) and include author, rank, military unit, title, and repository holding the journal.

1012. Day, James M. "Sources for Military History in the Texas State Archives." *Texas Military History* 2 (May 1962): 113-125.

Day provides many specific examples of manuscript collections, photographs, and maps relating to the Spanish, Mexican, and American periods of Texas history. Description includes record series, volume, and inclusive dates along with comments on research values.

1013. East, Ernest E. "Records of Illinois Soldiers at War." *Illinois Libraries* 41 (April 1959): 272-287.

    East mentions a few record series titles of Illinois records documenting the Black Hawk, Mexican, Civil, and Spanish-American Wars. Most of the article, though, reproduces selected data extracted from the records.

1014. Grimm, Verna. "The American Legion National Headquarters Library, Archives and Files." *Special Libraries* 39 (January 1948): 3-9.

    Only about one-third of this article is devoted to the legion's records, which Grimm describes in general terms. She concludes with a classification scheme for the headquarters' central files.

1015. Huber, Elbert L. "War Department Records in the National Archives." *Military Affairs* 6 (Winter 1942): 247-254.

    This is a review of military records accessioned into the National Archives during the first six years of its existence. Huber cites record groups, record series titles, and inclusive dates. The records date from the 18th-century to the 1930s.

1016. Lincoln, Charles H. "A Calendar of the Manuscripts of Col. John Bradstreet in the Library of the American Antiquarian Society." *Proceedings of the American Antiquarian Society* 19 (April 1908): 103-181.

    The Bradstreet letters date from 1755 to 1777. Entries include names of correspondents, place of origin, dates, length, and content notes. Most appear military related.

1017. Lincoln, Charles H. "Calendar of the Manuscripts of Sir William Johnson in the Library of the Society." *Proceedings of the American Antiquarian Society* 18 (October 1907): 367-401.

    The Johnson manuscripts date from 1755 to 1774. Entries include names of correspondents, place of origin, date, and content notes. Most of the letters appear related to frontier military affairs.

1018. "Manuscript Records of the French and Indian War in the Library of the Society." *American Antiquarian Society Transactions and Collections* 11 (1909): 1-177.

    This entire issue is a calendar of letters and documents from the Sir William Johnson and Col. John Bradstreet Collections; French and Indian War manuscripts; and the contents of Lt. William Henshaw's orderly book. Each entry has a content note.

1019. Miller, James C. "Les archives concernant la résistance européenne dans les dépôts d'archives fédérales de Etats-Unis d'Amérique." *Revue d'histoire de la deuxième guerre mondiale* 26 (Juillet 1976): 73-94.

Miller provides a through review of U.S. military and civil records in the National Archives and collections of personal papers in the Library of Congress. He also includes a section on captured Axis records.

1020. Morton, Louis. "The Bibliography of a Defeat: The Search for Records on the Loss of the Philippines." *American Archivist* 16 (July 1953): 195-212.

This articles examines the extant records of the U.S. armed forces regarding the Japanese invasion of the Philippine Islands in 1941. The author discusses both official and unofficial records along with maps and captured Japanese records.

1021. Morton, Louis. "Sources for the History of World War II." *World Politics* 13 (April 1961): 435-453.

Morton provides a thorough review of both published and unpublished records. His discussion covers pre-war records, wartime records, manuscript collections, captured enemy records, unit histories, memoirs, and reference works.

1022. Novossiltzeff, George A. "Soviet Union War Posters." *Quarterly Journal of Current Acquisitions* 2 (February 1945): 68-79.

The Library of Congress holds a collection of 477 WWII Russian war posters. This article describes twenty-six produced by TASS, the Soviet news agency. The description includes artists and content analysis.

1023. Spector, Ronald H. "'In the Nam' and 'Back in the World': American and Vietnamese Sources on the Vietnam War." *Journal of American History* 75 (June 1988): 209-214.

The author describes records and personal papers found in presidential libraries; U.S. military records; and non-military federal records, along with records of groups opposed to the war and those providing North Vietnamese viewpoints.

1024. Srinivasachary, Mudumbhi S. "Sources for the Study of United States Mutual Security Policy towards South Asia, 1951-1960." *Military Affairs* 39 (December 1975): 208-209.

The author reviews personal papers and oral histories in the Truman and Eisenhower presidential libraries along with the transcripts of the Dean Acheson Princeton Seminars. Some references are described down to the folder level.

1025. Zobrist, Benedict K. "Resources of Presidential Libraries for the History of Post World War II American Military Government in Germany and

Japan." *Military Affairs* 42 (February 1978): 17-19.

Zobrist cites specific collections in the Hoover, Roosevelt, Truman, Eisenhower, and Kennedy presidential libraries. He also notes which record series in these collections may be useful for research on post-war military governments.

1026. Zobrist, Benedict K. "Resources of Presidential Libraries for the History of the Second World War." *Military Affairs* 39 (April, 1975): 82-85.

Zobrist calls attention to Herbert Hoover's papers documenting U.S. relief efforts early in WWII and regarding the Japanese attack on Pearl Harbor. He also cites papers of presidential assistants in the Roosevelt, Truman and Eisenhower Libraries.

Air Force and Army

1027. Agnew, James B. "USAMHRC--The Mother Lode for Military History." *Military Affairs* 39 ((1975): 146-148.

This article relates mostly historical information about the U.S. Army Military History Research Collection. However, it does call attention to the papers of Generals Lewis B. Hershey and Matthew B. Ridgway and the collection's 55,000 pages of oral history transcripts.

1028. Atkinson, Gloria L. "The Archives of the USAF Historical Division." *Special Libraries* 59 (July/August 1968): 444-446.

Description is limited to comments on selected record series, topical strengths, and sources of materials donated to the archives.

1029. Boles, Nancy G. "The Bladensburg and Washington Campaigns." *Maryland Historical Magazine* 66 (Fall 1971): 300-302.

Boles reviews the manuscript collections of Generals William H. Winder and John Stricker for materials documenting these War of 1812 campaigns.

1030. "Catalogue of the William Barclay Parsons Collection." *Bulletin of the New York Public Library* 45 (January 1941): 95-108; and (July 1941): 585-658.

Parsons was a career military engineer and this two-article series is a catalog of his private library. While mostly published materials, it contains an interesting group of Robert Fulton's manuscripts and correspondence described on pages 656-658.

1031. Coker, Kathyrn R. "The U.S. Army Signal Center and Fort Gordon, a Military Archives in Georgia." *Provenance* 9 (Spring/Fall 1991): 66-76.

While mostly an overview of archival policies and services, the author concludes with a review of army records and manuscript collections held by the archives. She limits description to record series and collection titles.

1032. Dawson, Joseph G., III. "Government Documents and Manuscript Collections." In *The Late 19th Century U.S. Army, 1865-1898: A Research Guide*, edited by Joseph G. Dawson. Westport, Conn.: Greenwood Press, 1990. 15-48.

1033. Eells, Richard. "Strategic Bombing Photographs." *Quarterly Journal of Current Acquisitions* 5 (November 1947): 9-11.
  This collection in the Library of Congress is part of a larger General Carl Spaatz Collection. It consists of nineteen volumes of photos taken during and after bombing raids on German targets between January, 1944 and February, 1945.

1034. Ellis, A. V. "U.S.A.F. Historical Division Archives." *Special Libraries* 54 (March 1963): 169-171.
  Ellis reviews the types of materials held and their subject strengths.

1035. Evans, Charles. "Itemized List of the Whipple Collection." *Chronicles of Oklahoma* 28 (Autumn 1950): 231-234.
  A list of Lt. Amiel Weeks Whipple's papers created while he was a member of the 1851 Mexican Boundary Survey and the Pacific Railroad Survey of 1853. The papers include original journals, maps, and manuscripts, plus drawings and paintings by H. B. Möllhausen.

1036. Haight, David J., and George H. Curtis. "Abilene, Kansas and the History of World War II: Resources and Research Opportunities at the Dwight D. Eisenhower Library." *Military Affairs* 41 (December 1977): 195-200.
  The authors focus on Eisenhower's pre-presidential papers, referred to as the sixteen-fifty-two file (1916-1952). They also cite the library's extensive collection of personal papers of Eisenhower's chief lieutenants in WWII.

1037. Hanna, Archibald, Jr. "The General James Duncan Graham Papers." *Yale University Library Gazette* 39 (April 1965): 186-187.
  Graham was in the U.S. Army's Corps of Topographical Engineers early in his military career. His papers document his role in the Mexican Boundary Survey of 1851, and, later, his work on harbor improvements on the Great Lakes.

1038. Hanna, Archibald, Jr. "The Richard Henry Pratt Papers." *Yale University Library Gazette* 34 (July 1959): 38-42.

Pratt was the founder of the Indian Industrial School at Carlisle, Pennsylvania, and a career army officer. His papers include Civil War diaries; correspondence; scrapbooks; unpublished memoirs; and photographs.

1039. Hasdorff, James C. "Sources in Aerospace History: The USAF Oral History Collection." *Aerospace Historian* 23 (June 1976): 103-104.
Hasdorff describes the scope and content of the 876 interviews in the collection and cites names of informants in selected subject areas.

1040. Horowitz, Israel. "Army Air Forces Keep Pictorial Records." *Library Journal* 71 (December 15, 1946): 1751-1754.
This article describes the voluminous holdings of the U.S. Army Air Forces Photographic Library. In 1946, this library, founded in 1919, contained 1.5 million still photographs and 7.5 million feet of motion picture film of army aviation from 1908 forward.

1041. Kennedy, Marguerite K. "The Archives of the Historical Division, USAF." *American Archivist* 17 (April 1954): 123-134.
Kennedy discusses the formation of the Historical Division and, in general terms, some of its holdings. The inclusion of categories of the decimal classification system indicates how division personnel arranged material.

1042. LeRoy, Bruce. "The Chittenden Papers." *Pacific Northwest Quarterly* 50 (January 1959): 28-30.
Hiram M. Chittenden was a U.S. Army engineer and historian. His papers at the Washington State Historical Society include diaries and journals, correspondence, and scrapbooks documenting his engineering activities in the West and his historical scholarship.

1043. McFarland, Marvin W. "The General Spaatz Collection." *Quarterly Journal of Current Acquisitions* 6 (May 1949): 23-55.
A review of the provenance and various subdivisions of the Carl Spaatz papers. The article concludes with an analysis of the papers and their research values. Carl Spaatz ended his career as USAF chief of staff.

1044. McFarland, Marvin W. "The H. H. Arnold Collection." *Quarterly Journal of Current Acquisitions* 9 (August 1952): 171-181.
Henry H. Arnold led the U.S. Army Air Forces during WWII and retired in 1950 as general of the Air Force. The papers described in this article date from 1930 to 1950 and document his pre-WWII service, his leadership during the war, and his post-war career.

1045. McFarland, Marvin W. "The Papers of Ira C. Eaker." *Quarterly Journal of Current Acquisitions* 11 (February 1954): 63-68.

Eaker was an army aviator whose career spanned the period from WWI through WWII. Most of the papers are WWII-related and include correspondence, reports, photographs, and manuscripts of articles and books written by Eaker.

1046. Monaghan, Frank. "The Webb Manuscripts." *Yale University Library Gazette* 11 (July 1936): 1-7.

This collection contains the papers of three generations of Webbs, Gen. Samuel Blatchley Webb, Gen. James Watson Webb, and Gen. Alexander Stewart Webb. The article cites many of the Webbs' correspondents.

1047. Newberry Library. "The Papers of General Judson." *Newberry Library Bulletin* 3 (December 1945): 8-12.

The papers of Brig.Gen. William V. Judson document his military engineering career in Puerto Rico and Panama; his role as observer in the Russo-Japanese War and head of the U.S. military mission in Russia during the Bolshevik Revolution; and other assignments.

1048. Owen, Arthur F. "Opportunities for Research: The Early Records of the Office of the Inspector General, 1814-48." *Military Affairs* 7 (Fall 1943): 195-196.

Owen reviews the types of information found in these U.S. Army records. He recommends field inspection reports as a particularly rich source for frontier army life.

1049. Phillips, Helen C. "Signal Corps Historical Collection." *Military Affairs* 18 (Summer 1954): 88-89.

Phillips calls attention to historical materials held by the U.S. Army Signal Corp's Historical Branch at Fort Monmouth, New Jersey. Archival records, historical manuscripts, maps, and photographs are among the holdings.

1050. Pogue, Forrest C. "General Marshall and the Pershing Papers." *Quarterly Journal of the Library of Congress* 21 (January 1964): 1-11.

This article reviews materials, especially correspondence, in the John J. Pershing papers that are critical for researching the life and career of Gen. George C. Marshall. Pogue also cites other high-ranking U.S. Army officers represented in the Pershing papers.

1051. Schubert, Frank N. "Legacy of the Topographical Engineers: Textual and Cartographic Records of Western Exploration, 1819-1860." *Government Publication Review* 7A (March/April 1980): 111-116.

Schubert comments on the research values of U.S. Army topographers' correspondence, reports, maps, and drawings that describe their travels in the western U.S. He also explains how to access many of these records.

1052. Smith, G. Herbert. "Some Sources for Northwest History: The Archives of Military Posts." *Minnesota History* 22 (September 1941): 297-301.
   Smith describes federal records of Fort Ridgely and Fort Snelling. The originals are in the U.S. National Archives with microfilm copies at the Minnesota Historical Society.

1053. Sunderman, James F. "Documentary Collections Related to the U.S. Air Forces. A Guide for Military Writers." *Air University Review* 13 (Summer 1961): 110-126.
   A thorough overview of archives and historical sources at USAF and federal museums and libraries and at colleges and universities. Types of sources identified include records and manuscripts, photos, motion pictures, and published materials.

1054. Walker, Dale L. "Marshall Collection Adds Major Resource to U.T. El Paso." *Texas Libraries* 36 (Winter 1974): 179-183.
   Walker describes military-related correspondence; speeches; movie and T.V. scripts; interviews with military leaders and writers; sound recordings; photographs; and published materials assembled by Brig.Gen. Samuel L. A. Marshall.

Marine Corps and Navy

1055. Allard, Dean C. "The Naval Historical Center and the Resources of Naval History." In *Versatile Guardian: Research in Naval History*, edited by Richard A. von Doenhoff. Washington, D.C.: Howard University Press, 1979. 23-32.
   The author reviews published materials, archives and manuscripts, and photographs held by the center. The treatment is general, but some specific collections are mentioned.

1056. Armstrong, William J. "United States Naval Aviation History: A Guide to Sources." *Aerospace Historian* 27 (June 1980): 109-112.
   While not describing record groups or manuscript collections, the author identifies major repositories holding naval records and tells readers what may be found in each.

1057. Bauer, K. Jack. "The Navy in an Age of Manifest Destiny: Some Suggestions for Sources and Research." In *Versatile Guardian: Research in Naval History*, edited by Richard A. von Doenhoff, Washington, D.C.: Howard University Press, 1979. 161-175.

Bauer identifies and locates federal records and manuscript collections for U.S. Navy operations in the Mexican War. Description is limited to collection titles.

1058. Boles, Nancy G. "The Hammond Dugan Collection." *Maryland Historical Magazine* 68 (Spring 1973): 89-91.
Dugan was a career officer in the U.S. Navy's lighter-than-air aviation program. This collection includes his correspondence, scrapbooks, and photographs relating to his service aboard *Akron*.

1059. Cox, Richard J. "Two Marylanders in the Early Navy: The Hambleton Family Papers, MS. 2021." *Maryland Historical Magazine* 69 (Fall 1974): 317-321.
Samuel Hambleton's papers reflect U.S. Navy life for the period 1813-1832. The letters of his brother, John N. Hambleton, document shipboard life and routine for the period 1820-1832.

1060. Fishwick, Marshall W. "A Note on World War II Naval Records." *American Historical Review* 55 (October 1949): 82-85.
Description of the records is limited, but the author does identify key record groups and series and the repositories that hold them.

1061. Glenn, Bess. "Navy Department Records in the National Archives." *Military Affairs* 7 (Winter 1943): 247-260.
Glenn presents a checklist of sixteen record groups. Under each record group, she includes an administrative history of the record creating unit along with record series titles, and inclusive dates.

1062. Hayes, John D. "The Papers of Naval Officers: Where Are They?" *Military Affairs* 20 (Summer 1956): 102-103.
Hayes identifies repositories holding collections of naval officers' papers. He limits description to collection titles.

1063. Mcaulay, Neill. "Material on Latin America in the United States Marine Corps Archives." *Hispanic American Historical Review* 46 (May 1966): 179-181.
The author calls attention to records in the National Archives and the Marine Corps Historical Archives relating to USMC operations in Panama, Cuba, Nicaragua, Dominican Republic, and Haiti.

1064. Merrill, James M. "The Naval Historian and His Sources." *American Archivist* 32 (July 1969): 261-268.
Merrill comments on naval records in the National Archives, Library of Congress, University of North Carolina at Chapel Hill, Eleutherian Mills Historical Library, Syracuse University Library, New York

Historical Society, and many other manuscript repositories.

1065. Morgan, William T. "Documenting the American Navies of the Revolution: A Scattered but Fruitful Seedbed." In *Versatile Guardian: Research in Naval History*, edited by Richard A. von Doenhoff. Washington, D.C.: Howard University Press, 1979. 149-159.
   Morgan identifies and locates many manuscript collections in U.S. historical societies and university libraries. He cites collection and record series titles and comments on their research values.

1066. Ray, Thomas W. "Naval Aviation Photographs in the National Archives." *Military Affairs* 15 (Winter 1951): 207-209.
   This article calls attention to a collection of more than 100,000 images relating to naval aviation. Ray identifies aircraft types and aviation subjects documented by these photos.

1067. Thomas, Dorothy M. "Still Pictures Library, Navy Department." *Special Libraries* 36 (April 1945): 123-126.
   While this article does not describe holdings, it does explain how the Navy classified and filed its photos. This information may be useful for facilitating access to U.S. Navy photograph collections.

1068. Walker, Dale L. "Parsons Papers at U.T. El Paso Library: Ted Parson of the Lafayette Escadrille." *Texas Libraries* 38 (Winter 1976): 173-178.
   This collection contains manuscripts of Ted Parson's writings; radio scripts; his correspondence; scrapbooks; and photographs, all relating to Parson's service with the Lafayette Escadrille in WWI and as a U.S. Navy aviator during WWII.

American Revolution

1069. Adams, Randolph G. "A New Library of American Revolutionary Records." *Current History* 33 (November 1930): 234-238.
   Adams reviews the Landsdowne papers; the British Headquarters papers; and the Gage papers, all purchased by William L. Clements and given to the University of Michigan. The papers document British military affairs during the American Revolution.

1070. Beers, Henry P. "The Papers of the British Commanders in Chief in North America." *Military Affairs* 13 (Summer 1949): 79-94.
   Beers notes that the papers of the British commanders are the richest source for information about military affairs in colonial America. He lists each commander from 1754 to 1783 and locates and briefly describes their papers.

1071. Bell, Whitfield J., Jr. "The Stuart W. Jackson Lafayette Collection." *Yale University Library Gazette* 34 (October 1958): 49-56.

Jackson collected materials about the Marquis de Lafayette. This article describes 400 letters by, to, and about Lafayette. They date from 1773-1850 and relate to the military, social, political, and economic history of France and the U.S.

1072. Berthelsen, Barbara. "The Sparks Map Collection." *Special Libraries* 69 (April 1978): 164-168.

This article describes the manuscript maps of the American Revolution in the Jared Sparks Collection at Cornell University.

1073. Boles, Nancy G. "A Checklist of Loyalist Manuscripts in the Maryland Historical Society." *Maryland Historical Magazine* 68 (Summer 1973): 196-198.

The checklist includes collection and record series titles, volume, inclusive dates, and content notes for fourteen major collections containing Loyalist materials.

1074. Boles, Nancy G. "The John Hanson Collection." *Maryland Historical Magazine* 65 (Fall 1970): 304-305.

Boles describes a collection of fifty-two letters of John Hanson, a U.S. Revolutionary War leader.

1075. Bonnel, Ulane Z. "Resources in France for the American Historian: The Dobrée Papers at Nantes." *Quarterly Journal of the Library of Congress* 28 (October 1971): 253-259.

The Dobrées were a banking and shipping family operating from the port of Nantes. Their business records and personal papers help document French support of the American Revolution.

1076. Bonnel, Ulane Z. "Maps and Rare Books at the Library of the Ministère d'Etat chargé de la Défense nationale." *Quarterly Journal of the Library of Congress* 30 (October 1973): 256-261.

Bonnel reviews the French war department's maps relating to military operations during the French and Indian War and the Revolutionary War. This library holds American-related maps from Great Britain as well.

1077. Bridgwater, Dorothy W. "The Wetmore Manuscripts." *Yale University Library Gazette* 19 (July 1944): 10-13.

This is a collection of 263 items dating from 1702 to the early 19th century describing political, economic, and social events in Massachusetts. It contains materials relating to the American Revolution, Shays' Rebellion, and Aaron Burr.

1078. Brown, Sanborn C. "The Rumford Collection." *Dartmouth College Library Bulletin* 20 (November 1979): 25-28.

Benjamin Thompson (Count Rumford) was a Loyalist during the American Revolution and a member of George III's government. His papers at Dartmouth include over 1,000 letters and 20 reels of micro-filmed documents from European repositories.

1079. Bryan, Jennifer A. "The Tilghman Papers." *Maryland Historical Magazine* 88 (Fall 1993): 297-299.

These papers include those of Edward Tilghman and his son Edward Jr.; and James Tilghman and his sons Richard and William. Most of the collection focuses on the American Revolutionary period.

1080. Camden, Thomas E. "The Langdon-Elwyn Family Papers." *Historical New Hampshire* 36 (Winter 1981): 350-356.

This collection contains the correspondence and accounts of John Langdon and Elizabeth and Alfred Elwyn. It spans the years 1762-1792 and is especially rich in sources for the American Revolution in New Hampshire. A collection inventory concludes the article.

1081. Cavanagh, John C. "The Papers of Benjamin Lincoln." *Massachusetts Historical Society Miscellany* 8 (November 1963): 1-5.

1082. Chinard, Gilbert. "The Berthier Manuscripts: New Records of the French Army in the American Revolution." *Princeton University Library Chronicle* 1 (November 1939): 3-8.

Alexandre Berthier was a cartographer and aide to Gen. Jean de Rochambeau. Berthier's papers include his detailed diaries and journals and 119 original maps documenting the activities of the French army in America during 1781-1782.

1083. Cox, Richard J. "A Checklist of Revolutionary War Manuscript Collections Accessioned and Catalogued Since Publication of the Manuscript Collections of the Maryland Historical Society." *Maryland Historical Magazine* 71 (Summer 1976): 252-263.

Cox lists fifty-five collections. Entries include collection and record series titles; inclusive dates; volume; and content notes.

1084. Daniels, Mary F. "The Lafayette Collection at Cornell." *Quarterly Journal of the Library of Congress* 29 (April 1972): 95-137.

Daniels describes and provides representative examples of the more than 10,000 items of the Marquis de Lafayette Collection donated to Cornell by Arthur H. and Mary Dean. Daniels' examples cover all major areas of the Marquis' life and career.

1085. D'Innocenzo, Michael and John Turner. "The Peter Van Gaasbeek Papers: A Resource for Early New York History, 1771-97." *New York History* 47 (April 1966): 153-159.

Van Gaasbeek was active in politics during the American Revolution and early federal period. Central to the collection are some 1,000 letters to and from Van Gaasbeek dated from the 1770s to the 1790s.

1086. Dippel, Horst. "Sources in Germany for the Study of the American Revolution." *Quarterly Journal of the Library of Congress* 33 (July 1976): 199-217.

Dippel identifies German archives containing records and papers reflecting German opinion toward the American Revolution and relating to its commerce, military operations, and politics.

1087. Hamer, Philip M. "Henry Laurens of South Carolina -- the Man and His Papers." *Massachusetts Historical Society Proceedings* 77 (1965): 3-14.

Laurens was active in political affairs during the American Revolution and served as South Carolina's representative to the Continental Congress. Hamer provides an overview of Laurens' papers and identifies repositories holding them.

1088. Lacrocq, Nelly. "Maps and Drawings at the Bibliotèque de l'Inspection du Génie." *Library of Congress Quarterly Journal* 30 (October 1973): 253-255.

This article describes, in general terms, eight-two maps of North America and the Antilles depicting military operations during the U.S. Revolutionary War.

1089. Leventhal, Herbert and James E. Mooney. "A Bibliography of Loyalist Source Material in the United States: Part I." American Antiquarian Society *Proceedings* 85 (April 1975): 73-308; Part II, (October 1975): 405-460; Part III, 86 (October 1976): 343-390; Part IV, 90 (April 1980): 101-162; and Part V, (October 1980): 393-439.

A series of articles describing manuscript collections in the U.S. relating to Loyalists of the Revolutionary War. Using a state-by-state approach, parts 1-3 describe materials in Atlantic coast states, with part 4 covering the remainder of the U.S. Part V is an index to parts 1-4.

1090. Metzdorf, Robert F. "The Chauncey Family Papers." *Yale University Library Gazette* 29 (April 1955): 168-169.

These papers date from the 1700s to the 1820s and document the American Revolution in Connecticut; legal and church history; and the early history of Yale University.

1091. "North Carolina Revolutionary Military Papers." *North Carolinian* 7

(December 1961): 886-898.

1092. Peckham, Howard H. "Military Papers in the Clements Library."
Military Affairs 2 (Fall 1938): 126-130.
   Peckham describes twenty-three collections of papers and records
relating to the U.S. Revolutionary War. Many of these papers are
particularly valuable for documenting the British side of the war.

1093. Pognon, Edmond and Edwige Archier. "Maps and Plans in the Biblio-
thèque Nationale." *Quarterly Journal of the Library of Congress* 30
(October 1973): 248-251.
   The authors provide a checklist of twenty-nine manuscript maps relating
to the U.S. Revolutionary War. Entries include title, size, a repository
location, and brief descriptive comments.

1094. "Principal Manuscript Collections in the Emmet Library." *Bulletin of the
New York Public Library* 1 (February 1897): 62-63.
   This is a checklist of what appears to be a small collection of individual
manuscripts bound into one volume. Most are dated from the mid-to-late
18th century and relate to military events of the American Revolution.

1095. Ristow, Walter W. "Maps of the American Revolution: A Preliminary
Survey." *Quarterly Journal of the Library of Congress* 28 (July 1971):
196-215.
   Ristow reviews the types of maps that may be found in the Library of
Congress collection documenting the Revolutionary War. He includes
military survey maps; tactical maps; navigation and harbor maps; cities
and town maps; road maps; and published atlases.

1096. Schwartz, Gregory C. "The Haldimand Papers on Microfilm." *Dartmouth
College Library Bulletin* 25 (April 1985): 110-116.
   Sir Frederick Haldimand served in the British army from 1750-1785.
The 115-roll microfilm set of his papers documents British military
activities during the American Revolution.

1097. Sellers, John R. "Lafayette Papers at the Library of Congress." *Quarterly
Journal of the Library of Congress* 29 (April 1972): 138-154.
   Sellers identifies several collections that contain letters and related
documents to, from, or about the Marquis de Lafayette. He comments
on the research values of each in the narrative and ends the article with
a checklist of these collection titles.

1098. Swem, Earl G. "Newly Discovered George Rogers Clark Material."
Mississippi Valley Historical Review 1 (June 1914): 95-97.
   This is a checklist of record series titles of the George Rogers Clark

papers discovered in the Virginia State Auditor's Office and subsequently deposited in the Virginia State Library. The materials date from 1766 to 1787.

1099. Thomas, William S. "American Revolutionary Diaries, also Journals, Narratives, Autobiographies, Reminiscences, and Personal Memoirs." *New York Historical Society Quarterly Bulletin* 6 (April 1922): 32-35; (July 1922): 61-71; (October 1922): 101-107; (January 1923): 143-147; and 7 (April 1923): 28-35; and (July 1923): 63-71.

This series cites diaries and similar accounts, both published and unpublished, alphabetically by authors' surnames. Most are held by the New York Historical Society. The last installment is an index to the previous five.

Civil War

1100. Bentley, Esther F. "A Diplomat's Mailbag: William Lewis Dayton in Paris, 1861-1864." *Princeton University Library Chronicle* 20 (Spring 1959): 145-153.

The Dayton Collection at Princeton University contains mostly his correspondence and personal financial papers from Paris, France, where he was U.S. minister between 1861-1864. The article focuses on his letters concerning France's reactions to the U.S. Civil War.

1101. Black, Patti C., and Maxyne M. Grimes. "Civil War Manuscripts in the Mississippi Department of Archives and History." *Journal of Mississippi History* 23 (July 1961): 164-195.

The authors list manuscript collections alphabetically by title with entries including volume, type of materials statement, inclusive dates, and content note. This article was published as a separate guide in 1962.

1102. Booth, A. B. "Louisiana Confederate Military Records." *Louisiana Historical Quarterly* 4 (July 1921): 369-418.

This article provides some insight to CSA military records in Louisiana. It includes a checklist of CSA military units organized in Louisiana and an index to battles fought in the state.

1103. Callahan, J. Morton. "The Confederate Diplomatic Archives -- The 'Pickett Papers.'" *South Atlantic Quarterly* 2 (January 1903): 1-9.

Callahan relates the provenance of a body of Confederate States of America diplomatic correspondence sold to the U.S. government after the Civil War by John T. Pickett. The article concludes with a checklist of record series.

1104. Cappon, Lester J. "A Note on Confederate Ordnance Records." *Military Affairs* 4 (1940): 94-102.

   The author relates the provenance of these records which are now in the U.S. National Archives. He reviews their informational content and concludes the article with a checklist of the 147 volumes of Confederate ordnance records.

1105. Carter, George E. "The Breyfogle Papers." *Dartmouth College Library Bulletin* 11 (November 1970): 40-45.

   Carter describes the diaries and letters of Joshua D. Breyfogle. Among the diaries is one kept on a journey to California in 1849, but the rest, plus the correspondence, document his service in the Union army during the Civil War.

1106. Decker, Eugene D. "A Selected, Annotated Bibliography of Sources in the Kansas State Historical Society Pertaining to Kansas in the Civil War." *Emporia State Research Studies* 9 (June 1961): 7-95.

   Most of the citations are published works, but section five, pages 67-92, describes unpublished materials including diaries, correspondence, military records, and reminiscences.

1107. Donnelly, Ralph E. "Confederate Muster Rolls." *Military Affairs* 16 (Fall 1952): 132-135.

   Donnelly relates the purpose, use of, and content of Confederate army muster rolls. He concludes his article with a checklist of muster rolls in the Library of Congress' Manuscript Division.

1108. Harwell, Richard B. "A Brief Calendar of the Jefferson Davis Papers in the Keith M. Read Confederate Collection of the Emory University Library." *Journal of Mississippi History* 4 (January 1942): 20-30.

   The calendar lists sixty-eight letters to, from, or about Davis dated from the 1850s to 1905. Most are Civil War-related. Harwell also includes a brief description of other Confederate material in the Read Collection.

1109. Hecht, Arthur. "Confederate Postal Records in the National Archives." *Georgia Historical Quarterly* 45 (June 1961): 186-189.

   Hecht provides a short history of the Confederate postal service and concludes the article by listing seventeen extant record series with inclusive dates and volume.

1110. Irvine, Dallas D. "The Archives of the War Department: Repository of Captured Confederate Archives." *Military Affairs* 10 (Spring 1946): 93-111.

   This is a history of the capture and disposition of Confederate military records by Union forces and the federal government. Irvine briefly describes some of the records in the narrative.

1111. Irvine, Dallas D. "The Fate of Confederate Archives." *American Historical Review* 44 (July 1939): 823-841.

The article traces the provenance of the personal and official papers of Jefferson Davis, Robert E. Lee, and the CSA Departments of State, War, Navy, Treasury, the Post Office, and the Congress.

1112. Jones, Robert H. "The American Civil War in the British Sessional Papers: Catalogue and Commentary." *Proceedings of the American Philosophical Society* 107 (October 1963): 415-426.

Jones has identified British governmental correspondence and reports relating to the Civil War and provided citations in a catalog format that includes item numbers, title or content statements, and the volume and page numbers of Sessional Papers.

1113. Joyner, Fred B. "A Brief Calendar of Jefferson Davis Papers in the Samuel Richey Confederate Collection of the Miami University Library, Oxford, Ohio." *Journal of Mississippi History* 25 (January 1963): 15-32.

There are 178 letters to and from Jefferson Davis calendared in this article. Several of those to Davis are from CSA generals Beauregard, Bragg, Joseph Johnston, Kirby Smith, William Thomas, and others. The letters date from 1847 to 1890.

1114. Kaplan, Milton. "The Case of the Disappearing Photographers." *Quarterly Journal of the Library of Congress* 24 (January 1967): 41-45.

An article about a small collection of Civil War photographs taken by an unknown photography studio, Hass & Peale of Morris Island, and Hilton Head, South Carolina. The article concludes with a checklist of the fifty-eight photos in the collection.

1115. Lokke, Carl L. "The Captured Confederate Records Under Francis Lieber." *American Archivist* 9 (1946): 277-319.

A lengthy article explaining the capture of Confederate records by the U.S. after the Civil War, the selection of an archivist to care for them, brief descriptions of the records, and how they were used.

1116. McMurry, Richard M. "Disappointment in History: The Papers of John Bell Hood." *Prologue* 4 (Fall 1972): 161-164.

The papers of CSA general John B. Hood are in the U.S. National Archives in Record Group 109. This article describes how they got there and a little about what is in them and what is missing.

1117. Milhollen, Hirst. "The Brady-Handy Collection." *Quarterly Journal of Current Acquisitions* 13 (May 1956): 135-142.

Milhollen describes a collection of nearly 10,000 photographic images of Washington, D.C., and Civil War scenes and personalities taken by Levin C. Handy and his uncle Mathew B. Brady. The article concludes with a series checklist noting specific names and places.

1118. Milhollen, Hirst. "The Mathew B. Brady Collection." *Quarterly Journal of Current Acquisitions* 1 (April 1944): 15-19.
This article is mostly about the provenance of the Brady photograph collection held by the Library of Congress, but does provide some descriptive information about the collection's contents.

1119. Parker, Elmer O. "Confederate Muster Rolls." *Military Affairs* 28 (Summer 1964): 78-82.
Parker explains the purpose, the different types, use, and content of muster roles prepared by the Confederate forces.

1120. "Personal Narratives of the Civil War in the Collection of the Vermont Historical Society." *Vermont History* 31 (April 1963): 117-121.
This is a checklist presented alphabetically by title or author. Entries include volume, document type, dates, military units, and place of origin.

1121. Robinson, William M., Jr. "Confederate Judicial Records." *American Archivist* 4 (April 1941): 117-121.
An account of Robinson's personal search for court records of the Confederacy. The article identifies some of the record series he found, but many of the records could not be located during the Federal Records Survey of the late 1930s.

1122. Weathersford, John. "Ohio and the Civil War in Manuscripts." *Civil War History* 3 (September 1957): 307-313.
The article describes two groups of manuscripts, those of Ohioans in the war and those describing the war in Ohio. The author cites collection titles and indicates the quality and quantity of the manuscripts in each.

1123. Winschel, Terrence J. "The Archival Holdings of Vicksburg National Military Park: A Brief History." *Civil War Regiments* 2 (No. 1 1992): 75-77.
The holdings include Confederate and Union soldiers' reminiscences and correspondence; diaries; and regimental historical files.

1124. Young, James H. "Alexander H. Stephens Papers in the Emory University Library." *Emory University Quarterly* 2 (March 1946): 30-37.
Stephens was vice president of the Confederate States of America. His papers include his correspondence and a diary kept while he was a prisoner at Fort Warren after the Civil War.

Political Collections

General

1125. Bander, Ingram. "Sidney Edward Mezes and 'The Inquiry.'" *Journal of Modern History* 11 (June 1939): 199-202.

   "The Inquiry" was a U.S. committee formed to represent U.S. interests in negotiating the peace treaty of WWI. Mezes was its director. This article describes a collection of the group's papers.

1126. Bassett, T. D. Seymour. "The George Perkins Marsh Papers." *Dartmouth College Library Bulletin* 10 (November 1969): 9-14.

   Marsh was a 19th-century politician and man of letters. Bassett locates Marsh papers in several collections and repositories.

1127. Brand, Katherine E. "The Papers of Oscar S. Straus." *Quarterly Journal of Current Acquisitions* 7 (February 1950): 3-6.

   Straus was an American diplomat and envoy in the 1890s and early 1900s and again after WWI. His papers include twenty feet of correspondence, diaries, photographs, scrapbooks, and manuscripts of his books. The materials date from 1856 into the 1920s.

1128. Brescia, Anthony M. "Richard Rush (1780-1859): A Checklist of Sources." *Princeton University Library Chronicle* 32 (Spring 1971): 145-152.

   Brescia locates Rush manuscript material in thirty-five foreign and U.S. repositories. Entries note the titles of collections containing Rush correspondence or manuscripts.

1129. Brescia, Anthony M. "Richard Rush (1780-1859): Manuscript Letters in English Repositories." *Princeton University Library Chronicle* 35 (Spring 1974): 314-316.

   Brescia identifies manuscript collections that contain Richard Rush correspondence in four British libraries, plus letters that may be found in the Boston Public Library.

1130. Bryson, Thomas A. "The Walter George Smith Papers in the Archives of the American Catholic Historical Society." *Records of the American Catholic Historical Society of Philadelphia* 80 (December 1969): 203-209.

Smith was an attorney specializing in divorce law and active in Republican politics. His papers (1900-1922) cover his youth, his legal practice, and his service at the Paris Peace Conference, the League of Nations, and with the Department of the Interior.

1131. Camden, Thomas E. "The John Parker Hale Papers." *Historical New Hampshire* 38 (Winter 1983): 244-250.

Hale was an abolitionist, early Republican, and U.S. presidential nominee in 1852. His papers span the years 1814-1915 and include correspondence, speeches, certificates, and scrapbooks. An inventory of the collection concludes the article.

1132. Cox, Steven. "Nathaniel P. Rogers and the Rogers Collection." *Historical New Hampshire* 33 (Spring 1978): 52-61.

Nathaniel P. Rogers was an abolitionist. His correspondence in the Haverford College Library documents his life and the course of the abolitionist movement. Cox includes an inventory of his letters.

1133. Danky, James P., ed. "Resources for Scholars: Collections of Alternative and Left Materials: Parts I and Part II." *Library Quarterly* 59 (January 1989): 47-63; and (April 1989): 148-161.

The collections described in this two-part article are the Southern California Library for Social Studies and Research, Los Angeles; the Alternative Press Collection, University of Connecticut at Storrs; and the Tamiment Institute and the Robert F. Wagner Labor Archives at New York University. All contain both published and unpublished materials.

1134. Frantz, Joe B. "The Sam Houston Letters: A Corner of Texas in Princeton." *Princeton University Library Chronicle* 33 (Autumn 1971): 18-29.

This article describes an unspecified number of Houston letters covering the period 1838-1861.

1135. Hutson, James H. "Pierce Butler's Records of the Federal Constitutional Convention." *Quarterly Journal of the Library of Congress* 37 (Winter 1980): 64-73.

Hutson analyzes Butler's papers as a contemporary source of the convention's proceedings and reports on the types of information they contain. Pierce Butler was a South Carolina delegate to the convention.

1136. Lee, Charles E., and Ruth S. Green. "A Guide to the Upper House Journals of the South Carolina General Assembly, 1721-1775." *South Carolina Historical Magazine* 67 (October 1966): 187-202.

This is the first in a series of guides to South Carolina's colonial legislative assemblies. The compilers provide an introductory essay in which they relate the provenance of the records and note the location of archival copies. The entries are presented in assembly number order and include extant journals and their locations. Similar guides to other South Carolina legislative bodies follow in order of their appearance:

1. "A Guide to South Carolina Council Journals, 1671-1775." *South Carolina Historical Magazine* 68 (January 1967): 1-13.

2. "A Guide to the Commons House Journals of the South Carolina General Assembly, 1692-1721." *South Carolina Historical Magazine* 68 (April 1967): 85-96.

3. "A Guide to the Commons House Journals of the South Carolina General Assembly, 1721-1775." *South Carolina Historical Magazine* 68 (July 1967): 165-183.

1137. Neubeck, Deborah K. "MHS Microfilms the Papers of John Lind's Mission to Mexico." *Minnesota History* 42 (Winter 1971): 301-308.
John Lind was Woodrow Wilson's special envoy to Mexico in 1913-1914. Lind's papers for this period include correspondence, reports, and published materials, all relating to Mexican public affairs.

1138. Newberry Library. "The Papers of Lambert Tree." *Newberry Library Bulletin* 8 (December 1947): 3-8.
Tree was an Illinois judge, politician, and diplomat. His papers consist mostly of correspondence dating from the 1850s to 1910.

1139. Norton, Margaret C. "The General Assembly and Its Records." *Illinois Libraries* 22 (January 1940): 25-29; (April 1940): 17-22; (May 1940): 22-28; and (June 1940): 23-28.
A series of articles relating the history of the Illinois legislature and offering a checklist of records from 1809 to the 1930s. Checklist entries include record series titles, volume, inclusive dates, and explanatory notes.

1140. Otto, Kathryn. "The Richard Olsen Richards Papers at the South Dakota Historical Research Center." *South Dakota History* 9 (Spring 1979): 153-156.
Richards was a Progressive Republican active in state politics. His papers include correspondence and clipping files documenting his political activities and especially his sponsorship of a direct primary law.

1141. Riggs, John B. "The Henry L. Stimson Collection." *Yale University*

Library Gazette 27 (October 1952): 55-65.

Stimson's papers reflect his early life; his position in William Howard Taft's cabinet; as governor-general of the Philippines; secretary of state in the Hoover administration; and his role in Nicaraguan affairs, the London Naval Conference, and politics in general from 1900-1933.

1142. Shewmaker, Kenneth E. "The Sherman Adams Papers." *Dartmouth College Library Bulletin* 9 (April 1969): 88-92.

Adams' papers date from 1918 to the 1950s and include press releases, correspondence, speeches, memoranda, notes of telephone conversations and meetings, appointment books, and scrapbooks.

1143. Sommer, Linda M. "Dakota Resources: The Pickler Family Papers and the Humphrey Family Papers at the South Dakota Historical Society." *South Dakota History* 24 (Summer 1994): 115-134.

These two families were early settlers of Faulkton, Dakota Territory. Both were involved in territorial and national Republican politics, temperance societies, and the state's women's suffrage movement. The papers date from the 1880s to the 1940s.

1144. Stewart, Kate M. "The Daniel Scott Lamont Papers." *Quarterly Journal of Current Acquisitions* 17 (February 1960): 63-83.

Lamont was Grover Cleveland's private secretary and secretary of war in Cleveland's second administration. Stewart provides examples of how Lamont's letters illustrate his political career and his business ventures in the railroad industry.

1145. Tunis, Mildred C. "The Papers of James Fairbanks Colby." *Dartmouth College Library Bulletin* 10 (November 1969): 55-61.

Colby was an attorney, professor of law at Dartmouth, and active in Republican politics. His papers include a diary/cashbook and his correspondence. The materials date from the 1860s to 1910.

1146. Vance, Joseph C. "The William Gibbs McAdoo Papers." *Quarterly Journal of Current Acquisitions* 15 (May 1958): 168-176.

McAdoo is remembered as Woodrow Wilson's treasury secretary and as a leader in the Democratic Party. McAdoo's papers include reports, speeches, memoranda, correspondence, scrapbooks, and clipping files. Vance notes many of the topics and events covered by the papers.

1147. Wight, Ruth. "The Papers of Grenville Clark." *Dartmouth College Library Bulletin* 9 (November 1968): 57-61.

Clark was an attorney and active in Democratic politics. His papers document his work in President Roosevelt's New Deal programs; the civil rights movement of the 1960s; legal causes and civic projects; and international peace conferences.

1148. Wilensky, Norman M. "The Charles Dewey Hilles Papers." *Yale University Library Gazette* 36 (July 1961): 1-12.

Hilles was a Republican Party leader during the early decades of the 20th century. His papers include mostly correspondence and clipping files documenting his work as secretary to Pres. William H. Taft and as chairman of the Republican National Committee.

1149. Winther, Oscar O. "The Joseph Lane Papers in the Robert S. Ellison Collection." *Indiana University Bookman* 1 (January 1956): 16-26.

Originally from Indiana, Lane went west and became active in Oregon politics. His papers date 1848-1861. Specific documents are cited, but the article describes Lane's political views more than his papers.

Communists and Socialists

1150. Aptheker, Herbert. "The W.E.B. DuBois Papers." *Political Affairs* 44 (March 1966): 36-45.

Aptheker cites thirteen record series that make up the DuBois papers. He describes the correspondence in some detail and concludes the article by locating other DuBois collections.

1151. Barghoorn, Frederick C. "Letters from and to Leon Trotsky." *Yale University Library Gazette* 57 (October 1982): 72-77.

The author calls attention to a collection of 112 letters to and from Trotsky dating from the 1930s. In describing their contents, Barghoorn notes that they focus primarily on the Communist movement in America and reflect Trotsky's Communist orthodoxy.

1152. Buhle, Paul and Robin D. G. Kelley. "The Oral History of the Left in the United States: A Survey and Interpretation." *Journal of American History* 76 (September 1989): 537-550.

While more interpretive than descriptive, this article does identify interviews with prominent leftists in the U.S., and names the repositories and collections holding the interviews.

1153. Friedberg, Gerald. "Sources for the Study of Socialism in America." *Labor History* 6 (Spring 1965): 159-165.

This article serves as a directory to Socialist sources by listing collections under states and repositories therein. Cited in most entries are collection titles, volume, inclusive dates, and brief content notes.

1154. "Material for the Study of U.S. Socialist and Labor History at the

Newberry Library." *Socialism and Democracy* 10 (1990): 169-173.

1155. Pratt, Norma F. "Archival Resources and Writing Immigrant American History: The Bund Archives of the Jewish Labor Movement." *Journal of Library History* 16 (Winter 1981): 166-176.
Pratt does not describe individual collections, but provides an overview of the holdings which document 19th- and 20th-century Socialist and labor movements in the U.S. and eastern Europe.

1156. Reed, Dale. "Holdings on United States Socialism and Communism at the Hoover Institution on War, Revolution, and Peace." *Labor History* 27 (Fall 1986): 506-528.
Reed provides record series titles, volume, inclusive dates, and content notes for the papers of George D. Herron, Alice Park, Eric Hass, Wallace Stegner, Boris I. Nicolaevsky, David Starr Jordan, Carl Gershman, Jay Lovestone, and many others.

1157. Schrecker, Ellen W. "Archival Sources for the Study of McCarthyism." *Journal of American History* 75 (June 1988): 197-208.
The author cites federal records such as FBI case files; collections of papers in presidential libraries, historical societies, and universities; and records of professional groups, labor unions, radio, T.V., and the motion picture industry.

1158. Swanson, Evadene B. "Some Sources for Northwest History: The Dight Papers." *Minnesota History* 25 (March 1944): 62-64.
Charles F. Dight was a physician who is best known for his Socialist politics and advocacy of socialized medicine. His papers include records of the Minnesota Eugenics Society and extensive personal correspondence reflecting his views.

1159. Van Heijenoort, Jean. "The History of Trotsky's Papers." *Harvard Library Bulletin* 28 (July 1980): 291-298.
The author relates how Leon Trotsky's papers came to Harvard, the reason some series were closed, and concludes with comments on the significance of the 17,500 letters opened to research in 1980.

Governors

1160. Bordin, Ruth B. "The G. Mennen Williams Papers." *American Archivist* 26 (July 1963): 345-354.
Bordin calls attention to Williams' papers at the University of Michigan. They include his correspondence, reports, speeches, press releases, financial records, photographs, and printed materials, mostly relating to

Williams' terms as governor of Michigan.

1161. Butterfield, Margaret. "Report on the Papers of Thomas E. Dewey." *University of Rochester Library Bulletin* 13 (Autumn 1957): 7-8.
    While brief, this article identifies correspondents represented in Dewey's personal correspondence files (1930-1950s) and calls attention to an accretion to his speech and clipping files.

1162. "Calendar of the Barbour Papers, 1811-1841." *Bulletin of the New York Public Library* 6 (January 1902): 22-33.
    This is a collection of correspondence to James Barbour, governor of Virginia, secretary of war, minister to England, and U.S. senator, from prominent American statesmen of the early 19th century. The calendar concludes with a list of correspondents.

1163. Cummings, Charles M. "The Scott Papers: An Inside View of Reconstruction." *Ohio History* 79 (Spring 1970): 112-118.
    Robert K. Scott was an Ohio physician and Civil War general, best known for his political activities while a Reconstruction governor in South Carolina. His papers mostly document his military, political, and business activities from the 1860s to the 1880s.

1164. "Descriptive List of the Papers of Governor Austin Blair." *Michigan History Magazine* 1 (October 1917): 133-148.
    The list identifies record series and volume, with occasional dates. The papers appear to be in the Detroit Public Library's Burton Historical Collection.

1165. Hanna, Archibald, Jr. "Governor John G. Brady's Alaska Papers." *Yale University Library Gazette* 32 (April 1958): 158-159.
    Hanna calls attention to the availability and research value of Brady's papers. Brady served as a missionary in Alaska, and, later, as territorial governor.

1166. Lacy, Harriet S. "The Langdon Papers, 1716-1841." *Historical New Hampshire* 22 (Autumn 1967): 55-65.
    These are the papers of John Langdon, American Revolution patriot, governor of New Hampshire, and U.S. senator. They document his business interests and his political activities.

1167. Lacy, Harriet S. "The Wentworth Papers, 1717-1940." *Historical New Hampshire* 23 (Spring 1968): 25-30.
    This collection is significant for the correspondence of Benning Wentworth and John Wentworth, both governors of New Hampshire. Most of the article is an inventory of the papers.

1168. Land, Robert H. "The Shelby Family Papers." *Quarterly Journal of Current Acquisitions* 11 (May 1954): 140-153.

These are mostly the papers of Isaac Shelby, Revolutionary War officer and governor of Kentucky. Dating from 1738 to 1865, the papers document his career and, according to Land, are especially useful for documenting early 19th-century frontier life.

1169. McConnell, Edward N., and James J. Julich. "The William L. Harding Collection Held by the State Archvies of Iowa." *Annals of Iowa* 45 (Winter 1980): 574-575.

Harding was governor of Iowa and the archives holds thirty-seven feet of his papers for the period 1917-1921. The collection includes correspondence, papers relating to Iowa's WWI war effort and agencies, and records concerning crime and criminals.

1170. McCree, Mary Lynn. "The Illinois Governors' Correspondence, 1933-1961." *Illinois Libraries* 44 (June 1962): 427-430.

The correspondence described is that of Governors Henry Horner, John H. Stelle, Dwight H. Green, Adlai E. Stevenson, and William G. Stratton. McCree lists several topical divisions found within the correspondence series.

1171. Mulroy, Kevin. "Papers of Selected New Jersey Politicians: A Summary Guide." *Journal of the Rutgers University Libraries* 48 (December 1986): 95-105.

The authors describe twenty-two collections of people who have served as governor of New Jersey or represented New Jersey in the U.S. House of Representatives or Senate. Entries include record series titles, volume, inclusive dates, and content notes.

1172. Norton, Margaret C. "Correspondence of Illinois Governors." *Illinois Libraries* 21 (September 1939): 14-16.

This correspondence series dates from 1809 to 1905 and represents records that were originally filed in the secretary of state's office. Norton discusses some of the subjects treated in the correspondence and concludes with an inventory of the records.

1173. Olsgaard, John N. "Dakota Resources: The Richard F. Kneip Papers at the University of South Dakota." *South Dakota History* 11 (Spring 1981): 142-144.

Kneip was a businessman, state legislator, governor of South Dakota, and ambassador to Singapore. His gubernatorial papers are described in this article. They date 1971-1978.

1174. Robrock, David P. "The James Allred Papers." *Texas Libraries* 41 (Fall

1979): 140-144.

Allred was an attorney, a former Texas governor, and active in state Democratic politics. His papers, dated 1921-1959, reflect his private law practice and his political service as a district attorney, attorney general of Texas, governor, and a federal judge.

1175. Schnare, Robert and Herbert Janick. "Buried Treasure: The Official Correspondence of the Connecticut Governors." *American Archivist* 34 (October 1971): 359-365.

The authors describe the correspondence files of nineteen Connecticut governors in the Connecticut State Library, Hartford, Connecticut. In doing so they comment on the strengths and weaknesses in the records of specific governors.

1176. Sorensen, Scott and John LeDoux. "The William Lloyd Harding Papers in the Sioux City Public Museum." *Annals of Iowa* 45 (Winter 1980): 568-573.

Harding was a two-term Republican governor of Iowa from 1916 to 1921. His papers include correspondence (1905-1934); biographical materials; photographs; scrapbooks; and diaries (1907-1965), kept by his wife Carrie Harding.

1177. Taylor, P. A. M. "A Politician's Life: The Papers of John Davis Long." *Proceedings of the Massachusetts Historical Society* 101 (1989): 71-96.

Long was an attorney, Republican governor and congressman from Massachusetts, and secretary of navy in the administration of Pres. McKinley. His papers include correspondence, scrapbooks, and journals. Most of the article is biographical.

1178. Winkler, Paul W. "The Pacific Northwest Collection of Winlock W. Miller, Jr." *Yale University Library Gazette* 26 (October 1951): 43-52.

This collection contains manuscripts documenting martial law in Washington Territory (1856); Washington territorial governor Isaac I. Stevens' correspondence; papers of Stevens' secretary, Elwood Evans; and papers relating to other Washington Territory personalities.

1179. Wolf, George D. "The Scranton Papers." *Western Pennsylvania Historical Magazine* 51 (October 1968): 365-376.

William W. Scranton was a governor of Pennsylvania and U.S. congressman. Wolf reviews key record series and the personalities and topics represented in them.

1180. Zorn, Roman J. "Arkansas Manuscripts: The Collected Papers of Charles H. Brough and Harmon L. Remmel." *Arkansas Historical Quarterly* 12 (Autumn 1953): 278-285.

Brough was governor of Arkansas 1916-1920. His papers reflect his political career and Democratic politics for the period. Remmel was a Republican and businessman. His papers, dated 1896-1925, reflect his career in Arkansas politics and business.

Presidents and Vice Presidents

1181. Adams, Thomas R. "The Bloomfield Moore-Monroe Manuscripts." *Pennsylvania University Library Chronicle* 19 (Spring 1953): 99-105.

Adams describes a small collection of letters of James Monroe, John Quincy Adams, John C. Calhoun, and Andrew Jackson found within a collection of books accumulated by Bloomfield Moore.

1182. Alsobrook, David E. "Resources for Recent Alabama History in the Jimmy Carter Library: A Preliminary Survey." *Alabama Review* 43 (April 1990): 122-134.

The author reviews record series that relate to Alabama in the Carter papers. He notes that four sources provide most records. They include the White House central file, Ray Jenkins White House file, and the White House subject and name files.

1183. Ashton, Kristina V. "The George Washington Papers." *Dartmouth College Library Bulletin* 16 (April 1975): 71-81.

Ashton provides a chronological calendar of Washington letters and reports at Dartmouth. Entries include correspondents names, length, and content notes.

1184. Bragdon, Henry W. "The Woodrow Wilson Collection." *Princeton University Library Chronicle* 7 (November 1945): 7-18.

This article describes the scope and content of Wilson materials at Princeton. It includes books, manuscript materials, and related items.

1185. Brand, Katherine E. "The Woodrow Wilson Collection." *Quarterly Journal of Current Acquisitions* 2 (February 1945): 3-10.

Brand relates the provenance of the Wilson papers in the Library of Congress, reviews the key record series in the collection, and mentions other collections of people associated with Wilson.

1186. Buford, Rowland. "The Papers of the Presidents." *American Archivist* 13 (July 1950): 195-211.

Buford locates the papers of George Washington through Franklin D. Roosevelt. His description includes volume, inclusive dates, and occasional access notes.

1187. Bullock, Helen Duprey. "The Papers of John G. Nicolay, Lincoln's Secretary." *Quarterly Journal of Current Acquisitions* 7 (May 1950): 3-8.

Most of this collection is correspondence, both copies and originals, of letters to and from Lincoln. There are also scrapbooks and manuscripts of Nicolay's historical writings.

1188. Bullock, Helen Duprey. "The Papers of Thomas Jefferson." *American Archivist* 4 (October 1941): 238-249.

The author discusses the dispersal of Jefferson's papers and the principal collections of them at the Library of Congress, the Massachusetts Historical Society, the University of Virginia, and the Missouri Historical Society.

1189. Bullock, Helen Duprey. "The Robert Todd Lincoln Collection of the Papers of Abraham Lincoln." *Quarterly Journal of Current Acquisitions* 5 (November 1947): 3-5.

This collection opened for research in 1947 had been closed for twenty-one years after Robert Lincoln's death. Bullock relates the collection's provenance and analyzes the types of materials found among its 18,000 items.

1190. Butterfield, Lyman H. "The Jefferson-Adams Correspondence in the Adams Manuscript Trust." *Quarterly Journal of Current Acquisitions* 5 (February 1948): 3-6.

This author describes an exchange of correspondence between Thomas Jefferson, John Adams, Abigail Adams, and John Quincy Adams from 1785 to 1826. The article also publicizes the availability of a microfilm edition of this correspondence.

1191. "Calendar of the Jackson-Lewis Letters, 1806-1864." *Bulletin of the New York Public Library* 4 (September 1900): 292-320.

The calendar is alphabetical by surname of author with entries including place of origin, date, name of recipient, and content note. The letters are primarily between Pres. Andrew Jackson and William B. Lewis, but there are other correspondents too.

1192. Clark, Alexander P. "The Woodrow Wilson Collection, a Survey of Additions since 1945." *Princeton University Library Chronicle* 17 (Spring 1956): 173-182.

Clark reviews the Wilson materials, mostly manuscripts, which Princeton has acquired since Henry Bragdon described the collection in 1945. Most of the acquisitions came from people associated with Wilson. Clark cites many of these small collections.

1193. Cox, Richard J. "Presidential Letters." *Maryland Historical Magazine* 68

(Winter 1973): 438-439.
Cox reviews collections in the Maryland Historical Society that contain
letters of U.S. presidents. The David Baile Warden and William Wirt
Collections are noted as the richest in presidential correspondence.

1194. Culbertson, Thomas J. "The Hayes Presidential Center Library and
Archives." *Hayes Historical Journal* 10 (Winter 1991): 40-49.

1195. Dailey, Wallace F. "The Theodore Roosevelt Collection at Harvard."
Manuscripts 29 (Summer 1977): 146-154.
Dailey provides a description of the Roosevelt manuscript collection at
Harvard while noting that it contains photographs, sketches, rare books,
printed materials, and research notes of Roosevelt's biographers.

1196. Eaton, Dorothy S. "George Washington Papers." *Quarterly Journal of the
Library of Congress* 22 (January 1965): 3-26.
Mostly a description of the scholarly uses of Washington papers and
their provenance. The footnotes of this article are useful for understanding the papers' provenance and locating Washington items in private
collections and in other repositories.

1197. Edelstein, J. M. "Lincoln Papers in the Stern Bequest." *Quarterly
Journal of Current Acquisitions* 19 (December 1961): 7-14.
Edelstein reviews a large accretion of Abraham Lincoln legal documents
and correspondence. The article identifies and reproduces excerpts of
some of the more significant items.

1198. Elzy, Martin I. "LBJ Library: Local History Resources Found Nowhere
Else." *History News* 35 (February 1980): 9-11.
Elzy points out presidential papers, oral histories, and related national
sources that are rich in local history.

1199. Fitzgerald, Carol B. "The Presidential Papers, George Washington to
Calvin Coolidge: An Introduction to the Presidential Papers Microfilm
Series." *History Teacher* 17 August 1984): 545-566.
Fitzgerald's description of the microfilm editions of presidential papers
held by the Library of Congress includes number of reels and documents
filmed, inclusive dates, gaps in holdings, and citations for guides,
biographies, and letter press editions.

1200. George, Jr., Joseph. "Lincoln Family Documents in the F.J. Dreer
Collection." *Illinois Historical Journal* 79 (Summer 1986): 139-142.
The author cites Lincoln-related items in the Dreer Collection, a 15,000
item collection originally known as the Ferdinand J. Dreer Autograph
Collection. Dreer donated the materials to the Historical Society of

Pennsylvania in 1890.

1201. Gillespie, Veronica M. "T. R. on Film." *Quarterly Journal of the Library of Congress* 34 (January 1977): 39-51.

Gillespie describes the Library of Congress' collection of motion pictures with footage of Theodore Roosevelt. She reports that there are 375 titles in the Roosevelt Collection. Her article concludes with a checklist of selected film titles.

1202. Haight, David J. "The Papers of C.D. Jackson: A Glimpse at President Eisenhower's Psychological Warfare Expert." *Manuscripts* 28 (Winter 1976): 27-37.

Charles D. Jackson was a publishing executive who joined the Eisenhower administration in 1953. The papers are rich in correspondence between Eisenhower and Jackson on foreign affairs and economic policy and psychological warfare.

1203. Hill, Robert W., and Lewis M. Stark. "Washingtoniana in the New York Public Library." *Bulletin of the New York Public Library* 61 (February 1957): 73-80.

An overview of George Washington manuscripts, correspondence, art, music, notebooks and journals, and books from Washington's library.

1204. Hirshon, Arnold. "The Scope, Accessibility and History of Presidential Papers." *Government Publications Review* 1 (Fall 1974): 363-390.

This article concludes with a checklist locating and commenting on the scope of presidential papers from those of George Washington to those of Richard Nixon.

1205. Johnson, Neil M., and Phillip Lagerquist. "Resources at the Harry S. Truman Library on Western Issues and Programs." *Government Publications Review* 7A (March/April 1980): 159-166.

The authors cite manuscript collections and oral histories relating to Indians, water resources, migratory labor, and relocation of the Japanese living in the U.S. during WWII. The records cited date from 1942 to the 1960s.

1206. Little, Thomas. "The Theodore Roosevelt Collection at Harvard." *Harvard Library Bulletin* 5 (Autumn 1951): 376-378.

A review of the types of materials found in the Roosevelt papers in Harvard's Widener and Houghton Libraries.

1207. Lloyd, David D. "Presidential Papers and Presidential Libraries." *Manuscripts* 8 (Fall 1955): 4-15.

Most of this article discusses presidential libraries in general. It concludes, however, with a listing of known presidential papers, their volume, and institutions holding them.

1208. Marchman, Watt P. "The Hayes Memorial Library." *Autograph Collectors Journal* 3 (October 1950): 6-10.
    The library holds the correspondence, diaries, scrapbooks, and photographs of President Rutherford B. Hayes and his wife. Strengths in publishing holdings are also mentioned.

1209. Marchman, Watt P. "The Rutherford B. Hayes Memorial Library." *College and Research Libraries* 17 (May 1956): 224-227.
    An overview of the library's holdings with an emphasis on the Hayes papers. The author also mentions the titles of several other manuscript collections of Hayes' associates.

1210. Marchman, Watt P., and James H. Rodabaugh. "Collections of the Rutherford B. Hayes State Memorial." *Ohio History* 71 (July 1962): 151-157.
    This article describes museum collections as well as the library and manuscript holdings. The description of manuscript collections includes many collection titles with mention of record series, volume, inclusive dates, and content notes.

1211. Newland, Chester A. "The Lyndon Baines Johnson Library: New Dimensions of the Presidency and Presidential Papers." *Library Chronicle of the University of Texas at Austin* New Series 1 (March 1970): 13-23.
    Newland, then director of the newly opened presidential library, gives an overview of the holdings.

1212. Owsley, Harriet C. "Jackson Manuscripts in the Tennessee Historical Society and the Manuscript Division of the Tennessee State Library and Archives: A Bibliographical Note." *Tennessee Historical Quarterly* 26 (Spring 1967): 97-100.
    A review of Andrew Jackson correspondence that has been found or collected by the society and archives between 1935 and 1967.

1213. Pitzer, Donald E. "An Introduction to the Harding Papers." *Ohio History* 75 (Spring/Summer 1966): 76-84.
    Pitzer relates the provenance of President Warren Harding's papers from family control, to the Harding Memorial Association, and to the Ohio Historical Society. He comments on both the strengths and weaknesses of the papers, along with their research values.

1214. Pratt, Harry Edward. "Lincolniana in the Illinois State Historical Library." *Journal of the Illinois State Historical Society* 46 (Winter

1953): 373-400.

The article describes the more than 1,000 letters and documents in Lincoln's hand; the papers of the Abraham Lincoln Association; the National Lincoln Monument Association papers; and several collections of personal papers from Lincoln's associates.

1215. Reeves, Thomas C. "The Search for the Chester A. Arthur Papers." *Wisconsin Magazine of History* 55 (Summer 1972): 310-319.

An article relating the provenance of the extant Arthur papers. Probably a key article for anyone planning research on Arthur. It was reprinted in *Manuscripts* 25 (Summer 1973): 171-185.

1216. Richards, Gertrude. "New Letters of George Washington to Benjamin Lincoln." *Harvard Library Bulletin* 10 (Winter 1956): 30-72.

Richards gives the provenance of fifty-six Washington letters in the Galen L. Stone Collection at Harvard. She concludes the article with a calendar of the letters noting their dates, place of origin, the correspondents, and content notes.

1217. Rogers, Earl M. "The Papers of Henry A. Wallace." *Books at Iowa* 21 (November 1974): 43-51.

The University of Iowa's collection includes over 50,000 pieces of Wallace's correspondence, speeches, memoranda, political cartoons, diaries, scrapbooks, photographs, clippings, and other published materials dating from the 1880s to the 1960s.

1218. Rowland, Buford. "The Papers of the Presidents." *American Archivist* 13 (July 1950): 195-211.

Rowland locates and describes the papers of U.S. presidents from George Washington through Franklin D. Roosevelt.

1219. Shelley, Fred. "The Chester A. Arthur Papers." *Quarterly Journal of Current Acquisitions* 16 (May 1959): 115-122.

Shelley notes the paucity of Arthur papers and reviews the efforts of the Library of Congress to locate the materials it holds. He identifies some of the key items in the library's collection, most of which came from the president's grandson, Chester A. Arthur III.

1220. Shipman, Fred W. "The Roosevelt Papers." *Quarterly Journal of Speech* 34 (April 1948): 137-142.

This article describes the papers of Franklin D. Roosevelt. While noting they include Roosevelt's family and private papers, Shipman focuses on the papers documenting Roosevelt's political career.

1221. Sifton, Paul G. "Recent Additions to the James Madison Papers at the

Library of Congress." *Quarterly Journal of the Library of Congress* 37 (Spring 1980): 265-273.

Sifton reports on Madison papers acquired since the library microfilmed its Madison Collection in 1964. New materials cover topics such as the arts, agricultural societies, the Bonus Bill, Russian-American relations, and the Virginia Convention of 1829.

1222. Smith, Russell M. "The Andrew Johnson Papers." *Quarterly Journal of Current Acquisitions* 17 (November 1959): 13-16.

Smith notes that the majority of the papers document Johnson's presidency. He reviews the provenance of the papers and identifies correspondence files, speeches, amnesty records, scrapbooks, and military records as the key record series.

1223. Smith, Thomas A. "Before Hyde Park: The Rutherford B. Hayes Library." *American Archivist* 43 (Fall 1980): 485-488.

The article calls attention to the research potential of the Hays Library in Fremont, Ohio, with the 164 linear feet of Rutherford B. Hayes' papers as its key collection.

1224. Snyder, Charles M. "Forgotten Fillmore Papers Examined: Sources for Reinterpretation of a Little Known President." *American Archivist* 32 (January 1969): 11-14.

Snyder calls attention to some newly found Millard Fillmore papers and relates their provenance. He limits description to volume, inclusive dates, and selected content statements.

1225. Stewart, Kate M. "The William Howard Taft Papers." *Quarterly Journal of Current Acquisitions* 15 (November 1957): 1-11.

The Taft papers document the president's public career and that of his family from the 1870s to the 1930s. Record series include letterbooks, family papers, general correspondence, presidential files, and miscellaneous papers, all described briefly by Stewart.

1226. Thweatt, John H. "The James K. Polk Papers: A Bibliographic Note." *Tennessee Historical Quarterly* 33 (Spring 1974): 93-98.

Thweatt describes a collection of materials from Polk's home in Columbia, Tennessee, and now located in the Tennessee State Library and Archives. The papers (1825-1849) include financial records, reports, correspondence, and appointment papers.

1227. Toner, J. M. "Some Account of George Washington's Library and Manuscript Records and Their Dispersion from Mount Vernon, with an Excerpt of Three Months from His Diary in 1774 While Attending the First Continental Congress, with Notes." *Annual Report of the American*

Historical Association for the Year 1892 (1893): 73-169.

Pages 73-111 give a thorough accounting of the dispersal of Washington's papers after his death. The diary is reproduced on pages 113-155 while pages 157-169 are an index to the entire report.

1228. Wanning, Andrews. "The Edward M. House Collection." *Yale University Library Gazette* 7 (July 1932): 4-9.

House was secretary and personal advisor to President Woodrow Wilson. Among House's papers are his diary; correspondence, including many letters from Wilson; meeting minutes; and photographs.

1229. Wetherbee, S. Ambrose. "Lincoln Collection: Illinois State Archives." *Illinois Libraries* 25 (February 1943): 114-125.

A checklist of materials relating to Abraham Lincoln presented alphabetically by document or record series title. Entries include correspondents' or authors' names, inclusive dates, and content statements.

1230. Wright, Marcia. "The Benjamin Harrison Papers." *Quarterly Journal of Current Acquisitions* 18 (May 1961): 121-125.

The Harrison papers span the years 1833 to 1901 and cover all aspects of the president's life. They include correspondence, telegrams, messages, reports, shorthand notebooks, and speeches.

Representatives and Senators

1231. Adams, Thomas R. "The Samuel J. Randall Papers." *Pennsylvania History* 21 (January 1954): 45-54.

Randall was a U.S. congressman from Pennsylvania and leader in the Democratic Party in the late 19th-century. His papers are mostly correspondence files from the 1840s to the 1890s reflecting the major political issues of that period.

1232. Bowen, Laurel G., and Mary Michals. "The Scott Wike Lucas Collection: Manuscripts and Audiovisual Resources." *Illinois Historical Journal* 77 (Autumn 1984): 193-196.

Scott Lucas was an Illinois congressman and senator. His papers include over 600 boxes of correspondence, reports, subject files, photographs, sound recordings, and motion pictures dating from 1918 to 1968 and documenting his political career.

1233. Brown, Deward C. "The Sam Rayburn Papers: A Preliminary Investigation." *American Archivist* 35 (July/October 1972): 331-336.

Brown writes about the Rayburn papers in the Sam Rayburn Library in

Bonham, Texas. He notes that the papers date from 1906 to 1961, but 85 percent of the collection dates from 1940. He also reports on strengths and weaknesses of the collection, with comments on specific series and topics.

1234. Clark, Alexander P. "The Samuel L. Southard Papers." *Princeton University Library Chronicle* 20 (Autumn 1958): 45-47.
Clark calls attention to Southard's papers at Princeton University. Dating from 1820-1840, they include his political correspondence along with papers from his legal practice. Southard was governor of New Jersey, a U.S. senator, and U.S. secretary of the navy.

1235. Colley, Charles C. "The Papers of Carl T. Hayden: Arizona's 'Silent Senator' on Record." *Journal of the West* 14 (October 1975): 5-14.
In this article, Colley emphasizes the papers that document Hayden's support of minority groups in the West. The Hayden papers date from 1904 to 1968 and are held by Arizona State University, Tempe, Arizona.

1236. Colley, Charles C. "The Papers of Senator Carl T. Hayden of Arizona: The Monumental Record of a Distinguished Career." *Manuscripts* 28 (Fall 1976): 272-283.
The political career of Carl Hayden spanned a period of fifty-six years as a U.S. congressman and senator. His papers total over 700 linear feet. This article reviews his career and the legislation he sponsored with occasional reference to the papers.

1237. Coode, Thomas H., and Agnes M. Riggs. "The Private Papers of West Virginia's 'Boy Senator,' Rush Dew Holt." *West Virginia History* 35 (July 1974): 296-318.
Holt was active in state politics, served as a U.S. senator, and was a critic of the New Deal. His papers document his public career in West Virginia, 1920-1955, and include correspondence; speeches; sound recordings; press releases; and clipping files.

1238. Felt, Thomas E. "The Stephen A. Douglas Letters in the State Historical Library." *Journal of the Illinois State Historical Society* 56 (Winter 1963): 677-691.
Felt writes about 128 letters held by the Illinois State Historical Library. He cites the collections in which Douglas correspondence is found and provides excerpts from a few letters.

1239. Graffagnino, Jonathan K. "The Asa Lyon Papers." *Dartmouth College Library Bulletin* 19 (April 1979): 57-64.
Lyon was a Congregational minister active in Vermont politics who served as a U.S. congressman for Vermont in 1814. His papers include

sermons, college papers and journals, political speeches, and correspondence.

1240. Harbaugh, William H. "The Papers of John W. Davis." *Yale University Library Gazette* 37 (July 1962): 13-18.

Davis was an attorney, U.S. congressman, ambassador to England, and presidential candidate in 1924. His papers include correspondence, legal briefs, personal reminiscences, scrapbooks, speeches, and clipping files, all of which document his public career.

1241. Lacy, Harriet S. "Jeremiah Mason Papers (1796-1913)." *Historical New Hampshire* 21 (Autumn 1966): 38-45.

Mason was an attorney, U.S. senator, and attorney general of New Hampshire. His papers consist mostly of correspondence with an autobiography and reminiscences of others about Mason. Lacy lists the principal correspondents.

1242. Lacy, Harriet S. "The William E. Chandler Papers, 1829-1917." *Historical New Hampshire* 23 (Autumn 1968): 51-63.

Chandler was a 19th-century attorney active in Republican politics and served as a U.S. senator from New Hampshire. His papers include diaries, correspondence, scrapbooks, speeches, and appointment papers. An inventory concludes the article.

1243. Lange, Janet M. "Everett Dirksen's Legacy: A Research Center Devoted to the Study of Congress and Congressional Leadership." *Illinois Libraries* 63 (March 1981): 266-269.

The article is mostly a review of the center's history and mission. It, however, does describe briefly Dirksen's papers and mentions the titles of related political collections held.

1244. McCormick, Richard L. "The Thomas Collier Platt Papers." *Yale University Library Gazette* 50 (July 1975): 46-58.

Platt was a three-term U.S. senator from New York and political boss of the New York Republican Party in the 1880s and 1890s. His papers consist mostly of correspondence and clippings from the years 1896 to 1902.

1245. Miller, David H. "The E. Y. Berry Papers: An Unexpected Resource for Students of Recent South Dakota History." *South Dakota History* 3 (Winter 1972): 31-40.

Berry was a U.S. congressman. His papers include correspondence, subject files, sound recordings, motion picture films, and photographs. Many of Berry's papers document Indian-related legislation from 1951 to 1971.

1246. Murray, Keith. "The Wesley L. Jones Papers." *Pacific Northwest Quarterly* 36 (January 1945): 65-68.

Jones was a long-time senator for the state of Washington. His papers at the University of Washington include correspondence, legislation files, research files, and appointment and patronage materials.

1247. Olsgaard, John N. "Dakota Resources: The Peter Norbeck Papers at the University of South Dakota." *South Dakota History* 10 (Spring 1980): 147-151.

Norbeck was a Republican state senator, governor of South Dakota, and three-term U.S. senator. His papers include financial records, political correspondence, and personal papers.

1248. Olson, Gary D. "Dakota Resources: The Richard F. Pettigrew Papers." *South Dakota History* 12 (Summer/Fall 1982): 182-187.

Pettigrew was an early settler in South Dakota and one of the state's first U.S. senators. His papers, dating from 1876 to 1926 and mostly political in nature, are in the Pettigrew Museum, Sioux Falls.

1249. Peters, Werner. "The McCarthy Historical Project." *American Archivist* 33 (April 1970): 155-161.

The project systematically collected archival materials about Eugene McCarthy's campaign for the presidency. The article identifies the types of materials collected.

1250. Riggs, Joseph H. "The McKellar Collection." *Tennessee Librarian* 14 (January 1962): 37-38.

Riggs calls attention to the papers of U.S. senator Kenneth D. McKellar at the Memphis Public Library and notes the collection's strengths.

1251. Schmavonian, Arsine. "The Ralph E. Flanders Papers at Syracuse University." *Vermont History* 37 (Spring 1969): 128-131.

Flanders was an engineer and U.S. senator from Vermont. His papers include correspondence; radio broadcasts; voting record notebooks; speeches; literary manuscripts; scrapbooks; photographs; and published materials. The papers date from 1903 to 1958.

1252. Sewell, Richard H. "The John P. Hale Papers." *Dartmouth College Library Bulletin* 10 (April 1970): 70-80.

Hale was active in 19th-century New Hampshire politics and represented the state in the U.S. Senate. His papers at Dartmouth include correspondence, speeches, and biographical materials.

1253. Tregle, Joseph G., Jr. "The Josiah Stoddard Johnston Papers." *Pennsylvania Magazine of History and Biography* 69 (October 1945): 326-329.

Johnston was active in Louisiana politics and served in the U.S. Congress. His papers include correspondence with leading Southern politicians and agricultural leaders and document the development of a plantation economy in the 1830s.

1254. Wakefield, Ann. "The Broussard Papers of the University of Southwestern Louisiana: New Light on Louisiana Progressivism." *Lousiana History* 31 (Summer 1990): 293-300.

These papers reflect the political career of Robert F. Broussard and his brother, Edwin S. Broussard, who served Louisiana in the U.S. House of Representatives and Senate in the early 20th century. There are about fifty feet of papers dating from 1900 to the 1930s.

1255. Williams, Harry and John Milton Price. "The Huey P. Long Papers at Louisiana State University." *Journal of Southern History* 36 (May 1970): 256-261.

The authors describe a forgotten cache of Long's papers discovered in the basement of LSU's library. The article concludes with a list of record series, inclusive dates, and content notes.

Professional Groups and Organizations

General

1256. Brichford, Maynard. "The Context for a History of the American Library Association." *Libraries and Culture* 26 (Spring 1991): 348-355.
    In the first one-third of this article, Brichford cites record groups, record series titles, volume, and inclusive dates for American Library Association records.

1257. Brichford, Maynard. "Original Source Materials for the History of Librarianship." *Journal of Library History* 5 (April 1970: 177-181.
    Brichford lists record series titles and inclusive dates of records from the University of Illinois (Urbana) Graduate School of Library Science and the University Library director's office. The records date from the 1890s to the 1960s.

1258. Brooks, Richard. "Manuscripts Pertaining to Carlyle's Frederick the Great." *Yale University Library Gazette* 9 (October 1934): 38-41.
    Brooks describes eight categories of manuscript materials Thomas Carlyle used to write his *History of Friedrich II of Prussia, Called Frederick the Great.* They include Carlyle's notes and journals, correspondence, and drafts and manuscripts of the book.

1259. Cummings, Hubertis M. "James D. Harris, Canal Engineer: Notes on His Papers and Related Canal Papers." *Pennsylvania History* 18 (January 1951): 31-45.
    Harris' papers date from the 1820s and include correspondence; map books; reports; commissioners journals; minutes; and surveys. The author provides detailed comments about the map books.

1260. Eberhard, Wallace B. "Georgia Archives in Mass Media History." *Georgia Archive* 3 (Winter 1975): 45-52.
    The author cites collection titles of media-related collections at the Atlanta Historical Society; Emory University; Georgia State University; University of Georgia; and the Georgia State Archives.

1261. Finneran, Helen T. "Records of the National Grange in its Washington Office." *American Archivist* 27 (January 1964): 103-111.

    Finneran describes two record groups: 1) fragmentary records of Grange officials brought to the national headquarters after it was established, and 2) administrative records created after establishment of the Washington, D.C., office.

1262. Flint, Richard W. "A Selected Guide to Source Material on the American Circus." *Journal of Popular Culture* 6 (Spring 1972): 615-619.

    Flint identifies eleven repositories that have significant circus collections and provides summaries of their holdings.

1263. Hardwick, Bonnie. "The Sierra Club Collection at the Bancroft Library." *California History* 71 (Summer 1992): 254-268.

    After a short introduction, Hardwick provides traditional guide entries for the records, manuscript collections, photographs, motion pictures, and published materials relating to the Sierra Club.

1264. Higbie, Charles. "Mass Communications Manuscripts Trace Creation of Public Attitudes." *Manuscripts* 11 (Fall 1959): 40-42.

    Higbie cites several collections of papers from leaders in the broadcasting and journalism fields. The materials are held by the Mass Communications History Center at the Wisconsin State Historical Society, Madison, Wisconsin.

1265. Lurie, Maxine N. "Library History Materials at Rutgers, Including Archives Relating to the New Jersey College for Women Library School and the Founding of the Rutgers Graduate School of Library and Information Studies." *Journal of the Rutgers University Library* 43 (December 1981): 41-65.

    This article reviews record series in three collections, that of the New Jersey College for Women Library School; the John B. Kaiser Collection; and a manuscript by Ethel M. Fair on the history of the library school. The Fair manuscript is published in this article.

1266. Milhollen, Hirst. "The American Red Cross Collection of Photographs and Negatives, Library of Congress." *Quarterly Journal of Current Acquisitions* 2 (February 1945): 32-38.

    This article describes 50,000 photographs documenting Red Cross work from 1900 to 1933. While containing images of major disasters in the U.S., much of the collection emphasizes Red Cross activities during WWI.

1267. Neill, Wilfred T. "Surveyors Field Notes as a Source of Historical Information." *Florida Historical Quarterly* 34 (April 1956): 329-333.

Neill calls attention to the wealth of historical and geographical information that can be found in surveyors' notes. He provides several Florida-related examples.

1268. Peterson, Peter L. "Some Research Opportunities in the Papers of Edwin T. Meredith, 1876-1928." *Books at Iowa* 7 (November 1967): 32-40.

Peterson provides biographical information about Meredith and his association with the Meredith Publishing Company. Meredith's papers, according to the author, offer research opportunities in politics, publishing, farm relief, and land development.

1269. Rich, Paul J. "East Bridgewater's Scouting Museum. A Survey of the First Year." *Manuscripts* 26 (Spring 1974): 89-95.

The museum, located in East Bridgewater, Massachusetts, collects materials relating to Boy Scouts and Girl Scouts. The article describes its holdings of correspondence by Lord Baden-Powell, founder of the scouting movement, and related scouting material.

1270. Samuels, Joel L. "The John M. Wing Foundation on the History of Printing at the Newberry Library." *Library Quarterly* 58 (April 1988): 164-189.

While focusing on printed materials, the article describes several individual manuscripts, calligraphic manuscripts, and manuscript collections and archives relating to the history of printing.

1271. Yates, Barbara. "The Joseph L. Wheeler Papers." *Journal of Library History, Philosophy, and Comparative Librarianship* 8 (April 1973): 96-98.

Wheeler was a librarian and library consultant. His papers, dated 1925-1970, include materials accumulated during 150 library surveys; correspondence; scrapbooks; library policy statements; and manuscripts of his books and articles.

Architects

1272. Bullock, Helen Duprey. "The Personal and Professional Papers of Frederick Law Olmstead." *Quarterly Journal of Current Acquisitions* 6 (November 1948): 8-15.

Bullock describes the papers of landscape architect Frederick Olmstead by noting some of his achievements and commenting on the papers that document those aspects of his career. The papers include correspondence, drawings, and project files, 1819-1923.

1273. Carter, Edward C., III. "The Papers of Benjamin Henry Latrobe and the

Maryland Historical Society, 1885-1971: Nature, Structure and Means of Acquisition." *Maryland Historical Magazine* 66 (Winter 1971): 436-455.

This article describes the Latrobe papers with an emphasis on the process of editing them for publication.

1274. Cullison, William R. "Architectural Records--Recent Acquisitions at Tulane." *Louisiana History* 21 (Spring 1980): 196-200.

A short article describing six architectural collections adding more than 250,000 items to Tulane's existing collection of architectural records. The collections described are from New Orleans architectural firms, dating from the 1830s to the 1960s.

1275. Engelbrecht, Marie F. "A Catalogue of the Henry C. Trost Drawings." *Library Chronicle of the University of Texas at Austin* New Series 16 (1981): 93-102.

Trost was an El Paso, Texas, architect who achieved professional recognition for his designs in Arizona, New Mexico, and western Texas. This catalog lists seventy-three of his drawings.

1276. Ganelin, Susan S. "The Drawings of Robert Morris Hunt: Foundation Organizes Invaluable Collection of Prominent Architect's Work." *American Preservation* 2 (April/May 1979): 18-25.

The author notes that Hunt's drawings constitute the premier collection of the Architectural Archives of the American Institute of Architects Foundation. While primarily a biographical article, it does describe several examples of Hunt's work.

1277. Gilchrist, Agnes A. "Notes for a Catalogue of the John McComb (1763-1853) Collection of Architectural Drawings in the New York Historical Society." *Society of Architectural History Journal* 28 (October 1969): 201-210.

The McComb Collection consists of more than 500 architectural and engineering drawings and building plans and sketches. The article includes several illustrations with descriptive notes.

1278. Mearns, David C. "Architects and Poets and Prophets: Notes on the Letters of Benjamin Henry Latrobe to John Lenthall, 1803-1808." *Quarterly Journal of Current Acquisitions* 1 (October 1943): 9-17.

Mearns describes a letterbook containing 150 letters from the architect Benjamin Latrobe to his assistant John Lenthall. The author provides several examples of the type of information found in the letters.

1279. Peatross, C. Ford. "Architectural Collections of the Library of Congress." *Quarterly Journal of the Library of Congress* 34 (July 1977): 249-284.

Peatross describes some of the rich architectural holdings of the Prints and Photographs Division. It is this division that holds architectural photographs and negatives, measured drawings, and related prints and drawings of significant buildings.

1280. Sterner, Carl J. "The Marshall-Walton Papers." *Library Chronicle of the University of Texas at Austin* New Series 9 (1978): 61-65.
Benjamin Howard Marshall and Lewis B. Walton were Chicago-based architects. This article describes a collection of architectural drawings and papers from Marshall's firm, Walton and Walton. The records date from the beginning of Marshall's career in the 1890s.

1281. Zukowsky, John. "Burnham's Gift to Chicago: The Burnham Library of Architecture." *Illinois Libraries* 63 (April 1981): 298-300.
Along with traditional published materials, this library contains papers and drawings of Chicago-area architects. The drawings of Peter Bonnet Wight, Louis Sullivan, and the firm of Percier and Fontaine are among those Zukowsky cites.

Education

1282. Boatner, Maxine T. "The Gallaudet Papers." *Quarterly Journal of Current Acquisitions* 17 (November 1959): 1-12.
This article reviews Thomas Gallaudet's and his son Edward Gallaudet's work in educating the deaf. Boatner also identifies the diaries and journals that document the work of both.

1283. Boles, Nancy G. "Baltimore City College Records." *Maryland Historical Magazine* 66 (Summer 1971): 194-199.
The City College is an all-male high school founded in 1839. This article cites record series documenting its administration and operations. The records date from the 1830s to the 1950s.

1284. Copeley, William. "Manuscript School Records at the New Hampshire Historical Society." *Historical New Hampshire* 42 (Summer 1987): 150-152.
This is a checklist arranged alphabetically by town and by district thereunder. Entries include inclusive dates and occasional volume statements.

1285. East, Sherrod. "St. Albans Archives." *American Archivist* 34 (October 1971): 373-376.
This article uses the archival program of St. Albans School for Boys in Washington, D.C., as a model for retaining school records. In doing so,

it lists extant record series at St. Albans along with some description of
the series.

1286. Fuller, Grace P. "Papers of Rector Williams." *Yale University Library
Gazette* 1 (January 1927): 42-45.
    This article calls attention to a small collection of letters and papers by
Elisha Williams, rector of Yale, 1726-1739. The papers describe events
during Williams' time at Yale.

1287. Mulhern, James. "Manuscript School-Books." *Papers of the Bibliographic
Society of America* 32 (1938): 17-37.
    Mulhern defines the four basic types of manuscript school-books,
comments on the research value of each type, and concludes with a
checklist of these books in Pennsylvania repositories.

1288. Schmitt, Martin. "The Papers of Henry D. Sheldon." *Oregon Historical
Quarterly* 52 (March 1951): 57-60.
    Sheldon was an educator who retired in 1948 as dean of the School of
Education at the University of Oregon. His papers include more than
5,000 letters, unpublished manuscripts, an autobiography, and a diary.

1289. Schneider, Herbert W. "A Note on the Samuel Johnson Papers."
American Historical Review 31 (July 1926): 724-726.
    Schneider offers a brief description of the papers with comments on
their research value. Johnson was the first president of Kings College,
the forerunner of Columbia University.

1290. Swanson, Carl A. "The Arthur Livingston Papers at the University of
Texas." *Library Chronicle of the University of Texas* 3 (Spring 1950):
220-222.
    Livingston was a professor of Italian at Columbia University. His
papers consist mostly of correspondence (1918-1944) documenting his
interest in U.S.-Italian relations and the development of Italian studies in
this country.

1291. Walch, Timothy. "Archival Research Opportunities in American
Educational History." *History of Education Quarterly* 16 (Winter 1976):
479-486.
    This article contains a lengthy checklist of education-related collections.
Entries include collection and record series titles, inclusive dates, volume,
and repository names.

1292. Whitney, Dorman H. "The Ashbel Smith Papers." *Library Chronicle of
the University of Texas* 7 (Fall 1961): 32-34.
    Smith is known for his efforts to establish the University of Texas and

for his promotion of general education in Texas. His papers include correspondence, legislative materials, speeches, writings, and scrapbooks, all dating form the 1820s to the 1880s.

Health Fields

1293. Andersen, Kathleen S., and Daniel M. Fox. "History of Medicine Archives in New York State." *New York State Journal of Medicine* 90 (January 1990): 23-31.

This is a directory to thirty archives with substantial holdings of medical records. Entries include access and services information, and scope and content notes about holdings.

1294. Berlin, Ira R. "The Northwestern Memorial Hospital Archives." *Illinois Libraries* 63 (April 1981): 333-334.

Berlin cites collection titles and dates of records relating to Chicago-area hospitals and training programs for health-care personnel; collection titles of personal papers of health-care professionals; and a photo collection dating from the 1880s.

1295. Burns, David D. "Michael Reese Hospital: Archives and Public Affairs." *Illinois Libraries* 63 (April 1981): 335-336.

This article describes sixty feet of records, manuscript materials, and photographs relating to the operation of the hospital, its out-patient clinics, and a school of nursing.

1296. Corner, George W. "Rush Manuscripts." *American Philosophical Society Library Bulletin* (1943): 82-84.

Primary among the Benjamin Rush manuscripts is the series of eight notebooks he wrote as a memoir of his life and career. The Rush materials also include several of his letters, and a commonplace book which he kept between 1792 and 1813.

1297. Devlin, Mary and Marguerite Fallucco. "The Archives of the American Medical Association." *Illinois Libraries* 63 (April 1981): 337-338.

The authors limit description to record series titles and inclusive dates of AMA records and publications.

1298. Donato, Anne K., and Harlan Greene. "The Waring Historical Library Manuscript Guide." *South Carolina Historical Magazine* 86 (April 1985): 128-152.

The Waring Library of the Medical University of South Carolina collects manuscripts concerning physicians and medical science. The entries to this guide include collection titles, volume, inclusive dates, record series titles, and content notes.

1299. Field, William. "The Beaumont Letters." *Yale University Library Gazette* 60 (October 1985): 58-62.

    Field calls attention to a collection of sixty-one letters William Beaumont wrote to his family between 1804 and 1835. Beaumont was a physician and is known for his research on gastric physiology.

1300. Frank, Robert G., Jr. "The Joseph Erlanger Collection at Washington University School of Medicine, St. Louis." *Journal of the History of Biology* 12 (Spring 1979): 193-201.

    Erlanger won a Nobel Prize in medicine in 1944. His papers include correspondence; lecture and research notes; administration and teaching records; and biographical information, all dating from 1910 and relating to physiology of nerves, muscles, and the heart.

1301. Griffenhagan, George. "Structure of the Archives of the American Pharmaceutical Association." *Pharmacy in History* 7 (No. 3 1962): 35-42.

    Many would call this an index. It is an alphabetical listing of subjects, organizations, people, publications, and things found in the archives. It is useful for those planning research in pharmacy.

1302. Klemperer, Wolfgang W. "The Felix Klemperer Collection of German Medical Letters, Their History and Background." *Yale University Library Gazette* 48 (July 1973): 56-61.

    This collection holds correspondence (1900-1910) from Austrian, German, and Swiss physicians who were asked to contribute essays to *Die Deutsche Klinik.*

1303. Lacy, Harriet S. "Nathaniel Peabody Papers, 1767-1815." *Historical New Hampshire* 22 (Summer 1967): 39-46.

    Peabody was an Atkinson, New Hampshire, physician who also served in the Revolutionary War. Most of the collection is Peabody's correspondence dating from the 1770s to the 1820s. A checklist of his letters and miscellaneous papers concludes the article.

1304. Lawson, Brenda M. "Manuscripts on the History of Medicine at the Massachusetts Historical Society." *Proceedings of the Massachusetts Historical Society* 103 (1991): 157-190.

    Lawson cites collection and record series titles with inclusive dates for medically-related manuscripts under three periods: the colonial period through the American Revolution; the early national period through the Civil War; and modern medicine, 1866 forward.

1305. McCall, Nancy and Harold Kanarek. "The Alan Mason Chesney Medical Archives of the Johns Hopkins Medical Institutions." *Bulletin of the History of Medicine* 56 (Spring 1982): 88-92.

The authors review the history of the archives and its holdings. They cite key record groups and collections, record series titles, and, occasionally, inclusive dates.

1306. Norwood, Terrence S. "The Cook County Hospital Archives." *Illinois Libraries* 63 (April 1981): 338-339.

Norwood notes that the archives contain records from Cook County Hospital and its school of nursing; the Health and Hospitals Governing Commission; and Cermak Memorial Hospital. He limits description to record series titles and inclusive dates.

1307. Sonnedecker, Glenn. "The Papers of Rho Chi: Honor Society in the AIHP Collection." *Pharmacy in History* 16 (No. 3 1974): 108-109.

The records include minutes, committee reports, annual meeting proceedings, and chapter records, all dating from 1922. They are held by the American Institute of the History of Pharmacy at the Wisconsin State History Society.

1308. Sonnedecker, Glenn. "The Papers of Rufus Ashley Lyman (1875-1957)." *Pharmacy in History* 19 (No. 2 1977): 89-91.

Lyman was a professor of pharmacology and dean of the Pharmacy College at the University of Nebraska. His papers reflect his career in education and include correspondence, speeches, reports, committee minutes, and published materials, all dated 1900-1950.

1309. Wittman, Elisabeth. "The Historical Records and Archives of the University of Illinois at the Medical Center." *Illinois Libraries* 63 (April 1981): 339-342.

Wittman provides a history of the archives and cites record series titles it holds, along with collections of personal papers of health-care professionals.

Journalists

1310. Abbott, Mabel. "The George William Curtis Collection." *Proceedings of the Staten Island Institute of Arts and Sciences* 12 (1950): 68-72; 13 (1951): 82-85; and 18 (1956): 22-26.

1311. Anthony, Robert O. "A Walter Lippman Collection." *Yale University Library Gazette* 22 (October 1947): 39-41.

Much of this collection is Lippman's published works, but it also includes manuscripts of his column "Today & Tomorrow," several of his books, and magazine articles.

1312. Armstrong, William M. "The Letters of Edwin L. Godkin: A Calendar and Locator File." *Bulletin of the New York Public Library* 75 (September 1971): 311-326.

Godkin is known as a journalist and founding editor of *The Nation*. Armstrong identifies thirty-three institutions holding Godkin's papers and concludes the article with a to-and-from listing of his correspondence at these repositories.

1313. Barrett, Kayla. "The Paul Miller Papers at Oklahoma State University." *Chronicles of Oklahoma* 68 (Winter 1990): 434-439.

Miller was a journalist who rose to be president and chairman of the Gannett Company. The papers date from the 1940s to the 1970s and include correspondence files, scrapbooks, speeches, photographs, sound recordings, and published materials.

1314. Brand, Katherine E. "The Josephus Daniels Papers." *Quarterly Journal of Current Acquisitions* 7 (August 1950): 3-10.

Daniels was a journalist who is, perhaps, best known as U.S. ambassador to Mexico, 1933-1942. His papers include over 400 feet of correspondence, subject files, and scrapbooks, of which Brand identifies highlights.

1315. Brand, Katherine E. "The Personal Papers of Ray Stannard Baker." *Quarterly Journal of Current Acquisitions* 5 (August 1948): 3-9.

Baker was a journalist and official biographer of Woodrow Wilson. Brand provides a description of the types of materials found in the Baker Collection. The materials date from the 1870s to 1940s.

1316. Burr, Nelson R. "The Papers of William Allen White." *Quarterly Journal of Current Acquisitions* 4 (November 1946): 10-14.

Burr describes some of the materials in the Library of Congress' White Collection. He focuses upon White's correspondence with political and literary personalities and upon White's involvement in public affairs from the 1890s to the 1940s.

1317. Newberry Library. "The Herman Raster Papers." *Newberry Library Bulletin* 3 (December 1945): 24-29.

Raster was a German-American journalist credited with winning Germany to the Union side during the Civil War. His papers include a series of pro-Union articles published in the *National Zeitung* in the 1860s, and his personal correspondence.

1318. Newberry Library. "The Letters of Victor Fremont Lawson." *Newberry Library Bulletin* 5 (September 1946): 15-28.

   Lawson was a journalist who founded the *Chicago Daily News*. This article describes a collection of more than 75,000 of his letters.

1319. Newberry Library. "The Private Papers of a Foreign Correspondent." *Newberry Library Bulletin* 2nd Series 1 (July 1948): 1-11.

   The correspondent was Edward Price Bell who wrote for the *Chicago Daily News* and *Literary Digest*. His papers include correspondence, scrapbooks, clipping files, and speeches.

Judicial and Legal

1320. Ames, Susie M. "Law-in-Action: The Court Records of Virginia's Eastern Shore." *William and Mary Quarterly* 3rd Series 4 (April 1947): 177-204.

   The author notes that court records in Virginia's eastern counties date from 1632 to the 1940s. She lists extant record series and comments on the types of information found in the records and their research value.

1321. Boles, Nancy G. "The Joseph Nathan Ulman Collection." *Maryland Historical Magazine* 67 (Fall 1972): 307-309.

   Ulman was a Baltimore municipal judge and advocate for prisoners and Afro-Americans. His papers contain correspondence, scrapbooks, notebooks of cases tried, and photographs, mostly from the 1920s to the early 1940s.

1322. Browning, James R., and Bess Glenn. "The Supreme Court Collection at the National Archives." *American Journal of Legal History* 4 (July 1960): 241-256.

   The authors review the background of early transfers of court records to the National Archives in the 1950s. The article concludes with a guide to twenty-five record series transferred. Entries include volume, inclusive dates, and content summaries.

1323. Butt, Marshall W. "The Colonial Court Records of Lower Norfolk and Norfolk Counties." *William and Mary Quarterly* 2nd Series 19 (July 1939): 286-292.

   The author lists extant record series of 17th- and 18th-century Virginia court records. The entries include inclusive dates with occasional content notes.

1324. Carp, Robert A. "The Public and Private Papers of Judge William F. Riley." *Books at Iowa* 11 (November 1969): 19-29.

Riley was a federal judge active in Iowa Democratic politics in the 1930s, and in public affairs throughout his life. His papers, dated 1932-1956, consist mostly of correspondence with national and state public figures.

1325. Chadbourn, Erika S. "Documenting the American Legal Scene: The Manuscript Division of the Harvard Law School Library." *Harvard Library Bulletin* 30 (January 1982): 55-73.

Chadbourn notes that there are over 100 manuscript collections in the law library dating from the 1860s to the 1980s. She then describes key collections representing judges, lawyers, law professors, and those documenting well-known cases.

1326. Davis, W. N., Jr. "Research Uses of County Court Records, 1850-1879, and Incidental Intimate Glimpses of California Life and Society." Part 1 *California Historical Quarterly* 52 (Fall 1973): 241-266; and Part 2, (Winter 1973): 338-365.

The author devotes most of the article to providing the "intimate glimpses," but still useful for anyone interested in doing research in court records, especially, California records.

1327. Destler, Chester M. "The Roger Sherman (Titusville, Pennsylvania) Collection." *Yale University Library Gazette* 21 (January 1947): 39-43.

Sherman was an attorney who practiced in the Pennsylvania petroleum producing region. His papers include his correspondence, both professional and private, business records from his law practice, scrapbooks, and published materials about the petroleum industry.

1328. Drummey, Peter. "Manuscripts on American Legal History at the Massachusetts Historical Society." *Proceedings of the Massachusetts Historical Society* 101 (1989): 97-116.

The author lists collections and record series titles with dates under three headings: the colonial period through 1774; the new nation through 1864; and the modern period 1865-1980s.

1329. Durel, John W. "New Hampshire County Court Records." *Historical New Hampshire* 31 (Spring/Summer 1976): 56-59.

Durel does not describe records held, but identifies the record series created by county courts, the records' original purpose, and the types of information they contain.

1330. Feichtmeir, Karl. "Defending the Bill of Rights--the ACLU Archives at CHS." *California History* 58 (Winter 1979/1980): 362-364.

The article calls attention to the richness of the American Civil Liberties Union of Northern California Collection. The collection contains correspondence, organizational and legal records, scrapbooks, and published materials.

1331. Flaherty, David H. "A Select Guide to the Manuscript Court Records of Colonial New England." *The American Journal of Legal History* 11 (April 1967): 107-126.

The guide identifies and locates court records dated from the 1660s to 1776 in Massachusetts, Connecticut, and Rhode Island. Flaherty lists records by court and, then, by record series, volume, and inclusive dates.

1332. Flaherty, David H. "A Select Guide to the Manuscript Court Records of Colonial Virginia." *American Journal of Legal History* 19 (April 1975): 112-137.

Flaherty lists court records dating from the 1640s through the 1850s by county and for the Virginia colonial towns of Alexandria, Fredericksburg, Norfolk, Petersburg, and Richmond. Entries include record series titles, inclusive dates, and microfilm reel numbers.

1333. Gersack, Dorothy Hill. "Colonial, State, and Federal Court Records: A Survey." *American Archivist* 36 (January 1973): 33-42.

The author locates court records in the U.S. and comments on their potential use for historical research.

1334. Grigg, Susan. "The Alexander M. Bickel Papers." *Yale University Library Gazette* 52 (October 1977): 66-69.

Bickel was known as an authority on the U.S. constitution and the U.S. judicial system. His papers, which Grigg describes, document his writings, his legal work, his work with the U.S. Congress, and his political activities.

1335. Hayes, Catherine. "The Papers of Colonel William Emerson." *University of Rochester Library Bulletin* 18 (Spring 1963): 41-45.

While Emerson served in both world wars, his career was as an attorney for the city of Rochester, N.Y. His papers include early family diaries and correspondence, his wartime correspondence, and his correspondence as a city attorney.

1336. Hiden, Martha W. "Seventeenth Century Virginia Parochial and County Records." *Virginia Magazine of History and Biography* 56 (April 1948): 135-141.

This is a county-by-county review of extant 17th-century court records in Virginia. The author identifies record series and their inclusive dates. She also notes missing records known to have been lost or destroyed.

1337. Hiden, Martha W. "Virginia County Court Records: Their Background and Scope." *Virginia Magazine of History and Biography* 54 (January 1946): 3-16.

   While this article does not identify specific record holdings, it does examine, in detail, the types of court records created, the information they contain, and their research values. A useful article for those planning research in colonial legal records.

1338. House, Albert V. "The Samuel Latham Mitchill Barlow Papers in the Huntington Library." *Huntington Library Quarterly* 28 (August 1965): 341-352.

   Barlow was a 19th-century New York City attorney. His papers, dated 1849-1889, contain personal and business correspondence and legal and business records, all relating to his practice, national and New York state politics, and social activities.

1339. Lacy, Harriet S. "The Cyrus King Sanborn Papers (1845-1887)." *Historical New Hampshire* 22 (Spring 1967): 28-38.

   Sanborn was a 19th-century Rochester, New Hampshire, attorney. His papers include his personal and professional correspondence; docket books and other records from his legal practice; and financial records. The article ends with an inventory of the collection.

1340. Main, Gloria L. "Probate Records as a Source for Early American History." *William and Mary Quarterly* 3rd Series 32 (January 1975): 89-99.

   Main describes probate records generically, identifies the types of information they contain, and comments on their research values. She cites several examples from property inventories and wills found during her research in Massachusetts and Maryland.

1341. Massie, Larry. "Circuit Court Records: Witness for the Past." *Chronicle: The Magazine of the Historical Society of Michigan* 15 (Winter 1980): 26-33; and 16 (Spring 1980): 23-32.

   The author identifies circuit court record series, comments on the types of information found in each, and cites available holdings of these records.

1342. McCarthy, Jack, Laurie Rofini, and Barbara Weir. "Chester County Probate Records, 1713-1850." *Pennsylvania History* 54 (October 1987): 283-303.

   The authors note that Chester County was one of Pennsylvania's three original counties and its probate records date from 1713-1850. They identify seven probate record series and illustrate the type of information found in each.

1343. McReynolds, Michael. "Documentary Sources for the Study of U.S. Supreme Court Litigation: Part III---Materials in the National Archives." *Law Library Journal* 69 (November 1976): 448-452.

McReynolds first reviews record series from U.S. Supreme Court records and the information they contain. He then notes other federal agencies whose records contain litigation files.

1344. Mevers, Frank C. "Matthew Patten Papers." *Historical New Hampshire* 30 (Summer 1975): 115-116.

Patten was an 18th-century New Hampshire justice of the peace. His papers are from his office and include depositions, complaints, and wills and estate inventories, all dating from the 1730s to 1820.

1345. Morris, Richard B. "The Salzer Collection of Mayor's Court Papers." *American Journal of Legal History* 2 (October 1958): 314-315.

This collection contains 2,000 court documents dated 1681-1819. Morris notes they are especially illustrative of colonial maritime and admiralty law and litigation during the American Revolution.

1346. Noble, John. "The Early Court Files of Suffolk County." *Colonial Society of Massachusetts Publications* 3 (1895-97): 317-326.

Noble relates the provenance of these records, argues for their preservation, and provides topical examples of their richness for historical research. The records date from 1629 to 1800.

1347. Owens, James K. "'Untouched Mines' for the Legal Scholar: Records of the Massachusetts Federal Courts in the National Archives." *Massachusetts Law Review* 74 (December 1989): 279-287.

Owens reviews federal court records held in the National Archives regional branch at Waltham, Massachusetts. He discusses maritime records; civil liberties disputes; and patent and bankruptcy cases. He describes specific cases from each record series as examples.

1348. Read, William E., and William C. Berman. "Papers of the First Justice Harlan at the University of Louisville." *American Journal of Legal History* 11 (1967): 57-68.

These papers of John Marshall Harlan, mostly correspondence and clipping files, document his service on the U.S. Supreme Court from 1877 to 1911.

1349. Reed, H. Clay. "The Court Records of the Delaware Valley." *William and Mary Quarterly* 3rd Series 4 (April 1947): 192-202.

Reed identifies the extant court records of the Delaware River valley counties in Pennsylvania, New Jersey, and Delaware, and notes those that have been published. He also comments on the research values of 17th-

and 18th-century court records.

1350. Riley, Glenda. "Divorce Records: Linn County, Iowa, 1928-1944."
      Annals of Iowa 50 (Winter 1991): 787-800.
          Riley analyzes two record series, divorce registers and case files, and
      includes several comments on the contents of the records.

1351. Roberts, Martin A. "Records of the United States District Courts, 1790-
      1870, Deposited in the Copyright Office of the Library of Congress."
      Annual Report of the American Historical Association for the Year 1937
      1 (1939): 93-105.
          Prior to 1870, publishers and authors recorded their copyrights in U.S.
      district courts. This article describes these early records. It concludes
      with a checklist by state, with the number of volumes for each and their
      dates.

1352. Surrency, Erwin C. "Records of the United States Court for China."
      American Journal of Legal History 1 (July 1957): 234-236.
          This was a special U.S. court operating in China from 1906 to the
      1940s. The records, left behind when the U.S. broke diplomatic relations
      with the Chinese Communists, are presumed lost.

1353. Thalken, Thomas T. "The Papers of Charles Evans Hughes." *Quarterly
      Journal of Current Acquisitions* 11 (November 1953): 1-6.
          The Hughes papers include voluminous correspondence files spanning
      his entire life and career; biographical subject files; scrapbooks; and
      autobiographical memoirs and memoranda.   Thalken emphasizes the
      correspondence series in his description.

1354. Vanorny, Patricia M. "Records of the Baltimore Judicial System."
      Working Papers from the Regional Economic History Research Center 4
      (Nos. 1/2 1981): 65-74.

1355. Waters, James F. "Brooklyn's Earliest Court Records." *American Journal
      of Legal History* 2 (October 1958): 315-320.
          Waters reports on extant court records of Kings County, New York.
      Dating from 1646 to the 1790s, they include court minutes, town meeting
      proceedings, deeds, and other miscellaneous records.

1356. Wiltsey, Thomas E. "Territorial Court Records and Local History: New
      Mexico as a Case Study." *Prologue* 15 (Spring 1983): 43-54.
          Wiltsey discusses how selected records series of bankrupcy, naturaliza-
      tion, and land records from territorial courts might be useful for historical
      research.

1357. Wrigley, Linda. "The Jerome N. Frank Papers." *Yale University Library Gazette* 48 (January 1974): 163-177.

Frank was a corporate and federal attorney, federal judge, and chair of the Securities and Exchange Commission. His papers include his correspondence, court opinions, manuscripts of his writings, speeches, and research and teaching notes.

Natural and Physical Sciences

1358. Beck, Clark L., Jr. "Rutgers' Manuscript Collections on the History of Science and Technology." *Journal of the Rutgers University Libraries* 45 (June 1983): 48-50.

Beck lists thirteen collections in this article. Entries include collection and record series titles, volume, inclusive dates, and content notes.

1359. Bell, Whitfield J., Jr. "Papers for the History of Science." *Library of Congress Quarterly Journal* 24 (July 1967): 162-170.

This article describes the microfilming of science-related collections in the American Philosophical Society. Bell cites the titles of several filmed collections.

1360. Bird, Randall D., and Allen Garland. "The Papers of Harry Hamilton Laughlin, Eugenicist." *Journal of the History of Biology* 14 (Fall 1981): 339-353.

Laughlin's papers (1920s-1943) include correspondence; records relating to his work as superintendent of the Eugenics Record Office; research files on race horses and date palms; and papers relating to the Nazi Rassenhygiene Movement.

1361. Boewe, Charles. "The Manuscripts of C. S. Rafinesque (1783-1840)." *Proceedings of the American Philosophical Society* 102 (December 1958): 590-595.

Boewe describes the society's holdings of Rafinesque's papers, which he claims is the largest group extant. He also locates Rafinesque manuscripts in other repositories. Rafinesque was a naturalist, mostly known for his botanical studies.

1362. Bradley, A. Day. "The Mathematical Manuscripts in the Schwenkfelder Historical Library." *Scripta Mathematica* 7 (No. 2 1940): 49-58.

Bradley describes a collection of 200 mathematical copybooks dating 1731 to 1872. Categories of books include arithmetic, algebra, dialing, and geometry. The author notes the books illustrate methods used in the Schwenkfelder schools.

1363. Brasch, Frederick E. "Two Important Manuscripts by Albert Einstein."
       Quarterly Journal of Current Acquisitions 2 (February 1945): 39-48.
       Brasch analyzes the content and significance of Einstein manuscripts
       entitled "Zur Elektrodynamik bewegter Körper," and "Das Bi-Vektor
       Feld." Both are in the Library of Congress.

1364. Burchsted, Frederic F. "Archives of American Mathematics." *Historia
       Mathematica* 14 (November 1987): 366-374.
       Burchsted calls attention to the opening of the archives and lists
       manuscript collections alphabetically by title. Entries include volume,
       record series titles, inclusive dates, and content notes.

1365. Chase, Laurence B. "Space Travel Since 1640." *Princeton University
       Library Chronicle* 30 (Autumn 1968): 1-9.
       Chase describes the G. Edward Pendray Collection which includes
       correspondence; photographs; motion pictures; radio and T.V. scripts;
       and published materials about rocketry and space travel. It also contains
       Pendray's personal papers about public relations.

1366. Clagett, Marshall and John E. Murdoch. "Medieval Mathematics,
       Physics, and Philosophy: A Revised Catalogue of Photographic Repro-
       ductions." *Manuscripta* 2 (October 1958): 131-154; and 3 (February
       1959): 19-37.
       A two-part listing of microfilmed manuscripts and published books
       relating to the disciplines named in the title of this article. The list
       includes authors, manuscript or book titles, and locations of the original
       document and the microfilmed copy.

1367. Conklin, Edwin G. "Letters of Charles Darwin and Other Scientists and
       Philosophers to Sir Charles Lyell, Bart." *Proceedings of the American
       Philosophical Society* 95 (June 1951): 220-222.
       A preliminary description of the society's collection of 177 letters from
       Darwin to Lyell, along with 277 letters from other scientists to Lyell.
       Most of the Darwin letters discuss Darwin's *Origin of Species*....

1368. Daly, John F. "Mathematics in the Codices Ottoboniani Latini."
       Manuscripta 8 (March 1964): 3-17; and 9 (March 1965): 12-29.
       A two-part checklist of manuscripts in the Vatican Library and also
       available on microfilm in the Knights of Columbus Vatican Film Library
       at St. Louis University.

1369. Dobbs, B.J.T. "Newton Manuscripts at the Smithsonian Institution." *Isis*
       68 (March 1977): 105-107.
       This article calls attention to, and describes, a small collection of Isaac
       Newton manuscripts and letters. Description focuses on the content of

the documents.

1370. Elliott, Clark A. "Sources for the History of Science in the Harvard
University Archives." *Harvard Library Bulletin* 22 (January 1974): 49-
71.
      Elliott cites manuscript collection titles and key record series with
inclusive dates for material relating to the history of science in general,
and then for individual scientific disciplines such as mathematics, physics,
chemistry, etc.

1371. Fisher, Irving N. "The O. C. Marsh Papers." *Yale University Library
Gazette* 46 (July 1971): 35-40.
      Othniel Marsh was a paleontologist and heir to the George Peabody
fortune. His correspondence and papers document his lifelong passion
for collecting fossils.

1372. Gieseker, Brenda R. "A New Dimension for Mr. Shaw's Garden."
Manuscripts 24 (Summer 1972): 208-213.
      This article describes the manuscript holdings of the Missouri Botanical
Garden established by Henry Shaw whose personal papers form the
nucleus of the collections. The papers of the garden's directors and
visiting botanists are also in the archives.

1373. Grattan-Guinness, I. "The Manuscripts of Emil L. Post." *History of
Philosophy and Logic* 11 (No. 1 1990): 77-84.

1374. Halas, Christine D. "The James A. Van Allen Papers." *Books at Iowa* 51
(November 1989): 53-61.
      Van Allen is the space scientist for whom the earth's radiation belt is
named. His papers document his own research and the expanded role of
government in scientific research, especially in the area of space
exploration.

1375. Jeffrey, Thomas E. "The Thomas A. Edison Papers: Publishing the
Records of an American Genius." *Journal of the Rutgers University
Libraries* 47 (June 1985): 23-38.
      This article describes a microfilm edition of the Edison papers. Jeffrey
identifies many record series and comments on their research values.

1376. Long, Charles R. "Natural History Manuscripts and Related Materials in
the Archives of the New York Botanical Garden." *Journal of the Society
for the Bibliography of Natural History* 8 (May 1978): 343-349.
      Long identifies manuscript collections, mostly of botanists, in the
archives. He cites collection titles, inclusive dates, and record series, and
comments on research values of the materials.

1377. Lurie, Edward. "Some Manuscripts in the History of Nineteenth Century American Natural Science." *Isis* 44 (December 1953): 363-370.
      Lurie provides collection and record series titles, inclusive dates, and content notes for collections at thirty-five repositories in Connecticut, Massachusetts, New York, Maryland, Pennsylvania, Washington, D.C., and Wisconsin.

1378. Mugridge, Donald H. "Scientific Manuscripts of Benjamin Franklin." *Quarterly Journal of Current Acquisitions* 4 (August 1947): 12-21.
      Mugridge describes and analyzes sixteen Franklin manuscripts on scientific themes. The materials date from 1775 to 1785.

1379. Murphy, Robert C. "The Sketches of Titan Ramsay Peale (1799-1885)." *Proceedings of the American Philosophical Society* 101 (December 1957): 523-531.
      Peale was an artist-naturalist. Murphy describes his work and the contents of the Peale Collection at the society. It consists of over 250 sketches, along with notebooks, and miscellaneous family papers.

1380. Pace, Antonio. "The Manuscripts of Giambatista Beccaria, Correspondent of Benjamin Franklin." *Proceedings of the American Philosophical Society* 96 (August 1952): 406-416.
      Beccaria was an 18th-century physics professor at the University of Turin, Italy, and an early experimenter with electricity. Pace writes about Beccaria's work and ends the article with a listing of his manuscripts in Philadelphia and the Vatican.

1381. Parker, Nancy B. "Huxley Papers Acquired by Rice University." *Texas Libraries* 42 (Summer 1980): 67-70.
      Parker reviews the contents of fifty-five feet of Julian S. Huxley's papers. They include manuscripts of his writings; diaries and travel journals; photographs and sketches; correspondence; and published materials.

1382. Reingold, Nathan. "A Good Place to Study Astronomy." *Quarterly Journal of Current Acquisitions* 20 (September 1963): 211-217.
      This article describes the papers of Cleveland Abbe, a 19th-century U.S. astronomer. His papers include correspondence, research notes, photographs, and biographical materials relating to the Abbe family.

1383. Reingold, Nathan. "Jacques Loeb, the Scientist: His Papers and His Era." *Quarterly Journal of Current Acquisitions* 19 (June 1962): 119-130.
      Loeb was known as one of the country's leading physiologists. His papers include over 10,000 letters, notebooks, manuscripts, and publications dating from the 1890s to 1920s. The article lists many of his

correspondents and offers excerpts from key letters.

1384. Reingold, Nathan. "Manuscript Resources for the History of Science and Technology in the Library of Congress." *Quarterly Journal of Current Acquisitions* 17 (May 1960): 161-169.

Reingold cites collection titles, record series and inclusive dates of papers relating to the physical sciences; exploration; sciences of man; life sciences; and technology. He notes that the library has more than 140 collections relating to science.

1385. Reingold, Nathan. "Research Possibilities in the U.S. Coast and Geodetic Survey Records." *Archives Internationales d'Histoire des Sciences* 45 (October/December 1958): 337-346.

The author identifies the record series created by the survey which include administrative correspondence; astronomical observations; and observations of coastlines, tides, and currents. Reingold also comments on the research values of these records.

1386. Ron, Moshe. "The Sidney M. Edelstein Collection in the History of Chemistry and Chemical Technology." *Technology and Culture* 19 (July 1978): 491-494.

While mostly published materials, the collection does contain some manuscript materials relating to alchemy and chemistry.

1387. Root, Nina J. "The Thomas Baillie MacDougall Collection in the American Museum of Natural History." *Curator* 18 (December 1975): 276-280.

MacDougall was an amateur botanist who spent a lifetime collecting botanical and zoological specimens in Mexico. In this article, Root describes his papers at the record series level. The papers date from 1918 to the 1970s.

1388. Swann, John P. "Manuscript Resources in the History of Chemistry at the National Library of Medicine." *Annals of Science* 46 (May 1989): 249-262.

The materials Swann describes include the personal papers of chemists and biochemists; instructors' notes for chemistry courses dating from the 17th century; oral histories; and records of the U.S. Public Health Service's Division of Chemistry.

1389. Tunis, Mildred C. "The Gordon Ferrie Hull Papers." *Dartmouth College Library Bulletin* 12 (November 1971): 23-26.

Hull was a physics professor at Dartmouth. His papers include his personal and professional correspondence; manuscripts of writings; research notes; and photographs.

1390. Weaver, Warren. "The Mathematical Manuscripts of Lewis Carroll."
Princeton University Library Chronicle 16 (Autumn 1954): 1-9.
Lewis Carroll (the Rev. Charles L. Dodgson) was also a lecturer on
mathematics at Oxford University. This article describes these papers
which reflect his efforts to improve his teaching techniques rather than
original research in mathematics.

1391. Weiner, Charles. "Oral History of Science: A Mushrooming Cloud?"
Journal of American History 75 (September 1988): 548-559.
Weiner describes oral history projects relating to physics, chemistry,
and computers, as examples of this burgeoning field. He also cites
several repositories that hold rich oral history collections relating to
science.

Social Sciences

1392. Barry, John M. "The Roper Center: The World's Largest Archive of
Survey Data." *Reference Services Review* 16 (Nos. 1/2 1988): 41-50.
Barry reports on the center which holds the records of public opinion
surveys collected by Roper Research Associates. He includes a review
of holdings and information on how to access the survey data.

1393. Batts, Grover C. "The James McKeen Cattell Papers." *Quarterly Journal
of Current Acquisitions* 17 (May 1960): 170-174.
Cattell is known for his work in experimental psychology and as a
publisher of scientific journals. Cattell's papers include his correspondence, speeches, and articles he published. The article concludes with a
list of scientists with whom he corresponded.

1394. Coville, Bruce. "Treasure in the Library Attic: Von Ranke at Syracuse."
Wilson Library Bulletin 59 (October 1984): 98-102.
This article calls attention to the private library and papers of German
historian Leopold von Ranke, held by Syracuse University. Coville
focuses on the acquisition of the collection rather than the description of
its contents.

1395. Crawford, William R. "Sociological Research in the National Archives."
American Sociology Review 6 (April 1941): 203-216.
Crawford examined records from the Departments of State, War,
Treasury, Justice, Navy, Interior, Agriculture, Commerce, and several
others. He identifies and comments on the types of records that contain
data of interest to sociologists.

1396. Crosson, David. "The Papers of Edward Thomas Devine at the University of Wyoming." *Annals of Iowa* 44 (Spring 1978): 315-319.

The Devine papers document his career in social work and philanthropy and consist of manuscripts, correspondence, personal journals, and publications.

1397. Ehernberg, Ralph E. "The Archives of the Association of American Geographers." *Professional Geographer* 28 (May 1976): 181-185.

The author reviews the history of the archives, describes the association's records at the record series level, and comments on the research possibilities of the records in the archives.

1398. Fisher, Irving N. "The Charles McLean Andrews Collection." *Yale University Library Gazette* 42 (July 1967): 34-40.

The collection contains Andrews' correspondence; manuscripts of his books and essays; notebooks; and scrapbooks. Andrews was known as a historian and for his guides to British and American archives.

1399. Fisher, Irving N. "The Irving Fisher Collection." *Yale University Library Gazette* 36 (October 1961): 45-56.

Fisher wrote on a wide range of topics, but is, perhaps, best known for his writings on economics. Most of the collection consists of his publications, but also includes his correspondence and speeches.

1400. Friguglietti, James. "The Louis Gottschalk Papers." *French Historical Studies* 17 (Spring 1992): 802-803.

Gottschalk was a historian specializing in French history. Although brief, this article locates Gottschalk's papers and provides a listing of the eleven record series in the collection.

1401. Jimerson, Randall C. "The Papers of Three Hiram Binghams." *Yale University Library Gazette* 54 (October 1979): 85-90.

The Bingham family papers and the Yale Peruvian Expedition papers, dating from 1815-1967 and spanning three generations of Binghams, document missionary work, archaeology, and linguistic studies, and contain correspondence, diaries, manuscripts, photos, and maps.

1402. Kane, Lucile M. "Gilman Family Papers." *Social Service Review* 39 (March 1965): 92-95.

These papers document the activities of Robbins and Catheryne Gilman, social workers in Minneapolis, Minnesota. Most of the papers date from 1914 to the 1940s and include scrapbooks, minutes, reports, correspondence, speeches, and financial records.

1403. Knatz, Lothar and Hans-Arthur Marsiske. "Die Wilhelm Weitling Papers: Neue Quellen Und Dokumente Aus Dem Nachlass Wilhelm Weitlings In

Der Public Library, New York." *International Review of Social History* 29 (No. 1 1984): 62-91.

This article concludes with an inventory of Weitling correspondence, sewing machine patents and plans, astronomical papers, poetry and plays, and materials relating to the Communia, Iowa, colony. Weitling was a 19th-century social reformer.

1404. Martin, Geoffrey. "The Ellsworth Huntington Papers." *Yale University Library Gazette* 45 (April 1971): 185-195.

Huntington was an American geographer. His papers include his correspondence, diaries, photographs, manuscripts of his writings, and published materials.

1405. Patterson, Jerry E. "Checklist of Prescott Manuscripts." *Hispanic American Historical Review* 39 (February 1959): 116-128.

Patterson's approach is to list Prescott correspondence and manuscripts by repository. The list is national in coverage. For letters, he includes correspondents' names, dates of the letter or manuscript, and volume statements.

1406. Plakas, Rosemary F. "Social Science Sources in the Library of Congress Rare Book and Special Collections Division." *Social Science Journal* 25 (January 1988): 105-110.

While mostly an overview of published holdings, Plakas also identifies key manuscript collections such as the papers of Henry Harrisse, Margaret Mead, and Sigmund Freud, and the records of the Federal Writers Project and Historical Records Survey.

1407. Reichard, Gladys A. "The Elsie Clews Parsons Collection." *Proceedings of the American Philosophical Society* 94 (June 1950): 308-309.

Parsons was an anthropologist whose papers contain field notebooks, southwestern American Indian art, folklore of the Antilles, and published materials.

1408. Robson, Charles B. "Papers of Francis Lieber." *Huntington Library Bulletin* 3 (February 1933): 135-155.

Lieber was a German educator and sociologist who lived in the U.S. from 1827-1872. His papers include extensive correspondence, manuscripts of his writings, lecture notes and schedules, and published materials. The article ends with a list of correspondents.

1409. Smiley, David. "A Slice of Life in Depression America: The Records of the Historical Records Survey." *Prologue* 3 (Winter 1971): 153-159.

The correspondence files of the survey are noted as being especially rich with letters from the leading historians, bibliographers, archivists, and librarians of the 1930s.

1410. Stark, Bruce P. "The Robert Mearns Yerkes Papers." *Yale University Library Gazette* 59 (April 1985): 162-167.

Yerkes is known as a leading American psychologist of the 20th century. His papers include extensive correspondence, reports, research files, diaries, photographs, and his published writings.

1411. Tucker, Sarah J. "Archival Materials for the Anthropologist in the National Archives, Washington, D.C." *American Anthropologist* 43 (October/December 1941): 617-644.

Tucker reviews federal records containing data of interest to anthropologists. The article uses a record group approach, describing the types of records found in each, and frequently mentions specific record series and inclusive dates.

1412. Valderrama, Lucila. "Squier Manuscripts in the Biblioteca Nacional del Perú." *Hispanic American Historical Review* 36 (August 1956): 338-341.

Ephraim G. Squier was a U.S. journalist and amateur archaeologist interested in the antiquities of the Americas. The author describes six of Squier's manuscripts on Latin American topics.

1413. Vandersee, Charles. "Henry Adams: Archives and Microfilm." *Resources for American Literary Study* 9 (Spring 1979): 70-79.

The author locates the major repositories holding original Adams papers; comments on which papers have and have not been published and which were not microfilmed; and cites principal non-family correspondents represented in the Adams papers.

Regional Collections

Alaska, Hawaii, Puerto Rico, and Pacific Island Trust Territories

1414. Bell, Janet. "Hawaiian Manuscripts in the University of Hawaii Library, Honolulu, Hawaii." *Journal of Pacific History* 3 (1968): 174-177.
   Bell lists eight collections. Entries include record series titles, volume, inclusive dates, and biographical and content notes.

1415. Castro Arroyo, María de los Angeles. "Guía descriptiva de los fondos documentales existentes en el Centro de Investigaciones Históricas." *Cuadernos de la Facultad de Humanidades* 10 (1983): 91-115.
   This article was not available for annotation, but it apparently describes Puerto Rican resources.

1416. Conrad, Agnes. "The Archives of Hawaii--Records Prior to 1900." *Hawaii Historical Review* 1 (January 1963): 36-39.

1417. Conrad, Agnes. "The Archives of Hawaii." *Journal of Pacific History* 2 (1967): 191-197.
   Conrad first provides a brief history of the archives and then lists fifteen key record groups with their inclusive dates, volume, and content notes. She concludes the article by citing collection titles of personal papers also in the archives.

1418. Falk, Marvin W. "The Alaska and Polar Regions Collection at the Elmer E. Rasmuson Library." *Alaska Journal* 9 (Winter 1979): 65-70.
   Falk gives the history of the collection and provides an overview of its holdings. He limits description of holdings to subject strengths.

1419. Ford, Worthington C. "Public Records in our Dependencies." *Annual Report of the American Historical Association for the Year 1904*. 1 (1904): 129-147.
   Described are selected Spanish records in the Puerto Rican and Philippine archives. Ford mentions record series and inclusive dates for each series. Generally, the records date from the 1600s to 1898.

1420. "The Hawaiian Mission Children's Society Library." *Journal of Pacific History* 16 (January 1981): 53-56.

This article cites collections of personal papers and missionary records of U.S. missionaries operating in Hawaii from the 1820s to 1909. Entries include record series, dates, volume, and content notes.

1421. Hori, Joan. "A Survey of Indexes to Hawaiiana." *Journal of the Hawaii Library Association* 28 (December 1971): 10-16.

The author identifies photograph and manuscript collections in Hawaii for which there are indexes or detailed finding aids.

1422. Kadooka-Mardfin, Jean T. "The Municipal Archives of the City and County of Honolulu--Its Creation and Collection." *Records Management Quarterly* 11 (April 1977): 38-40.

This article offers a very brief review of holdings which include city records, maps, and photographs. A few collection titles are mentioned.

1423. La Fuse, George L. "The Puerto Rico Food Administration: Its Organization and Papers." *Hispanic American Historical Review* 21 (August 1941): 499-504.

The author names the many administrative subdivisions of this WWI agency and identifies and describes the significant record series of each.

1424. McGrath, Thomas B. "The Joachim deBrum Papers." *Journal of Pacific History* 8 (1973): 181-185.

Joachim deBrum operated a shipping business in the Marshall Islands prior to WWII. His papers (1886-1936) include information on German, Japanese, and protestant missionary influences in the islands. The article concludes with a reel list of the microfilmed papers.

1425. McGrath, Thomas B. "Records of the American Naval Period on Guam, 1898-1950." *Journal of Pacific History* 16 (January 1981): 42-53; and 18 (October 1983): 269.

McGrath provides a checklist of records and personal papers found in the U.S. National Archives; Naval Operations Archives; Marine Corps Historical Center; and the Military History Institute. Citations include record group/collection titles, record series, dates, box and folder numbers, and content notes.

1426. McGrath, Thomas B. "Records in Spain of the Augustinian Recollects in the Marianas: An Inventory." *Journal of Pacific History* 24 (April 1989): 106-109.

The citations of records relating to the Mariana Islands are from "Bound Volumes of Communications, 1843-1904," in the Recollects' archives at Marcilla, Spain. Entries include volume and page numbers, sender, date, and subjects treated.

1427. McGrath, Thomas B. "Whalers in the Marianas." *Journal of Pacific History* 21 (April 1986): 104-109.
The author lists whaling ship logs held by the Mystic Seaport Whaling Museum; the Providence (Rhode Island) Public Library; and the Kendall Whaling Museum.

1428. Robertson, James A. "Notes on the Archives of the Philippines." *Annual Report of the American Historical Association for the Year 1910* 1 (1912): 421-425.
A narrative report mentioning some of the principal record series and their location in the Philippines.

1429. Rodríguez Cruz, Juan. "Documentos sobre Puerto Rico que se encuentran en los archivos nacionales de Estados Unidos (R.G. 186)." *Caribbean Studies* 5 (October 1965): 32-50.
A checklist of documents dating from the 1750s to the 1890s arranged under the headings of civil and political affairs; financial affairs; military affairs; naval affairs; ecclesiastical affairs; records of federal agencies; and municipal records.

1430. Silvestrini-Pacheco, Blanca and María de los Angeles Castro Arroyo. "Sources for the Study of Puerto Rican History." *Latin American Research Review* 16 (Summer 1981): 156-171.
This article reviews Puerto Rico's Archivo General and its district and municipal archives. It describes, in general terms, the types of records that may be found at each level of archives and concludes with a checklist of archives and selected record groups.

1431. Vázquez Sotillo, Nelly. "Relación de mapas, planos, y fotografías existentes en el Centro de Investigaciones Históricas." *Boletin del Centro de Investigaciones* 1 (1985-1986): 127-154.
This article reviews maps, plans and photographs at the University of Puerto Rico.

East (Connecticut, Delaware, Maine, Massachusetts, New Hampshire, New Jersey, New York, Pennsylvania, Rhode Island, Vermont)

1432. Anderson, Bart. "The Chester County Historical Society." *Pennsylvania History* 19 (April 1952): 194-197.
Anderson provides a brief overview of the society's holdings, both published and unpublished. Description of manuscript material is limited to collection and record series titles and inclusive dates.

1433. "Annotated List of the Principal Manuscripts in the New York State Library." *University of the State of New York Library Bulletin* 3 (June 1899): 209-237.

There are seventy-nine documents described in this list with entries including titles, inclusive dates, volume, and content notes. The dates range from 17th-century Dutch records to state records of the 1870s. The list is indexed.

1434. Babb, James T. "Manuscripts at Yale." *Manuscripts* 10 (Fall 1958): 8-12.

This article focuses on the different manuscript collections at Yale such as the collection on American literature; western Americana; the Franklin Collection; the historical manuscripts collection; the medical collection; and the map collection.

1435. Babb, James T. "The Yale University Library: Its Early American Collections." *William and Mary Quarterly* 3rd Series 2 (October 1945): 397-401.

Babb reviews both published and unpublished materials. He cites key manuscript collections by title and inclusive dates while noting the research values of specific collections.

1436. Barck, Dorothy C. "The New York Historical Society." *Autograph Collectors' Journal* 3 (April 1951): 9-11.

Barck describes manuscript collections in the society noting several 18th-century collections; diaries; 19th-century collections of papers of well-known New Yorkers; military collections; and business collections.

1437. Bassett, T. D. Seymour. "The Dorothy Canfield Collection in the Wilbur Library of the University of Vermont." *News and Notes* 10 (December 1958): 27-29.

1438. Bassett, T. D. Seymour. "Sources for the Study of Vermont at the University of Vermont." *Vermont Libraries* 4 (September/October 1975): 105-108.

Bassett describes the university's special collection holdings in general terms by noting topical strengths and citing collection and record series titles for photographs, manuscripts, and university archives.

1439. Baughman, Roland. "Columbia University's Department of Special Collections." *Manuscripts* 15 (Winter 1963): 22-28.

Baughman reviews the manuscript holdings. Description is limited to collection titles with occasional comments on a collection's scope.

1440. Baumann, Roland M. "The Pennsylvania State Archives and Research Opportunities in the Era of the American Revolution." *Pennsylvania*

Heritage 11 (September 1976): 11-16.

1441. Bell, Whitfield J., Jr. "American Philosphical Society Library Offers Scholars an Exciting Cache." *Manuscripts* 11 (Spring 1959): 39-47.
Bell emphasizes the manuscripts from the early years of the society with its Thomas Jefferson correspondence, its Benjamin Franklin correspondence, 18th-century documentation on Indians, the papers of Richard Henry Lee, and the Lewis and Clark papers.

1442. Bell, Whitfield J., Jr. "Archives and Autographs in the American Philosophical Society Library." *Proceedings of the American Philosophical Society* 103 (December 1959): 761-767.
The author describes some of the society's early correspondence files which, because of the prominence of the correspondents, are now records with historical research value. He also reviews some key manuscript collections of the society.

1443. Blake, Theresa. "Microfilm Publications Sponsored or Published by the Dartmouth College Library." *Dartmouth College Library Bulletin* 16 (November 1975): 34-41.
There are several manuscript collections in this bibliography. Entries include extensive content notes, collection titles, inclusive dates, and the number of reels in the set.

1444. Blatt, Genevieve. "Sources for Pennsylvania History in the Department of Internal Affairs." *Pennsylvania History* 24 (January 1957): 1-13.
Blatt, Pennsylvania's secretary of internal affairs, cites several record series created by Pennsylvania's Bureau of Land Records. The article also comments on her role in preserving these records.

1445. Blier, Carol. "The Pierpont Morgan Library: Changing of the Guard." *Wilson Library Bulletin* 62 (April 1988): 41-44.
Blier provides an overview of the library's holdings which include 120,000 manuscripts dating from the Middle Ages to the 1850s.

1446. Bond, W. H. "Manuscript Collections in the Houghton Library." *Autograph Collectors' Journal* 4 (Spring 1952): 32-39.
Bond reviews the extremely rich holdings of Harvard's Houghton Library noting strengths in literature, American history, music, and theatre. Description is limited to collection titles and volume.

1447. Bowden, Karen. "The Archives: Its Strengths and Its Silences." *Pittsburgh History* 74 (Winter 1991): 157-159.
This is a brief overview of public records, manuscripts, and photograph collections in the Historical Society of Western Pennsylvania. The author

cites a few collections by title with a scope and content note.

1448. Boyce, George K. "The Pierpont Morgan Library." *Library Quarterly* 22 (January 1952): 21-35.
   While mostly a review of the library's book strengths, Boyce also gives an overview of its holdings of renaissance, medieval, literary, and historical manuscripts.

1449. Boyd, Julian P. "Notes on Some Early Post Office Records." *American Philosophical Society Library Bulletin* (1943): 84-88.
   This article describes postal records accumulated by Ebenezer Hazard, deputy postmaster of New York. The records consist of letters sent by, and received at, the Philadelphia post office between 1764 and 1768.

1450. Bressler, Nancy. "The Seeley G. Mudd Manuscript Library: A Home Fit for Statesmen." *Princeton University Library Quarterly* 39 (Autumn 1977): 1-10.
   Bressler provides an overview of the library and its holdings with description limited to collection titles.

1451. Bressor, Julie. "The Shelburne Farms Archives and Webb Family Collection." *Vermont History* 59 (Summer 1991): 180-183.

1452. Cahn, Walter and James Marrow. "Medieval and Renaissance Manuscripts at Yale: A Selection." *Yale University Library Gazette* 52 (April 1978): 173-283.
   This entire issue is devoted to a catalog and concordance and author and title indexes to Yale's collection. Catalog entries include author, title, place of origin, physical attributes, provenance, content notes, and publication notes.

1453. Clark, Alexander P. "The Manuscript Collections of the Princeton University Library: An Introductory Survey." *Princeton University Library Chronicle* 19 (Spring/Summer 1958): 159-190.
   Clark provides collection titles under categories such as the ancient world; medieval and renaissance manuscripts; Eastern and Mideastern manuscripts; English manuscripts; and modern Europe and American manuscripts.

1454. Cox, Richard J., and Anne S. K. Turkos. "Local History Research and the Records of Baltimore's Housing and Community Development Agency." *Prologue* 16 (Spring 1984): 49-61.
   Many of the record series in this record group are useful for studying housing types, architectural styles, construction materials, and structural condition. The records may also be used for social history as they

contain data about the residents of Baltimore housing.

1455. Dawson, Edgar. "Public Archives of Delaware." *Annual Report of the American Historical Association for the Year 1906* 2 (1908): 129-148.
This report includes records kept at both the state and county levels. There are court records, colonial council records, land records, wills, and records relating to orphans. Most date from the 1770s to the 1850s.

1456. "The Department of Special Collections: A Survey." *University of Rochester Library Bulletin* 24 (Fall 1968): 5-15.
This article cites record series and collection titles from the university archives, historical manuscript, literary manuscript, and theatre and drama manuscript sections of the department.

1457. Dienstag, Jacob F. "The Mendal Gottesman Library of the Yeshiva University." *Jewish Book Annual* 22 (1964/1965): 51-57.
Dienstag's overview of the library includes a section on manuscript holdings in which he lists titles of some key collections.

1458. Dojka, John. "The Yale-China Collection." *Yale University Library Gazette* 53 (April 1979): 211-216.
Dojka describes the official records of the Yale-China Association and the personal papers of the association's key administrators. The records and papers date from 1901 to the 1950s.

1459. Dunn, James T. "Manuscript Diaries in the New York State Historical Association Library." *New York History* 32 (October 1951): 488-492.
Entries in this checklist include author, birth and death dates, author's home, inclusive dates, length of diary, and content notes.

1460. Eberstadt, Edward. "The William Robertson Coe Collection of Western Americana." *Yale University Library Gazette* 23 (October 1948): 41-130.
This entire issue is devoted to a review of the Coe Collection at Yale. Materials relating to eleven western states, British Columbia, and "exploration of the interior" are examined. Both published and unpublished materials are cited.

1461. Eddy, Henry H., and Frank B. Evans. "Materials Available at the State Archives." *Pennsylvania History* 28 (January 1961): 58-63.
The authors note the archives holds the original records published in *Colonial Records* and the *Pennsylvania Archives* series, along with "voluminous" records from state agencies. There is almost no identification of record groups or series in this article.

1462. Farnham, Charles W. "Rhode Island Colonial Records." *Rhode Island*

History 29 (Winter/Spring 1970): 36-45.

Farnham identifies archives and manuscript repositories and public libraries holding colonial Rhode Island records. He concludes his article with a list of town records in Providence, Kent, Washington, Newport, and Bristol Counties.

1463. Freiberg, Malcolm. "The Winthrops and Their Papers." *Massachusetts Historical Society Proceedings* 80 (1968): 55-70.

The papers of the Winthrop family date from the early 17th century to the 1960s. They include correspondence and letterbooks; diaries and journals; speeches; financial records; scrapbooks; and medical records from nine generations of Winthrops.

1464. Graffagnino, Jonathan K. "Sources for Vermont Historians: The Manuscript Holdings of the Wilbur Collection." *Vermont History* 48 (Summer 1980): 155-172.

The James B. Wilbur Collection is at the University of Vermont. The author identifies subject strengths and concludes with a list of processed manuscript collections relating to Vermont. Entries include record series, inclusive dates, and volume.

1465. Hall, Vernon, Jr. "The Scaliger Family Papers." *Proceedings of the American Philosophical Society* 92 (May 1948): 111-114.

There are two parts to this article. The first traces the family from its 15th-century European orgins to its demise in America in 1888. Part two describes the papers at the record series level.

1466. Halstead, Vera C. "Newly Found New Canaan Records." *New Canaan Historical Society Annual* 4 (June 1955): 26-31.

1467. Hanna, Archibald, Jr. "An American West Treasure Hunt in Connecticut: The Frederick W. Beinecke Collection, Yale University." *American West* 9 (September 1972): 12-17.

A brief review of the western Americana holdings of the Beinecke Collection at Yale University. Hanna mentions selected manuscript collections and comments on their strengths.

1468. Hanna, Archibald. "Manuscript Sources in the Yale University Library for the Study of Western Travel." In *Travelers on the Western Frontier*, edited by John F. McDermott. Urbana: University of Illinois Press, 1970. 79-88.

Hanna reviews some of the better collections documenting travel in the western U.S. during the 19th century. His description is limited to collection titles and short content summaries.

1469. Hanna, Archibald. "Western Americana at Yale." *Western Historical Quarterly* 2 (October 1971): 405-408.
Brief descriptions of the major collections relating to Texas and the Mississippi River valley; the Louisiana Purchase area; the Pacific Northwest; and California and the American Southwest.

1470. Harpster, John W. "The Manuscript and Miscellaneous Collections of the Historical Society of Western Pennsylvania--A Preliminary Guide." *Western Pennsylvania Historical Magazine* 49 (January 1966): 67-78; (October 1966): 345-358; 50 (April 1967): 161-169; (July 1967): 256-268; (October 1967): 339-359; 51 (January 1968): 80-97; (April 1968): 198-208; (July 1968): 309-326; (October 1968): 417-430; 52 (January 1969): 89-98; 53 (January 1970): 90-104; (April 1970): 199-206; (July 1970): 305-315; (October 1970): 400-407; 54 (January 1971): 88-109; (April 1971): 225-243; (July 1971): 327-329; 55 (January 1972): 103-116; and (April 1972): 203-211.
Harpster provides a serialized guide in nineteen parts. Entries include collection title, inclusive dates, volume, record series titles, and detailed content notes.

1471. Heindel, Richard H. "Historical Manuscripts in the Academy of Natural Sciences, Philadelphia." *Pennsylvania History* 5 (January 1938): 30-32.
Heindel cites some of the lesser known manuscript holdings of the academy in this article. He includes the collections of L.O. von Schweinitz; Samuel S. Haldeman; S. G. Morton; and Constantine Rafinesque.

1472. Hill, Robert W. "The Liebmann Collection of American Historical Documents." *New York Public Library Bulletin* 58 (August 1954): 386-391.
The Alfred J. Liebmann Collection contains over 200 manuscripts relating the history of distilling and sale of spirituous liquors in the U.S. This article is reprinted in *Manuscripts* 6 (Summer 1954): 210-214.

1473. Hirsch, Rudolf. "Catalogue of Manuscripts in the Libraries of the University of Pennsylvania to 1800: Supplement A." *University of Pennsylvania Library Chronicle* 35 (Winter/Spring 1969): 3-32 and 36 (Winter 1970): 3-36; (Spring 1970): 79-104; 37 (Winter 1971): 3-23; (Spring 1971): 91-115; 38 (Spring 1972): 99-122; and 45 (Winter 1981): 5-29.
This is a supplement to the catalog published by Hirsch in 1965. Entries are arranged by the language of the manuscript and include author, titles, dates, physical characteristics, and content notes. The manuscripts cover a wide range of topics and time periods.

1474. "Inventory of Nims Family Papers, 1763-1910." *Historical New Hampshire* 25 (Spring 1970): 39-45.

The article offers no information on the Nims family beyond its members being farmers and small businessmen. The collection contains diaries and journals, correspondence, school records, account books, and biographical papers.

1475. Isaac, Ephraim. "The Princeton Collection of Ethiopic Manuscripts." *Princeton University Library Chronicle* 42 (Autumn 1980): 33-52.

This collection contains 330 manuscripts. Isaac divides his description into two parts, codices and scrolls, and provides content notes for each.

1476. Jacobsen, Edna L. "Manuscript Treasures in the New York State Library." *New York History* 20 (July 1939): 265-276.

The author reviews the library's George Washington and Abraham Lincoln documents; New York constitutional convention records; diaries and journals of civil and military personalities; governors' correspondence; and literary manuscripts.

1477. Johnson, Allen. "Report of the Archives of the State of Maine." *Annual Report of the American Historical Association for the Year 1908* 1 (1909): 257-318.

A thorough checklist for the time including record series titles and inclusive dates for state, county, proprietary, and local records.

1478. Joyce, William L. "The Manuscript Collections of the American Antiquarian Society." *Proceedings of the American Antiquarian Society* 89 (April 1979): 123-152.

A review of the society's acquisition history in which the author identifies some significant manuscript collections acquired. The article also describes a then recently-published catalog to the society's manuscript holdings and how to use it.

1479. Koenigsberg, Lisa. "Renderings from Worcester's Past: Nineteenth-Century Architectural Drawings at the American Antiquarian Society." *Proceedings of the American Antiquarian Society* 96 (October 1986): 367-434.

The author reviews each architect represented in the collection and concludes with a catalog of drawings held. Entries include architect, name of edifice, description of drawings, and date.

1480. Kreutzberger, Max. "The Library and Archives of the Leo Baeck Institute in New York." *Jewish Book Annual* 29 (1971/1972): 47-54.

This is a general review of the institute's holdings in which the author mentions a few key manuscript collections and comments on their contents and research values.

1481. Lane, Carl A. "Guide to the Manuscript Collections of the New Jersey Historical Society: Supplement Number 1." *New Jersey History* 99 (Fall/ Winter 1981): 209-214.

   This is a supplement to the guide published by Don Skemer and Robert Morris in 1979. Entries include collection and record series titles, inclusive dates, volume and content notes. No additional supplements were noted.

1482. Lewis, William D. "A Finding List of Material on the History of Newark, Delaware, and the University of Delaware, Its Predecessors and Associated Institutions." *Delaware Notes* 32 (1959): 33-69.

   The list contains both published and unpublished material presented three ways, alphabetically by author, chronologically, and by subject.

1483. Lewis, Wilmarth S. "Address at the Dedication of the Beinecke Rare Book and Manuscript Library." *Yale University Library Gazette* 38 (April 1964): 123-126.

   This article serves as an introduction to the Beinecke Library and is followed by a series of articles describing the library's holdings. Those describing manuscripts are:

   1. Gallup, Donald. "The Yale Collection of American Literature." 151-159.

   2. Hanna, Archibald, Jr. "The Yale Collection of Western Americana and the Benjamin Franklin Collection." 160-166.

   3. Liebert, Herman and Marjorie G. Wynne. "The General Collection of Rare Books and Manuscripts." 131-137.

1484. Lincoln, Charles H. "The Manuscript Collections of the American Antiquarian Society." *Papers of the Bibliographical Society of America* 4 (1909): 59-72.

   A general review of the society's unpublished holdings. The author cites collection titles and comments on the volume and research value of several collections. The manuscripts described date from the 17th century through the Civil War.

1485. Lingelbach, William E. "The American Philosophical Society Library from 1942 to 1952 with a Survey of Its Historical Background." *Proceedings of the American Philosophical Society* 97 (October 1953): 471-492.

   Part one of the article provides the historical background, part two

238 EastEast

describes the holdings, including manuscript collections.

1486. López, Jeanne B. "The Louis Wiley Collection." *University of Rochester Library Bulletin* 9 (Autumn 1953): 4-11.

1487. Lovett, Robert W. "The Collection of W. Cameron Forbes," *Harvard Library Bulletin* 5 (Autumn 1951): 381-385.
This is a description of the better record series in the Forbes Collection. The collection is particularly rich in Forbes' correspondence and journals relating to his travels and diplomatic career in the Philippines and Japan.

1488. "Manuscript Collections in the New York Public Library." *Bulletin of the New York Public Library* 5 (July 1901): 306-336; and 19 (February 1915): 135-165.
This is a guide in two parts, with entries appearing alphabetically by collection title under broad geographical headings. Each entry includes record series titles, inclusive dates, volume, and content notes.

1489. Martz, Louis L. "The Beinecke Rare Book and Manuscript Library." *Yale University Library Gazette* 48 (April 1974): 221-283.
This entire issue of the *Gazette* is devoted to the collections of the Beinecke Library. Individual articles include:

1. Gallup, Donald. "The Collection of American Literature." 241-252.

2. Hanna, Archibald, Jr. "The Collection of Western Americana." 261-266.

3. Liebert, Herman W., and Marjorie G. Wynne. "The General Collection of Rare Books and Manuscripts." 227-240.

4. Parks, Stephen. "The Osborn Collection." 277-283.

5. Sammons, Christa A. "The German Literature Collection." 267-276.

1490. McDaniel, Jane G. "Julius A. Skilton Papers." *Hispanic American Historical Review* 36 (August 1956): 342-344.
Skilton was a U.S. citizen living in Mexico and serving as U.S. consul between 1867 and 1878. His papers include correspondence relating to U.S. claims against Mexico and other papers relating to his consular duties. The papers are at Cornell University.

1491. McDermott, John F. "The Western Journals of George Hunter, 1796-1805." *Proceedings of the American Philosophical Society* 103 (December 1959): 770-773.

A review of the society's holdings of Hunter's journals describing his travels to Kentucky, Illinois, Arkansas, Louisiana, and St. Louis, Missouri, between 1796 and 1805.

1492. Mead, Nelson P. "Public Archives of Connecticut. County, Probate, and Local Records." *Annual Report of the American Historical Association for the Year 1906* 2 (1908): 53-127.

Mead includes record series titles, inclusive dates, and volume of records with notes on missing records. The local records are those of municipalities.

1493. Metzdorf, Robert F. "Manuscripts at Yale." *Manuscripts* 6 (Winter 1954): 81-85.

The author cites a few of Yale's outstanding collections such as the early Babylonian, Egyptian, and Greek materials; Ezra Stiles' papers; Jonathan Edwards' manuscripts; Eli Whitney's papers; Benjamin Franklin's papers; and others.

1494. Mevers, Frank C., and Harriet S. Lacy. "Early Historical Records (c.1620-c.1817) at the New Hampshire State Archives." *Historical New Hampshire* 31 (Fall 1976): 108-118.

The authors cite record series titles, volume, inclusive dates, publication information, and content notes for manuscripts and records from the colonial, American Revolutionary, and early national periods.

1495. Miner, Dorothy E. "The Collections of Manuscripts and Rare Books in the Walters Art Gallery." *Papers of the Bibliographical Society of America* 30 (1936): 104-109.

The author describes the private collection of Henry Walters among which are 750 illuminated manuscripts dating from the 9th to the 18th centuries, along with 75 letters of Catherine the Great and an early manuscript copy of the "Star-Spangled Banner."

1496. Moody, Robert E. "Boston University's Growing Manuscript Collections." *Manuscripts* 18 (Spring 1966): 40-43.

This short article cites the titles of some of the collections held by the university library.

1497. "New York City Collections." *Wilson Library Bulletin* 54 (June 1980): 625-639.

The holdings of eleven special libraries which have manuscript collections are briefly described, including the Julliard School, the Schomburg Center, and the Pierpont Morgan Library.

1498. New York Historical Society. "Old New York Inventories of Estates,

1717-1800." *New York Historical Society Quarterly Bulletin* 6 (January 1923): 130-137; and 8 (April 1924): 43-46.

After reprinting one inventory in its entirety as an example, the article presents an alphabetical checklist of inventories in the society.

1499. New York State Library. "Annotated List of the Principal Manuscripts in the New York State Library." *State Library Bulletin. History* 3 (June 1899): 209-237.

While listing this article in his 1951 bibliography in the *Mississippi Valley Historical Review*, Ray Allen Billington notes that a 1911 fire destroyed many of the papers described in the article.

1500. Paltsits, Victor H. "Manuscript Sources for the History of Central and Western New York in the New York Public Library." *New York History* 19 (January 1938): 53-63.

The author lists, alphabetically by title, thirty collections and individual items. Entries include record series titles, inclusive dates, volume, and content notes. Most materials date from the 1740s to the 1850s.

1501. Pennsylvania Historical Society Library. "Supplement to the Guide to the Manuscript Collections in the Historical Society of Pennsylvania." *Pennsylvania Magazine of History and Biography* 67 (January 1943): 108-112; 68 (January 1944): 98-111; 69 (January 1945): 50-59; 70 (April 1946): 181-184; 71 (July 1947): 283-287; and 72 (July 1948): 276-283.

These guide supplements are presented without introduction. Each entry is numbered, apparently continuing a series in the published guide. The entries include collection and record series titles, volume, inclusive dates, provenance statements, and content notes.

1502. Powers, Zara J. "American Historical Manuscripts in the Historical Manuscript Room." *Yale University Library Gazette* 14 (July 1939): 1-11.

Powers reviews 18th- and 19th-century manuscripts housed in the then newly-opened historical manuscript room. Many of the collections relate to Connecticut, the Western Reserve, and the American Revolution.

1503. Reed, H. Clay. "Manuscript Books in the Historical Society of Delaware." *Delaware History* 11 (1964): 65-82.

This article offers a checklist of account books, journals, diaries, minutes, copybooks, and similar manuscript records. Entries appear under subject headings such as business, churches, military, etc.

1504. Riggs, John B. "A Summary Report on Manuscripts Accessioned by the Eleutherian Mills Historical Library Through 1975." *Working Papers from the Regional Economic History Research Center* 2 (No. 1 1978): 1-30.

1505. Riley, Edward M. "The Deborah Franklin Correspondence." *Proceedings of the American Philosophical Society* 95 (June 1951): 239-245.
Riley describes the society's collection of over 200 letters between Benjamin Franklin and his wife during the years 1751-1774.

1506. Riley, Stephen T. "Manuscripts in the Massachusetts Historical Society." *Proceedings of the Massachusetts Historical Society* 92 (1980): 100-116.
This is a review of the society's acquisition program. Riley cites many significant items and collections that have made the society an important manuscript repository. Description is limited to collection titles, volume, and comments on research strengths.

1507. Roach, George W. "Guide to Depositories of Manuscript Collections in New York State: Supplements No. 1-5." *New York History* 24 (April 1943): 265-270; (July 1943): 417-422; (October 1943): 560-564; 25 (January 1944): 64-68; and (April 1944): 226-227.
This five-part guide series supplements the Historical Record Survey's *Guide to Depositories of Manuscript Collections in New York State (Exclusive of New York City)* published in 1941. The series lists collection entries under repository headings. Entries include collection and record series titles, volume, and inclusive dates.

1508. Root, Nina J. "The Rare Book and Manuscript Collection of the American Museum of Natural History Library." *Curator* 20 (June 1977): 121-152.
The author devotes most of this article to the museum's published rarities, describes several manuscript collections on pages 147-152.

1509. Rothert, Otto A. "Shane, the Western Collector." *Filson Club Historical Quarterly* 4 (January 1930): 1-16.
John D. Shane, a contemporary of Lyman C. Draper, collected materials relating to pioneer life and the Presbyterian Church in Kentucky. The article lists his papers that are in the Draper Collection and in the Presbyterian Historical Collection, Philadelphia.

1510. Russell, John R. "The William E. Werner Collection." *University of Rochester Library Bulletin* 9 (Winter 1954): 21-28.

1511. Salisbury, Ruth. "Survey of the Darlington Library." *Western Pennsylvania Historical Magazine* 48 (January 1964): 19-29.
The author reviews local, state, and national history resources held by the library. She includes many manuscripts and records. Description includes collection and record series titles, inclusive dates, volume, and content notes.

1512. Sellers, Charles C. "Manuscripts at Dickinson College." *Manuscripts* 6 (Summer 1954): 202-204.

    The article mentions a few key collections at Dickinson, the most noteworthy, perhaps, the papers of President James Buchanan, a graduate of its class of 1809. Description is limited to titles of collections and their volume.

1513. Severance, Frank H. ed. "Rough List of Manuscripts in the Library of the Buffalo Historical Society." *Buffalo Historical Society Publications* 14 (1910): 421-485.

    The list, which is appendix B of volume 14, is alphabetical by collection title. Entries include record series titles, volume, inclusive dates, and content notes.

1514. Shearer, Augustus H. "Report on the Archives of the State of Vermont." *Annual Report of the American Historical Association for the Year 1915* 1 (1917): 311-355.

    Shearer provides record series titles and inclusive dates along with some descriptive comments about records found in Vermont state offices.

1515. Shearer, Augustus H. "Resources in Buffalo for the Study of American History." *Papers of the Bibliographical Society of America* 16 (1922): 6-9.

    While brief, this article does cite some key collections in Buffalo, New York, repositories.

1516. Shipton, Clifford K. "The American Antiquarian Society." *William and Mary Quarterly* 3rd Series 2 (April 1945): 164-172.

    The author reviews the research strengths of several subject collections of the society. He describes, in general terms, both published and unpublished holdings while citing some specific manuscript collections by title.

1517. Shipton, Clifford K. "Collections of the Harvard University Archives." *Harvard Library Bulletin* 1 (Spring 1947): 176-184.

    The three-hundred year accumulation of university records at Harvard begins in 1643 and includes correspondence and minutes of the Overseers, financial records, faculty records, student and class records, and publications of the university.

1518. Spofford, Ernest. "Some of the Manuscript Resources of the Historical Society of Pennsylvania." *Pennsylvania History* 1 (April 1934): 88-97.

    Spofford reviews the scope and content of the papers of William Penn; James Logan; Isaac Norris; Edward Shippen; John Pemberton; William Rawle; Thomas Wharton; Joshua Humphreys; and several others.

1519. Stapleton, Darwin. "The American Philosophical Society Library Holdings in Early American Technology." *Technology and Culture* 23 (July 1982): 430-434.

This is an overview of the library's topical strengths. The author mentions both published and manuscript materials.

1520. Swan, Bradford F. "The Providence Town Papers." *Rhode Island History* 11 (July 1952): 65-70.

Swan describes a collection of municipal records dating from the 1640s to the 1830s. He reports that the records are rich in correspondence and documents by Roger Williams.

1521. Tolles, Bryant F., Jr. "Dartmouth College Manuscript Materials at the New Hampshire Historical Society." *Dartmouth College Library Bulletin* 13 (April 1973): 74-94.

Tolles provides four checklists of collections, documents, letters, and miscellaneous manuscript items. Entries include collection or document titles, record series titles, correspondents' names, inclusive dates, and content notes.

1522. Turner, Silvie. "The Connecticut Archives." *Connecticut Historical Society Bulletin* 33 (July 1968): 81-89.

This is a mini-guide to Connecticut records held by the Connecticut State Library in Hartford. Entries include record series titles, volume, inclusive dates, and a detailed content summary for forty-nine record series.

1523. Van Deusen, Glyndon G. "The Thurlow Weed Collection." *University of Rochester Library Bulletin* 1 (February 1946): 21-25.

1524. Wainwright, Nicholas B. "The Penn Collection." *Pennsylvania Magazine of History and Biography* 87 (October 1963): 393-419.

A lengthy article, mostly about the provenance of the Penn family papers at the Historical Society of Pennsylvania. Description of the papers is limited.

1525. Wallace, Marlene. "A Guide to the Vermont State Papers." *Vermont Libraries* 4 (July/August 1975): 89-92.

This article discusses the papers held and created by Vermont's secretary of state office. The records date from 1775 to the 1970s. A more complete description of these records may be found in Wallace's 1970 article in *Vermont History* cited below.

1526. Wallace, Marlene and John Williams. "Vermont State Papers: Rich Sources for the Study of Vermont History." *Vermont History* 38

(Summer 1970): 214-249.

These papers include session laws; treasurers' orders; orders and allowances of the courts; petitions; land records; public letters; General Assembly members credentials; constable certificates; resolutions; and committee reports.

1527. Wallace, R. Stuart. "The State Papers: A Descriptive Guide." *Historical New Hampshire* 31 (Fall 1976): 119-128.

Stuart explains that "State Papers" is a frequently used short title for forty volumes of published New Hampshire records entitled *Documents and Records Relating to New Hampshire, 1623-1800*. The article also reviews the contents of the forty volumes.

1528. Wax, Bernard. "Rhode Island Materials in the American Jewish Historical Society Collections." *Rhode Island Jewish Historical Notes* 7 (November 1975): 171-174.

1529. Weber, David C. "Non-Book Materials in the Harvard Library." *Harvard Library Bulletin* 9 (Spring 1955): 268-273.

This article is an overview of microform holdings, sound recordings, sheet music, maps, photographs, broadsides, and manuscripts in several of Harvard's libraries.

1530. White, Leslie A. "The Lewis Henry Morgan Collection." *University of Rochester Library Bulletin* 2 (June 1947): 48-51.

1531. Wolfe, Richard J. "Early New York Naturalization Records in the Emmett Collection, with a List of Aliens Naturalized in New York, 1802-1814." *Bulletin of the New York Public Library* 67 (April 1963): 211-217.

The article calls attention to, and identifies two manuscripts lists of immigrants to New York state who were naturalized between 1740-1769 and 1802-1814. The lists are published as a conclusion to the article.

1532. Wroth, Lawrence C. "Source Materials of Florida History in the John Carter Brown Library of Brown University." *Florida Historical Quarterly* 20 (July 1941): 3-46.

The author cites published and unpublished maps; early travel accounts; narratives of exploration; and early accounts by settlers and military officers. French, Spanish, and British sources are the most numerous.

Midwest (Illinois, Indiana, Iowa, Kansas, Michigan, Minnesota, Missouri, Nebraska, North Dakota, Ohio, Oklahoma, South Dakota, Wisconsin)

1533. Abbott, John C., and John N. Hoover. "Regional and Music Research

Collections at Lovejoy Library, Southern Illinois University at Edwards-ville." *Illinois Libraries* 66 (April 1984): 174-178.

The authors describe the John Francis McDermott Collection; the microfilm collection relating to Mormons in Illinois; ethnic collections; and the library's music collection.

1534. Alvord, Clarence W., and Theodore C. Pease. "The Archives of the State of Illinois." *Annual Report of the American Historical Association for the Year 1909* 1 (1911): 383-463.

The authors provide record series titles and inclusive dates for records held in state offices at Chester, Belleville, and Springfield, Illinois.

1535. Ander, O. Fritiof. "The Augustana College Archives." *Illinois Libraries* 37 (June 1955): 168-175.

Ander reviews the records of the Augustana Theological Seminary and manuscript collections in the archives. See his 1958 article below for a slightly more recent description of this repository's holdings.

1536. Ander, O. Fritiof. "The Augustana College Archives." *Illinois Libraries* 40 (April 1958): 279-286.

The article begins with a review of the records of the Augustana Theological Seminary and closes with an alphabetical checklist of manuscript collections in the college archives. Entries include record series titles, inclusive dates, and content notes.

1537. Bamberger, Mary Ann and Mary Lynn McCree. "The Manuscript Collection at the University of Illinois at Chicago Circle." *Illinois Libraries* 63 (April 1981): 301-304.

This article updates a 1975 article by Bamberger and Stewart by citing collection titles of new acquisitions. The repository is noted for its holdings related to women and social welfare. Description is limited to collection titles.

1538. Bamberger, Mary Ann and Virginia R. Stewart. "The Manuscript Collection at University of Illinois at Chicago Circle." *Illinois Libraries* 57 (March 1975): 216-219.

The authors note the collection's strengths by citing records and papers relating to social welfare and ministries; ethnic groups; women; politics; community services; and the archives of the university.

1539. Baumann, Karen J. "State Historical Society of Wisconsin: Manuscript Resources on Georgia History." *Georgia Archive* 2 (Summer 1974): 103-111.

Baumann describes eight labor collections; twelve civil rights collections; and nine miscellaneous collections. Entries include record series titles, inclusive dates, volume, and content notes.

1540. Bauxar, J. Joe. "Northern Illinois University Archives." *Illinois Libraries* 57 (March 1975): 230-232.

Bauxar reviews, in general terms, holdings of university records; state and local governmental records; and regional manuscript collections. Description is limited to record series titles.

1541. Beatty, John D. "Genealogical Research in Indiana." *National Genealogical Society Quarterly* 79 (June 1991): 100-122.

This article should be useful to those planning research in Indiana. It identifies and locates many types of records in the state, comments on the information found within record series, notes the existence of indexes, and provides other access tips.

1542. Becker, Carl. "Public Archives of Kansas." *Annual Report of the American Historical Association for the Year 1904* 1 (1905): 597-601.

A checklist of record series titles with inclusive dates along with a listing of published records.

1543. Biggert, Elizabeth C. "The Library of the Ohio State Archaeological and Historical Society." *Autograph Collectors' Journal* 5 (Spring 1953): 46-48.

The author notes that the library has over 1,100 collections with strengths in the Revolutionary War, the Civil War, business, and religion. Description is limited to collection titles.

1544. Bishop, Beverly D. "Eyewitnesses of the Past: The Archival Collections." *Gateway Heritage* 1980 (Summer 1980): 40-45.

This article reviews specific manuscript collections held by Missouri Historical Society in St. Louis. The collections document the early fur trade, exploration in the West, the St. Louis area, and a variety of personal careers.

1545. Bishop, Beverly D. "The Writingest Explorers: Manuscripts of the Lewis and Clark Expedition." *Gateway Heritage* 2 (Fall 1981): 22-29.

The Missouri Historical Society archives at St. Louis holds about 200 Lewis and Clark-related manuscripts including letters, legal documents, official orders, and notebooks. The materials are in the William Clark, Meriwether Lewis, and Thomas Jefferson Collections.

1546. Blazier, George J. "The Marietta College Collections of Historical Manuscripts." *Manuscripts* 9 (Winter 1975): 35-38.

Highlighting this collection are records of the Ohio Company formed in 1786 and including minute books, surveys, and deeds. Also noted are the papers of General Rufus Putnam and the diary of Joseph Buell, a soldier at Fort Harmar in 1786-1787.

1547. Bowen, Laurel G. "The Manuscripts Department of the Illinois State Historical Library: The 1980s." *Illinois Libraries* 69 (October 1987): 582-583.
     A review of selected collection titles under the topical headings of religion, labor, agriculture, women, Afro-Americans, business, public services, law, and the 1970 state constitutional convention.

1548. Bowen, Laurel G. "The Manuscripts Section of the Illinois State Historical Library." *Illinois Libraries* 63 (March 1981): 250-253.
     Bowen notes that the library has significant collections relating to Abraham Lincoln and the Civil War; business and organized labor; medicine; social services; law; education; and religion. Description is limited to collection titles.

1549. Brichford, Maynard. "The Illiarch." *Illinois Libraries* 52 (February 1970): 182-204.
     While mostly a history of the University of Illinois-Urbana archives and its operations, the article closes with a checklist of personal papers and archival record groups in the archives.

1550. Brown, Margaret Kimball. "The Kaskaskia Manuscripts." *Illinois Libraries* 62 (April 1980): 312-324.
     A thorough review of the provenance of the Kaskaskia records, their volume, and the types of information they contain. The Kaskaskia records are French notarial and court records created in what is now Illinois. They date from 1708 to 1816.

1551. Browne, Valerie G. "Loyola University of Chicago Archives." *Illinois Libraries* 69 (October 1987): 587-588.
     Browne notes that most of the university records date from the 1920s forward. She also cites several key manuscript collections of faculty and prominent individuals. Her description includes content notes and inclusive dates.

1552. Brubaker, Robert L. "The Development of an Urban History Research Center: The Chicago Historical Society's Library." *Chicago History* 7 (Spring 1978): 22-36.
     In this history of the library, Brubaker gives an overview of the library's holdings which include a large manuscript collection. He cites subject strengths and many collection titles.

1553. Brudvig, Glenn. "The Catalog of the Orin G. Libby Historical Manuscripts Collection of the University of North Dakota Library." *North Dakota Historical Quarterly* 31 (January 1964): 79-90.

A standard guide with entries alphabetical by collection title and including record series titles, volume, inclusive dates, and content notes.

1554. Brunvand, Jan H. "Norwegian-American Folklore in the Indiana University Archives." *Midwest Folklore* 7 (Winter 1975): 221-228.

This article reports on the types of Norwegian folklore found in the archives. The holdings are organized by categories such as customs, songs, poems, games, beliefs, and informant sketches.

1555. Burton, Clarence M. "The Burton Historical Collection of the Public Library, Detroit." *Papers of the Bibliographical Society of America* 16 (Part 1 1922): 10-16.

A review of published and unpublished resources in the Burton Collection. Description of manuscript collections is limited to titles and brief content notes.

1556. Caldwell, Norman W. "Additional Kaskaskia Manuscripts." *Illinois Libraries* 34 (May 1951): 192-204.

A listing, under record series titles, of individual 18th-century documents discovered in the circuit court office at Chester, Illinois. Entries include the names of people mentioned in the documents, dates, and content summaries.

1557. Caldwell, Norman W. "Manuscript Holdings of Southern Illinois University Library." *Illinois Libraries* 40 (April 1958): 333-339.

Caldwell describes county and university records and manuscript records under general headings of public records; university archives; and private papers. Entries include collection titles, record series titles, inclusive dates, volume, and content notes.

1558. Cassady, Theodore J. "Record Holdings of Illinois State Archives." *Illinois Libraries* 40 (April 1958): 295-304.

Cassady lists record groups of state agency records under which he then lists record series titles and inclusive dates. He also includes listings of county records. The article is most useful for identifying record series from Illinois governmental units.

1559. Cloud, Patricia D. "The Northwestern University Archives." *Illinois Libraries* 69 (October 1987): 595-597.

Cloud provides an overview of the archives and its services and lists many collections of faculty papers along with inclusive dates.

1560. Colket, Meredith B., Jr. "The Western Reserve Historical Society." *Ohio*

History 72 (April 1963): 140-149.

This article reviews the society's artifact holdings, manuscript collections, exhibits, and published materials. Colkett identifies subject strengths and closes the article by citing twenty-four manuscript collections with their inclusive dates.

1561. Crouse, Moses C., and Doris K. Colby. "The Aurora College Archives." *Illinois Libraries* 63 (April 1981): 304-307.

The authors describe the two categories of materials that are in the archives: the Orrin Roe Jenks Collection relating to the history and development of the Adventist Movement in the U.S., and the records of the college.

1562. Daly, John. "The Illinois State Archives." *Illinois Libraries* 63 (March 1981): 253-257.

One-half of this article relates the history and goals of the archives. The other half cites record groups, record series titles, volume, and inclusive dates for state records held. Daly notes the archives also holds county and municipal records.

1563. DeBolt, Dean. "Education and Public Affairs: Documenting Illinois' First Senior University." *Illinois Libraries* 63 (March 1981): 257-260.

Textual and audio-visual records in the archives document the growth and administration of the university, local history, and the public affairs educational programs at the university. The archives also holds county and municipal records from central Illinois.

1564. Conger, John L. "Report on the Public Archives of Michigan." *Annual Report of the American Historical Association for the Year 1905* 1 (1906): 369-376.

A brief report in general terms. The article may be useful for identifying selected record series titles.

1565. Davenport, John B. "The Manuscript Collections of the University of North Dakota." *Great Plains Journal* 15 (Spring 1976): 134-143.

Among the holdings at the University of North Dakota are the papers of North Dakota's congressmen, senators, and governors; the White Bull manuscript; an oral history collection; 1,500 photographs; a map collection; and university records.

1566. DeWitt, Donald L. "The University of Oklahoma's Western History Collections." *Journal of the West* 29 (January 1990): 89-92.

DeWitt provides an overview of resources in the University of Oklahoma's Western History Collections. Description is limited to areas of strengths and collection titles for book, manuscript, and photograph collections, and sound recordings.

1567. Dorson, Richard M. "The Michigan State University Folklore Archives."
Midwestern Folklore 5 (Spring 1955): 51-59.
    Dorson provides a brief history of the archives and comments on its
    usefulness to research. The article concludes with a list of more than 800
    interviews noting their geographical origins and subject content.

1568. Downs, Robert B. "University of Illinois Library." *Illinois Libraries* 47
(November 1965): 861-868.
    This article is a description of special collections. Downs describes
    mostly published works, but cites important manuscript holdings by
    collection title.

1569. Dunlap, Leslie W., and Hallet Gildersleeve. "University of Illinois
Library Manuscript Collections." *Illinois Libraries* 40 (April 1958): 349-
352.
    The authors describe several key collections including the Herbert
    George Wells papers; the records of English publisher George Bentley;
    and the Carl Sandburg papers, along with smaller collections of British
    writers.

1570. Dunn, Lucia S. "The New Trier Township High School Archives."
Illinois Libraries 69 (October 1987): 592-593.
    Dunn's article describes administrative records, photographs, and
    memorabilia held by this Winnetka, Illinois, high school. The materials
    date from 1913 to the 1970s.

1571. East, Ernest E. "Historical Treasures of Randolph County." *Illinois
Libraries* 35 (April 1953): 161-170.
    East describes 18th-century French records and 18th- and 19th-century
    U.S. records microfilmed by the state archives. His description includes
    record series titles, dates, volume, and types of information found in the
    records.

1572. East, Ernest E. "History in County Archives: Peoria County's Plan for
a County Archives Department." *Illinois Libraries* 22 (February 1940):
27-31.
    East reviews some early records found in the Peoria County court
    house. They include marriage and divorce records; French claims for
    losses during the U.S. Revolutionary War; documents relating to
    Abraham Lincoln; probate records; and county commissioner files.

1573. East, Ernest E., and Margaret C. Norton. "Randolph County Records:
An Inventory of Microfilm Copies in the Illinois State Library." *Illinois*

Libraries 35 (June 1953): 256-262.

This is a checklist of microfilmed record series described in the April, 1953 article by East in entry 1571. The checklist includes record series titles, volume, and inclusive dates.

1574. Edstrom, James A. "The Champaign County Historical Archives: 'Keeper of the Collective Memory.'" *Illinois Libraries* 70 (September 1988): 524-527.

This article describes the holdings and services of a local history and genealogical collection in the Urbana Free Library. The holdings, described by record series and inclusive dates, include oral histories, photographs, and county vital records.

1575. Elliott, J. M. "The Owen Family Papers." *Indiana Magazine of History* 60 (December 1964): 331-352.

Elliott describes the papers of the descendents of Robert Owens, the founder of New Harmony, Indiana, and others associated with the community. The papers, dating from the 1790s to the 1950s, include correspondence, business records, journals, and diaries.

1576. Erney, Richard A. "Wisconsin's Area Research Centers." *American Archivist* 29 (January 1966): 11-22.

Mostly a review of the organizational structure of the research center network. The article concludes, however, by citing key collections and strengths of the centers.

1577. Fish, Carl R. "Report on the Public Archives of Wisconsin." *Annual Report of the American Historical Association for the Year 1905* 1 (1906): 377-419.

Fish lists record series titles with inclusive dates under the state office in which the records were created and held.

1578. Frey, Charles J. "The Virginius H. Chase Special Collection Center." *Illinois Libraries* 66 (April 1984): 185-188.

While mostly a description of published materials, the author does cite the Philander Chase correspondence; the records of the Associated Public-Safety Communications Officers; and a number of other manuscript materials.

1579. Giaquinta, Joyce and Billie Peterson. "The Irish-Preston Papers, 1832-1972." *Annals of Iowa* 44 (Fall 1978): 475-479.

These are the papers of two Iowa families. They include diaries, drawings, manuscripts, correspondence, photographs, scrapbooks, and financial records. The collection is held by the Iowa State Historical Society, Iowa City, Iowa.

1580. Gibson, Michael D. "The Archival Collections at the Center for Dubuque History." *Annals of Iowa* 50 (Spring 1990): 389-393.

The center is at Loras College, Dubuque, Iowa. The materials cited include municipal and county records, personal papers, maps, clipping files, and photographs.

1581. Gildemeister, Glen. "The Early W. Hayter Regional History Center." *Illinois Libraries* 69 (October 1987): 593-594.

Located on the campus of Northern Illinois University, DeKalb, the center holds and collects regional manuscript materials and university records. Description is limited to collection titles.

1582. Golter, Robert and Ruth James Cording. "Wheaton College Library." *Illinois Libraries* 47 (November 1965): 872-875.

This is a description of special collections at Wheaton College in which description of unpublished materials is limited to record series titles in the college archives.

1583. Grace, Michael. "Loyola University of Chicago Archives." *Illinois Libraries* 63 (April 1981): 307-308.

University records; the Samuel Insull papers; the records of the Catholic Church Extension Society; the files of the Institute of Jesuit History; and a Chicago-area clipping file are the collections Grace describes in this article.

1584. Haring, Jacqueline. "Manuscript Collections in the Knox College Archives." *Illinois Libraries* 63 (March 1981): 260-262.

Haring notes that the archives holds nearly 200 collections of personal papers relating to development of the college and central Illinois history. She cites inclusive dates and titles of significant collections.

1585. Harlan, Edgar R. "Alphabetical List of Manuscript Collections in the Historical Memorial and Art Department of Iowa." *Annals of Iowa* 3rd Series 16 (April 1929): 617-621.

This is a list of collection titles with no additional information. It is useful only if seeking a specific surname or corporate entity.

1586. Harper, Josephine L. "Searching for Ancestors in the Draper Manuscripts or the Draper Collection as a Source for Genealogical Research." *Indiana History Bulletin* 37 (September 1960): 107-119.

These are the papers of Lyman Draper. A useful article in that it identifies those series in the collection most useful from a genealogical perspective. Harper also provides information on access and what types of data researchers may expect to find.

1587. Haskell, Diana. "Midwest Manuscripts at the Newberry Library." *Illinois Libraries* 63 (April 1981): 287-289.

Haskell describes key collections in the Midwest Collection, a grouping of 170 manuscript collections relating to the Chicago area and midwestern states. She cites collection titles under categories of politics, literature, music, journalism, and family papers.

1588. Haskell, Diana. "The Newberry Library's Manuscript Holdings: Second Report." *Illinois Libraries* 57 (March 1975): 232-235.

This article is an update of the 1958 article by Stanley Pargellis (entry 1640). Haskell provides some new volume statements and cites collection titles and inclusive dates for collections acquired since 1958.

1589. Hickerson, Joseph C. "Hoosier Materials in the Indiana University Folklore Archive." *Midwest Folklore* 11 (Summer 1961): 75-83.

The author reviews Indiana-related folklore data in the Archives of Folk and Primitive Music; the University Folklore Archives; and the Michigan State University Folklore Archives transferred to Indiana in 1957.

1590. Hoehn, Richard A. "The Stuckenberg Collection." *Concordia Historical Institute Quarterly* 58 (Summer 1985): 89-93.

1591. Holden, Thomas R. "Canal Park Marine Museum." *Inland Seas* 48 (Fall 1992): 216-218.

Holden reviews museum library holdings which include records of the Duluth Customs District, U.S. Steel's Great Lakes Fleet records, and Corps of Engineers records. The library also has 50,000 photos of lake vessels and drawings of port facilities.

1592. Holli, Melvin G. "The Urban Historical Collection at the University of Illinois--Chicago Circle." *Illinois Libraries* 52 (February 1970): 163-166.

Holli reviews the 110 collections making up the Urban Historical Collection. He limits description to collection titles. Many of the collections relate to ethnic groups in the Chicago area.

1593. Howren, Robert. "Iowa Materials for the Linguistic Atlas of the Upper Midwest." *Books at Iowa* 6 (April 1967): 29-35.

Howren explains the informational content of 574 worksheets collected in a 1939 linguistic survey. Also included among these survey materials are 200 lexical questionnaires collected from informants then over sixty years old.

1594. Hubach, Robert R. "Unpublished Travel Narratives on the Early Midwest, 1720-1850: A Preliminary Bibliography." *Mississippi Valley Historical Review* 42 (December 1955): 525-548.

Hubach's bibliography has 199 entries from 30 repositories. The entries include author; document type; title, which incorporates geographical area covered; dates; and content note.

1595. Hunt, Carol. "Manuscript Collections: The Putnam Museum in Davenport." *Annals of Iowa* 44 (Summer 1978): 388-393.
Hunt describes eleven collections with entries including collection title, volume, inclusive dates, content notes, and biographical information where appropriate.

1596. Hurst, Roger A. "The New Harmony Manuscript Collections." *Indiana Magazine of History* 37 (March 1941): 45-49.
These manuscripts reflect the development of the Rappite and Owenite communities in New Harmony, Indiana. The papers include town records, correspondence, music, biographical information, maps, and drawings, all dated 1821-1938.

1597. Iben, Icko. "Notes from the Work Shop, Marriage in Old Cahokia." *Illinois Libraries* 24 (November 1944): 473-483.
The author provides a thorough analysis of seventy French marriages recorded in Cahokia (in what is now Illinois) between 1763 and 1802, including the types of data found in these records.

1598. James, Thelma. "Report on Wayne University Archives." *Midwestern Folklore* 5 (Spring 1955): 62-64.
This brief article identifies the locale and topical content of some 250 folklore interviews at Wayne State University in Detroit.

1599. Jewell, Frank. "The Ryerson and Burnham Libraries." *Chicago History* 8 (Spring 1979): 58-60.
These two libraries are part of the Art Institute of Chicago. Jewell provides a history of their development and comments on their holdings. The Burnham Library holds the papers of architects Louis H. Sullivan, Daniel H. Burnham, and John W. Root.

1600. Jordan, H. Glenn. "The Western History Collections of the University of Oklahoma Library." *Great Plains Journal* 15 (Fall 1975): 55-64.
The second part of this article describes the unpublished holdings including manuscripts, photo collections, maps, oral histories, and the archives of the University of Oklahoma. Description is limited to collection titles and scope.

1601. Jordan, H. Glenn. "Western History Collections at the University of Oklahoma." *Chronicles of Oklahoma* 54 (Fall 1976): 370-392.
A thorough description of this University of Oklahoma special

collection. The article cites book, manuscript, photograph, sound recording, microfilm, and map collections along with the university archives.

1602. Josephson, Bertha. "Catalogue of Manuscript Collections at the Library of the Ohio State Archaeological and Historical Society." *Ohio State Archaeological and Historical Quarterly* 55 (January/March 1946): 44-67.

This is a partial alphabetical listing of manuscript collections and records by title. It runs 'A' through Camp. Entries include record series titles, inclusive dates, and volume. There is no indication that the catalog was continued.

1603. Kane, Lucile M. "The Autograph Collection." *Minnesota History* 33 (Autumn 1953): 298-300.

Kane calls attention to the Minnesota Historical Society's collection of signatures of America's prominent people.

1604. Kane, Lucile M. "The Autograph Collection of the Minnesota Historical Society." *Autograph Collectors' Journal* 5 (Fall 1952): 36-37.

A short review describing the scope of the society's 3,000-plus autograph collection of famous personages.

1605. Kane, Lucile M. "The Papers of John Harrington Stevens." *Minnesota History* 34 (Winter 1954): 144-148.

Stevens was an early settler in Minnesota, a land developer, and active in state politics. This article reviews his career and the collection of over 500 of Stevens' letters dating from 1839 to 1890 in the Minnesota Historical Society.

1606. Kellar, Herbert A. "A Preliminary Survey of the More Important Archives of the Territory and State of Minnesota." *Annual Report of the American Historical Association for the Year 1914* 1 (1916): 385-476.

Kellar lists record series titles, inclusive dates, volume, and, occasionally provides descriptive notes for records found in state offices.

1607. Kent, Donald H. "Sources for Pennsylvania History in the William L. Clements Library." *Pennsylvania History* 14 (January 1947): 23-29.

This article describes the papers of Jeffery Amherst; Generals Thomas Gage and Josiah Harmar; Loammi Baldwin; the Moravian papers; and the Maps and Plans Collection. Entries include inclusive dates, record series titles, volume, and content notes.

1608. Koch, David V. "The University Archives of Southern Illinois University at Carbondale." *Illinois Libraries* 63 (March 1981): 263-265.

The author reviews the growth of the archives and cites the titles of many of its significant collections.

1609. Koch, David V. "The University Archives of Southern Illinois University at Carbondale." *Illinois Libraries* 69 (October 1987): 598-600.
An update of Koch's 1981 article. He again cites the titles of the archives' significant collections.

1610. Krasean, Thomas. "Guide to the Indiana Sesquicentennial Manuscript Project, Part I." *Indiana Magazine of History* 64 (June 1968): 113-148.
An alphabetical presentation by collection title of collections of personal papers, business records, and organizational records relating to Indiana history. Entries include type of materials, volume, and the location of the materials.

1611. Krasean, Thomas. "Guide to the Indiana Sesquicentennial Manuscript Project, Part II." *Indiana Magazine of History* 64 (September 1968): 211-246.
A continuation of Krasean's June, 1968 article. See entry 1610 above.

1612. Leonard, Kevin B. "The Northwestern University Archives." *Illinois Archives* 63 (April 1981): 308-311.
Leonard cites record series titles in the university archives and collection titles of personal papers to describe the holdings at Northwestern University in Evanston. He also notes the existence of an extensive photograph collection.

1613. Lindley, Harlow. "Report on the Archives of the State of Indiana." *Annual Report of the American Historical Association for the Year 1910* 1 (1912): 315-330.
A checklist of record series titles with inclusive dates from the Offices of the Governor, Secretary of State, Auditor, Supreme Court Clerk, Treasurer, Superintendent of Public Instruction, Adjutant General, the State Library, and the Board of Charities.

1614. Lindley, Harlow. "The Woodbridge-Gallaher Collection." *Ohio History* 44 (October 1935): 443-450.
This is a collection of papers of families who originally settled in the Marietta, Ohio, area in the late 18th century. The papers include correspondence; financial records; personal journals; and land and military records. The materials date from the 1750s-1880s.

1615. Maher, William J. "The Illini Archives: A Laboratory for Retrospective Research." *Illinois Libraries* 63 (March 1981): 269-273.
About one-third of this article describes the holdings of the University

of Illinois at Urbana-Champaign archives. Maher notes the records of the university, the American Library Association, and the titles of several collections of faculty papers.

1616. Maher, William J. "The Illini Archives in the 1980s." *Illinois Libraries* 69 (October 1987): 584-587.
Maher reviews significant manuscript collections and record groups in the archives. Description is limited to collection and record series titles with occasional content summaries.

1617. "Manuscript and Local History Collections in Illinois: A Survey." *Illinois Libraries* 40 (April 1958): 353-392.
A checklist of manuscript materials in Illinois public libraries; college and university libraries; special libraries; historical societies; and private collections. The list concludes with an index to the manuscripts.

1618. Marchman, Watt P. "Ohio Rich in Manuscript Repositories." *Autograph Collectors Journal* 5 (Spring 1953): 50-53, 58.
This article is a directory to nineteen libraries and archives in Ohio. The author includes a scope and content note for each which includes titles of key collections.

1619. Martin, Dorothy V. "Archives of an Albany Family: The Horatio Seymour Papers in the Burton Historical Collection, Detroit Public Library." *New York History* 39 (July 1958): 268-272.
Martin describes a complex collection of documents and papers of the Bleecker-Collins family and of General Jonathan Foreman. Foreman served during the American Revolution and helped suppress the Whiskey Rebellion. Seymour married into the Bleecker family.

1620. McCoy, Ralph E. "Manuscript Collections in Morris Library." *ICarbS* 1 (Spring/Summer 1974): 153-162.
McCoy lists manuscript collections of public and literary figures; philosophers; the theatre; and local history. Entries include record series titles and content notes.

1621. McCoy, Ralph E. "Morris Library and Lovejoy Library, Southern Illinois University." *Illinois Libraries* 47 (November 1965): 854-860.
While mostly a review of published holdings, the article does cite manuscript collections too. These include papers of James Joyce, William Butler Yeats, R. Buckminster Fuller, and Mordecai Gorelik.

1622. McCree, Mary Lynn. "Illinois State Archives Guide to Records Holdings." *Illinois Libraries* 46 (May 1964): 319-363.
Arranged by record groups, the entries include administrative histories

of state offices; record series titles; inclusive dates; and volume statements. McCree also includes county records and some federal records
such as Illinois census schedules.

1623. "Microfilm Collections of Periodicals, Manuscripts and Miscellany in the
Illinois State Historical Library." *Illinois Libraries* 47 (March 1965): 276-
281.
   This article includes collection titles, record series titles, and inclusive
dates of microfilmed manuscript collections held by the Illinois State
Historical Library.

1624. Moore, Karl. "New Uses for Some Old Records: Genealogical Resources
of the Illinois Regional Archives." *Illinois Libraries* 68 (April 1986): 274-
279.
   The author analyzes tax records; county commissioners proceedings;
election records; registers of licensed professionals; and selected
municipal records for their research values. The article concludes with
the addresses of Illinois regional archives.

1625. Morales, Phyllis S. "Milner Library, Illinois State University." *Illinois
Libraries* 47 (November 1965): 834-841.
   Morales describes the library's special collections which include several
manuscript collections. Her description includes record series titles,
inclusive dates, and content notes.

1626. Motley, Archie. "Chicago Historical Society." *Illinois Libraries* 57
(March 1975): 223-226.
   Motley describes the Charles F. Gunther Collection and mentions other
collections by title that relate to Chicago and Illinois; the early U.S.
federal period; labor unions and movements; politics, including radical
organizations; and social work.

1627. Motley, Archie. "The Chicago Historical Society." *Illinois Libraries* 69
(October 1987): 572-574.
   Another review of the society's holdings in which Motley cites
collection titles and occasionally includes content statements.

1628. Motley, Archie. "The Chicago Historical Society Manuscripts Collection." *Illinois Libraries* 63 (April 1981): 291-292.
   Description in this article is limited to citing titles of manuscript
collections acquired since the author's 1975 article.

1629. Motley, Archie. "Manuscript Sources on Frontier Chicago." *Chicago
History* 9 (Summer 1980): 122-127.
   Motley cites collection and record series titles and inclusive dates of

manuscripts relating to Fort Dearborn, the fur trade, Indian affairs, business and commerce, travel, and the social life and culture of the Chicago-area frontier.

1630. Nauen, Lindsay B. "Dakota Resources: School Census Records at the South Dakota Archives Resource Center." *South Dakota History* 10 (Winter 1979): 59-65.
      The author reviews the types of information found in the records and provides several examples. The article concludes with a list of South Dakota counties and years for which the archives has censuses.

1631. Newberry Library. "The Hamill Calligraphic Collection." *Newberry Library Bulletin* 3 (April 1954): 148-151.
      This article describes manuscripts from the private collection of Alfred E. Hamill. Included are manuscripts of Nicolas Jarry, Esther Inglis, Johann Neudorffers, and several others.

1632. Norton, Margaret C. "Census Records in the Archives Department of the Illinois State Library." *Illinois Libraries* 26 (May 1944): 178-184.
      This article lists Illinois and U.S. census records held by the archives beginning with the territorial census of 1818 and ending with the Illinois schedule of the U.S. census of 1880. Entries comment on data found in each census and the availability of indexes.

1633. Norton, Margaret C. "The Nick Perrin Collection." *Illinois Libraries* 22 (October 1940): 22-24.
      Perrin, a Belleville, Illinois, attorney, discovered a cache of old records in the courthouse of St. Clair County, Illinois. Also known as the Cahokia records, the 5,000 items document French, British, and U.S. activities in the St. Clair area for the period 1737-1850.

1634. Norton, Margaret C. "The Resources of the Illinois State Archives." *Illinois Libraries* 36 (January 1954): 33-41.
      This article presents an overview of state archival holdings beginning with the Kaskaskia and Cahokia records and including county records, state records, the Illinois & Michigan Canal records, and genealogical-related records.

1635. Nyholm, Amy Wood. "Newberry's Modern Manuscripts." *Manuscripts* 19 (Winter 1967): 33-39.
      The modern manuscript collections include the Newberry Library's archives; railroad records; materials relating to printing; and collections relating to midwestern states. It is the latter group that Nyholm addresses in this article.

1636. Olson, Richard D., and Hans E. Panofsky. "Charles Deering Library, Northwestern University." *Illinois Libraries* 47 (November 1965): 845-853.

While mostly a description of published materials, the authors do include manuscript materials and maps.

1637. O'Neill, Robert K. "The Federal Writers' Project Files for Indiana." *Indiana Magazine of History* 76 (June 1980): 85-96.

A review of the origins of Indiana's Federal Writers Project with comments on the twenty-four linear feet of files created. The article notes the records are housed in the Cunningham Memorial Library, Indiana State University, Terre Haute, Indiana.

1638. Oster, Harry. "The Edwin Ford Piper Collection of Folksongs." *Books at Iowa* 1 (October 1964): 28-33.

Piper collected folksongs, mostly from Iowa and Nebraska. His collection at the University of Iowa contains 828 different songs. Oster reviews the categories of songs represented.

1639. Overman, William D. "Ohio Archives." *American Archivist* 5 (January 1942): 36-39.

After a brief history of the state archives, Overman lists selected state record series with inclusive dates accessioned by the archives.

1640. Pargellis, Stanley M. "Manuscript Collections in the Newberry Library." *Illinois Libraries* 40 (April 1958): 314-320.

Pargellis describes individual items and collections under nine divisions: medieval and renaissance manuscripts; music; post-1600 manuscripts; Philippine manuscripts; the Ayer Collection; the Midwest Collection; calligraphic manuscripts; railroads; and genealogy.

1641. Parker, John. "Manuscripts and Books, a Natural Partnership." *Manuscripts* 26 (Spring 1974): 79-87.

This article is about holdings of the James Ford Bell Library at the University of Minnesota. It reviews manuscripts relating to European expansion, which is the collecting theme of the library.

1642. Patterson, Robert D., and David H. Thomas. "Michigan Technological University Library Archives." *Historical Society of Michigan Chronicle* 9 (First Quarter 1973): 6-9.

This is a brief overview of the scope and contents of the archives' holdings. Description is limited to citing subject strengths and collection titles.

1643. Pease, Marguerite J. "Archives in Randolph County: A Revised

Inventory." *Illinois Libraries* 3 (June 1961): 433-448.

A review of the Kaskaskia papers and other records of the same time period, followed by a list of both microfilmed and unfilmed records. The list includes reel numbers, record series titles, inclusive dates, and number of items filmed per reel.

1644. Pease, Marguerite J. "Early Illinois Records in Randolph County: A Progress Report." *Illinois Libraries* 46 (May 1964): 364-366.

Pease reviews the provenance of these records which include the Kaskaskia records and lists Randolph County court records and notarial papers that have been microfilmed. The list includes reel numbers, inclusive dates, and case numbers.

1645. Pease, Marguerite J. "The Illinois Historical Survey Library, University of Illinois." *Illinois Libraries* 36 (October 1954): 298-301.

This article describes the survey's manuscript materials that document the roles of France, England, and Spain in the upper-Mississippi River valley; the U.S. colonial and early federal periods; the Civil War; the New Harmony community; and Illinois state and local history.

1646. Pease, Marguerite J. "The Illinois Historical Survey, University of Illinois." *Illinois Libraries* 40 (April 1958): 289-294.

Pease explains the mission of the survey; its relationship to the university library; and describes the manuscript collections it has published, microfilmed, or holds. Pease cites specific collections and notes their scope and content.

1647. Pollak, Felix. "The Manuscript Collections at Northwestern University Library." *Illinois Libraries* 40 (January 1958): 321-332.

Among the materials Pollak describes are the Bolivian Collection; French Republic documents; and the James B. Pinker, Ralph Straus, Lew Sarett, Abraham D. Groves, Manasseh Cutler, Charles G. Dawes, and Anaïs Nin Collections, along with other individual documents.

1648. Pratt, Harry Edward. "Manuscripts in the Illinois State Historical Library." *Autograph Collectors' Journal* 5 (Winter 1953): 38-41.

Pratt notes that the library's strength is in two areas, Civil War records and manuscripts and Lincolniana. He provides the collection titles, volume, and inclusive dates of several key collections in both groups.

1649. Pratt, Marion Dolores. "Preliminary Report of the Land Records." *Illinois Libraries* 41 (April 1959): 258-271.

Pratt provides historical information about public lands in Illinois, along with a listing of land record series titles in the state archives. The list is by land district and also includes volume of records and inclusive dates.

1650. Prinster, Inez D. "Dakota Resources: The Harriet Montgomery Water Resources Collection at Northern State College." *South Dakota History* 16 (Spring 1986): 67-69.

The article describes the collection as sixty cubic feet of maps, correspondence, videotapes and films, photographs, reports, news releases, clipping files, and published materials dating from the 1940s and relating to water use and resources in South Dakota.

1651. Quinn, Patrick M. "Profile in Purple: The Northwestern University Archives." *Illinois Libraries* 57 (March 1975): 220-223.

Mostly a history of the archives with concluding remarks on future needs and goals. However, about one-fourth of this article does cite record series titles held by the archives.

1652. Rau, Louise. "Sources for the History of Wayne County in the Burton Historical Collection." *Michigan History Magazine* 26 (Spring 1942): 223-232.

Rau cites records of individual churches; papers of families who settled in the county; business records; and British colonial government records. Most of the materials date from the early 1700s to the 1830s.

1653. Reed, Doris M. "Manuscripts in the Indiana University Library." *Indiana Magazine of History* 49 (June 1953): 191-196.

Reed gives an overview of manuscript collections relating to Indiana. She concludes with a checklist of collections, their volume, and inclusive dates.

1654. Reiter, Edith S. "Manuscripts in Marietta." *Manuscripts* 3 (Winter 1956): 117-120.

The collections noted in this article are in the Campus Martius State Memorial Museum in Marietta, Ohio. They include the papers of General Rufus Putnam; municipal and early state records; and several other collections of personal papers.

1655. Rose, Margaret. "The Archives of Dakota Territory." *American Archivist* 26 (July 1963): 307-313.

Rose describes the procedure used to divide the records of Dakota Territory when it became North and South Dakota. She provides a list of the records divided and a summary of which record series remained in North Dakota.

1656. Rose, Margaret. "Manuscript Collections of the State Historical Society of North Dakota." *North Dakota History* 30 (January 1963): 17-61.

This is an indexed guide with entries including collection titles, record series titles, volume, inclusive dates, and content summaries.

1657. Rosenthal, Robert. "Chicago's Manuscripts." *Manuscripts* 10 (Summer 1958): 43-52.
This article describes the manuscript holdings of the University of Chicago's library. Description is limited to collection title along with a comment on scope and content.

1658. Rosenthal, Robert. "Harper Library, University of Chicago." *Illinois Libraries* 47 (November 1965): 821-829.
While mostly a description of published sources, this article does contain information on the university's collections of political, social services, journalism, and literary papers. Rosenthal limits description to collection titles.

1659. Rosenthal, Robert. "Manuscripts in the University of Chicago Library." *Illinois Libraries* 40 (April 1958): 340-348.
Among the collections the author describes are the S. Calvary & Co. Collection of renaissance manuscripts, the Reuben T. Durrett Collection of Americana and Kentuckiana; the Martin Ryerson purchases; the Stephen A. Douglas papers; and several others.

1660. Rowley, Margaret. "Inventory of Records in the Kent County Courthouse." *Michigan Heritage* 1 (Spring 1960): 101-103.

1661. Running, Jane. "The Illinois State Library." *Illinois Libraries* 68 (April 1986): 264-266.
This article concludes with a checklist of microfilmed Illinois census schedules; state record series; and records from other states.

1662. Scheffler, Emma M. "Maps in the Illinois State Archives." *Illinois Libraries* 44 (June 1962): 418-426.
The author notes several collections of maps including those of the Illinois & Michigan Canal; the Chiperfield Collection of Illinois lake shorelines; highway maps; WWI expeditionary forces; and the atlas collection.

1663. Schoeweler, Susan Prendergast. "The Chicago Public Library Special Collections Division." *Illinois Libraries* 63 (April 1981): 293-296.
The author notes that the library's Civil War and American History Collections; its Chicagoana Collection; and the library's own records are the most frequently sought materials. Description of each category is limited to record series titles.

1664. Scrivin, Margaret. "The Manuscript Collection of the Chicago Historical Society." *Manuscripts* 16 (Spring 1964): 45-47.
The author provides collection titles and inclusive dates of several

collections at the society relating to French discovery and exploration, Indian affairs, politics, Mormon history, the arts, and the history of Chicago.

1665. Scriven, Margaret. "[Manuscripts in the] Chicago Historical Society." *Illinois Libraries* 40 (April 1958): 287-288.
    Description is limited to noting the names of significant personalities and events in U.S. history about which the society holds manuscripts.

1666. Sheldon, Addison E. "Report on the Archives of the State of Nebraska." *Annual Report of the American Historical Association for the Year 1910* 1 (1912): 365-420.
    A checklist of record series titles, inclusive dates, and volume statements of records in Nebraska's state offices.

1667. Siebert, Susan. "The Herbert Marshall Collection." *ICarbS* 4 (Spring/ Summer 1978): 41-48.

1668. Smith, Dwight L. "The Westward Traveler: Unexploited Manuscript Resources of the Newberry Library." In *Travelers on the Western Frontier*, edited by John Francis McDermott. Urbana: University of Illinois Press, 1970. 89-99.
    Smith identifies 19th-century travel accounts in the western U.S. He cites the collections from which they come and provides several extracts to illustrate the types of information they contain.

1669. Sommerfield, Marcia. "The Northern Illinois Regional History Center." *Illinois Libraries* 63 (March 1981): 274-276.
    The center is on the campus of Northern Illinois University at DeKalb. Sommerfield notes its strengths as being manuscript collections and local records relating to agriculture; business and industry; religion; politics; women; and the university.

1670. Steele, Leah J., and Richard C. Bjorklund. "Genealogical Resources of Conrad Sulzer Library." *Illinois Libraries* 74 (November 1992): 442-443.
    Records (1874-1976) of the Ravenswood community and Lake View district in Chicago are cited in this article. Included are church, school, and homeowners association records; oral histories; and photographs.

1671. Stevenson, Richard T. "A Preliminary Report on the Ohio Archives." *Annual Report of the American Historical Association for the Year 1906* 2 (1908): 165-196.
    The description is on a state office-by-office basis with a brief summary of the types of records found in each. Record series and inclusive dates are sometimes included. County court records are described best.

1672. Stoler, Mildred C. "Indiana Historical Society Manuscript Collections."
Indiana Magazine of History 30 (September 1934): 267-269.
A description of several collections in the William Henry Smith
Memorial Library. Most relate to military and political events in late
18th-century and early 19th-century Indiana.

1673. Stoler, Mildred C. "Manuscripts in Indiana State Library." *Indiana
Magazine of History* 27 (September 1931): 236-239.
A description and listing of several manuscript collections newly opened
for research. Foremost was a collection of 1,200 letters (1850-1929) of
Lucius B. Swift, civil service reformer.

1674. Storm, Colton. "The William L. Clements Library." *Autograph
Collectors' Journal* 2 (January 1950): 10-12.
A brief review of the holdings of the library of which Storm notes
strength in manuscripts relating to early European exploration and
colonization in North America and the American Revolution, especially
from the British perspective.

1675. Streeter, Floyd B. "The Burton Historical Collection of the Detroit Public
Library." *Americana Collector* 1 (January 1926): 124-134.

1676. Sutton, Robert M. "The Illinois Historical Survey: A Half-Century of
Selective Acquisitions." *Illinois Libraries* 52 (February 1970): 205-210.
Sutton reviews the survey's mission, its collection strengths, and cites
specific holdings relating to French, British, and Spanish activities in the
upper Mississippi River valley and several collections of personal papers
dating from the 1790s to the 1930s.

1677. Sutton, Robert P. "Western Illinois University Archives and Special
Collections." *Illinois Libraries* 63 (March 1981): 279-281.
Western Illinois University at Macomb is a regional repository for
county and local governmental records. This article cites record series
titles from governmental sources, along with titles of significant
manuscript collections.

1678. Swanson, Jeffrey. "The Franklin J. Meine Collections at the University
of Illinois." *Resources for American Literary Study* 5 (Spring 1975): 59-
68.
Meine collected materials relating to American humor. While mostly
published items, his collection does contain some Mark Twain manuscripts along with Meine's correspondence and speeches, cartoon art,
photographs, and sheet music.

1679. Swierenga, Robert P. "The Iowa Land Records Collection: Periscope to the Past." *Books at Iowa* 13 (November 1970): 25-30.

Swierenga describes the types of information found in 7,500 county land records dating from 1838 to 1900, and the project designed to convert the data to a machine-readable format.

1680. Teleky, Elizabeth Stege. "The University Archives and Manuscript Collections in University of Chicago Library." *Illinois Libraries* 63 (April 1981): 311-314.

Teleky cites record series in the university archives along with collections of faculty papers. She also notes collections of medieval, Civil War, renaissance, literary, Spanish, Italian, and Chicago-area manuscripts.

1681. Temple, Wayne C. "Government Records as Historical Sources." *Illinois Libraries* 52 (February 1970): 167-175.

The author comments in some detail on the research values of census records; state auditor's receipt books; land records; and military records held by the Illinois State Archives.

1682. Thompson, Harry F. "Dakota Resources: Historical Collections at the Center for Western Studies." *South Dakota History* 15 (Fall 1985): 234-242.

Thompson's narrative reviews and identifies manuscript collections and organizational records relating to South Dakota. He cites collection titles, inclusive dates, volume, record series, and comments on collection contents and research values.

1683. Tucker, Louis Leonard. "The Historical and Philosophical Society of Ohio: Its Resources." *Ohio History* 71 (October 1962): 254-261.

The society is primarily a library and archive. Tucker gives an overview of both published and unpublished holdings. He cites collection titles with their inclusive dates, along with the names of significant personalities represented in the collections.

1684. University of Missouri Library. "Western Historical Manuscripts Collection." *University of Missouri Library Bulletin* No. 5 (July 1949): 1-77.

1685. Utley, George B. "Source Material for the Study of American History in the Libraries of Chicago." *Papers of the Bibliographical Society of America* 16 (Part 1 1922): 17-46.

Utley cites many manuscript collections and specific documents while reviewing the published and unpublished holdings of the Chicago Historical Society, the Newberry Library, the University of Chicago Library, and the Chicago Public Library.

1686. Viles, Jonas. "Report on the Archives of the State of Missouri." *Annual Report of the American Historical Association for the Year 1908* 1 (1909): 319-364.

The report includes records series titles and inclusive dates, with some description of the records, for Missouri state offices.

1687. Volkel, Lowell M. "Genealogical Sources in the Illinois State Archives." *Illinois Libraries* 68 (April 1986): 279-284.

Volkel analyzes land records; Illinois census schedules; state military records; and selected county records for their research values.

1688. Walton, Clyde C. "Manuscripts in the Illinois State Historical Library." *Illinois Libraries* 40 (April 1958): 305-313.

This article is an alphabetically presented list of manuscript collections with entries including record series titles, volume, inclusive dates, and content notes. The article closes with a description of the library's Abraham Lincoln Collection.

1689. Warren, Paula Stuart. "Genealogical Research in Minnesota." *National Genealogical Society Quarterly* 77 (March 1989): 22-42.

This article should be useful to those planning research in Minnesota. It identifies and locates many types of records in the state, comments on the information found in record series, notes the existence of indexes, and provides other access tips.

1690. Wendel, Carolynne and Dorothy Riker. "County Records in the Genealogy Division of the Indiana State Library." *Indiana Magazine of History* 53 (June 1957): 181-196; and 54 (March 1958): 57-65 .

The authors have prepared a checklist presented alphabetically by county and, then, by record series. Inclusive dates and the availability of indexes are included.

1691. Wheat, Helen and Brad Agnew. "Special Collections Department at Northeastern Oklahoma State University." *Chronicles of Oklahoma* 56 (Spring 1978): 73-84.

The article describes the growth of the department and cites many of its manuscript collections. The primary sources noted relate mostly to Cherokee Indians.

1692. Wilson, Steve. "Documenting Our Heritage: Manuscript Collections of the Museum of the Great Plains." *Great Plains Journal* 17 (January 1978): 2-23.

Among the materials cited by Wilson are municipal and local business records of Lawton, Oklahoma; political collections; the papers of Lawton attorneys; and a photograph collection documenting Lawton and Fort Sill,

Oklahoma, and Indian tribes.

1693. Winther, Oscar O. "The Robert S. Ellison Collection." *Indiana Quarterly for Bookmen* 4 (January 1948): 7-19.

The Ellison Collection at Indiana University contains mostly published western Americana. It does include, however, Joseph Lane's papers; diaries of Joel Palmer and J. Robert Brown; and papers relating to the Bozeman Trail.

1694. Woltz, L. O. "Source Material of the Detroit Public Library as Supplied by the Acquisition of the Burton Historical Collection." *Michigan History Magazine* 6 (1922): 386-399.

Woltz provides an overview of the manuscript collections that are a part of the Burton Historical Collection. While describing some individual 18th-century items, he mostly cites collection titles.

1695. Wood, Thomas J. "Archives and Manuscript Collections at Sangamon State University." *Illinois Libraries* 69 (October 1987): 597-598.

A review of record series titles; collections of faculty papers; and non-university collections, all with volume statements and inclusive dates.

1696. Young, Sandra F., and Mary Ann Bamberger. "Special Collections Department at the University of Illinois at Chicago." *Illinois Libraries* 74 (November 1992): 433-436.

The authors review materials that might be useful to genealogists. They cite collection titles and inclusive dates of manuscript holdings; record series titles and inclusive dates of university, county, and municipal records in the university archives; and maps.

South (Alabama, Arkansas, District of Columbia, Florida, Georgia, Kentucky, Louisiana, Maryland, Mississippi, North Carolina, South Carolina, Tennessee, Texas, Virginia, West Virginia)

1697. Allen, Winnie and Helen Hunnicutt. "The Archives Collection." *Library Chronicle of the University of Texas* 4 (Fall 1950): 11-18.

This article reviews some of the personal papers and Spanish records held by the Eugene C. Barker Texas History Center. Foremost are the Bexar Archives and the Stephen F. Austin papers. The authors also cite other key collections by title.

1698. Angevine, Erma Miller. "Genealogical Research on Families of the District of Columbia." *National Genealogical Society Quarterly* 78 (March 1990): 15-32.

This article should be useful to those planning research in Washington,

D.C. It identifies and locates many types of records in the area, comments on the information found in record series, notes the existence of indexes, and provides other access tips.

1699. "Archives and Manuscripts in North Carolina." *North Carolina Libraries* 19 (Winter 1961): 1-29.
This is a series of articles giving overviews of major repositories in the state. Authors and titles of the articles include:

1. Jones, H. G. "Archives and Manuscripts in North Carolina." 2-4.

2. Jones, H. G. "Special Manuscript Repositories in North Carolina." 28-29.

3. Jones, H. G. "The State Department of Archives and History." 5-15.

4. Russell, Mattie. "Manuscript Collections in the Duke University Library." 21-27.

5. Wallace, Carolyn A. "The Southern Historical Collection." 16-20.

1700. Austin, Deborah W., and Allen W. Jones. "Georgia Manuscripts in the Auburn University Archives." *Georgia Archive* 2 (Winter 1974): 33-35.
The authors provide descriptions for the J.E.D. Shipp; Madison Kilpatrick; Emily Smith York; Bethel Baptist Church; and Georgia Confederate Letters Collections. Entries include record series titles, volume, and inclusive dates.

1701. Bach, William E. "Fayette County, Kentucky, Records." *Register of the Kentucky Historical Society* 47 (July 1949): 250-252.
This is an inventory of record series found in the Fayette County court house in 1949. Entries show inclusive dates, but volume is not included. The records date from the 1780s to 1823.

1702. Bassett, John S., Charles L. Raper, and J. H. Vaughan. "North Carolina County Archives." *Annual Report of the American Historical Association for the Year 1904* 1 (1905): 603-627.
A checklist of record series titles with inclusive dates. The counties included are Beaufort, Brunswick, Cartelret, Chowan, Craven, Cumberland, Guilford, Martin, Mecklenburg, New Hanover, Onslow, Orange, Pasquotank, Perquimans, Rowan, Tyrrell, and Wake.

1703. Bedsole, V. L. "Collections in the Department of Archives and Manuscripts, Louisiana State University." *Louisiana History* 1 (Fall 1960): 328-334.

Bedsole cites collection titles with inclusive dates and volume statements. The collections are grouped by period, i.e., Civil War, or
occupation, i.e., planters, authors, etc. Also included is a group of
Louisiana state records.

1704. Berkeley, Francis L., Jr. "The University of Virginia Library." *Autograph Collectors' Journal* 4 (Winter 1952): 32-36.
Berkeley mentions many collection titles that make the library a rich
source for regional manuscript collections, photographs, and maps with
strengths in the Civil War, literature, and Americana. The university
archives contains many Thomas Jefferson items.

1705. Bethel, Elizabeth. "Material in the National Archives Relating to the
Early History of the District of Columbia." *Records of the Columbia
Historical Society* 42/43 (1942): 169-187.

1706. Boswell, George W. "The Several Folklore Archives at Oxford."
Mississippi Folklore Register 6 (Spring 1972): 9-17.

1707. Browne, Henry J. "Manuscript Collections at the Catholic University of
America." *Manuscripts* 6 (Spring 1954): 166-168.
Browne notes that Catholic University's collections are divided into two
groups, labor-related, and the history of Catholicism in America.
Description is limited to collection titles and inclusive dates of the more
prominent collections at the university.

1708. Bush, Robert D., and Blake Touchstone. "A Survey of Manuscript
Holdings in the Historic New Orleans Collection." *Louisiana History* 16
(Winter 1975): 89-96.
The authors use narrative to describe broad topical groupings of
manuscripts. They cite collection titles, record series, volume, inclusive
dates, and comment on research values.

1709. Campbell, Randolph. "Local Archives as a Source of Slave Prices:
Harrison County, Texas, as a Test Case." *Historian* 36 (August 1974):
660-669.
The author comments on the research values of property appraisals in
probate records at the county level for establishing the monetary value of
slaves in the 19th-century U.S.

1710. Cappon, Lester J. "The Blathwayt Papers of Colonial Williamsburg Inc."
William and Mary Quarterly 3rd Series 4 (July 1947): 317-331.
William Blathwayt was a 17th-century clerk and administrator for the
Lords of Trade and Plantations. Cappon relates the provenance of his
papers, identifies record series, and comments on their research value.

1711. Cappon, Lester J., and Patricia H. Menk. "The Evolution of Materials for Research in Early American History in the University of Virginia Library." *William and Mary Quarterly* 3rd Series 3 (July 1946): 370-382.

This article is mostly a history of the library's development, but it concludes with a checklist of nineteen of its better manuscript collections. Entries include collection title, inclusive dates, and content notes. Most appear to be Virginia-related.

1712. Carleton, Don E. "The Houston Public Library's Houston Metropolitan Research Center." *Texas Libraries* 39 (Summer 1977): 64-68.

Carleton provides the historical background of the center and describes its holdings which, then, included 2,500 linear feet of archives and manuscript collections. Description is limited to collection titles and inclusive dates.

1713. Carson, Jane. "Historical Manuscripts in Williamsburg." *Manuscripts* 5 (Summer 1953): 9-15.

Carson reviews the many manuscript collections in the Colonial Williamsburg library, at the library of William and Mary College, and at the Institute of Early American History and Culture. Collection titles, inclusive dates, and volume are mentioned.

1714. Cashin, Mary Ann. "Selected Manuscripts in the Special Collections Room of Reese Library, Augusta College." *Richmond County History* 16 (No. 2 1984): 21-27.

1715. Chapman, David L. "Aggie Archives, New But Origins Old." *Texas Libraries* 39 (Fall 1977): 103-108.

Chapman gives the background of the archives and provides an overview of its holdings. He limits description to collection titles and inclusive dates.

1716. Clark, Thomas D. "Reuben T. Durrett and His Kentuckiana Interest and Collection." *Filson Club History Quarterly* 56 (October 1982): 353-378.

Durrett collected Kentuckiana, published and unpublished. This article details some of the materials he collected and recounts how his collection went to the University of Chicago library.

1717. Cobb, Maud B. "Check List of the Georgia Archival Material in Certain Offices of the Capitol." *Georgia Historical Association Proceedings* (1917): 49-63.

A list of records by series and inclusive dates under the offices of their origin. The article may be useful for identifying record series that should now be in the state archives.

1718. Coles, Harry L., Jr. "The Federal Food Administration of Tennessee and Its Records in the National Archives, 1917-1919." *Tennessee Historical Quarterly* 4 (March 1945): 23-57.

Coles' article reviews the Tennessee field office records of the Federal Food Administration in considerable detail.

1719. Colket, Meredith B., Jr. "The Public Records of the District of Columbia." *Records of the District of Columbia Historical Society* 48/49 (1949): 281-299.

1720. College of William and Mary. "Historical Manuscripts in the Library of the College of William and Mary." *William and Mary College Quarterly Historical Magazine*. 2nd Series 20 (July 1940): 388-390.

This article is an announcement that the college had completed inventorying and cataloging its manuscript collections. It concludes with an alphabetical listing of collections by surname.

1721. Connor, Seymour V. "A Preliminary Guide to the Archives of Texas." *Southwestern Historical Quarterly* 59 (January 1956): 255-334.

Collection titles and record groups appear alphabetically with each entry including volume statement, record series titles, inclusive dates, and a short content note.

1722. "Cook Collection Provides Panorama of Texas." *Texas Libraries* 36 (Winter 1974): 187-192.

This article describes the Texas State Library's L. L. Cook photograph collection of Texas towns. The images date from the 1930s through the 1950s. A list of towns represented concludes the article.

1723. Cox, Lynn and Helena Zinkham. "Picture Research at the Maryland Historical Society: A Guide to the Sources." *Maryland Historical Magazine* 76 (Spring 1981): 1-21.

This article lists the divisions within the society that hold graphic materials and describes the types of images that many be found in each. A few key collections are named, but, generally, description is limited to volume and types of materials.

1724. Cox, Richard J. "Notes on Maryland Historical Society Manuscript Collections: A Description of the Vertical File." *Maryland Historical Magazine* 69 (Spring 1974): 86-90.

Cox reviews significant items under the topics of literature; fine arts; politics; religion; ethnic and women's studies; and business. He also notes the society has large accumulations of documents about the American Revolution, the War of 1812, and the Civil War.

1725. Cox, Richard J. "Resources and Opportunities for Research at the Baltimore City Archives." *Working Papers from the Regional Economic History Research Center* 4 (Nos. 1/2 1981): 1-18.

1726. Cox, Richard J., and Patricia M. Vanorny. "The Records of a City: Baltimore and Its Historical Sources." *Maryland Historical Magazine* 70 (Fall 1975): 286-310.
     After a review of record keeping in Baltimore, the authors present checklists of manuscript collections and public records relating to the city. Cox locates manuscript collections and identifies them by title, Vanorny cites record series titles with volume and inclusive dates.

1727. Dabrishus, Michael J. "Customs Department Papers Available in Texas Archives." *Texas Libraries* 40 (Spring 1978): 23-26.
     Dating from 1836 to 1846, the record series in this collection include correspondence; bonds; oaths; passenger lists; financial records; and shipping manifests.

1728. Dart, Henry P. "The Archives of Louisiana." *Louisiana Historical Quarterly* 2 (October 1919): 351-367.
     A review of the dispersal of Louisiana's colonial records and an appeal for better treatment of records. The article locates a few record groups in New Orleans and Spain, but it is more useful to those researching the history of archives in the state.

1729. Davis, Robert S., Jr. "The Joseph M. Toomey Collection of Wilkes County Records." *Georgia Archive* 8 (Spring 1980): 34-37.
     Davis calls attention to a collection of early 19th-century county records previously thought lost or destroyed. While commenting on their research values, the article does not identify record series.

1730. Dobson, John. "Preservation of Historical Materials in Tennessee College and University Libraries." *Tennessee Librarian* 14 (January 1962): 33-36.
     Dobson cites subject strengths and key manuscript collections in the state's special collections. Description is limited to collection titles.

1731. Dunn, Roy Sylvan. "The Southwest Collection at Texas Tech." *American Archivist* 28 (July 1965): 413-419.
     Dunn names and describes several significant collections held by the Southwest Collection at Texas Technical University in Lubbock, Texas. The collections relate to the development of the university and to the history of the Texas panhandle region.

1732. Eltzroth, Richard T. "The Atlanta Historical Society: Its Archival and Library Holdings." *Georgia Archive* 1 (Fall 1972): 3-14.

The author provides a checklist of record groups and manuscript collections with entries including record series titles and inclusive dates.

1733. Everett, Diana. "Preliminary Inventory of Resources for New Mexico History in the Panhandle-Plains Historical Museum Research Center." *Panhandle-Plains Historical Review* 63 (1990): 75-84.

1734. "Federal Census Records at the South Carolina Archives." *South Carolina Historical Magazine* 85 (July 1985): 253-256.
This article provides a checklist of the available schedules from each census from 1790 through 1910.

1735. Filby, P. William. "Washington, D.C. Material in the Collections of the Maryland Historical Society." *Records of the Columbia Historical Society of Washington, D.C.* 69/70 (1971): 371-379.
The author identifies and describes twelve manuscript collections. He includes record series titles, inclusive dates, and content notes.

1736. Filby, P. William and Sandra M. Kamtman. "Manuscripts in the Maryland Historical Society, Baltimore." *Manuscripts* 18 (Summer 1966): 40-46.
The authors cite several collections held by the society in this short article. They also provide inclusive dates and limited content notes for the collections cited.

1737. Flisch, Julia A. "Report on the Local Records of Georgia." *Annual Report of the American Historical Association for the Year 1906* 2 (1908): 159-164.
The brevity of this report limits its usefulness. It contains summaries of the types of records found in offices of Richmond County, Georgia, and in the Ordinary's Office in Augusta.

1738. Gracy, David B., II. "Data in the Raw: A Guide to Atlanta's Archives." *Georgia Archive* 3 (Summer 1975): 116-124.
Gracy identifies the key repositories in Atlanta and provides an overview of their holdings.

1739. Griffith, Connie G. "Collections in the Manuscript Section of Howard-Tilton Memorial Library, Tulane University." *Louisiana History* 1 (Fall 1960): 321-327.
Griffith cites collection titles with inclusive dates and volume statements. She groups the collections by period, i.e., Civil War, or by occupation, i.e., planters, authors, etc.

1740. Griffith, Connie G. "Summary of Inventory: Louisiana Historical

Association Collection." *Louisiana History* 9 (Fall 1968): 355-370.

This is a summary of a longer, and presumably more detailed, inventory of the collections of the Louisiana Historical Association. Griffith groups them by topic with record series titles, inclusive dates, and volume.

1741. Guertler, John T. "A Brief Description of the Collections of the Baltimore Region Institutional Studies Center." *Working Papers from the Regional Economic History Resource Center* 4 (Nos. 1/2 1981): 19-23.

1742. Hagy, James W. "The Death Records of Charleston." *South Carolina Historical Magazine* 91 (January 1990): 32-44.

The author relates the provenance of this municipal record series, identifies the types of information the records contain, and comments on their value to social history. He also provides information on how to access them.

1743. Hamer, Collin B., Jr. "Records of the City of Jefferson (1850-70) in the City Archives Department of the New Orleans Public Library." *Louisiana History* 17 (Winter 1976): 51-67.

Among the records specifically listed and described are city council minutes and correspondence; financial ledgers for cash receipts and tax collections; financial reports; cemetery records; vital records; and law enforcement records.

1744. Hamer, Collin B., Jr. "Records of the City of Lafayette (1833-52) in the City Archives Department of the New Orleans Public Library." *Louisiana History* 13 (Fall 1972): 413-431.

The record series described in this article are similar in title and volume to those described in the entry above including those of the city council; law enforcement agencies; vital records; and financial records.

1745. Hamilton, William B. "The Sources of History of the Mississippi Territory." *Journal of Mississippi History* 1 January 1939): 29-36.

Much of this article is devoted to citing collections of state and territorial records and manuscript collections in the Mississippi Department of Archives and History and other repositories.

1746. Henderson, Thomas W. "Georgia Manuscripts in the Mississippi Department of Archives and History." *Georgia Archive* 1 (Spring 1973): 6-11.

Henderson identifies collections by title and annotates each entry with information about how the materials relate to Georgia.

1747. Historical Records Survey. "Guide to Depositories of Manuscript

Collections in Louisiana." *Louisiana Historical Quarterly* 24 (April 1941): 305-353.

This article publishes a list of repositories, with summaries of their holdings, in New Orleans, Shreveport, and Baton Rouge.

1748. Hruneni, George A., Jr. "Bicentennial Potpourri in The Catholic University of America Archives." *Manuscripts* 28 (Winter 1976): 17-26.

This article reviews collections and documents that relate to areas which are not strengths of the archives, but still signifcant. Included are materials relating to colonial America, western Americana, and the Civil War.

1749. Josel, Nathan A. "Special Collections of the Memphis and Shelby County Public Library." *Tennessee Librarian* 22 (Summer 1970): 162-163.

Josel reviews the contents of the Kenneth D. McKellar Collection; Memphis municipal and Shelby County records; the William Lockhart Clayton papers; the Mississippi River Collection; the papers of Sarah and Walker Kennedy; and an oral history collection.

1750. Kendall, John S. "Historical Collections in New Orleans." *North Carolina Historical Review* 7 (October 1930): 463-476.

Among the records Kendall describes are the French colonial Superior Council and Spanish colonial judicial records; New Orleans municipal government records; the Louisiana Historical Society's manuscripts relating to the Mississippi River; and others.

1751. King, George H.S. "A Survey of Stafford County Records." *Virginia Magazine of History and Biography* 53 (July 1945): 215-218.

This is a checklist of record series, with inclusive dates, then held by the Stafford County, Virginia, clerk's office.

1752. Kuehn, Claire R., and Bill Neeler. "Historic Research Center Provides Resources on Panhandle-Plains." *Texas Libraries* 40 (Fall 1978): 138-143.

The authors provide the background for the center and an overview of its holdings. They limit description to collection titles and inclusive dates.

1753. Kunstling, Frances W. "The Cooper Family Papers: A Bibliographic Note." *Tennessee Historical Quarterly* 28 (Summer 1969): 197-205.

Kunstling describes the papers of this Maury County, Tennessee, family. The papers, dating from 1716 to 1968, are especially rich in 19th-century political, social, and economic data. The Tennessee State Library and Archives holds the collection.

1754. Lentz, Lamar. "The Parsons Collection Revisited." *Library Chronicle of the University of Texas at Austin* New Series 30 (1985): 73-81.

    While mostly published materials, the Edward A. Parsons Collection in the Humanities Research Center contains 8,000 manuscripts dating from the 14th century, but focusing on the Louisiana area from the 17th century through the U.S. Civil War.

1755. Lich, Glen E. "German Emigration Contracts in the General Land Office." *Texas Libraries* 38 (Spring 1976): 19-21.

    Lich provides a brief description of the record series created by the German Emigration Company in the 1840s. The records, now in the Texas General Land Office, Austin, Texas, contain biographical information about immigrants, including their origins.

1756. Long, Edith E. "The Historic New Orleans Collection. A New Exhibition Center and Reference Library for the Colorful Creole City." *Manuscripts* 24 (Spring 1972): 101-107.

    The mission of the library is to collect materials relating to Louisiana and New Orleans. The author notes that the L. Kemper Williams Collection relating to the Battle of New Orleans is the base with the Edward Butler Collection a valued addition.

1757. Lovelace, Lisabeth. "The Southwest Collection of the El Paso Public Library." *Great Plains Journal* 11 (Spring 1972): 161-166.

    While devoting most of this article to published holdings, the author notes that the Southwest Collection also has more than 9,000 photographs and several archival collections. The Otis Aultman Collection is outstanding for its photos of the Mexican Revolution.

1758. Manucy, Albert C. "Florida History (1650-1750) in the Spanish Records of North Carolina State Department of Archives and History." *Florida Historical Quarterly* 25 (April 1947): 319-332; and 26 (July 1947): 77-91.

    Besides commenting on the research values of records at North Carolina, Manucy also identifies Florida-related records at the Florida Historical Society and the National Park Service. Much of this two-part series is devoted to research opportunities.

1759. Manucy, Albert C. "Notes on the Catálogo de los Fondos de las Floridas and the Distribution of Other Florida Archival Material for the Second Spanish Period." *Florida Historical Quarterly* 25 (July 1946): 44-63.

    Manucy identifies Florida-related records in Cuban archives; the Library of Congress; the Florida Historical Society; North Carolina archives; and several other state and university libraries.

1760. "Manuscript Collections of the South Carolina Historical Society." *South Carolina Historical Magazine* 78 (July 1977): 253-261.

This is a checklist of the society's holdings under fourteen categories. Entries include collection title, inclusive dates, and volume. There are also references to where more detailed descriptions of these collections may be found. See entry 1763 also.

1761. Martin, Cindy. "The Southwest Collection: New Materials, New Directions." *West Texas Historical Association Year Book* 63 (1987): 171-177.

This is an update on volume of materials held along with comments on key acquisitions between 1977 and 1987. Description is limited to collection and record series titles, inclusive dates, and research value of the collections.

1762. Maxwell, Robert S. "Manuscript Collections at Stephen F. Austin State College." *American Archivist* 28 (July 1965): 421-426.

The collections at Austin State College in Nacogdoches, Texas, relate to the history of Texas, and to business interests of the east Texas region. The timber and lumber industries are particularly well represented.

1763. McCormack, Helen G. "A Provisional Guide to Manuscripts in the South Carolina Historical Society." *South Carolina Historical and Genealogical Magazine* 45 (April 1944): 111-115; (July 1944): 172-176; 46 (January 1945): 49-53; (April 1945): 104-109; (July 1945): 171-175; (October 1945): 214-217; 47 (January 1946): 53-57; (July 1946): 171-178; 48 (January 1947): 48-52; and (July 1947): 177-180.

The entries to this serialized guide include collection title, inclusive dates, volume, record series titles, and detailed content notes.

1764. Melnick, Ralph. "College of Charleston Special Collections: A Guide to Its Holdings." *South Carolina Historical Magazine* 81 (April 1980): 131-153.

Melnick provides an alphabetical presentation by collection title. Entries include record series titles, inclusive dates, volume, and detailed content notes.

1765. Ming, Virginia. "Southwest Archives: The Texas Collection of Baylor University." *Password* 17 (Spring 1972): 41-44.

This is a review of the holdings of the Texas Collection including library, university archives, and manuscript and photograph collections. Description of unpublished materials is limited to collection titles.

1766. Mississippi Historical Commission. "An Account of the Manuscripts, Papers, and Documents Pertaining to Mississippi in the Public Repositories Within the State of Mississippi." *Mississippi Historical Society Publications* 5 (1902): 51-291.

This survey locates and describes Mississippi-related manuscript collections and official records in Mississippi, in private hands, and in other states. Description is limited to record series titles and inclusive dates.

1767. Moore, Mary T. "The Kentuckiana Library Collection at Western Kentucky State College." *Register of the Kentucky Historical Society* 49 (April 1951): 113-132.

Moore provides an extensive listing of books, maps, manuscript collections, photographs, and sound recordings, all relating to Kentucky history.

1768. Murray, Barbara S. "The Archer-Mitchell-Stump-Williams Family Papers." *Maryland Historical Magazine* 68 (Fall 1973): 330-332.

Among this family collection are the papers of George E. Mitchell, a Maryland politician; Stevenson Archer, congressman and judge; Frederick Stump, judge; and Lewis J. Williams, a naval surgeon. The papers date from the 18th century to the 1850s.

1769. Myers, Irene T. "Report on the Archives of the State of Kentucky." *Annual Report of the American Historical Association for the Year 1910* 1 (1912): 331-364.

Myers' report includes record series titles, inclusive dates, and volume statements for records from Kentucky's pre-statehood period and for records of its state offices.

1770. Neal, Ellen B. "Resources for Georgia Studies in the Southern Historical Collections." *Georgia Archives* 2 (Winter 1974): 2-19.

Neal cites more than forty collections relating to Georgia. Her description includes collection and record series titles; volume; inclusive dates; and comments on the relationship to Georgia.

1771. Oliphant, Dave. "Introduction." *Library Chronicle of the University of Texas at Austin* 22 (Number 3 1992): 7-9.

This entire issue of the *Chronicle* is devoted to the holdings and development of the Nettie Lee Benson Latin American Collection. This article provides an overview of the collection and calls attention to the themes expressed in the following articles:

1. Gibbs, Donald L. "The Development of the Literary Holdings of the Benson Latin American Collection." 11-21.

2. Gutiérrez, Margo. "The Mexican American Library Program and Its

Archival Collection." 133-153.
This program is charged with collecting materials relating to
Hispanic culture in the U.S.

3. Gutiérrez-Witt, Laura. "Mapping Mesoamerica in the Sixteenth
Century: The Merger of Traditions in the 'Relaciones Geográficas.'"
55-67.

4. Ortega, Julio. "The Manuscript of *Rayuela*." 35-39.
Rayuela is a novel by Julio Cortázar.

5. Schwaller, John F. "Nahuatl Holdings in the Benson Latin American
Collection." 41-53.

1772. Owen, Thomas M. "Alabama Archives." *Annual Report of the American
Historical Association for the Year 1904* 1 (1905): 487-553.
The presentation is by state office with record series titles and inclusive
dates listed thereunder. Volume frequently is listed too. The article also
cites some county and municipal records and some university records.

1773. Owsley, Harriet C. "The Fergusson Family Papers: A Bibliographical
Note." *Tennessee Historical Quarterly* 28 (Fall 1969): 324-329.
These papers (1784-1927) in the Tennessee State Library and Archives
include correspondence, diaries, photographs, legal records, biographical
and genealogical materials, and published materials documenting the
family's social and economic affairs.

1774. Owsley, Harriet C. "The Rugby Papers: A Bibliographical Note."
Tennessee Historical Quarterly 27 (October 1968): 225-228.
This article describes the records held by the Tennessee State Library
and Archives of the colony at Rugby, Tennessee. The records include
surveys, maps, church records, legal records, and the correspondence of
Thomas Hughes and other founders.

1775. Parsley, Gertrude M. "Special Collections in College and University
Libraries in Tennessee." *Tennessee Librarian* 3 (April 1951): 11-13.
Parsley reviews the subject strengths and key collections in the state.
Description is limited to collection titles.

1776. Phillips, Ulrich B. "Georgia Local Archives." *Annual Report of the
American Historical Association for the Year 1904* 1 (1905): 555-596.
This article describes county and municipal records from Oglethorpe,
Habersham, and Clarke Counties and the city of Athens.

1777. Phillips, Ulrich B. "Public Archives of Georgia." *Annual Report of the*

American Historical Association for the Year 1903 1 (1904): 439-474.
This description includes records of the Georgia Department of State and the records of Milledgeville, Georgia.

1778. Radoff, Morris L. "Early Annapolis Records." *Maryland Historical Magazine* 35 (March 1940): 74-78.
After a short introduction, Radoff lists 18th- and 19th-century Annapolis, Maryland, records in the Maryland Hall of Records. The list includes record series titles and dates only.

1779. Radoff, Morris L. "The Maryland Hall of Records." *Manuscripts* 20 (Spring 1968): 16-19.
This brief article reviews some record groups in the Hall of Records as opposed to describing the records.

1780. Reynolds, John H. "An Account of Books, Manuscripts, Papers and Documents Concerning Arkansas in Public Repositories." *Arkansas Historical Association Publications* 1 (1906): 43-273.
This is a summary of a statewide survey to locate and identify Arkansas manuscripts and records. It includes public, religious, and organizational records and private papers.

1781. Reynolds, John H. "Public Archives of Arkansas." *Annual Report of the American Historical Association for the Year 1906* 2 (1908): 23-51.
Reynolds cites record series titles and inclusive dates, and includes an annotation about the purpose and content of the records. Descriptions of county and municipal records are more general.

1782. Roberts, Warren. "The Humanities Research Center at the University of Texas." *Manuscripts* 27 (Fall 1975): 256-261.
Roberts briefly mentions several manuscript collections acquired by the center, most of them literary in nature. Description is limited to collection titles with occasional comments about their contents.

1783. Robertson, James A. "The Archival Distribution of Florida Manuscripts." *Florida Historical Society Quarterly* 10 (July 1931): 35-50.
The author identifies Florida-related records and the repositories holding them in Spain, France, England, Cuba, Canada, Washington, D.C., New York, Massachusetts, Wisconsin, Louisiana, and Florida.

1784. Rundell, Walter, Jr. "Guides to Maryland's Past: Eight Society Microfilm Projects." *Maryland Historical Magazine* 70 (Spring 1975): 92-97.
Rundell reviews the guides to the microfilmed papers of the Calvert family; David Baile Warden; William Wirt; the Maryland State Colonization Society; Robert Goodloe Harper; John Pendleton Kennedy; Charles

Carroll; and the Lloyd family.

1785. Russell, Mattie. "The Manuscript Department in the Duke University Library." *American Archivist* 28 (July 1965): 437-444.
An overview of holdings with specific mention of outstanding collections and subject strengths.

1786. Sánchez, Irene. "Index to Census and Manuscript Microfilm Materials in Texas State Archives." *Texas Libraries* 23 (May/June 1961): 60-71.
Sánchez indexes 19th-century consular dispatches from Mexican border towns; Texas census records (1850 to 1880); 19th-century military post medical reports; Texas Confederate service records; and other 19th-century Texas state records.

1787. Santos, Richard G. "A Preliminary Survey of the San Fernando Archives." *Texas Libraries* 28 (Winter 1966/1967): 152-172.
Santos provides a history of the Church of San Fernando, San Antonio, Texas, along with a description of its records. The records include birth, death, baptism, and marriage records for the period 1703-1860.

1788. Schaadt, Robert. "Collections Document Houston Family." *Texas Libraries* 48 (Summer 1987): 79-81.
After providing a brief overview of the Sam Houston Regional Library and Research Center, Schaadt notes collection titles in the center that relate to Sam Houston.

1789. Schinkel, Peter E. "Archival and Manuscript Holdings in Georgia Outside Atlanta: A Preliminary Survey." *Georgia Archive* 4 (Summer 1976): 105-118.
This is a directory to repositories. Entries appear under the headings of colleges and universities; historical societies; public libraries; and special libraries, and include access information and holdings summaries.

1790. Scisco, Louis Dow. "Colonial Records of Charles County." *Maryland Historical Magazine* 21 (September 1926): 261-270.
This appears to be the first of several checklists of colonial Maryland county records compiled by Scisco over a period of years. The last list noted was in volume 36 (1941), but later ones may exist. The lists are by geographical entity, record group, such as courts, land offices, etc., and record series. The lists may be useful in that entries are dated and have limited content notes.

1791. Scroggs, William O. "The Archives of the State of Louisiana." *Annual Report of the American Historical Association for the Year 1912* 1 (1914): 275-293.

Scroggs lists record series titles, inclusive dates, and volume of Louisiana state records found in New Orleans and Baton Rouge repositories and in the parishes of Natchitoches and East Baton Rouge.

1792. Sioussat, St. George L. "Preliminary Report upon the Archives of Tennessee." *Annual Report of the American Historical Association for the Year 1906* 2 (1908): 197-238.
Records in state offices are described, usually listing record series titles and inclusive dates. The author also includes some county records and state records held by the Tennessee Historical Society.

1793. Slate, Joseph Evans. "The 'Journal-American' Morgue." *Library Chronicle of the University of Texas at Austin* New Series 2 (November 1970): 82-89.
This article reviews the types of materials in the library of the *Journal-American*, the New York newspaper that ceased publication in 1966. Of particular interest is the substantial collection of photographs of events and people.

1794. Smither, Harriet. "The Archives of Texas." *American Archivist* 3 (July 1940): 187-200.
Smither comments on the early transfer of Spanish and Mexican records into the archives. She also describes some of the more contemporary record series held and concludes the article by citing several publications of records held by the Texas State Archives.

1795. "Southwest Archives: The El Paso Public Library." *Password* 17 (Summer 1972): 86-88.
This short article calls attention to a substantial collection of manuscripts relating to the history of Mexico and the American Southwest. Description is limited to collection titles.

1796. Standard, William G. "Virginia Archives." *Annual Report of the American Historical Association for the Year 1903* 1 (1904): 645-664.
The description is limited to record series titles and inclusive dates. Some Virginia records held by the Library of Congress are included.

1797. Sullivan, Larry E. "Sources for the Study of Baltimore History at the Maryland Historical Society." *Working Papers from the Regional Economic History Research Center* 4 (Nos. 1/2 1981): 24-64.

1798. Swem, Earl G. "A List of Manuscripts Recently Deposited in the Virginia State Library by the State Auditor." *Bulletin of the Virginia State Library* 7 (January 1914): 3-32.
This is a mixture of state and county records and personal papers listed

alphabetically by record series, surnames, and subjects. They date from the 1780s to the 1870s. The list is indexed.

1799. Teel, Cora P. "Manuscript Collections in the Special Collections Department, Marshall University." *West Virginia History* 43 (Summer 1982): 329-341.
Teel provides information about services available with an overview of the collection's holdings. She concludes with a list of record groups, manuscript collections, and photograph collections. Entries include record series titles, dates, volume, and content notes.

1800. Thomas, David Y. "Report on the Public Archives of Florida." *Annual Report of the American Historical Association for the Year 1906* 2 (1908): 149-158.
Thomas uses narrative to describe the records while occasionally mentioning record series and inclusive dates. The lack of detail limits the usefulness of this state report.

1801. Thomas, David Y. "Report upon the Historic Buildings, Monuments, and Local Archives of St. Augustine, Florida." *Annual Report of the American Historical Association for the Year 1905* 1 (1906): 339-352.
The archives include minutes and ordinances of the city council 1821-1905; court records of St. Johns County 1846-1905; and scattered marriage, slave, and financial records for the same time periods. Records are described on pages 344-352.

1802. Thomas, Samuel W. "An Inventory of Jefferson County Records." *Filson Club History Quarterly* 44 (October 1970): 321-355.
Most of the citations seem to be court records with vital records and records of the city of Louisville, Kentucky, included. Listings include record series titles, dates, volume, and content notes.

1803. Tindol, Lucila A. "Archival Material in the North Louisiana Historical Association Collection Being Cataloged at Centenary College." *North Louisiana Historical Association Journal* 2 (No. 1 1970): 7-9.

1804. "Typescripts of Manuscripts Made by Florida Historical Records Survey." *Florida Historical Quarterly* 18 (January 1940): 216-224.
These copied documents include diaries and personal narratives; letters; public records; Spanish records; library catalogs; and miscellaneous items.

1805. Viccars, Marion. "The First One Hundred." *Manuscripts* 25 (Winter 1973): 27-33.
The author describes a few of the better collections held by the

University of West Florida library. The descriptions include collection titles, record series titles, inclusive dates and the scope of the collection.

1806. Wallace, Carolyn A. "The Southern Historical Collection." *American Archivist* 28 (July 1965): 427-436.

Wallace relates the background of the collection while describing its holdings in general terms with occasional references to specific collections.

1807. Watson, Elbert L. "Tennessee State Library and Archives Manuscript Section." *Tennessee Librarian* 16 (Spring 1964): 82-85.

Watson describes ten categories of records. They include 18th- and 19th-century records; church records; school-related records; personal papers; fine arts collections; civic and social clubs; medical records; military records; and turnpike and bridge records.

1808. Weaks, Mabel C. "Manuscript Collections of the Filson Club." *Filson Club Historical Quarterly* 33 (July 1959): 251-256.

The article is limited to noting the collection titles of some of the club's more significant collections relating to the history of Kentucky.

1809. Webb, Carol. "The Southwest Collection: A Success Story." *Southwest Heritage* 8 (Summer 1978): 2-7.

Webb provides an overview of archival holdings at Texas Technical University in Lubbock, Texas. Ranching and agriculture, railroads and aviation, politics, and oil are among the topics covered by the manuscript collections, oral histories, maps, and photographs.

1810. Whatley, William A. "The Historical Manuscript Collections of the University of Texas." *Texas History Teachers' Bulletin* 9 (November 1920): 19-25.

While outdated, this article describes the Stephen Austin papers and the Bexar Archives, while mentioning a collection of Sam Houston correspondence and a few other smaller collections.

1811. Wilson, Louis R., and Robert B. Downs. "Special Collections for the Study of History and Literature in the Southeast." *Papers of the Bibliographical Society of America* 28 (1934): 97-131.

A three-part article of which part two is a review of archives and manuscript sources in Alabama, Florida, Georgia, Kentucky, Mississippi, North Carolina, South Carolina, Tennessee, and Virginia.

1812. Winfrey, Dorman H. "Genealogical Research in the Texas State Archives." *Texas Libraries* 22 (May/June 1960): 80-83.

Winfrey reviews record series that are rich in genealogical information such as Republic of Texas military claim files; enlistment papers; muster rolls; pension files; Confederate military records; and other vital records.

1813. Winfrey, Dorman H. "The Texas State Archives." *Texas Libraries* 22 (September/October 1960): 112-118.
  The author provides an overview of the archives' holdings citing many record groups and series with their inclusive dates.

1814. Woody, R. H. "The Public Records of South Carolina." *American Archivist* 2 (October 1939): 244-263.
  Woody provides a history of the care and keeping of South Carolina's records from colonial times to the 20th century. While intended to be an overview, there are many references to specific record series, both in the text and in the footnotes.

West (Arizona, California, Colorado, Idaho, Montana, Nevada, New Mexico, Oregon, Utah, Washington, Wyoming.)

1815. Abajian, James de T. "Preliminary Listing of Manuscript Collections in the Library of the California Historical Society." *California Historical Society Quarterly* 33 (December 1954): 372-376.
  This is a checklist of collection titles with inclusive dates only. The list is divided into personal papers, business records, organizational records, and ships' logs.

1816. Abraham, Terry and Richard C. Davis. "Directory of Manuscript and Archival Repositories in Idaho." *Idaho Yesterdays* 34 (Fall 1990): 21-33.
  The directory follows the format of the *Directory of Archives and Manuscript Repositories in the United States* with repositories listed under cities. Entries include holdings statements and access information.

1817. Arden, Sylvia. "The San Diego Historical Society Research Archives." *California History* 61 (Summer 1982): 140-145.
  A general account of the society's holdings that mentions record series titles. The most specific descriptions are of San Diego municipal records and the photograph collection.

1818. Artel, Linda. "California History on Film." *California History* 58 (Fall 1979): 264-268.
  A description of film and video tape holdings at the Sacramento Museum and History Division; the Oakland Museum; the Bancroft Library; University Art Museum, UC Berkeley; the National Maritime Museum; Hoover Institute; and the California Historical Society.

1819. Austin, Judith and Gary Bettis. "A Preliminary Checklist of Guides to Sources in Idaho History." *Idaho Yesterdays* 21 (Fall 1977): 19-26.

While not describing individual collections, this article identifies many Idaho-related collections and should be useful to anyone planning research in or about that state.

1820. Avery, Mary W. "The W. Park Winans Manuscripts." *Pacific Northwest Quarterly* 47 (January 1956): 15-20.

Winans was a businessman, Indian agent, and local politician in Colville, and Walla Walla, Washington. His papers are held by Washington State University, Pullman, and include diaries, financial records, and correspondence for the period 1857-1915.

1821. Bisceglia, Louis R. "Primary Sources of Anti-English Activities in California, 1916-1936: The John Byrne Collection." *Southern California Quarterly* 64 (Fall 1982): 227-237.

The Byrne Collection contains published and unpublished materials relating to Irish nationalist organizations in California. The materials, dating 1916-1936, are in the San Jose State University library.

1822. Bliss, Leslie E., Robert G. Cleland, and Godfrey Davies. "The Research Facilities of the Huntington Library: Americana." *Huntington Library Quarterly* 3 (October 1939): 135-141.

The authors provide an overview of the library's holdings. They cite numerous manuscript collections and comment on their scope and content. Americana and English history and literary materials are emphasized.

1823. Bond, Robert. "Bare Legs and Pinafores: The American Heritage Center." *Wilson Library Bulletin* 62 (January 1988): 54-57.

Bond reviews subject strengths and cites the titles of some collections in the University of Wyoming's American Heritage Center.

1824. Bowman, Jacob N. "The Parochial Books of the California Missions." *Historical Society of Southern California Quarterly* 43 (September 1961): 303-315.

Bowman explains what mission parochial books were and locates and describes the contents of baptism, marriage, and death volumes in California.

1825. Bowman, Jacob N. "Report on the Archives of the State of Washington." *Annual Report of the American Historical Association for the Year 1908* 1 (1909): 365-398.

A checklist of record series titles and inclusive dates of records in Washington state offices, including the state university at Seattle and the normal schools at Bellingham and Cheney.

1826. Bowman, Jacob N. "The State Archives at Olympia." *Washington Historical Quarterly* 2 (April 1908): 241-249.

Bowman provides an overview of state records held by the archives. Description is limited to record series titles and inclusive dates.

1827. Brand, Joanna. "Laguna Greenbelt Archives." *Journal of Orange County Studies* 5/6 (1990/1991): 42-48.

1828. Brennan, John A. "The University of Colorado's Western Historical Collections." *Great Plains Journal* 11 (Spring 1972): 154-160.

The author provides an overview of the collections' holdings. Most manuscript collections have a Colorado emphasis and relate to organized labor, mining, agriculture, and politics. Brennan cites specific collection titles noting the strength of each.

1829. Bridge, Kathryn. "The Maynard Northwest Coast Photographs at the Southwest Museum: The History of a Collection." *Masterkey* 61 (Winter 1988): 3-10.

Bridge describes a collection of photographs of the northwest California coast area taken by Richard and Hannah Maynard in the late 19th century.

1830. Cahoon, John M., and Katharine E.S. Donahue. "The Western History Collection of the Los Angeles County Museum of Natural History." *California History* 62 (Spring 1983): 67-69.

This article is too brief to be of use to most researchers. It does cite, however, collection titles of the more important collections at the museum.

1831. Chávez, Angélico. "Some Original New Mexico Documents in California Libraries." *New Mexico Historical Review* 25 (July 1950): 244-253.

The documents listed by date and title in this article are from the Ritch Collection in the Huntington Library; the "New Mexico Originals," and the "Southwest Originals" Collections in the Bancroft Library; and the Santa Barbara mission archives.

1832. Crawford, Richard W., Susan A. Painter, and Sarah B. West. "Local History Materials in the Research Archives of the San Diego Historical Society." *Journal of San Diego History* 37 (No. 2 1991): 129-148.

1833. Crawford, Richard W., and Clare V. McKanna, Jr. "Crime in California: Using State and Local Archives for Crime Research." *Pacific Historical Review* 55 (May 1986): 95-110.

The authors review crime-related records at the California State Archives and the San Diego Historical Society, including state prison records; pardons; county court records; coroners' inquest records; and arrest records.

1834. Davis, W. N., Jr. "California Local History in the State Archives." *California Historian* 13 (No. 3 1967): 89-93.

1835. Díaz, Albert J. "University of New Mexico Special Collections." *New Mexico Historical Review* 33 (July 1958): 235-251; and (October 1958): 316-321.
    A two-article series that is actually a guide to the collections with entries arranged in alphabetical order by collection title, volume statements, record series titles, inclusive dates, and detailed content notes.

1836. Donovan, Lynn Bonfield and Linda Chiswick. "Day-by-Day Records: Diaries from the CHS Library." *California Historical Quarterly* 54 (Winter 1975): 359-372; and 56 (Spring 1977): 73-81.
    Donovan reports that the library holds about 100 diaries. Following a short introduction, this two-article series lists diaries alphabetically by author's surname with entries including writer's occupation, place of origin, dates, length, and content note.

1837. Ellsworth, S. George. "A Guide to Utah Manuscripts in the Bancroft Library." *Utah Historical Quarterly* 22 (July 1954): 197-247.
    The guide is divided into two parts: manuscripts collected by Bancroft, and additions since 1905. Collections are cited alphabetically by title with entries including volume statements, record series titles, and content notes.

1838. Enright, John S. "The Breens of San Jaun Bautista with a Calendar of Family Papers." *California Historical Society Quarterly* 33 (December 1954): 349-359.
    The Breen family came to California in 1846 with the Donnor party. The family papers at San Francisco University library include diaries, correspondence, financial records, and photographs of several family members.

1839. Fante, Thomas M. "Fragments of California's Past: The Manuscript Collections of the State Library's California Section." *News Notes of California Libraries* 74 (No. 1 1979): 1-37.
    After an overview of the manuscript holdings in the California Section, a checklist of manuscript collections begins on page 19. Entries include collection titles, record series titles, volume, inclusive dates, and content notes.

1840. Freeze, Alys H. "The Western History Collection of the Denver Public

Library." *Great Plains Journal* 11 (Spring 1972): 101-115.
Freeze provides a review of the types of materials in the collection
including books, newspapers, photographs, maps, and manuscripts. The
library also has a special collection on the frontier theatre.

1841. Gerlach, Larry R., and Michael L. Nicholls. "The Mormon Genealogical
Society and Research Opportunities in Early American History." *William
and Mary Quarterly* 3rd Series 32 (October 1975): 625-629.
This article reviews record groups and series relating to colonial
America that may be found on microfilm at the society's library. The
records filmed are from both U.S. and European archives.

1842. Grenier, Judson A. "Addenda to J. N. Bowman's 'History of the
Provincial Archives of California.'" *Southern California Quarterly* 66
(Fall 1984): 257-261.
Grenier provides a checklist of record series and inclusive dates of
records held by the Office of the U.S. Surveyor General for California
in 1857. He noted that Bowman did not mention this inventory in his
"History of the Provincial Archives...."

1843. Gressley, Gene M. "The American Heritage Center: A Resource, as a
Resource." *Wyoming Annals* 64 (Winter 1992): 22-26.
A review of the center's premier collections written by the person who
did the collecting. Gressley cites collections in water rights; the mining,
geology, petroleum, and livestock industries; western writers; performing
arts; conservation; and transporation.

1844. Gressley, Gene M. "Oil and History Do Mix: The Petroleum History and
Research Center of the University of Wyoming." *Special Libraries* 61
(October 1970): 433-440.
Lengthy quotes from three sources take up one-half of the article.
Gressley, however, cites many petroleum-related collections and several
record series that may be found at the center.

1845. Haines, Aubrey. "The Yellowstone Archives: A Unique Source of
History." *Proceedings of the Montana Academy of Sciences* 22 (1962):
98-100.
The official records of Yellowstone National Park date from 1872 and
include correspondence files, outpost reports, ranger diaries, cemetery
records, law enforcement reports, financial records, and miscellaneous
park maintenance records.

1846. Hammond, George P. "Manuscript Collections in the Bancroft Library."
American Archivist 13 (January 1950): 15-26.
Hammond describes some of the outstanding collections at the

University of California. The Thomas O. Larkin papers, the Benjamin Hayes papers, the records of the Glenn Ranch, the Marcel E. Cert Collection, and the George C. Pardee papers are a few of those mentioned.

1847. Hanson, James A. "The Historical Records Survey in Wyoming." *Annals of Wyoming* 45 (Spring 1973): 69-91.
   This article is a history of the survey in Wyoming. It closes with an appendix that lists the survey's field records, inventories produced, and other archival work accomplished.

1848. Haselden, R. B. "Manuscript Collections in the Huntington Library." In *Archives and Libraries: Papers Presented at the 1939 Conference of the American Library Association*, edited by A. F. Kaufman. Chicago: American Library Association, 1939. 71-79.
   This essay notes four major British collections, the Battle Abbey papers; the Hastings papers; the Ellesmere papers; and the Stowe papers, along with key U.S. collections relating to exploration, colonial development, the American Revolution, westward expansion, and the Civil War and Reconstruction.

1849. Head, Edwin L. "Report on the Archives of the State of California." *Annual Report of the American Historical Association for the Year 1915* 1 (1917): 277-309
   A list of record series titles, inclusive dates, and volume statements of records found in California state offices.

1850. Hinckley, Kathleen W. "Genealogical Research in Colorado." *National Genealogical Society Quarterly* 77 (June 1989): 107-127.
   This article will be of assistance to anyone planning research in Colorado. It identifies and locates many types of records within the state, cites availability of indexes, comments on information found within record series, and provides other access tips.

1851. Hines, Donald M. "The History and Traditional Lore of the Inland Pacific Northwest: Archival Materials." *Journal of the Folklore Institute* 13 (No. 1 1976): 91-103.
   This is mostly a review of repositories that have manuscript collections and records relating to folklore of the Pacific Northwest. Hines cites a few key collections and comments on their research values.

1852. Hitchman, James H. "Primary Source Materials in Washington Maritime History." *Pacific Northwest Quarterly* 65 (April 1974): 79-84.
   Hitchman cites record series, and collection titles for materials held by federal and state archives; public libraries, museums, and historical

societies; county and municipal governments; and colleges and universities.

1853. Hodson, Sara C. "Checklist of Pre-Raphaelite Manuscripts in the Huntington Library." *Huntington Library Quarterly* 55 (Winter 1992): 148-219.
    There are 231 manuscripts or collections cited in the checklist. Entries include collection titles; authors or correspondents of letters and documents; volume; provenance notes; and inclusive dates.

1854. Kantor, J.R.K. "Sources in the Streets: The Sather Gate Handbill Collection of the University of California Archives." *California Historical Quarterly* 55 (Fall 1976): 270-273.
    The collection described dates from the 1930s to the 1970s. The author notes it is available as a five-roll microfilm set.

1855. Kelsey, Harry. "California History Resources: The Los Angeles County Museum of Natural History." *California Historical Quarterly* 54 (Fall 1975): 272-276.
    A brief overview of the museum's photograph, manuscript, map, and graphic arts collections. Description is limited to collection titles with indications of content and volume.

1856. Kessell, John L. "Sources for the History of a New Mexico Community: Abiquiú." *New Mexico Historical Review* 54 (October 1979): 249-285.
    Most of the citations are secondary sources, but the article also cites archival and manuscript sources in New Mexico, Mexico, and Spain. There is also a section locating photographs and oral histories relating to the town.

1857. Kurutz, Gary F. "The Sutro Library." *California History* 59 (Summer 1980): 173-178.
    While mostly discussing published materials, Kurutz does not neglect the manuscript, photographic, and map holdings of the library. He cites titles and notes the contents of the more significant collections.

1858. Lamb, Blaine P., and Ellen Halteman Schwartz. "The Paper Trail of the Iron Horse: The California State Railroad Museum Library." *California History* 70 (Spring 1991): 94-113.
    The article begins with a narrative about published and unpublished holdings of the library, including photographs, maps, and drawings. Descriptions of manuscript collections with content summaries, volume, dates, and record series titles follow the narrative.

1859. Lenzen, Connie. "Genealogical Research in Oregon." *National Genealog-

ical Society Quarterly 79 (March 1991): 33-55.

This article should be useful to those planning research in Oregon. It identifies and locates many types of records in the state, comments on the information found within record series, notes the existence of indexes, and provides other access tips.

1860. LeRoy, Bruce. "Go West, Young Man." *Manuscripts* 31 (Spring 1979): 138-141.

LeRoy cites areas of strength and key manuscript collections held by the Washington State Historical Society. He limits description to collection titles with occasional mention of record series and inclusive dates.

1861. Mahood, Ruth. "The Coronel Collection." *Los Angeles County Museum Quarterly* 14 (Autumn 1958): 4-7.

The Antonio Coronel Collection contains 19th-century documents and correspondence detailing life in Spanish and Mexican California.

1862. Marshall, Thomas M. "Report on the Public Archives of Idaho." *Annual Report of the American Historical Association for the Year 1917* 1 (1920): 137-172.

A checklist of record series titles, inclusive dates, and occasional volume statement of records in Idaho state offices. It includes records relating to Idaho's participation in the Columbian, Alaska-Yukon Pacific, and Panama-Pacific Expositions.

1863. Mathes, W. Michael. "Documents for the History of Sonoma, California, 1848-1906: A Calendar." *California History* 59 (Fall 1980): 255-264.

Mathes presents these municipal records first by office of origin, and chronological thereunder. Entries include names of people involved and general subjects of the documents.

1864. Mills, Hazel. "New Manuscript Collection in the Washington State Library: The Alanson Wesley Smith Papers." *Library News Bulletin* 38 (January/March 1971): 47-48.

Smith was a teacher at the Quillayute Indian Agency school in Washington state, and a farmer and businessman. His papers include correspondence, diaries, account books, and photographs, all dating from the 1850s to the 1930s.

1865. Mills, Todd. "Western Manuscripts in the University of Arizona Library." *Arizona and the West* 22 (Spring 1980): 5-66.

This is a guide to manuscript collections and sound recordings relating to the trans-Mississippi West and northern Mexico in the library's special collections. Entries include collection title, volume, inclusive dates, and content summary.

1866. Morgan, Dale L. "Western Travels and Travelers in the Bancroft Library." In *Travelers on the Western Frontier*, edited by John F. McDermott. Urbana: University of Illinois Press. 1970. 100-111.
Morgan cites many collections from the rich holdings of the Bancroft Library. His descriptions include collection titles and brief notes on the scope and content of the materials.

1867. Parish, John C. "California Books and Manuscripts in the Huntington Library." *Huntington Library Bulletin* 7 (April 1935): 1-58.
Parish divided the essay into two periods, Spanish and American. Under each, Parish first describes published materials followed by manuscript materials. His description is detailed and includes volume, inclusive dates, record series, and research values.

1868. Phillips, Paul C. "The Archives of the State of Montana." *Annual Report of the American Historical Association for the Year 1912* 1 (1914): 295-303.
A checklist of record series titles with inclusive dates and volume found in state offices including those of the governor, treasurer, secretary of state, auditor, clerk of the supreme court, the land office, railroad commission, and state boards.

1869. Priestley, Herbert I. "Manuscript Collections in the Bancroft Library." In *Archives and Libraries: Papers Presented at the 1939 Conference of the American Library Association*, edited by A. F. Kaufman. Chicago: American Library Association, 1939. 64-70.
Priestley comments on H. H. Bancroft's personal papers, the California-related documents he copied in Spanish and Mexican archives, the Mariano Guadalupe Vallejo papers, and several other collections documenting the Spanish and Mexican periods in California.

1870. Reingold, Nathan. "The Anatomy of a Collection: The Rhees Papers." *American Archivist* 27 (April 1964): 251-259.
The William Jones Rhees papers are in the Huntington Library in San Marino, California. Rhees was chief clerk and archivist for the Smithsonian Institution. Reingold analyzes the arrangement of the collection and notes the provenance of some materials within it.

1871. Rothwell, C. Easton. "Resources and Research in the Hoover Institute and Library." *American Archivist* 18 (April 1955): 141-150.
An overview of the library's holdings on a country-by-country approach. Germany, France, Russia, Italy, China, and Japan have the longer write-ups.

1872. Ruoss, G. Martin. "The Archives in the Special Collections of the

Zimmerman Library." *Great Plains Journal* 11 (Spring 1972): 116-124.

After a brief history of archival development in New Mexico, Ruoss reviews the holdings of the Zimmerman Library. He lists the ten best collections by title and provides a chronological and subject anaylsis of the other manuscript holdings.

1873. Shaw, Dorothy P. "The Cragin Collection." *Colorado Magazine* 25 (July 1948): 166-175.

This title refers to the papers of Francis W. Cragin of Colorado Springs, Colorado, who, prior to WWI, collected western Americana and interviews of "old timers" in southeastern Colorado. The article reveals more about Cragin than about his papers.

1874. Sherburne, George. "Huntington Library Collections." *Huntington Library Bulletin* 1 (May 1931): 33-106

This article reviews some of the key collections purchased by Henry E. Huntington and which formed the nucleus of the library. Many are manuscript collections, the description of which includes volume, dates, record series titles, and content notes. The article is indexed.

1875. Smith, Charles W. "The Bagley Collection of Pacific Northwest History." *Washington Historical Quarterly* 10 (April 1919): 83-87.

This collection is notable for its early Washington and Pacific Northwest imprints and many manuscripts relating to the Hudson's Bay Company and the Puget Sound Agricultural Company.

1876. Swensen, Rolf. "All the Fantastic Forms Possible to Imagine. The Haynes Yellowstone Park Collection at Montana State University." *Wyoming Annals* 65 (Spring 1993): 36-53.

The Haynes Collection contains photographs, clipping files, manuscripts, business records, and books documenting the career of the Haynes family as photographers and concessionaires in Yellowstone National Park.

1877. Tingley, Donald F. "Manuscript Materials Relating to Illinois in California's Henry E. Huntington Library." *Illinois Historical Society Journal* 60 (Autumn 1967): 313-319.

The author cites specific collections including those of Ward Hill Lamon; Samuel Barlow; Henry D. Bacon; John A. Rockwell; Charles H. Ray; John Brophy; Welborn Beeson; Charles M. Jones; James M. Forbes; and Abraham Lincoln. Most are Civil War-related.

1878. Vaughan, John H. "A Preliminary Report on the Archives of New Mexico." *Annual Report of the American Historical Association for the Year 1909* 1 (1911): 465-490.

Vaughan lists record series titles, inclusive dates, and volume for Spanish and Mexican records in New Mexico; U.S. territorial archives; county records; and selected church records.

1879. Vedeler, Harold C. "Historical Materials at the Southern Branch of the University of Idaho." *Pacific Northwest Quarterly* 27 (April 1936): 174-175.

1880. Wexler, Geoffrey B. "A Few More Pieces of the Puzzle: Collections Documenting San Diego History at the University of California, San Diego." *Journal of San Diego History* 37 (No. 1 1991): 52-67.

1881. Willard, James F. "The Public Archives of Colorado." *Annual Report of the American Historical Association for the Year 1911* 1 (1913): 365-392.
Willard lists record series titles, inclusive dates, and volume of Colorado's records from its state executive offices, judiciary, the legislature, and other state offices.

1882. Willard, James F. "The Public Archives of Wyoming." *Annual Report of the American Historical Association for the Year 1913* 1 (1915): 275-317.
A thorough listing of record series, inclusive dates, and volume of records found in Wyoming's state offices, including those of boards and commissions.

1883. Wyman, Leland C. "The Archives of the Museum of Northern Arizona." *Plateau* 39 (Spring 1967): 169-174.
Wyman provides an overview of holdings which includes photographs of Navajo and Hopi Indians, and anthropology-related manuscript collections. The author cites several collection and record series titles with inclusive dates.

Religious Groups

General

1884. Anderson, Gary C. "The American Missionary in the Trans-Mississippi West: Sources for Future Research in Indian History." *Government Publications Review* 7A (March/April 1980): 117-127.

Anderson describes the records and papers of missionary organizations and missionaries as they relate to American Indians. The article cites numerous collections in church archives, historical societies, and university libraries.

1885. Avery, Mary W. "Survey of Seattle Church Archives." *Pacific Northwest Quarterly* 28 (April 1937): 163-191.

This is a thorough listing of extant church records at the time of the survey. Denominations, including non-Christian ones, appear alphabetically with record series, volume, and inclusive dates listed under each.

1886. Borst, John C. "Dakota Resources: The Mary C. Collins Family Papers at the South Dakota Historical Resource Center." *South Dakota History* 12 (Winter 1982): 248-253.

Mary Collins was a missionary to the Sioux Indians, first at Oahe Mission and, later, at the Standing Rock Reservation. Her papers date from the 1870s to 1920 and include diaries, writings, correspondence, and genealogical materials on the Jacobson and Collins families.

1887. Brayer, Herbert O. "Church Records and History." *Bulletins of the American Association for State and Local History* 1 (April 1946): 257-258.

Brayer introduces a series of three articles in this issue of *Bulletins*. The articles provide overviews of records, manuscript collections, and publications of the Presbyterian, Mormon, and Catholic Churches in the U.S. The three articles are:

   1. O'Connor, Thomas F. "Historical and Archival Activities of the Roman Catholic Church in the United States." 287-304.

2. Peterson, Virgil. "Behold There Shall Be a Record Kept Among You." 272-286.

3. Spence, Thomas H., Jr. "The Historical Foundation of the Presbyterian and Reformed Churches." 259-271.

1888. Copeley, William. "Church Records at the New Hampshire Historical Society." *Historical New Hampshire* 39 (Fall/Winter 1984): 152-159.
Copeley provides a checklist arranged alphabetically by town. The entry then cites the churches from which the society has records, the record series titles, and the inclusive dates.

1889. Coté, Richard N. "South Carolina Religious Records: Other Denominations." *South Carolina Historical Magazine* 86 (January 1985): 50-61.
In this article, Coté reviews records of the African Methodist Episcopal Church; the Congregational, Unitarian, and Universalist Churches; Disciples of Christ; the Huguenot Church; the Lutheran Church; the Catholic Church; Society of Friends; and Jewish groups.

1890. Deutrich, Mabel E. "American Church Archives: An Overview." *American Archivist* 24 (October 1961): 387-402.
The last one-half of this article is a guide to depositories for church archives. It locates the archives for the Catholic, Protestant, and Jewish groups plus the repositories of selected missionary societies.

1891. Deutsch, Herman J. "Survey of Spokane Church Archives." *Pacific Northwest Quarterly* 28 (October 1937): 383-403.
Deutsch lists Spokane, Washington, denominations alphabetically with record series, volume, and inclusive dates listed under each.

1892. Dorosh, John T. "The Alaskan Russian Church Archives." *Quarterly Journal of Current Acquisitions* 18 (August 1961): 193-203.
The papers, dating from the mid-1700s to the 1930s, include ships journals; lists of settlers in Alaska; diaries and journals describing the region; church vital records; reports; financial records; and missionary correspondence and records.

1893. Hall, Manly P. "A Library of Obscure Knowledge." *Manuscripts* 8 (Spring 1956): 165-170.
The library referred to is that of the Philosophical Research Society in Los Angeles, California. The article cites several of its manuscripts and rare books on comparative religion, ancient Egypt, pre-Columbian Mexico, alchemy, and the occult.

1894. "The Thomas Lake Harris Collection of the Markham Archives."

Markham Review 4 (February 1969): 11-14.

Harris was a 19th-century U.S. mystical religious writer influenced by Emanuel Swedenborg and Ralph W. Emerson. This article provides a checklist of Harris' published works; his manuscripts and papers; and published material from his private library.

1895. "Inventory and Digest of Early Church Records in the Library of the Holland Society of New York." *Holland Society of New York Library Year Book* (1912): 1-52.

The inventory is alphabetical by town with entries including a provenance statement, record series titles, inclusive dates, and publication information.

1896. Jantz, Harold S. "The Samuel Miller Papers at Princeton." *Princeton University Library Chronicle* 4 (February/April 1943): 68-75.

Miller was a professor of theology and a historian, perhaps, best known for his biography of Jonathan Edwards. Jantz reviews the correspondence files that focus on Miller's exchange of letters with leading 18th-century European intellectuals.

1897. Jones, Clifton H. "Manuscript Sources on Religious History at the Historical Resource Center." *South Dakota History* 7 (Summer 1977): 325-333.

Jones lists both manuscript collections and church records in thirty-seven entries which include collection title, inclusive dates, volume, record series titles, and content notes.

1898. Kramer, William M., and Norton B. Stern. "Archival Sources for the History of Religion in California, Part 2: Jewish Religious Sources." *Southern California Quarterly* 72 (Fall 1990): 275-289.

The first four pages of this article lists five repositories along with contact information and brief content summaries. The remainder is a bibliographical essay on published sources relating to Jews in California. See entries 1935 and 1961 for parts 1 and 3.

1899. Parvis, Merrill M. "The Importance of the Michigan Manuscript Collection for New Testament Textual Studies." In *New Testament Manuscript Studies*, edited by M. M. Parvis and A. P. Wikgren. Chicago: University of Chicago Press, 1950. 125-136.

The author reviews New Testament manuscripts held by the University of Michigan, Ann Arbor, and comments on their values to Biblical scholarship.

1900. Pierson, R. M. "Denominational Collections in Theological Seminary and Church Historical Society Libraries." *Library Trends* 9 (October

1960): 213-230.

Pierson offers some general comments on church records in this article. Its value, however, is a concluding checklist of religious historical societies and archives in the U.S.

1901. Price, Frank W. "Specialized Research Libraries in Missions." *Library Trends* 9 (October 1960): 175-185.

While mostly about published materials, Price does cite several collections of missionary manuscript collections and records.

1902. Schnirring, E. Cheryl. "Church Collections in the Illinois State Historical Library Manuscript Section." *Illinois Libraries* 74 (November 1992): 456-458.

This author lists record series titles with inclusive dates of Illinois churches and religious organizations. Denominations represented are Baptist, Congregational, Presbyterian, Episcopal, Methodist, and Catholic.

1903. Shuster, Robert. "'Everyone Did What Was Right in His Own Eyes:' Nondenominational Fundamentalist-Evangelical-Pentecostal Archives in the United States." *American Archivist* 52 (Summer 1989): 366-375.

While not describing records in detail, this article does identify the major evangelical/pentecostal archives in the U.S. along with several collections of important evangelists.

1904. Starkes, M. Thomas. "The O.D. Foster Collection." *Books at Iowa* 6 (April 1967): 24-28.

Foster was a Congregational minister and consultant to the School of Religion at the University of Iowa. His papers include personal diaries, notebooks, personal correspondence, and photographs, all relating to his worldwide efforts to achieve Christian unity.

1905. Story, Cullen I. K. "Syriac Manuscripts of the New Testament." *Princeton University Library Chronicle* 22 (Winter 1961): 90-92.

Story calls attention to, and describes, five manuscripts used by Syriac-speaking Christians in the 5th century. A sixth manuscript is a 13th-century copy of the Gospels.

1906. Sweet, William W. "Church Archives in the United States." *Church History* 8 (March 1939): 43-53.

Sweet identifies the major repositories holding church records. He uses a denominational approach while providing repository scope and content notes for each collection.

1907. Thompson, Harry F. "Dakota Resources: The Riggs Family Papers at the

Center for Western Studies." *South Dakota History* 22 (Spring 1992): 64-74.

The Riggs papers document missionary work among the Sioux Indians and life at the Indian boarding schools at Oahe Mission and on the Santee Indian Reservation. The papers include photographs, correspondence, notes, and published materials.

1908. Weiser, Frederick S. "Eighteenth Century German Church Records from Maryland: A Checklist." *The Report: A Journal of German-American History* 38 (1982): 5-14.

1909. Wikgren, A. P. "Armenian Gospel MSS in the Kurdian Collection." *Journal of Biblical Literature* 55 (1936): 155-158; 64 (December 1945): 531-533; and 72 (June 1953): 115-126.

In this series of articles, Wikgren describes sixty manuscripts held by a private collector in Wichita, Kansas, Harry Kurdian. The concluding article lists and describes the most manuscripts, those numbered 24-60.

1910. Wright, Eugene Patrick. "A Catalogue of the Joanna Southcott Collection at the University of Texas at Austin." *Texas Quarterly* 12 (Spring 1969): 145-283.

Joanna Southcott was an 18th-century English mystic. This catalog is of her published and unpublished writings which include poems, notebooks, correspondence, "divine communications," songs, prayers, and sermons. The catalogue was also published as a monograph and is indexed.

Catholic

1911. "The Archives at Baltimore." *Records of the American Catholic Historical Society* 21 (June 1910): 85-95.

These archives are the papers of John Carroll, archbishop of Baltimore. The article offers little description beyond citing selected letters from the correspondence files of the early 1800s.

1912. Bannon, John F. "The Saint Louis University Collection of Jesuitica Americana." *Hispanic American Historical Review* 37 (February 1957): 82-88.

Bannon describes the Jesuit records microfilmed in the Archivo de Indias; the Jesuit archives in Rome; and materials from private collections in Mexico. He notes that most of the records date from the Spanish colonial period, but some are mid-19th century.

1913. "Checklist of Vatican Library Manuscript Codices on Microfilm in the

Knights of Columbus Vatican Film Library." *Manuscripta* 29 (July 1985): 91-117; (November 1985): 166-191; 30 (March 1986): 41-70; and (July 1986): 120-137.

A cumulative list of codex numbers assigned by the Vatican Library to documents in its key collections. Researchers having a specific codex number can consult this list to see if it is on microfilm at St. Louis University. This list supersedes the one published in *Manuscripta* volumes 1, 2, and 3 during the 1950s.

1914. D'Antoni, Blaise C. "The Church Records of North Louisiana." *Louisiana History* 15 (Winter 1974): 59-67.

This article describes extant 18th-century Catholic church records at the Church of St. François at Natchitoches and the Church of Nuestra Señora del Carmen at the Puesto de Avoyelles.

1915. Daly, Lowrie J. "Microfilmed Documents about the Southwest at Saint Louis University." *Manuscripts* 21 (Fall 1969): 251-256.

Daly describes four major collections, the Pablo Pastells Collection; the Archivum Romanum Societatis Iesu; De Propaganda Fide Collection; and the Missouri Province of the Society of Jesus Collection, all of which contain Southwestern materials.

1916. Daly, Lowrie J. "Microfilmed Materials from the Archive of the Sacred Congregation 'De Propaganda Fide.'" *Manuscripta* (November 1966): 139-144.

Daly calls attention to, and provides a narrative description of, a microfilm edition of the Propaganda Fide archives. The microfilm is held by St. Louis University, St. Louis, Missouri.

1917. Ellis, John T. "A Guide to the Baltimore Cathedral Archives." *Catholic Historical Review* 32 (October 1946): 341-360.

Ellis lists diocesan records by record series which include correspondence and papers of the archbishop's office, the chancery office, the metropolitan tribunal, the records of the cathedral, and miscellaneous records for the period 1780s-1940s.

1918. Fletcher, John E. "A Brief Survey of the Unpublished Correspondence of Athanasius Kircher, S.J., (1602-1680)." *Manuscripta* 13 (November 1969): 150-160.

Kircher was a German Jesuit known for his broad knowledge of the physical and natural sciences. In this article, Fletcher reviews the content of Kircher's correspondence, of which a microfilm set is available at St. Louis University's Vatican Film Library.

1919. Gómez Canedo, Lino. "Some Franciscan Sources in the Archives and

Libraries of America." *Americas* 13 (October 1956): 141-174.

The author locates Franciscan records and manuscripts in Argentina, Bolivia, Brazil, Central America, Chile, Colombia, Ecuador, Mexico, Paraguay, Peru, Uruguay, U.S., and Venezuela. His citations include record series, dates, and volume.

1920. "The Historical Archives of the Archdiocese of St. Louis." *St. Louis Catholic Historical Review* 1 (1918): 276-285.

This article continues the checklist prepared by the Rev. F. G. Holweck cited below.

1921. Holweck, F. G. "The Historical Archives of the Archdiocese of St. Louis." *St. Louis Catholic Historical Review* 1 (1918): 24-39.

After a brief history of the archives, the author provides a selective checklist of documents, petitions, letters, and Mexicana. Entries include names of correspondents or authors, dates, volume, and for the documents section only, content notes.

1922. House, Katherine L. "The John A. Lyons Collection in the Filson Club Library." *Filson Club History Quarterly* 64 (January 1990): 71-77.

The Lyons Collection consists of records from Catholic churches in Bullitt, Casey, Hardin, Jefferson, Marion, Meade, Nelson, and Washington Counties, Kentucky. The records mostly document baptisms, marriages, deaths, and burials from the 1820s to 1950s.

1923. Madaj, M. J. "The Chicago Archdiocesan Archives." *Illinois Libraries* 63 (April 1981): 322-325.

While mostly a history of the archives, the article does mention some record series and collections of personal papers by title.

1924. McAvoy, Thomas T. "Catholic Archives and Manuscript Collections." *American Archivist* 24 (October 1961): 409-414.

McAvoy identifies the major Catholic archives and manuscript collections in the U.S.

1925. McAvoy, Thomas T. "Manuscript Collections Among American Catholics." *Catholic Historical Review* 37 (October 1951): 281-295.

This article is mostly about James F. Edwards, librarian of the University of Notre Dame, and his efforts to establish the Catholic Archives of America at Notre Dame. McAvoy does mention however, the titles of a few key collections.

1926. McGloin, John B. "The Roman Propaganda Fide Archives: An Overview and Assessment." *Church History* 33 (March 1964): 84-91.

The author reviews both incoming and outgoing record series noting those that are rich in information concerning U.S. Catholicism.

1927. O'Connor, Thomas F. "Catholic Archives of the United States."
      Catholic Historical Review 31 (January 1946): 414-430.
      O'Connor locates and discusses the holdings of key archdiocesan and
      diocesan archives in the U.S. He notes, in general terms, the types of
      materials found in each and comments on their research values.

1928. O'Toole, James M. "Catholic Diocesan Archives: A Renaissance in
      Progress." *American Archivist* 43 (Summer 1980): 284-293.
      Mostly about a resurgence of interest in Catholic archives. The article,
      however, discusses the types of records that may be found in diocesan
      archives and the importance of diocesan records for historical research.

1929. Paschala, M. "Preluding History." *Illinois Libraries* 26 (June 1944): 238-
      244.
      While mostly about how the archives are arranged, this article does list
      the record series and some inclusive dates of the records of a Catholic
      teaching order held by St. Clara Convent in Sinsinawa, Wisconsin.

1930. Rahill, Peter J. "Archives of the Archdiocese of Boston." *American
      Archivist* 22 (October 1959): 427-432.
      The records described by the author include correspondence, diaries,
      reports, baptismal registers, indexes, and published materials from the
      1820s to the 1950s.

1931. Szczesniak, Boleslaw. "Material in the Archives of the University of
      Notre Dame Relating to the American Missions in the Far East."
      Catholic Historical Review 36 (July 1950): 190-211.
      Aside from a few miscellaneous documents, photographs, and small
      collections, this article calendars the papers of Father Daniel E. Hudson.
      The papers, dating from the 1840s to 1900, document Catholicism in
      China, India, Japan, Korea, and the Philippines.

1932. Thomas, M. Ursula. "Sources for the Study of Oklahoma Catholic
      Missions: A Critical Bibliography." *Chronicles of Oklahoma* 16 (Septem-
      ber 1938): 346-377.
      The first ten pages of this article provide an excellent commentary on
      Catholic manuscript sources relating to Oklahoma and Indian Territory.
      The remainder of the article treats published source material.

1933. Treanor, John J. "Genealogical Research Policy of the Archdiocese of
      Chicago Archives and Records Center." *Illinois Libraries* 74 (November
      1992): 477-480.
      Treanor briefly describes sacramental, orphanage, and school records;

chancery correspondence; records of parish churches; and papers of priests, bishops, and cardinals.

1934. Vollmar, Edward R. "The Archives of the Missouri Province of the Society of Jesus." *Manuscripta* 12 (November 1968): 179-189.

Dating from the 1820s, these records relate to the history of the Jesuits in the province; their educational efforts; government and spiritual life of the order; and include papers and correspondence of individual Jesuits, including Jean Baptiste DeSmet.

1935. Weber, Francis J. "Archival Sources for the History of Religion in California, Part 1: Catholic Sources." *Southern California Quarterly* 72 (Summer 1990): 157-171.

Actually a directory to Catholic archives in California, including missions, religious orders, diocesan and chancery repositories, and educational institutions. Some entries have content notes, all have basic contact information. See entries 1898 and 1961 for parts 2 and 3.

1936. Weber, Francis J. "The Catholic University of America Archives." *Records of the American Catholic Historical Society of Philadelphia* 77 (March 1966): 50-59.

The first part of this article outlines the administrative structure of the archives. It concludes with a checklist of collection titles with entries including record series titles, volume, and inclusive dates.

1937. Weber, Francis J. "The Chancery Archives of the Archdiocese of Los Angeles: An Historical Perspective." *Records of the American Catholic Historical Society* 82 (September 1971): 171-188.

While mostly a history of the archives, Weber does review the holdings in the concluding pages of the article.

1938. Weber, Francis J. "The Los Angeles Chancery Archives." *The Americas* 21 (April 1965): 410-420.

This is a guide to records relating to the Catholic Church in California for the period 1769-1964. It is divided into the Mission Period, 1769-1840, and the Diocesan Period, 1840-1960s, with sub-groups, record series, and inclusive dates listed under each.

1939. Weber, Francis J. "Printed Guides to Archival Centers for American Catholic History." *American Archivist* 32 (October 1969): 349-356.

A bibliographical essay about guides describing Catholic-related records.

1940. Weber, Francis J. "Roman Archives of Propaganda Fide." *American Catholic Historical Society Records* 76 (December 1965): 245-248.

After relating some of the history of the archives, Weber lists record groups and series relating to Catholicism in the U.S.

1941. Weber, Francis J. "The San Francisco Chancery Archives." *The Americas* 20 (January 1964): 313-321.
A guide divided chronologically into the Mission Period, 1769-1840, and the Diocesan Period, 1840-1962. Entries under each list sub-groups, record series, and inclusive dates. Some personal papers of priests and bishops are included.

1942. Weber, Francis J. "Sources for a Catholic History of California: A Biblio-Archival Survey." *Southern California Quarterly* 57 (Fall 1975): 321-335.
Weber cites guides and published descriptions of archives holding records and papers relating to Catholicism in California.

1943. Wright, Ralph. "Something New For Historians: Letters of the Notre Dame Archives Reveal New Facts about Catholic America." *Catholic Educational Review* 47 (June 1949): 380-383.
Wright cites key manuscript collections of prominent Catholics in the university archives including those of Joseph de Veuster (Father Damien), John B. Lamy, Orestes A. Brownson, Daniel E. Hudson, James A. McMasters, Edward N. Hurley, and others.

Protestant

1944. Andrews, Charles M. "The Newly Acquired Stiles Papers." *Yale University Library Gazette* 15 (April 1941): 65-70.
Andrews describes memoirs, letters, diaries, and sermons of Ezra Stiles, president of Yale from 1778-1795. He notes that these papers are especially illustrative of Stiles' religious convictions.

1945. Bellamy, V. Nelle. "The Library and Archives of the Church Historical Society." *Historical Magazine of the Protestant Episcopal Church* 36 (December 1967): 387-390.
This article begins a series of published inventories of major record groups in the Protestant Episcopal Church's archives. Each also offers a scope and content note for the record group. In this first article, Bellamy describes the records of the Domestic and Foreign Missionary Society Papers. Others that follow are:

1. Booth, Karen M. "The Constantinople Papers: 1835-1850." 40 (March 1971): 104-108.

2. Booth, Karen M. "The Puerto Rico Papers: 1870-1952." 42 (September 1973): 341-343.

3. Crosson, David. "The Philippine Papers: 1901-1968." 43 (March 1974): 65-68.

4. Davis, Patricia L. "The Alaska Papers: 1884-1939." 40 (June 1971): 197-199.

5. Dean, David M. "The China Papers: 1835-1951." 42 (September 1973): 333-339.

6. Dean, David. "The Greece Papers: 1829-1909." 40 (March 1971): 101-104.

7. Dean, David. "The Haiti Papers: 1855-1939." 39 (March 1970): 94-95.

8. Haywood, Dolores. "Liberia Papers: 1822-ca. 1911." 37 (March 1968): 77-82.

9. Haywood, Dolores. "Mexico Papers: 1878-1911." 37 (June 1968): 155-163.

10. Haywood, Dolores and Patricia L. Davis. "The Liberia Papers: 1822-1939." 39 (March 1970): 90-94.

11. Kinney, John M. "Archives of the General Convention: An Inventory of the Papers of the House of Bishops, and the House of Deputies, 1785-1958." 38 (September 1969): 290-326.

1946. Blodgett, Peter J. "Studying the Saints: Resources for Research in Mormon History at the Huntington Library." *Brigham Young University Studies* 32 (Summer 1992): 71-86.
Blodgett cites both published and unpublished materials. He limits description of manuscripts to collection and record series titles, inclusive dates, and the general subject contents of a collection. He mentions many diaries documenting the Mormon experience.

1947. Brackney, William H. "The American Baptist Historical Society." *American Baptist Quarterly* 1 (No 1 1982): 43-50.

1948. Brann, Harrison A. "Bibliography of the Sheldon Jackson Collection." *Presbyterian Historical Society Journal* 30 (September 1952): 139-164.
Sheldon Jackson was a Presbyterian missionary who served in the American West and Alaska. A biography of Jackson precedes the

bibliography, which begins on page 158 and includes manuscripts of his writings, letters, diaries and travel journals, and scrapbooks.

1949. Childs, Margaretta P., and Isabella G. Leland. "South Carolina Episcopal Church Records." *South Carolina Historical Magazine* 84 (October 1983): 250-263.
This article uses guide-like entries that include record series titles, inclusive dates, volume, location of records, and detailed content notes.

1950. Chrisman, Richard A. "Central Illinois Conference United Methodist Church Archives." *Illinois Libraries* 74 (November 1992): 476-477.
Chrisman cites the union list of ministers; general minutes; church vital records; published materials; and records of churchwomen's organizations as types of materials held by this archive.

1951. Clayton, J. Glen. "South Carolina Baptist Records." *South Carolina Historical Magazine* 85 (October 1984): 319-327.
The author reviews the Baptist presence in the state and identifies key repositories holding Baptist-related records and manuscript collections. He limits description to collection titles and occasional volume statements.

1952. Collison, Gary L. "A Calendar of the Letters of Theodore Parker." *Studies in the American Renaissance* (1979): 159-229; and (1980): 317-408.
Parker was a Unitarian minister known for his liberal religious views and humanitarianism. Collison has located and listed 1,999 Parker letters in sixty different collections. Entries include correspondents, dates, place of origin, and location of original.

1953. Coté, Richard N. "South Carolina Methodist Records." *South Carolina Historical Magazine* 85 (January 1984): 51-57.
The author gives a brief history of Methodism in the state and uses narrative to describe the denomination's historical resources. Description of records is limited to listing repositories, with limited scope and content statements for each.

1954. Coté, Richard N. "South Carolina Presbyterian Records." *South Carolina Historical Magazine* 85 (April 1984): 145-152.
Coté identifies repositories holding Presbyterian records and mentions a few specific collections.

1955. Cox, John, Jr. "Quaker Records in New York." *New York Genealogical and Biographical Record* 45 (1914): 263-269, 366-373.
Cox provides general information about Quaker records and their locations. The value of the article is in the checklist of monthly New

York meetings with their extant record series and dates.

1956. Curtis, Barbara L. "Searching the Sources: Quaker Archives in the Philadelphia Area." *Quaker History* 70 (Spring 1981): 40-46.
The author reviews Quaker records and manuscript collections at Haverford and Swarthmore Colleges. She cites many collection titles and comments on their subject strengths and research values.

1957. Deschamps, Margaret B. "The Presbyterian Church in the South Atlantic States, 1801-1861: A Bibliography." *Presbyterian Historical Society Journal* 30 (September 1952): 193-207.
The bibliography begins with manuscript collections listed alphabetically by title and noting the institution holding them. Diaries, journals, autobiographies, church records, and other unpublished materials follow the manuscript collections.

1958. Deutrich, Mabel E. "Archival Developments in the Lutheran Churches in the United States." *American Archivist* 15 (April 1952): 127-138.
This article identifies and locates many scattered archives of the Lutheran Church in the U.S.

1959. Drake, Thomas E. "The Quaker Collection, Haverford College Library." In *Then and Now: Quaker Essays, Historical and Contemporary*, edited by Anna Brinton. Philadelphia: University of Pennsylvania Press, 1960. 215-227.
Drake gives an overview of published and unpublished materials. He limits the description of manuscript collections to collection and record series titles with inclusive dates.

1960. Edwards, Paul M. "The Restoration History Manuscript Collection." *Annals of Iowa* 47 (Spring 1984): 377-381.
This article describes the records, manuscripts, and published materials relating to the Reorganized Church of Jesus Christ of Latter Day Saints; Mormonism in Iowa, and, especially, in Decatur County; and to Graceland College in Lamoni, Iowa, which holds the collection.

1961. Ernst, Eldon G. "Archival Sources for the History of Religion in California, Part 3: Protestant Sources." *Southern California Quarterly* 72 (Winter 1990): 373-391.
Ernst lists fifteen repositories, provides basic contact information, and includes titles of significant collections in the repository holdings summary. See entries 1898 and 1935 for parts 1 and 2.

1962. Esplin, Ronald K., and Max Evans. "Preserving Mormon Manuscripts. Historical Activities of the LDS Church." *Manuscripts* 27 (Summer

1975): 166-177.
The article discusses the types of materials the church's historical department collects. It also mentions specific collections held and their scope. The authors provide the most detail about the Brigham Young papers.

1963. Evans, Max J., and Ronald G. Watt. "Sources for Western History at the Church of Jesus Christ of Latter-day Saints." *The Western Historical Quarterly* 8 (July 1977): 303-312.
The authors review church records, manuscript collections, oral histories, photographs, and unpublished histories of the church, along with the themes documented in the different formats.

1964. "Extant Papers of Bishop Samuel Seabury." *Historiographer of the Episcopal Diocese of Connecticut* 83 (February 1973): 13-26.
This is a calendar of Seabury's sermons and correspondence in the General Theological Seminary, New York City, and of a microfilm set of Seabury's correspondence in Scottish repositories. Seabury was a bishop of the Episcopal Church in Connecticut.

1965. Fox, Donald H. "The Papers of Walter Lowrie." *Princeton University Library Chronicle* 39 (Winter 1978): 80-97.
Lowrie was an Episcopal priest and author known for his writings on the Christian Church and for his translations of the works of Søren Kierkegaard. His papers include correspondence, unpublished writings, and published materials.

1966. Glidden, Sophia Hall. "A Little-Known Friends Library." *Library Journal* 83 (November 1958): 3070-3071.
Glidden calls attention to a New York City collection of Quaker records dating back to the U.S. colonial period. The materials include discipline records; minutes of meetings; birth, death, and marriage records; and organizational records for Friends meetings.

1967. Hamilton, Kenneth G. "The Moravian Archives at Bethlehem, Pennsylvania." *American Archivist* 24 (October 1961): 415-423.
Hamilton comments on the major record groups in the Moravian Archives. He mentions records of the individual churches, missionary records, and personal papers of Moravians.

1968. Hamilton, Kenneth G. "The Resources of the Moravian Church Archives." *Pennsylvania History* 27 (July 1960): 263-272.
Records in the church archives include congregational diaries; maps and architectural drawings; mission reports; minutes; accounting records; photographs; individual diaries and journals; biographical accounts; and

correspondence files.

1969. Hamm, Thomas D., ed. "Resources for Scholars: Four Quaker Collections in the United States." *Library Quarterly* 60 (January 1990): 44-65; and (April 1990): 139-158.

Hamm serves as editor for this two-part series of four essays in which authors describe published and unpublished Quaker resources. Among the unpublished materials are Quaker college archives; yearly meeting records; personal papers; maps; and photographs. The four articles are:

1. Fowler, Albert W. "Friends Historical Library of Swarthmore College." 56-65.

2. Hamm, Thomas D. "The Friends Collection at Earlham College." 139-149.

3. Peterson, Diana F. "The Quaker Collection in the Haverford College Library." 149-158.

4. Treadway, Carole E. "Friends Historical Collection, Guilford College." 45-56.

1970. Heiss, Willard C. "Guide to Quaker Records in the Midwest." *Indiana History Bulletin* 39 (March 1962): 51-68; and 71-82.

Heiss explains the geographical division of the Society of Friends and its administrative structure and describes the types of records created and their informational content. The second part of the series locates Quaker records in the Midwest. Useful article.

1971. Heuser, Frederick. "Archival Resources." *Journal of Presbyterian History* 61 (Fall 1983): 373-386.

A series entitled "Archival Resources" begins in this issue. It presents, without introduction, detailed descriptions of manuscript collections and church records held by the Presbyterian Historical Society. The first installment contains fourteen descriptions while subsequent offerings appear irregularly and with as few as one collection described.

1972. Hicks, Muriel A., Mary Ogilvie, and Dorothy G. Harris. "Manuscript Resources of Friends Libraries." In *Then and Now: Quaker Essays Historical and Contemporary by Friends of Henry Joel Cadbury*, edited by Anna A. Brinton. Philadelphia: University of Pennsylvania Press, 1960. 203-228.

Hicks describes collections held by the Friends historical libraries in London and Dublin; Ogilvie in the Department of Records in Philadelphia; and Harris in the Friends library of Swarthmore College.

1973. Horn, Jason. "Seventh Day Adventist Archives." *American Archivist* 17 (July 1954): 221-224.
The article identifies the major record groups held in the General Conference headquarters at Takoma Park, Maryland.

1974. Hough, Brenda. "The Archives of the Society for the Propagation of the Gospel." *Historical Magazine of the Protestant Episcopal Church* 46 (September 1977): 309-322.
Hough reports on the pre-Revolutionary America information that can be found in missionary reports and accounts. She uses several quotes to illustrate the research value of these records.

1975. Howe, Charles A. "Materials at the Massachusetts Historical Society for the Study of Universalist History." *Proceedings of the Massachusetts Historical Society* 101 (1989): 117-119.
Howe cites collection titles of early Universalist Church records, personal papers of Universalist ministers, and published materials such as sermons and tracts.

1976. Keegan, G. Kearnie. "The Archival Resources of Dargan-Carver Library." *Baptist History and Heritage* 6 (July 1971): 164-170.
Keegan relates the scope of archival holdings and cites several key Baptist-related manuscript collections. Entries include collection title, volume, inclusive dates, record series titles, and content notes.

1977. Kimball, Stanley B. "Sources on the History of the Mormons in Ohio, 1830-38." *Brigham Young University Studies* 11 (Summer 1971): 524-540.
The author identifies and locates diaries, journals, and reminiscences; correspondence; state and county records; financial records; newspapers; and miscellaneous documents, in historical societies, colleges, federal repositories, and in private hands.

1978. Launius, Roger. "The American Home Missionary Society Collection and Mormonism." *Brigham Young University Studies* 23 (Spring 1983): 201-210.
Launius notes that most of the Mormon-related materials in this voluminous collection date from 1831 to 1893 and may be found in the outgoing correspondence files. He identifies these records by state, date, and volume.

1979. Lawrence, Harold. "Georgia Methodist Source Materials in South Carolina." *Milestones* 1 (No. 2 1988): 112-119.

1980. Leonard, Kevin B. "Northern Illinois Conference of the United Methodist

Church: Policies and Collections for Genealogical Research." *Illinois Libraries* 74 (November 1992): 474-475.

The author identifies Methodist-related records useful for genealogical research while commenting on their research values.

1981. Lind, William E. "Methodist Archives in the United States." *American Archivist* 24 (October 1961): 435-444.

The author locates many of the major repositories for Methodist Church records and papers of prominent Methodists. The article also identifies some significant record groups and series and manuscript collections.

1982. Lindley, Harlow. "Quaker Records of the Old Northwest." *Indiana History Bulletin* 16 (February 1939): 91-96.

Lindley identifies quarterly and yearly meeting records as the most useful Quaker records. Guilford College Library and Earlham College Library have two of the best collections of these records.

1983. "List of Letters in the Samuel Farmar Jarvis Collection Owned by the Church Historical Society, Austin 5, Texas, Available on Film in the Archives of the Diocese of Connecticut Episcopal Diocese of Connecticut." *Episcopal Diocese Connecticut Historiographer* 20 (May 1957): 12-20; and 21 (September 1957): 6-11.

The list is alphabetical by author with each entry also listing date, place of origin, and a brief content note.

1984. Lundeen, Joel W. "The Lutheran Church in America's Archives." *Illinois Libraries* 63 (April 1981): 315-318.

This article describes the records of the Lutheran Church in America, its constituent synods, and its predecessor churches. The article closes with addresses of related Lutheran archives.

1985. Lynch, James R. "Brethren Historical Library and Archives." *Illinois Libraries* 63 (April 1981): 319-322.

Lynch notes that the Church of the Brethren is one of three "historic peace churches." He describes Church records and many related manuscript collections using collection and record series titles and inclusive dates.

1986. Lynch, James R. "Brethren Historical Library and Archives." *Illinois Libraries* 69 (October 1987): 567-569.

In this update of his 1981 article, Lynch again surveys the holdings and services of this repository supported by the Church of the Brethren. He cites many different collection and record series titles along with inclusive dates.

1987. Manross, William W. "Resources of the Church Historical Society."
      Historical Magazine of the Protestant Episcopal Church 24 (June 1955):
      201-206.
         This article contains a short history of the society and concludes with
      a summary of its holdings. Manuscript collections and record groups are
      listed by title only.

1988. May, Lynn E., Jr. "A Baptist Research Center: The Dargan-Carver
      Library." *Baptist History and Heritage* 6 (October 1971): 222-225.
         This is an overview of the library's holdings. Some specific manuscript
      collections with inclusive dates and volume are cited along with other
      types of materials held by the library.

1989. McGovern, James R. "John Pierce: Yankee Social Historian." *Old-Time
      New England* 64 (Winter/Spring 1974): 77-86.
         Pierce was a Congregational minister, secretary for Harvard's Board of
      Overseers, and friend of many New England intellectuals. This article
      describes his papers which include memoirs, account books, sermons, and
      correspondence, all dating from the 1790s to 1840s.

1990. Miller, William B. "Manuscripts in the Presbyterian Historical Society."
      Manuscripts 17 (Summer 1965): 41-44.
         The author cites four areas in which the society holds significant
      manuscript collections: the Domestic Mission letters; the records of the
      Presbyterian Church; the American Indian Collection; and the Board of
      Aid for Colleges correspondence.

1991. Nute, Grace L. "The Edmund Franklin Ely Papers." *Minnesota
      History* 6 (December 1925): 343-354.
         Edmund Ely was a protestant missionary in the Lake Superior region
      in the 1830s. Nute describes the contents of Ely's correspondence and
      diaries for the period 1832 to the 1860s.

1992. O'Brien, Elmer J. "The Methodist Collections at Garrett Theological
      Seminary." *Methodist History* 8 (April 1970): 28-37.
         The author notes that manuscript collections at the seminary fall into
      two groups, the personal papers of seminary faculty, and those of
      prominent Methodists. O'Brien cites key collections in both groups and
      includes record series titles, dates, and content notes.

1993. O'Neal, Ellis E., Jr., and Diana Yount. "Andover Newton Theological
      School." *American Baptist Quarterly* 1 (No. 1 1982): 51-59.

1994. Olson, Adolf. "The Archives of the Historical Society, Baptist General
      Conference of America." *Swedish Pioneer Historical Quarterly* 5 (July

1954): 79-87.

Olson lists the types of materials the archives holds, which include early Swedish Baptist imprints; conference minutes; church histories; biographical materials; and diaries and journals. He provides content notes for each record series cited.

1995. Osborn, Walter. "The Moody Bible Institute Archives." *Illinois Libraries* 63 (April 1981); 326-327.

The article briefly describes the Dwight L. Moody papers; the Elizabeth Moody Washburn Collection; the Emma Moody Powell Collection; and the records of the Chicago Evangelization Society.

1996. Pennington, Edgar L. "Manuscript Sources of Our Church History." *Historical Magazine of the Protestant Episcopal Church* 1 (March 1932): 19-31.

Pennington identifies British repositories and the manuscript collections and records they hold that document Church of England operations in the American colonies. The author adds that many of these records have been copied and are in the Library of Congress.

1997. Pestana, Carla G. "Manuscripts in the Massachusetts Historical Society's Collections Relating to Religious Dissenters." *Proceedings of the Massachusetts Historical Society* 102 (1990): 148-163.

Pestana cites key collections containing information by and about individual religious leaders and their denominations. Baptists, Quakers, Anglicans, Huguenots, Rogerenes, Sandemanians, and Shakers are among those mentioned.

1998. Pike, Kermit J. "Shaker Manuscripts and How They Came to Be Preserved." *Manuscripts* 29 (Fall 1977): 227-236.

Much of this article is about the Shaker viewpoint of records and their preservation, but it also reports on the types of records created by Shakers and what may be found in the library of the Western Reserve Historical Society, Cleveland, Ohio.

1999. Reinford, Wilmer. "Index to the Jacob B. Mensch Collection of Letters, 1861-1912." *Mennonite Quarterly Review* 52 (January 1978): 77-85.

This is an alphabetical presentation of correspondents among the 1,600 letters in the Mensch Collection. Entries include place of origin, dates, and the number of letters by each correspondent.

2000. Riley, Lyman W., and Frederick B. Tolles. "A Guide to the Location of American Quaker Meeting Records." *Friends Historical Association Bulletin* 40 (Spring 1951): 33-37.

2001. Rosenberger, Francis C. "German Church Records of the Shenandoah Valley as a Genealogical Source." *Virginia Magazine of History and Bibliography* 66 (April 1958): 195-200.

    The author reviews the types of information in church birth, death, marriage, and baptismal records. The article closes with a checklist of Lutheran and German Reformed Church records held by the Virginia State Library's Archives Division.

2002. Sampley, Ethelene. "The Methodist Archives of Epworth-by-the-Sea." *Georgia Archive* 2 (Winter 1974): 36-42.

    This article lists record groups held by the archives with entries including record series titles and inclusive dates.

2003. Schwartz, Alan M. "Religious Archives at the Center for Western Studies." *South Dakota History* 13 (Fall 1983): 261-264.

    The center is at Augustana College in Sioux Falls, South Dakota. It holds some ninety feet of records of the Episcopal Church of South Dakota which includes correspondence, diaries, minutes, reports, school records, photographs, and church registers.

2004. Seaburg, Alan. "Some Unitarian Manuscripts at Andover-Harvard." *Harvard Library Bulletin* 26 (January 1978): 112-120.

    Seaburg describes the official records of the American Unitarian Association; Conference of Unitarian and Other Christian Churches; Unitarian Ministerial Union; and other Unitarian organizations, plus the private papers of Unitarian ministers.

2005. Seaburg, Alan. "The Universalist Collection at Andover-Harvard." *Harvard Library Bulletin* 28 (October 1980): 443-455.

    Similar in content to Seaburg's article above, but also containing citations of several different Unitarian record sets and papers of prominent Unitarian ministers.

2006. Selesky, Harold F. "Additional Material Relating to Ezra Stiles." *Yale University Library Gazette* 50 (October 1975): 112-122.

    Among the manuscript materials in this accretion are 18th-century sermons by leading clergymen, and correspondence with Thomas Jefferson.

2007. Shaw, Edward B. "Calendar of the Shane Papers: A Preliminary Report." *Presbyterian Historical Society Journal* 19 (December 1940): 183-192.

2008. Shepard, E. Lee. "Baptist Manuscripts at the Virginia Historical Society, an Update." *Virginia Baptist Register* 29 (1990): 1477-1481.

2009. Sherman, Stuart C., and Martha L. Mitchell. "Brown University."
American Baptist Quarterly 1 (No. 1 1982): 59-61.
This article reviews Baptist-related manuscripts at Brown.

2010. Shires, Winfield. "The Family Papers of Jedidiah Morse, D.D., Yale
1873." *Yale University Library Gazette* 10 (January 1936): 52-58.
While a clergyman, Morse is best known for his authorship of *American
Geography*. The article is mostly biographical, but it briefly describes
Morse's correspondence which is the core of the collection.

2011. Shuster, Robert. "The Archives of the Billy Graham Center." *Illinois
Libraries* 69 (October 1987): 566-567.
Shuster reviews major acquisitions since the publication of his 1981
article cited below. He cites collection titles of manuscript collections,
microfilmed sets, and oral histories.

2012. Shuster, Robert. "The Archives of the Billy Graham Center and the
Preservation of the History of Evangelicals." *Illinois Libraries* 63 (April
1981): 327-330.
The Billy Graham Center is located on the campus of Wheaton College,
Wheaton, Illinois. This article describes the center's holdings which
include Billy Graham's papers; the papers and records of other evangelists; evangelistic organizations; and of missionaries.

2013. Skaggs, David C., and F. Garner Ranney. "Thomas Craddock Sermons."
Maryland Historical Magazine 67 (Summer 1972): 179-180.
The authors report on 100 Craddock sermons added to the Maryland
Episcopal Diocesan Archives in the Maryland Historical Society.
Craddock was an 18th-century clergyman in Maryland.

2014. Springer, Nelson P. "General Catalogue of the Archives of the Mennonite
Church." *Mennonite History Bulletin* 10 (January 1949): 1-4.

2015. Sumners, Bill. "Selected Guide to Archival and Manuscript Collections
in the Dargan-Carver Library." *Baptist History and Heritage* 19 (April
1984): 4-21.
Sumners divides the guide into two sections. The first lists collections
relating to the Southern Baptist Historical Commission, the other to the
Sunday School Board. Entries include collection and record series titles,
dates, volume, and content notes.

2016. Tenney, S. M. "Materials on Kentucky History in the Library of
Historical Foundation of the Presbyterian and Reformed Churches
Montreat, North Carolina." *Filson Club History Quarterly* 5 (April 1931):
99-111.

Included are church records; unpublished reminiscences and historical papers; sermons; and published materials relating to the Presbyterian Church in Kentucky. Description is limited to series titles and inclusive dates.

2017. Thorne, Dorothy Gilbert. "The Guilford College Quaker Collection." *Quaker History* 58 (Autumn 1969): 108-112.

While much of this article describes published materials and artifacts, Thorne does devote a section to records and manuscripts which include minutes of monthly and yearly meetings dating from the 17th century, and manuscript collections identified by titles.

2018. Tolles, Frederick B. "Quakeriana in the Huntington Library." *Friends Historical Association Bulletin* 42 (Autumn 1953): 98-100.

2019. Turner, Joseph B. "A Catalogue of Manuscript Records in the Possession of the Presbyterian Historical Society." *Presbyterian Historical Society Journal* 8 (March 1915): 13-22.

2020. Umble, John. "Catalog of an Amish Bishop's 'Library.'" *Mennonite Quarterly Review* 20 (July 1946): 230-239.

This is a checklist of Amish manuscripts collected by Jacob Schwarzendruber, first bishop of Iowa, and his son Frederick. There are thirty-eight documents listed, most of which appear to document church affairs. Entries include content notes.

2021. Umble, John. "Manuscript Amish Ministers' Manuals in the Goshen College Mennonite Historical Library." *Mennonite Quarterly Review* 15 (October 1941): 243-253.

Umble describes in detail the informational contents and variations found in the manuals in the Goshen College library.

2022. Wade, Louise C. "The Graham Taylor Collection." *Newberry Library Bulletin* 3 (October 1953): 109-121.

Taylor was a Chicago minister and social reformer in the late-19th century and early-20th century. His papers include his writings; financial and administrative records relating to settlement houses and associations he founded; and his correspondence.

2023. Walker, Mary Alden. "The Archives of the American Board for Foreign Missions." *Harvard Library Bulletin* 6 (Winter 1952): 52-68.

Walker describes the correspondence, diaries, reports, journals, publications, and photographs dating from 1812 and reflecting the world-wide activities of this Congregationalist missionary group.

2024. Walker, Mary Alden. "India and Ceylon in the Archives of the American Board of Foreign Missions." *Indian Archives* 7 (July/December 1953): 95-99.

Walker provides the background of U.S. missionary interest in India, cites the areas in which they worked, reviews the record groups that contain materials relating to India, and describes the types of information that might be found in these records.

2025. Wallace, Paul A. W. "The John Heckewelder Papers." *Pennsylvania History* 27 (July 1960): 249-262.

Heckewelder was a Moravian missionary. His papers contain letters, manuscripts of his writings, and diaries and travel journals which provide insights on Indians and missionary society of 18th-century Pennsylvania and the West.

2026. Wallace, Paul A. W. "The Moravian Records." *Indiana Magazine of History* 48 (June 1952): 141-160.

A thorough analysis of the Moravian archives in Bethlehem, Pennsylvania. The author reviews the type of records created, their background and original use, and their value for research.

2027. Weimer, Ferne L. "The Billy Graham Center: Special Collections for Public Use." *Illinois Libraries* 66 (April 1984): 191-194.

Weimer describes the center and its services and lists the four major record groups in its archives.

2028. Weis, Frederick L., Christopher R. Eliot, and Robert D. Richardson. "Early Records of the Seventeenth-Century Churches in Massachusetts which Became Unitarian." *Proceedings of the Unitarian Historical Society* 7 (1941): 11-22.

2029. Wentz, A. R. "Collections of the Lutheran History Society." *Pennsylvania History* 3 (January 1936): 66-69.

Wentz reviews the holdings, both published and unpublished, of the society at the Gettysburg Theological Seminary. His description of records and manuscripts is limited to collection and record series titles with inclusive dates.

2030. Westberg, Sigurd F. "The Archives of the Evangelical Covenant Church of America." *Illinois Libraries* 63 (April 1981): 331-332.

Swedish immigrants founded the Covenant Church of America and its archives is located on the campus of North Park College, Chicago, Illinois. Most of this article relates the history of the archives with only a brief description of the records held.

2031. Williams, Marvin D., Jr. "The Disciples of Christ Historical Society: A Brief Summary." *Tennessee Librarian* 20 (Spring 1968): 101-108.

    Williams cites many of the key manuscript collections and church records the society holds. Description is limited to collections and record series titles and dates. The materials include records of local churches, education programs, and missionary papers.

2032. Winfrey, Dorman H. "Protestant Episcopal Church Archives." *American Archivist* 24 (October 1961): 431-433.

    This short article identifies the Episcopal Seminary of the Southwest in Austin, Texas, as a major archive of the Episcopal Church in the U.S. Winfrey lists ten record groups and series that he considered a significant part of the archives' holdings.

2033. Wittman, Elisabeth. "The Archives of the Lutheran Church in America on the Eve of the Evangelical Lutheran Church in America." *Illinois Libraries* 69 (October 1987): 589-590.

    The author comments on the archival ramifications of the merger of three groups of Lutheran Churches. She also cites significant acquisitions since 1981 and notes the location and types of records held by the merged churches.

2034. Zuck, Lowell H. "The Eden Archives." *Illinois Libraries* 74 (November 1992): 471-472.

    Eden Theological Seminary, Webster Groves, Missouri, holds reports, microfilmed correspondence, church records, and related materials of the Evangelical Synod of North America. The records include those of the synod's world-wide missions.

Foreign Repositories Holding U.S.-Related Records

Europe

2035. Bolkhovitinov, Nikolai N. "Materials on Russian-American Relations in the Archival Repositories of the USSR." *Soviet Studies in History* 25 (Fall 1986): 1-36.

    The author identifies the archives holding U.S.-related materials and subjects treated by the records. He also cites collection titles, record groups, record series titles, inclusive dates, and volume, along with titles of guides to the archives mentioned.

2036. Borges, Pedro. "Documentación americana en el Archivo General O.F.M. de Roma." *Archivo Ibero-Americano* 19 (enero/junio 1959): 5-119.

    This is a checklist of documents with citations including document title with author/correspondent name, date, origin, and content note. Documents identified refer to all of the Americas, but many relate to the Spanish borderlands, or what is now the U.S.

2037. Broneer, Oscar. "Records of the American School of Classical Studies at Athens." *American Archivist* 12 (January 1949): 42-44.

    A report on existing record series of the school. The author notes that the annual reports are the most useful for historical research.

2038. Burrus, Ernest J. "The Bandelier Collection in the Vatican Library." *Manuscripta* 10 (July 1966): 67-84.

    These papers of Adolph F. A. Bandelier contain archeological and ethnological sketches, maps, and a manuscript history, all relating to northwestern Mexico and the southwestern U.S. Burrus describes the materials in considerable detail.

2039. Calderón Quijano, José and Luis Navarro García. "Guía de los documentos, mapas, y planos sobre historia de América y España moderna en la Biblioteca Nacional de París, Museo Británico, y Public Record Office de Londrés." *Anuario Estudios Americanos* 18 (1961): 549-614.

    As in most articles of this scope, the materials relate to all of the

Americas, not just the U.S. However, it is possible to identify U.S.-related maps by using this guide.

2040. Dethan, Georges. "Les Archives des Affaires Etrangères." *French Historical Studies* (Fall 1965): 214-218.
    A report on the scope and content of the records of France's Ministry of Foreign Affairs. The author identifies record groups that are especially rich in U.S.-related records.

2041. Fleisher, Eric W. "Swedish American Diplomatic History: Some Sources in the Swedish National Archives (Sveriges Riksarkiv, Stockholm)." *Swedish Pioneer Historical Quarterly* 11 (July 1960): 116-123.
    Fleisher provides a short review of U.S.-Swedish relations, cites a few manuscript collections at Swedish university libraries, and concludes with a listing of record series in Sweden's national archives relating to U.S.-Swedish diplomatic relations.

2042. Hanke, Lewis. "Materials for Research on Texas History in European Archives and Libraries." *Southwestern Historical Quarterly* 59 (January 1956): 335-343.
    This is a bibliographic essay about published guides to foreign archives and transcription projects. The article does not describe records or manuscripts.

2043. Holmes, Jack D. "Maps, Plans, and Charts of Colonial Alabama in French and Spanish Archives." *Alabama Historical Quarterly* 27 (Spring/ Summer 1965): 9-21.
    Holmes lists seventy-two maps chronologically under geographical groupings such as the gulf coast, Alabama general, Mobile and Dauphin Island, and Tombigbee River posts. Entries include title, date, cartographer or publisher, and location.

2044. Holmes, Jack D. "Maps, Plans and Charts of Louisiana in Paris Archives: A Checklist." *Louisiana Studies* 4 (Fall 1965): 200-221.
    This article describes 120 maps. Entries include title, place and date of publication, if published; cartographer's name; archives and libraries holding a copy; and descriptive notes.

2045. Joshi, Manoj K. "Materials Pertaining to Indo-American Relations: An Archival Survey of Major Depositories in Delhi." *Indian Journal of American Studies* 14 (Winter 1984): 129-134.

2046. Karpinski, Louis C. "Manuscript Maps Relating to American History in French, Spanish, and Portuguese Archives." *American Historical Review* 33 (January 1928): 328-330.

A general article reporting the number and types of manuscript maps photographically reproduced and noting the libraries in which copies were placed.

2047. Le Moël, Michel. "Maps and Plans of the United States in the Archives Nationales." *Quarterly Journal of the Library of Congress* 30 (October 1973): 245-247.
The author identifies four record groups in the national archives of France that contain U.S. maps, mostly relating to Louisiana and the American Revolution. Le Moël also cites individual maps.

2048. Manigaulte, John W. "Sources for American History in Three Italian Archives." *American Archivist* 27 (January 1964): 57-61.
Manigaulte reviews record groups and specific record series in the Archivio di Stato in Naples, the Vatican Library and Archives, and the Archivio Storico del Ministero degli Affari Esteri in Rome.

2049. McGloin, John B. "European Archival Resources for the Study of California Catholic History." *Church History* 30 (March 1961): 103-105.
McGloin identifies European archives containing records and personal papers relating to California. He appears to have copied many of the materials for the University of San Francisco.

2050. Morales Padrón, Francisco, J. Gil-Bermejo, and María Teresa Garrido. "Cartografía sobre Puerto Rico en París, Londrés, y Madrid." *Anuario Estudios Americanos* 18 (1961): 615-649.
This is an easy-to-use checklist of Puerto Rican maps in the National Library of France; British Museum; British Public Record Office; British Admiralty Office; and the Spanish Naval Museum. In all, there are 115 maps described.

2051. Nasatir, Abraham P. "The Archives of the French Foreign Ministry: Opportunities for Research in American History." *American Archivist* 19 (July 1956): 203-213.
Nasatir describes four record groups containing U.S.-related records: correspondance politique; correspondance politique des consuls; mémoires et documents; and correspondance commerciale. He cites record series, volume, and inclusive dates for each.

2052. Parkman, Francis. "Early Unpublished Maps of the Mississippi and the Great Lakes." in *La Salle and the Discovery of Great West.* by Francis Parkman. Boston: Little, Brown, and Company, 1918. 449-458.
Appendix one of this book is a description of 17th-century maps, most of which Parkman said, were in the Dépôt des Cartes de la Marine et des Colonies in Paris, France. The description includes area, cartographer,

date, and title.

2053. Shur, Leonid A., and James R. Gibson. "Russian Travel Notes and Journals as Sources for the History of California, 1800-1850." *California Historical Quarterly* 52 (Spring 1973): 37-63.

The authors identify and comment on travel journals, notes and diaries, and correspondence of Russian visitors to California. They also identify the Russian archives holding the materials.

2054. Sluiter, Engel. "The Dutch Archives and American Historical Research." *Pacific Historical Review* 6 (January 1937): 21-35.

The first one-half of this article describes the establishment of a Dutch colonial empire. The remainder identifies Dutch archives holding records relating to what is now North America and the U.S.

2055. Smith, Ronald D. "Opportunities for Research on Louisiana in the Archives Nationales: A Survey of Manuscripts for the Years 1763-1803." *Social Science Journal* 14 (January 1977): 157-161.

Smith describes three key collections in the French National Archives, the records of the ministry of the colonies; the ministry of foreign affairs; and a grouping of Louisiana material in the Outre-Mer section.

2056. Spijkerman, Henri. "The Amsterdam Municipal Archives as a Source for the History of the United States of America." *American Archivist* 52 (Winter 1989): 88-95.

The author cites the value of notarial records for economic and social history, the banking and financial records of Hope and Company and the firm of Ketwich and Voombergh for investments in America, and the cartographic records of the Holland Land Company.

2057. Turner, Frederick J., ed. "Correspondence of the French Ministers to the United States, 1791-1797." *Annual Report of the American Historical Association for the Year 1903* 2 (1904): 5-1110.

This entire volume reproduces correspondence copied from the French Archives du Ministère des Affaires Etrangères. Part 2 is a "Calendar of Correspondence of Ternant, Genet, Fauchet, Adet, and Létombe."

Great Britain and the British Commonwealth

2058. Andrews, Charles M. "List of the Journals and Acts of the Councils and Assemblies of the Thirteen Original Colonies, and the Floridas, in America, Preserved in the Public Record Office, London." *Annual Report of the American Historical Association for the Year 1908* 1 (1909): 399-509.

The list includes a description of the type of document, i.e. acts, minutes, reports; general content notes; names of those involved; inclusive dates; and geographical areas covered. The arrangement is first by colony and then chronological.

2059. Andrews, Charles M. "List of Reports and Representations of the Plantation Councils, 1660-1674, the Lords of Trade, 1675-1696, and the Board of Trade, 1696-1782, in the Public Record Office." *Annual Report of the American Historical Association for the Year 1913* 1 (1915): 319-406.
The presentation is chronological with citations including subject of report, the names of principals involved, and the geographical area covered. All of the entries refer to England's American colonies.

2060. Bill, Geoffrey. "American Papers in Lambeth Palace Library." *Historical Magazine of the Protestant Episcopal Church* 28 (September 1959): 257-260.
Bill calls attention to records of the bishopric of London which contain many documents relating to the American colonies in the 18th century. He notes the records are of three series: letters of orders, correspondence, and missionary bonds.

2061. "British Records Relating to America on Microfilm." *CAAS Bulletin* 2 (Spring 1964): 40-41.
Cited in this short article are the papers of merchants John Sparling and William Bolden; the correspondence of Joseph Priestley and James Bryce; the Dalhousie muniments; and 19th-century cotton market reports.

2062. Carter, Clarence E. "Notes on the Lord Gage Collection of Manuscripts." *Mississippi Valley Historical Review* 15 (March 1929): 511-519.
This article reviews the papers of General Thomas Gage, commander-in-chief of British forces in colonial America from 1763 to 1775. Carter notes that Gage's correspondence with British officials is a rich source of information.

2063. Clark, Robert C. "The Archives of the Hudson's Bay Company." *Pacific Northwest Quarterly* 29 (January 1938): 3-15.
This article describes the company's records for operations west of the Rocky Mountains. While much of the operations area is now in Canada, Clark focuses on records documenting trading activities in what is now the northwestern U.S. for the period 1821-1847.

2064. Craig, Joan. "Three Hundred Years of Records." *The Beaver, Magazine of the North* Outfit 301 (Autumn 1970): 65-70.
The company's archivist reviews the records of the Hudson's Bay

Company. Most document operations in Canada, but some appear U.S.-related.

2065. Crick, Bernard R. "First List of Addenda to a *Guide to Manuscripts Relating to America in Great Britain and Ireland.*" *Bulletin of the British Association for American Studies* 5 (December 1962): 47-63.

This, and the following two entries, are additions to the book-length guide compiled by Crick and Miriam Alman in 1961. Crick cites, from public and private sources, British correspondence, diaries, business records, and reports relating to what is now the U.S.

2066. Crick, Bernard R. "Second List of Addenda to a *Guide to Manuscripts Relating to America in Great Britain and Ireland.*" *Bulletin of the British Association for American Studies* 7 (December 1963): 55-64.

2067. Crick, Bernard R., and others. "Third List of Addenda to a *Guide to Manuscripts Relating to America in Great Britain and Ireland.*" *Bulletin of the British Association for American Studies* 12/13 (December 1966): 61-77.

2068. Davenport, John B., and Dan Rylance. "Archival Note -- Sources of Business History: The Archives of the Hudson's Bay Company." *Business History Review* 54 (Autumn 1980): 387-393.

Most of the records document company activities in Canada, but many relate to areas now part of the U.S. The authors provide detailed descriptions of record series with content notes. The records described are in the Manitoba Provincial Archives.

2069. Kellaway, W. "Archives of the New England Company." *Archives* 2 (Michaelmas 1954): 175-182.

The New England Company was a missionary society founded in 1649 and operating in colonial America until the beginning of the American Revolution. This article identifies and locates extant pre-1770 records of the company.

2070. Leach, MacEdward. "Notes on American Shipping Based on Records of the Court of the Vice-Admiralty of Jamaica, 1776-1812." *American Neptune* 20 (January 1960): 44-48.

The records Leach describes are in the archives at Spanish Town, Jamaica, and include ships' logs; commissions; registry documents; manifests; and correspondence from U.S. ships seized during the American Revolution.

2071. Leveson-Grower, R.H.G. "The Archives of the Hudson's Bay Company." *The Beaver* 264 (December 1933): 40-42; 265 (June 1934): 19-21;

and 266 (September 1935): 22-24.

This series of three articles offers a description of the company's records from the 17th century to the 20th century. Most records document operations in Canada, but some appear related to the U.S. border states and the Puget Sound area.

2072. Rogers, George C., Jr. "The Papers of James Grant of Ballindalloch Castle, Scotland." *South Carolina Historical Magazine* 77 (1976): 145-160.

Grant was a British army officer and a colonial governor of East Florida. Rogers explains how Grant's papers are useful for the history of colonial South Carolina and Florida.

2073. Street, J. "The G. R. G. Conway Collection in the Cambridge University Library." *Hispanic American Historical Review* 37 (January 1957): 60-81.

The article lists the contents of eighty-one volumes of transcribed Spanish documents. Most relate to Mexico and the Inquisition. Some, however, are on California topics. See entries 2074, 2208, and 2271 also.

2074. Thornton, A. P. "The G. R. G. Conway MS. Collection in the Library of the University of Aberdeen." *Hispanic American Historical Review* 36 (August 1956): 345-347.

One of four Conway Collections. Like the others this contains mostly materials relating to colonial Mexico, along with some items about California. See entries 2073, 2208, and 2271 also.

Mexico and Spain

2075. Beerman, Eric. "A Checklist of Louisiana Documents in the Servicio Histórico Militar in Madrid." *Louisiana History* 20 (Spring 1979): 221-222.

Beerman lists twenty-three Louisiana-related documents in the Servicio Histórico Militar, the principal military archive of Spain. Entries include title, date, and what appears to be an archival control number.

2076. Beerman, Eric. "French Maps of Mississippi in Spanish Archives." *Journal of Mississippi History* 42 (February 1980): 43-47.

Beerman provides citations for sixteen maps found in the archives of the Servicio Geográfico del Ejército; the Servicio Histórico Militar; and the Biblioteca Nacional, all in Madrid, Spain.

2077. Bolton, Herbert E. "Materials for Southwestern History in the Central Archives of Mexico." *American Historical Review* 12 (April 1908): 510-527.

Bolton describes materials found in Mexico City's archives that relate to the history of the American Southwest. He limits his description to Spanish records prior to 1821 and to government archives as opposed to church or private collections.

2078. Bolton, Herbert E. "Notes and Fragments. Records of the Mission of Nuestra Señora del Refugio." *Texas Historical Association Quarterly* 14 (October 1910): 164-166.

In this short article, Bolton describes two record books from the Refugio Mission near Copano Bay, Texas, that were found in the church archives at Matamoros, Tamaulipas. One, a register of baptisms, the other a book of burials, date from 1807 to 1828.

2079. Bolton, Herbert E. "Some Materials for Southwestern History in the Archivo General de México." *The Quarterly of the Texas State Historical Association* 6 (October 1902): 103-112; and 7 (January 1904): 196-213.

These records describe policies, issues, and events in Spanish Texas, Louisiana, and New Mexico. The materials date from the 17th to the early 19th centuries. The first article is general in nature, the second focuses on Texas documents.

2080. Cardoso, Lawrence A. "Archival Sources in Mexico for the Study of Chicano History." *New Scholar* 7 (Fall 1978): 255-258.

Cardoso calls attention to five ramos within the Archivo Histórico de la Secretaría de Relaciones Exteriores in Mexico City. The ramos are: la revolución mexicana; legajos de numeración corrida; recortes de periódicos; Flores Magón; and servicios culturos de la secretaría.

2081. Carpenter, Edwin H., Jr. "Checklist of the Official Imprints of the Administration of Revilla Gigedo the Younger, 1789-1794." *Papers of the Bibliographical Society of America* 46 (1952): 215-263.

Revilla Gigedo was viceroy of New Spain. The checklist includes more than 275 imprints or broadsides. Entries are chronological with short titles, subject content notes, archival locations, and types of documents.

2082. Chapman, Charles E. "The Archivo General de Indias." *Southwestern Historical Quarterly* 21 (October 1917): 145-155.

A brief review of the Spanish colonial archives at Seville. Chapman explains how materials came to the archives, the type of records found there, how to use them, and their value to southwestern U.S. history.

2083. Cortés Alonso, Vicenta. "The Archive of the Indies." *Manuscripts* 21 (Winter 1969): 2-10.

After a short history of the archives, the author provides a list of its sections, or record groups, and briefly describes the contents of those that have information about the Americas.

2084. Cortés Alonso, Vicenta. "Fuentes documentales españolas para la historia de los Estados Unidos." *Revista de Historia de América* 94 (julio/ diciembre 1982): 151-174.
     This a bibliographical article in which the author cites published guides to the major archives of Spain.

2085. Gómez del Campillo, Miguel. "Madrid Archives, Chronological Statement of Papers and Documents Relative to Louisiana in the National Historical Archives of Madrid (1740-1832)." *Louisiana Historical Society Publications* 4 (1908): 121-144.
     There are two lists. The first contains the legajo numbers and years they cover. The second is a list which describes specific documents relating to Louisiana.

2086. Holmes, Jack D. "Maps, Plans and Charts of Louisiana in Spanish and Cuban Archives: A Checklist." *Louisiana Studies* 2 (Winter 1963): 183-203.
     Holmes lists and describes 123 maps. Entries include title; place and date of publication, if published; cartographer's name; archives and libraries holding a copy; and descriptive notes.

2087. Holmes, Jack D. "Research Opportunities in the Spanish Borderlands: Louisiana and the Old Southwest." *Louisiana Studies* 1 (Winter 1962): 1-19.
     The value of this article is its review of Spanish archives and their respective subject strengths.

2088. Mathes, W. Michael. "Sources in Mexico for the History of Spanish California." *California History* 61 (Fall 1982): 223-226.
     A review of the ramos, or record groups, and their contents in the archives in Mexico City; La Paz, Baja California; and Guadalajara, Jalisco. The article mentions microfilm holdings of these records in the Bancroft Library, University of California-Berkeley.

2089. Nasatir, Abraham P., and Ernest R. Liljegren. "Materials Relating to the History of the Mississippi Valley from the Minutes of the Supreme Councils of State, 1787-1797." *Louisiana Historical Quarterly* 21 (January 1938): 5-75.
     The compilers list each meeting of the Spanish council by date and include a one-line statement about the subjects discussed. Extensive footnotes provide information about the actions, people involved, and where additional documentation can be found.

2090. Piette, Charles J.G.M. "The Diarios of Early California, 1769-1784."
The Americas 2 (April 1946): 409-422.
   The diarios were travellers' accounts of Spanish land and sea explorations to unsettled areas from the 16th to 18th centuries. This article cites
nearly fifty of these accounts, both published and unpublished, relating
to Spanish California.

2091. Scholes, France V. "Manuscripts for the History of New Mexico in the
National Library in Mexico City." *New Mexico Historical Review* 3 (July
1928): 301-323.
   This article includes a calendar of several hundred 17th- and 18th-
century documents that Scholes encountered in Mexico's national library.
The records were from the archive of the Franciscan province of Santo
Evangelio.

2092. Scholes, France V. "Royal Treasury Records Relating to the Province of
New Mexico, 1596-1683." *New Mexico Historical Review* 50 (January
1975): 5-23; and (April 1975): 139-164.
   Scholes analyzes Spanish accounting records and identifies the legajos
that contain financial records concerning what is now New Mexico. The
article is useful for understanding the data in the records, and learning
where the records may be found.

2093. Shepherd, William R. "The Spanish Archives and Their Importance for
the History of the United States." *Annual Report of the American
Historical Association for the Year 1903* 1 (1904): 145-183.
   A review of the principal archives in Spain and the system used to
classify documents, followed by a description of the records relating to
U.S. history, and concluding with a bibliographic essay about the
archives and their finding aids.

2094. Wroth, Lawrence C. "The Frontier Presidios of New Spain: Books,
Maps, and a Selection of Manuscripts Relating to the Riviera Expedition,
1724-1728." *Papers of the Bibliographical Society of America* 45 (3rd
Quarter 1951): 191-218.
   Wroth describes and locates copies of eleven manuscripts and printed
documents and six manuscript maps relating to Pedro de Riviera y
Villalón's inspection trip of presidios in what is now the southwestern
U.S.

U.S. Repositories Holding Foreign Records or Manuscripts

Africa, Asia, and the Mideast

2095. Beal, Edwin G. "Microfilmed Archives of the Japanese Ministry of Foreign Affairs." *Quarterly Journal of Current Acquisitions* 11 (November 1953): 7-11.

This article notes which records were destroyed during WWII, the records that were filmed, and the subjects covered in the records filmed. Beal concludes the article with an analysis of selected record series.

2096. Beck, Clark L., Jr., and Ardath W. Burks "Additional Archives of the Yatoi." *Journal of the Rutgers University Libraries* 45 (June 1983): 25-42.

The authors review an accretion to the William E. Griffis papers which document late 19th-century Japanese culture. Much of the article treats the significance of the papers as opposed to describing their content.

2097. Bennett, Norman, George E. Brooks, and Alan R. Booth. "Materials for African History in the Peabody Museum and Essex Institute." *African Studies Bulletin* 5 (October 1962): 13-22.

The authors list forty-eight collections of papers and ships logs. Entries include collection title, or ship's name for logs, and inclusive dates. Each entry is annotated to indicate the materials' relationship to Africa.

2098. Bhagat, G. "Materials Relating to Eighteenth and Nineteenth Century Indo-American Trade and Consular Relations in Private Archives in the United States." *Indian Archives* 17 (January 1967/December 1968): 1-18.

Bhagat identifies U.S. repositories holding India-related papers and cites titles of major collections with record series titles and inclusive dates; minor collections by title; and ships' logs and journals by names of vessel and ships' masters and dates of voyage.

2099. Boullata, Issa J. "The Arabic Manuscript Collection at Hartford Seminary." *Hamdard Islamicus* 8 (Summer 1985): 91-95.

This is an overview of more than 1,200 manuscripts at the seminary. While providing some information on subjects, Boullata does not describe manuscripts individually.

2100. Bruno, N. J. "Press Reform in Occupied Japan (1945-1952): The Records of the Press and Publications Branch, Information Division, Civil Information and Education Section of the Supreme Commander for the Allied Powers at the National Archives and Records Administration, Suitland, Maryland." *Committee on East Asian Libraries Bulletin* 89 (February 1990): 1-15.

Bruno provides some specific references to U.S.-Japanese relations in a large collection. He describes the appropriate record series, and also cites the specific boxes containing these records.

2101. Furber, Holden. "A Preliminary Report on the Macartney Manuscripts." *Library Chronicle* 21 (Spring 1955): 43-50.

This article reports on a collection of personal correspondence of George, Lord Macartney, governor of Madras and England's first ambassador to China in 1792. The letters document, mostly, administrative affairs in southern India in the 1780s.

2102. Goodman, Roy E. "Benjamin Smith Lyman and the Geological Survey of Japan (1872-1879): Papers, Maps, and Charts at the American Philosophical Society in Philadelphia." *Committee on East Asian Libraries Bulletin* 84 (June 1988): 1-4.

The Lyman papers include correspondence; notes; sketches and maps; and reports on mineral deposits, all dated 1872-1883. Goodman also notes other Lyman papers at the University of Massachusetts, Amherst.

2103. Haywood, Carl. "American Contacts with Africa: A Bibliography of the Papers of the American Whalemen." *African Studies Bulletin* 10 (December 1967): 82-95.

Haywood locates two categories of papers: journals and logbooks. Collections of each are listed under the repositories holding them. Entries include titles, authors or names of keepers, inclusive dates, and the names of vessels where appropriate.

2104. Jabbour, Alan and Joseph C. Hickerson. "African Recordings in the Archive of Folk Song." *Quarterly Journal of the Library of Congress* 27 (July 1970): 283-288.

The authors cite several collection titles containing field recordings of African music and folklore. Their description includes names of those recording the music, the location and dates of the recordings, and the content of the recordings.

2105. Jamison, Martin. "The Archive of Turkish Oral Narrative at Texas Tech University." *Texas Libraries* 43 (Summer 1981): 51-53.

Jamison provides an overview of some 600 sound recordings of Turkish folktales. Description of the collection is limited to mention of finding aids available and the basic categories into which the folktales fall.

2106. Johns, Francis A. "A Collection of the Papers of Arthur Waley and Beryl de Zoete." *Rutgers University Library Journal* 29 (June 1966): 59-61.
   Johns gives a brief description of Waley's letters and manuscripts and Zoete's diaries and photographs. Waley is known for his expertise in Japanese and Chinese cultures, Zoete for her study of Asian dance.

2107. Levitt, Stephan H. "A Descriptive Catalogue of the Indic and Greater Indic Manuscripts in the Collection of the University Museum of the University of Pennsylvania." *Library Chronicle* 44 (Winter 1980): 97-152.
   The catalogue describes forty-seven manuscripts from India, Nepal, Tibet, Ceylon, Burma, and Thailand. Entries include date, language, author, title, physical characteristics, length, and content notes.

2108. Martinovitch, Nicholas N. "Arabic, Persian and Turkish Manuscripts in the Columbia University Library." *American Oriental Society Journal* 49 (September 1929): 219-233.
   There are forty-seven manuscripts described in this checklist. Entries include author, title, size, language, and, in most cases, content notes.

2109. Morley, James W. "Checklist of Seized Japanese Records in the National Archives." *Far Eastern Quarterly* 9 (May 1950): 306-333.
   Morley lists record series titles, inclusive dates, and content notes under broader record group headings.

2110. Needham, Wesley E. "Gifts of Manuscripts and Tankas to the Tibetan Collection." *Yale University Library Gazette* 58 (April 1984): 181-183.
   Needham calls attention to a collection of more than 100 Tibetan terma and nyingmapa manuscripts. The texts are religious in nature.

2111. Needham, Wesley E. "The Tibetan Collection at Yale." *Yale University Library Gazette* 34 (January 1960): 127-133.
   This collection includes several manuscripts which Needham reviews. Most of the manuscripts are religious in content.

2112. Nemoy, Leon. "The Rescher Collection of Arabic, Persian, and Turkish Manuscripts." *Yale University Library Gazette* 47 (October 1972): 57-99.
   Except for a short introduction and bio-bibliography of Oskar Rescher, this article is a checklist of manuscripts in Rescher's private collection, now at Yale. The list is divided into Arabic, Persian, and Turkish manuscripts in chronological order.

2113. Nunn, G. Raymond. "Research Materials on Southeast Asia in the United States." *Southeast Asian Archives* 3 (July 1970): 47-50.

2114. Phelan, John L. "The Philippine Collection in the Newberry Library." *Newberry Library Bulletin* 3 (March 1955): 229-236.
    These materials were originally part of Edward Ayer's collection. The article describes both 17th- and 18th-century manuscripts and books relating to the Philippine Islands. Linguistic materials are a strength of the collection.

2115. Rieger, Morris. "Africa-Related Papers of Persons and Organizations in the United States." *African Studies Bulletin* 8 (December 1965): 1-11.
    This article lists manuscript collections under broad headings such as politicians, diplomats, naval officers, missionaries, companies and businesses, sciences, etc. Each entry includes collection and record series titles, volume, inclusive dates, and content notes.

2116. Rosenbaum, Thomas. "The Archives of the China Medical Board and the Peking Union Medical College at the Rockefeller Archive Center." *Committee on East Asian Libraries Bulletin* 84 (June 1988): 5-19.
    Rosenbaum provides a thorough narrative description of these records that includes record series titles, inclusive dates, and information about related records and using the archives.

2117. Rubinstein, Murray A. "Olyphant's Island: China Trade Materials in Manhattan Library Collections--The New York Historical Society, the Union Theological Seminary, and the Research Division/New York Public Library." *Chin-tai Chung-kuo Shih Yen-chiu T'ung-hsün* 8 (1989): 148-161.
    The author cites both published and unpublished materials. Most of the primary sources are ships' logs and journals and missionaries' diaries.

2118. Schneider, Laurence A. "Using the Rockefeller Archives for Research on Modern Chinese Natural Science." *Chinese Science* 7 (December 1986): 25-31.
    Schneider describes mostly the records of the China Medical Board and the files of Project Series 601 -- China. His description includes record series, volume, inclusive dates, and content notes.

2119. Shih, Hu. "The Gest Oriental Library at Princeton University." *Princeton University Library Chronicle* 15 (Spring 1954): 113-141.
    Shih describes mostly published materials, but he also briefly reviews the library's 3,000 manuscripts on pages 136-141.

2120. Shih-Chia, Chu. "Chinese Documents in the United States National

Archives." *Far Eastern Quarterly* 9 (August 1950): 377-383.

The author identifies eight types of documents or record series including: credentials of emperors; treaties; communications of the Chinese foreign office and local governments; petitions of Chinese citizens; proclamations; Boxer Rebellion cartoons; and maps.

2121. Voorhoeve, P. "Four Batak Manuscripts in Princeton." *Princeton University Library Chronicle* 30 (Spring 1969): 158-170.

The author describes four manuscripts from the Robert Garrett and William H. Scheide Collections. The manuscripts are written in the Batak dialect, a Sumatran language.

2122. Witek, John W. "Seventeenth to Twentieth Century Cultural and Diplomatic Materials on East Asia in the Special Collections of the Lauinger Library, Georgetown University." *Committee on East Asian Libraries Bulletin* 89 (February 1990): 16-23.

The author cites collection and record series titles along with rare book holdings. China and Japan are the countries most obviously represented.

Europe

2123. Alvord, Clarence W. "Eighteenth Century French Records in the Archives of Illinois." *Annual Report of the American Historical Association for the Year 1905* 1 (1906): 353-366.

These records date from 1720 to 1799 and have become known as the Kaskaskia and Cahokia records. Alvord describes them by time period including the number of documents from each period and the types of businesses they document.

2124. Babcock, James. "Resources in Detroit for the History of the French in the Mississippi Valley." In *The French in the Mississippi Valley*, edited by John F. McDermott. Urbana: University of Illinois Press, 1965. 209-216.

Babcock describes manuscript sources in the Clarence Monroe Burton Collection held by the Detroit Public Library. He notes the collection is rich in materials relating to the fur trade; census records; missionaries to the area; and military accounts.

2125. Beer, William. "Calendar of Documents in a Volume Having on Back: French Mss., Mississippi Valley, 1679-1769." *Louisiana Historical Society Publications* 4 (1908): 4-120.

There are forty documents cited, all of which appear to be published following the calendar. Beer noted that the originals were in the Tilton Memorial Library, Tulane University.

2126. Betts, Raymond. "The Longwood Library." *French Historical Studies* 1
(Spring 1960): 360-362.
   This article emphasizes French-related manuscripts in the DuPont
family's Winterthur and Longwood Collections.

2127. Bispham, Clarence W. "New Orleans, A Treasure House for Historians."
Louisiana Historical Quarterly 2 (July 1919): 237-247.
   This article reviews some of the colonial records held by the Louisiana
Historical Society and includes a list of French and Spanish records and
manuscript collections.

2128. Bitton, Davis. "Research Materials in the Mormon Genealogical Society."
French Historical Studies 8 (Spring 1973): 172-174.
   A report on the scope and content of microfilmed French records in the
Genealogical Society of the Church of Jesus Christ of Latter-day Saints.

2129. Boxer, C. R. "The Naval and Colonial Papers of Dom Antonio de
Ataide." *Harvard Library Bulletin* 5 (Winter 1951): 24-50.
   Boxer describes 17th-century manuscripts of Antonio de Ataide in the
British Museum, Lisbon Academy of Sciences, Brazil's national library,
the Lynch Library in Rio de Janeiro, and at Harvard College's library.
He ranks Harvard's collection as the most extensive.

2130. Brasseaux, Carl A. "The Colonial Records Collection of the Center for
Louisiana Studies." *Louisiana History* 25 (Spring 1984): 181-188.
   The center's collection is divided into two sections of French and
Spanish colonial records, most of which have been microfilmed or
otherwise copied from European, Canadian, and Latin American
archives. The article cites key record groups and series.

2131. Brasseaux, Carl A. "French-Period Archival Resources in the Lower
Louisiana Territory." *Primary Sources & Original Works* 1 (Nos. 1/2
1991): 189-199.
   The author identifies records in French archives; microfilm sets of
French records; manuscript collections; and church records, all relating
to Louisiana for the period 1699-1769 and 1803.

2132. Brown, Elizabeth A. R. "The Library of Congress Microfilm Collection
of Unpublished Inventories of the Archives Nacionales, Paris." *French
Historical Studies* 15 (Fall 1988): 759-777.
   Brown relates the background of these inventories and how they were
acquired. This introductory material is followed by a listing of the
inventories by archival section or division.

2133. Bush, Robert D. "Documents on the Louisiana Purchase: The Laussat

Papers." *Louisiana History* 18 (Winter 1977): 104-107.
This article describes the papers of Pierre Clément de Laussat, French colonial perfect and commissioner, 1803-1804. The papers include correspondence, petitions, and a manuscript copy of Laussat's memoirs.

2134. Cobb, Gwendolin B. "Bancroft Library Microfilm: Portugal and Her Empire." *Hispanic American Historical Review* 34 (February 1954): 114-125.
Cobb provides the background of the microfilm project, describes the materials filmed in Portuguese repositories, and concludes with a checklist of microfilm reel titles and inclusive dates.

2135. Connelly, Owen. "The Beauharnais Papers at Princeton University." *French Historical Studies* 16 (Spring 1990): 700-701.
The papers, dating from 1804 to the 1850s, are those of Eugène de Beauharnais, a French viceroy of Italy. The article calls attention to their untapped research values.

2136. Daly, John and Edward R. Vollmar. "The Knights of Columbus Vatican Microfilm Library at Saint Louis University." *Library Quarterly* 28 (July 1958): 165-171.
The authors provide the historical background of the library, review the types of microfilmed manuscripts held, and discuss the research possibilities the holdings offer.

2137. Daly, Lowrie J. "Some Examples of Theological Materials Available on Microfilm." *Library Trends* 9 (October 1960): 246-251.
This article briefly describes Vatican manuscripts found in the Knights of Columbus Vatican Film Library at St. Louis University. It also contains information on available guides to the microfilm.

2138. Daly, Lowrie J. "Some Political Theory Tracts in the Vatican Barberini Collection." *Manuscripta* 5 (February 1961): 28-34; (July 1961): 88-95; and 16 (November 1972): 156-164.
A three-article series in which Daly identifies documents by codex number, most of which are available on microfilm at St. Louis University. In addition to codex numbers, Daly identifies authors, titles, and provides brief content summaries.

2139. Dennis, George T. "An Inventory of Italian Notarial Documents in the Sutro Library, San Francisco." *Manuscripta* 9 (July 1965): 89-103.
The inventory is of 168 documents which Dennis says pertain mostly to property settlements of Venetian families from the 15th to the 17th centuries. Entries include place of origin, date, language, size, and content statement, including names of those involved.

2140. DeVille, Winston. "Manuscript Sources in Louisiana for the History of the French in the Mississippi Valley." In *The French in the Mississippi Valley*, edited by John F. McDermott. Urbana: University of Illinois Press, 1965. 217-228.

DeVille calls attention to lesser known sources such as New Orleans notarial records; the Spanish cabildo records; the "Black Book" in the Louisiana State Museum; and church records scattered throughout Louisiana.

2141. Epstein, Fritz T. "Washington Research Opportunities in the Period of World War II." *American Archivist* 17 (July 1954): 225-241.

This articles describes captured German military records, records of German civilian agencies, and Nazi Party records held by U.S. agencies after WWII. It also discusses captured Japanese records and records relating to the Nuremberg trials.

2142. Ermatinger, Charles J. "Catalogues in the Knights of Columbus Vatican Film Library at Saint Louis University." *Manuscripta* 1 (February 1957): 5-21; and (July 1957): 89-101.

This two-article series offers a checklist of manuscript collections on microfilm that also have inventories available.

2143. Galloway, Patricia. "Louisiana Post Letters: The Missing Evidence for Indian Diplomacy." *Louisiana History* 22 (Winter 1981): 31-43.

While not locating the missing French outpost reports, Galloway does provide insights to extant French records, such as Série C13A, Corresponance général: Louisiane, in the National Archives of France, and the papers of Pierre de Rigaud de Vaudreuil.

2144. Gatzke, Wilhelm. "The Streseman Papers." *Journal of Modern History* 26 (March 1954): 49-59.

Gustav Streseman was German chancellor and minister of foreign affairs during the 1920s. Gatzke reviews Streseman's papers available on microfilm at the U.S. National Archives while commenting on their research values and noting missing segments.

2145. Gehring, Charles. "New Netherland Manuscripts in United States Repositories." *Halve Maen* 57 (No. 3 1983): 5-8.

2146. Gehring, Charles. "New York's Dutch Records: A Historiographical Note." *New York History* 56 (July 1975): 347-354.

Gehring reviews efforts to translate and publish Dutch records in the U.S. that relate to New York state.

2147. Gotlieb, Howard B. "Documenting the Third Reich: The Stutz Collection of Nazi Manuscripts." *Yale University Library Gazette* 37 (January 1963): 109-117.

This is a collection of 109 manuscripts accumulated by Rolf Stutz. The authors of these documents were prominent leaders of the Nazi Party and frequently were in Hitler's inner circle.

2148. Grant, W. Leonard. "Neo-Latin Materials at St. Louis." *Manuscripta* 4 (February 1960): 3-18.

This is a checklist of neo-latin literary, scientific, and miscellaneous manuscripts on microfilm in the Knights of Columbus Vatican Film Library at St. Louis University. Entries are keyed to the Vatican Library codex numbers.

2149. Grzybowski, Kazimierz. "The Jakhontov Papers." *Quarterly Journal of Current Acquisitions* 17 (August 1960): 227-230.

Arkadi Nikolaievitch Jakhontov was chief of the chancellery in Russia until the 1917 revolution. His papers include minutes of the Russian Council of Ministers and related documents and reports. The article analyzes their research values.

2150. Holschuh, Albrecht and Saundra Taylor. "The S. Fischer Verlag Papers in the Lilly Library, Indiana University." *Indiana University Bookman* 14 (March 1982): 1-99.

This entire issue is devoted to listing the records of this German publishing company. The materials date from 1889 to 1977. The collection is mostly correspondence with some manuscripts. No index, but the correspondence is presented alphabetically.

2151. "Index to the Judicial Records of the French Superior Council of Louisiana." *Louisiana Historical Quarterly* 5 (January 1922): 76-117.

This is a guide to French colonial records in Louisiana. It is similar in format to the "Index to Spanish Judicial Records of Louisiana" described below (entry 2235). The French guide begins with this issue and continues into the 1940s.

2152. Izbicki, Thomas M., and Patrick Lally. "Texts Attributed to Bartolus de Saxoterrato in North American Manuscript Collections." *Manuscripta* 35 (July 1991): 146-155.

The authors list eleven manuscripts in the U.S. and one in Canada.

2153. Kent, George O. "A Survey of German Manuscripts Pertaining to American History in the Library of Congress." *Journal of American History* 56 (March 1970): 868-881.

This article lists the titles, dates, and sources of German documents under the headings of emigration and colonization; political and diplomatic affairs; military and naval affairs; trade and economic affairs; and miscellaneous. The materials date from the 1700s to 1860.

2154. Kilbourne, John D. "French Manuscripts in the Archives of the Society of the Cincinnati." *Manuscripts* 27 (Winter 1975): 65-68.

The article calls attention to the correspondence and papers of French officers who served in the Continental Army during the American Revolution. The society's archive is in Washington, D.C.

2155. Leffler, Phyllis and John C. Rule. "French History Holdings in the Folger Library." *French Historical Studies* 9 (Spring 1976): 532-536.

Description in this article is evenly divided between rare books, the pamphlet collection, and manuscripts. The authors cite the titles of several key collections held by the library.

2156. Lich, Glen E. "Archives of the German Adelsverien, Beinecke Rare Book and Manuscript Library, Yale University." *Southwestern Historical Quarterly* 91 (January 1988): 361-368.

The author describes the records of the Society for the Protection of German Immigrants in Texas, a 19th-century organization designed to promote German migration. The article focuses on correspondence files in the collection.

2157. Lich, Glen E., Gunter Moltmann, and Michael T. Womack. "New Crowns to Old Glory: Archives of the German Adelsverien." *Yale University Library Gazette* 63 (April 1989): 145-157.

This archive of about fifteen linear feet of records and papers documenting the activities of a German immigration society in Texas includes immigrants' applications; records of the society; and descriptions and surveys of the area settled in Texas.

2158. Lobay, Halyna. "The Zdeněk Němeček Papers." *Yale University Library Gazette* 64 (October 1989): 76-82.

Němeček was a Czech writer and editor for Radio Free Europe. His collection includes correspondence, manuscripts of his writings, radio scripts, speeches, and photographs.

2159. Mancha, Philip E. "Heinrich Hoffmann: Photographer of the Third Reich." *Prologue* 5 (Spring 1973): 31-40.

Most of this article relates the rise of Hoffmann's fortunes as a friend of Adolf Hitler. The last page, however, describes the Hoffmann photograph collection held by the U.S. National Archives in its RG 242. The photos date from the WWI period to 1944.

2160. Mars, Anna M. "Americana in the Archives of the Jozef Pilsudski

Institute in New York." *Polish Review* 22 (December 1977): 65-75.

Mars lists manuscript collections containing U.S.-related materials under the headings of 19th century and WWI; period between the wars; WWII; and postwar immigration. Entries include collection and record series titles, inclusive dates, and content notes.

2161. McDonough, John J., and James E. O'Neill. "France in the Manuscript Division of the Library of Congress." *French Historical Studies* 4 (Spring 1965): 95-102.

The authors discuss two groups of collections, historical manuscripts from the 18th and 19th centuries, and official records copied in French archives. Description is limited to collection titles, inclusive dates, and research potentials.

2162. Mendelsohn, John. "Genealogy and the Holocaust: Selected Sources at the National Archives." *Prologue* 15 (Fall 1983): 179-187.

Mendelsohn emphasizes German concentration camp personnel records in this article. These include inmate questionnaires and record cards; entry registers; and deathbooks.

2163. Mulligan, Timothy. "Tracking *Das Boot*: Records of U-96 in the National Archives." *Prologue* 14 (Winter 1982): 202-211.

Among the captured German naval records in the U.S. National Archives are U-96's war diary, torpedo firing reports, route charts, patrol reports, and radio log extracts. Mulligan also notes related records held by the National Archives.

2164. Oliveira Lima, Manoel de. "The Portuguese Manuscripts in the Ibero-American Library at the Catholic University of America." *Hispanic American Historical Review* 8 (May 1928): 261-280.

The article provides detailed descriptions of documents and correspondence series relating to 17th- and 18th-century Portuguese diplomacy; genealogy; the administration of Brazil and Portuguese India; and miscellaneous diplomatic affairs.

2165. O'Neill, James E. "Copies of French Manuscripts for American History in the Library of Congress." *Journal of American History* 51 (March 1965): 674-691.

O'Neill lists copies of French documents at the record series level under broader repository or record group headings. The series entries include volume statements and inclusive dates.

2166. Palmer, R. R. "The Beauharnais Archives." *Princeton University Library Chronicle* 3 (February 1942): 45-51.

Eugene Beauharnais was a stepson of Napoleon Bonaparte and viceroy of Italy. His papers document his governance of Italy from 1805 to 1814. Palmer describes the papers and explains their historical context.

2167. Perman, Dagmar Horna. "Microfilming of German Records in the National Archives." *American Archivist* 22 (October 1959): 433-443.
An article explaining the division, disposition, and handling of captured German archives. The article concludes with a checklist of the German record groups filmed and titles of the first thirteen guides produced.

2168. Plante, Julian G. "The Monastic Manuscript Microfilming Program of Saint John's University (Collegeville)." *Manuscripta* 11 (November 1967): 158-161.
Plante relates the progress of this project to film pre-1600 manuscripts in European monasteries. He identifies many of the monasteries in which microfilming was completed.

2169. Plante, Julian G., and Donald Yates. "Manuscripts from Hungary on Microfilm at the Hill Monastic Manuscript Library." *Manuscripta* 24 (March 1980): 31-39.
The authors list 260 manuscripts filmed in the Metropolitan Ecclesiastical Library in Esztergom and the David Kaufmann Collection of Judaica in the Hungarian Academy of Sciences, Budapest.

2170. Plummer, Leonard B. "Research Materials on Early German Settlers in Texas." *Library Chronicle of the University of Texas* 6 (Spring 1958): 29-33.
Plummer cites archival records valuable for studying German immigration into Texas. He found especially useful a microfilmed set entitled the Solm-Braunfels Archives containing records of a colonization project.

2171. Sexton, Meta M. "The Cavagna Library at the University of Illinois." *Papers of the Bibliographical Society of America* 19 (1925): 66-72.
This is mostly a description of the published materials in the private library of Count Antonio Cavagna. It, however, does include a brief description of manuscripts maps and Italian manuscripts dating from the 12th century.

2172. Shad, Robert O. "The Estelle Doheny Collection." *New Colophon* 3 (1950): 229-242.
While mostly about published materials, Shad does describe in some detail the illuminated medieval and renaissance manuscripts in the collection along with mention of 18th- and early-19th-century Spanish materials relating to California.

2173. Stuurman, Douwe. "The Nazi Collection: A Preliminary Note."

Quarterly Journal of Current Acquisitions 6 (November 1948): 21-22.

This article calls attention to materials accumulated in Germany after the end of WWII. Among the primary materials are Nazi Party archives, police records, propaganda posters, chancellory records, the public's correspondence to Hitler, speeches, and other records.

2174. Swietek, Francis R. "Preserving Medieval Manuscripts and Promoting Research." *Manuscripts* 26 (Fall 1974): 255-260.

Swietek describes the type of materials and specific manuscripts found on microfilm at the Monastic Manuscript Microfilm Library of Saint John's University, Collegeville, Minnesota. The library films manuscripts predating 1600 for research.

2175. Timberlake, Charles E. "Source Materials on Russian and American History in the Alexander Petrunkevich Collection." *Yale University Library Gazette* 41 (January 1967): 120-130.

Petrunkevich was an expert arachnologist, but his papers are better known for their rich documentation of the liberal movement in Russia before the 1917 revolution.

2176. Vanderbilt, Paul. "Prints and Photographs of Nazi Origin." *Quarterly Journal of Current Acquisitions* 6 (August 1949): 21-27.

Vanderbilt describes a Library of Congress photograph collection of Nazi leaders and party activities accumulated after WWII. While some of the German photographs date back to WWI, most are from the 1932-1942 period.

2177. Wardrop, James. "Six Italian Manuscripts in the Department of Graphic Arts." *Harvard Library Bulletin* 7 (Spring 1953): 221-225.

The author describes six representative manuscripts from Harvard's calligraphic collection. This collection was formed for the penmanship examples used in the manuscript rather than its informational value.

2178. Williamson, John G. "Mussolini Collection." *Yale University Library Gazette* 53 (July 1978): 45-47.

Valerian Lada-Mocarski was an O.S.S. agent in Italy in April, 1945 where he accumulated these first-hand accounts describing the murder of Benito Mussolini and Clara Petacci. He interviewed most of the key participants involved in this closing drama of WWII.

Great Britain and the British Commonwealth

2179. Alvord, Clarence W. "The Shelburne Manuscripts in America." *Bulletin of the Institute of Historical Research* 1 (1924): 77-80.

An article about the provenance of Lord Shelburne's collection of
manuscripts now in the Clements Library of the University of Michigan.
The papers relate to British colonial activities in America and elsewhere
from the 1750s to the early 19th century.

2180. Blake, Theresa. "Claydon House Papers." *Dartmouth College Library
Bulletin* 6 (January 1964): 9-12.

This article describes a sixty-reel microfilm set of papers of the Verney
family, Claydon House, Buckinghamshire, England. The papers date
from 1500 to 1790 and include correspondence, legal documents, and
financial records.

2181. Bracher, Frederick. "The Letterbooks of Sir George Etherege." *Harvard
Library Bulletin* 15 (July 1967): 238-245.

Etherege was a 17th-century British playwright. The article describes
two of his letterbooks held by Harvard University. The letters, dated
1685-1689, are of the period when he was British ambassador to the
Imperial Diet of Ratisborn, Regensburg, Bavaria.

2182. Canada, Public Archives of. "Calendar of Manuscripts in the Archives
of the Chicago Historical Society." *Report on Canadian Archives 1905* 1
(1906): xxxii-xlvii.

The calendar of Canadian-related documents is included in the report of
the archivist. It lists mostly individual documents chronologically from
1480 to 1833. Entries include authors or correspondents, dates, type of
document, and content notes.

2183. Canada, Public Archives of. "Papers in the Possession of Mr. C. M.
Burton, of Detroit." *Report on Canadian Archives* 1905 1 (1906): xxiv-
xxxii.

This is a checklist of Canadian-related manuscript collections and
documents in the Burton Collection in the Detroit Public Library. Entries
summarize the contents, provide inclusive dates, and name correspondents.

2184. Hayman, John G. "The John Ruskin Collection." *Dartmouth College
Library Bulletin* 22 (November 1981): 2-10.

The author provides a checklist of selected letters and describes others
in this narrative about Dartmouth's Ruskin Collection.

2185. Hemlow, Joyce. "Preparing a Catalogue of the Burney Family Correspondence 1749-1878." *Bulletin of the New York Public Library* 1 (October
1967): 486-495.

While not the catalogue, this article reviews the provenance and content
of this collection of over 10,000 letters between the U.S. and British

branches of this family.

2186. Macomber, William F. "The Microfilming of Archives in Malta."
Manuscripts 27 (Spring 1975): 131-134.
A brief article describing the types of records filmed in the Archives of
the Episcopal Chancery; the Archives of the Cathedral of Malta; and the
Archives of the Inquisition of Malta for the Monastic Manuscript
Microfilm Library, St. John's University.

2187. Mowat, Charles L. "Material Relating to British East Florida in the Gage
Papers and Other Manuscript Collections in the William L. Clements
Library." *Florida Historical Quarterly* 18 (July 1939): 46-60.
Mowat provides a checklist of letters between General Gage and British
officers in Florida and also cites references in the Henry Clinton,
Shelburne, and William Knox papers, and the map collection.

2188. Mugridge, Donald H. "The Papers of Baron Howard of Effingham."
Quarterly Journal of Current Acquisitions 10 (February 1953): 63-71.
Francis, Baron Howard of Effingham was colonial governor of Virginia
from 1683 to 1689. Mugridge describes the Virginia legislative journals,
correspondence, and British "home office" papers in the collection.

2189. Nussbaum, Frederick L. "A Checklist of the Film Copies of Archival
Material in the University of Wyoming Library from the Public Record
Office, the India Office, the British Museum in London, and the Archives
Nationales in Paris." *University of Wyoming Publications* 2 (December
1, 1936): 213-243.
Description in the checklist is limited to document title, its location
within the original record group or series, and its placement on the
microfilm. The records relate to economic history and date from ca.
1700 to 1815.

2190. Pargellis, Stanley M., and Norma B. Cuthbert. "Loudoun Papers: (a)
Colonial, 1756-58, (b) French Colonial, 1742-53." *Huntington Library
Bulletin* 3 (February 1933): 97-107.
The Loudoun papers document British military activities in North
America from 1740 to 1758. These family papers also contain a group
of French records documenting the Marquis de Vaudreuil-Canagnal's
governorship of Louisiana from 1742 to 1753.

2191. "The Smyth of Nibley Papers, 1613-1676." *Bulletin of the New York
Public Library* 1 (July 1897): 186-190.
A calendar of the papers of John Smyth of Nibley, England, who was
an investor in the Virginia colony. The documents, primarily relating to
Virginia, are presented alphabetically by author.

2192. "Summary Report on the Hastings Manuscripts." *Huntington Library Bulletin* 5 (April 1934): 1-67.
    This is a detailed description of records and papers of the Hastings, a British family, dating from 1101 to 1892. There are twelve sub-groups of papers, each listing record series chronologically with brief content notes.

2193. Syrett, David. "A Checklist of Admiral Lord Howe's Manuscripts in United States Archives and Libraries." *Mariner's Mirror* 67 (August 1981): 273-284.
    Syrett lists Howe's correspondence in twenty libraries along with correspondents' names, dates, and occasional content notes. Lord Howe commanded the British Squadron at the start of the American Revolution and later served as first lord of the admiralty.

2194. Tyler, Lyon G. "London Company Records." *Annual Report of the American Historical Association for the Year 1901* 1 (1902): 543-575.
    Tyler writes about two volumes of court and assembly records from the Virginia Company of London relating to its Jamestown settlement. He attributes them to Sir John Danvers, an auditor of the company. The records are in the Library of Congress.

2195. Voigts, Linda E. "A Handlist of Middle English in Harvard Manuscripts." *Harvard Library Bulletin* 33 (Winter 1985): 5-96.
    This entire issue is devoted to middle English manuscripts at Harvard. There are 147 manuscripts listed under the libraries that hold them.

2196. Welke, William F. "The Papers of the Viscounts Melville." *American Archivist* 26 (October 1963): 449-462.
    The collection documents the Napoleonic Wars, the British navy, Anglo-American relations, naval hospitals, the Danish East India Company, the London metropolitian police, and naval warfare on the Great Lakes, during the period 1812-1814.

Latin America and Spain

2197. Anderson, Robert R. "A Note on the Archivo de Hidalgo del Parral." *Arizona and the West* 4 (Winter 1962): 381-385.
    This is a description of a microfilmed set of the Spanish archive at Hidalgo del Parral, Chihuahua, Mexico, held by the University of Arizona library. The records, dated 1631-1821, relate to civil and military administrative affairs, mining, and criminal cases.

2198. Arnade, Charles W. "Florida History in Spanish Archives: Reproductions

at the University of Florida. " *Florida Historical Quarterly* 34 (July 1955):
36-50.

The first part of this article traces the exodus of Spanish records from
Florida to various archives. The second part describes a set of records
copied in Seville, Spain, and placed at the University of Florida.

2199. Arnade, Charles W. "The Porfirio Díaz Papers of the William L.
Clements Library." *Hispanic American Historical Review* 33 (May 1953):
324-325.

This short article calls attention to a small collection of Díaz papers at
the University of Michigan. The papers focus almost entirely on
Mexican military operations for the year 1867.

2200. Bolton, Herbert E. "Spanish Mission Records at San Antonio." *The
Quarterly of the Texas State Historical Association* 10 (April 1907): 297-
307.

When Bolton wrote this article, the records were held by the Catholic
diocese of San Antonio, Texas. The materials he describes include
baptismal, marriage, and burial records for the period 1703-1783.

2201. Bowman, Jacob N. "History of the Provincial Archives of California."
Southern California Quarterly 64 (Spring 1982): 1-97.

The entire issue is devoted to Bowman's history of the Spanish and
Mexican records relating to California from the 1760s to the 1850s.
Bowman identifies and analyzes the records that survived the 1906 San
Francisco earthquake and fires.

2202. Boxer, C. R. "The Papers of Martín de Bertendoña, a Basque Admiral
of Spain's Golden Age, 1586-1604." *Indiana University Bookman* 10
(November 1969): 3-23.

Boxer describes selected documents in detail while noting that the
collection is mostly correspondence to Bertendoña with only four letters
from him and nothing on his early life.

2203. Boxer, C. R. "Preliminary Report on a Collection of Documents Looted
at Manila in 1762-64, and Now in the Lilly Library, Indiana University."
Southeast Asian Archives 2 (July 1969): 104-107.

These Spanish records dating from the 1580s to the 1760s are mostly
ecclesiastical in content with many relating to the China missions.

2204. Broussard, Ray E. "Family Letters of Ignacio Comonfort." *Library
Chronicle of the University of Texas* 6 (Spring 1959): 29-32.

Comonfort was a Mexican Liberal politician influential during the mid-
19th century. Broussard describes his papers dating from the 1840s to
the 1860s in the University of Texas' Latin American Collection.

2205. Brower, Philip P. "The U.S. Army's Seizure and Administration of
Enemy Records up to World War II." *American Archivist* 25 (April
1963): 191-207.
   Brower identifies and comments on the disposition of records seized by
U.S. military forces during the Revolutionary War, the War of 1812, the
First Seminole War, the Mexican War, the Civil War, the Spanish-
American War, and WWI.

2206. Bryan, Anthony. "The Mexican Revolution of 1910: Perspectives from
the Francisco Vázquez Gómez Papers." *ICarbS* 1 (Spring/Summer 1974):
145-152.
   Bryan calls attention to this collection at Southern Illinois University.
It contains 10,000 letters and telegrams, scrapbooks, and clipping files
relating to Gómez's role in the revolution.

2207. Buisseret, David. "Archival Research Opportunities in Discovery History
at the Newberry Library." *Terrae Incognitae* 13 (1981): 35-36.
   The author cites copies of Spanish records relating to the Spanish
borderlands; portolan charts and atlases; and an unpublished history of the
French navy.

2208. Cadenhead, Evie E., Jr. "The G. R. G. Conway Collection in the
Gilcrease Institute: A Checklist." *Hispanic American Historical Review*
38 (August 1958): 373-382.
   Cadenhead cites 125 manuscripts in chronological order.   Entries
include short titles, dates, and length of document. See entries 2073,
2074, and 2271 also.

2209. Callaghan, William S. "Gold Mining on the Brazilian Frontier: The
Archives of the St. John d'el Rey Mining Company." *Library Chronicle
of the University of Texas at Austin* New Series 10 (1978): 27-32.
   This mining company operated in the Brazilian state of Minas Gerais
from the 1830s to the 1960s. The firm's records include mining reports
and plans, maps, minutes, stockholder records, annual reports, financial
records, and photographs.

2210. Coker, William S. "Research in the Spanish Borderlands: Mississippi,
1779-1798." *Latin American Research Review* 7 (Summer 1972): 40-54.
   This is a historiographical article on Spanish Mississippi. It opens with
a five-page review of manuscript collections and Spanish records relating
to the Spanish period in Mississippi.

2211. Coker, William S. "Research Possibilities and Resources for a Study of
Spanish Mississippi." *Journal of Mississippi History* 34 (May 1972): 117-
128.

Coker identifies eight collections of copied Spanish records in Mississippi, Louisiana, and Florida that relate to Mississippi history.

2212. Coker, William S., and Jack D. L. Holmes. "Sources for the History of the Spanish Borderlands." *Florida Historical Quarterly* 49 (April 1971): 380-393.
The authors provide a thorough review of microfilmed French and Spanish records relating to Florida, Louisiana, Alabama, Texas, Mississippi, and New Mexico, and manuscript collections in historical societies and public and university libraries.

2213. Cortés Alonso, Vicenta. "Manuscripts Concerning Mexico and Central America in the Library of Congress, Washington, D.C." *The Americas* 18 (January 1962): 255-296.
The article lists, in guide-like entries, 145 separate documents or manuscript collections dating from the 16th century to the 1940s. The entries include titles, inclusive dates, record series, volume or length, and content notes.

2214. Coutts, Brian E. "An Inventory of Sources in the Department of Archives and Manuscripts, Louisiana State University for the History of Spanish Louisiana and Spanish West Florida." *Louisiana History* 19 (Spring 1978): 213-250.
There are 172 collections cited in this inventory. Entries include collection titles, inclusive dates, volume, record series titles, and content notes.

2215. Daly, Lowrie J. "Latin American Manuscripts at Saint Louis University." *Manuscripta* 21 (July 1977): 104-106.
Daly notes the microfilm collections of the Vatican Library and the Pastells Collections; the archives of the Jesuit Order in Rome and the Procurator General of Jesuits; La Biblioteca Ecuatoriana ... Polit; the European and private Mexican archives; and the De Propagande Fide Archives.

2216. Daly, Lowrie J. "Microfilming the Biblioteca Ecuatoriana 'Aurelio Espinosa Polit.'" *Manuscripta* 16 (March 1972): 34-36.
Aurelio Polit was a Jesuit serving in Ecuador where he accumulated published and unpublished materials relating to the country's history from 1800 to 1894. The latter includes hundreds of letters to, from, and about Educadorian president Gabriel García Moreno.

2217. Daly, Lowrie J., and Edward K. Burger. "Some Notes on the Pastells Collection at Saint Louis University." *Manuscripta* 24 (July 1980): 99-105.

The authors briefly describe a microfilm set of 17th- and 18th-century
Spanish records relating to the West Indies and the Americas. Pablo
Pastells, a Spanish Jesuit, originally accumulated the materials.

2218. Dunne, Peter M. "Jesuit Annual Letters in the Bancroft Library." *Mid-
America* 20 (October 1938): 263-272.
Dunne relates the history of these letters, explains their original
purpose, and comments on their content. He notes they are a rich source
for data about the Mexican frontier which includes the southwestern U.S.
The letters date from 1573 to 1763.

2219. Evans, G. Edward. "A Guide to Pre-1750 Manuscripts in the United
States Relating to Mexico and the Southwestern United States, with
Emphasis on Their Value to Anthropologists." *Ethnohistory* 17 (Win-
ter/Spring 1970): 63-90.
The guide is to repositories presented alphabetically by state. The
author cites some collection titles and individual documents, and
comments on the scope and contents of the repository's holdings.

2220. Evans, G. Edward and Frank J. Morales. "Fuentes de la historia de
México en archivos norteamericanos. *Historia Mexicana* 18 (enero/
marzo 1969): 432-462.
The authors use an institutional approach by listing repositories under
the state they are in. Description includes scope and content notes with
occasional mention of specific collection titles, record series, and volume.
Published holdings are described too.

2221. Friede, Juan. "Peruvian Manuscripts in the Lilly Library." *Indiana
University Bookman* 9 (April 1968): 3-38.
Friede divides the manuscripts into three categories: colonial, 1565-
1819; wars of independence, 1814-1828; and national period, 1825-1870.
He includes descriptions and record series titles for each group.

2222. Gannon, Michael V. "Documents of the Spanish Florida Borderlands: A
Calendaring Project at the University of Florida." *William and Mary
Quarterly* 38 (October 1981): 718-722.
Gannon describes four collections of Spanish records at Florida: the
John B. Stetson Collection, the East Florida papers, Papeles Procedentes
de Cuba, and the Residencias.

2223. Geiger, Maynard J. "History of the Santa Barbara de la Guerra Family
Documents." *Southern California Quarterly* 54 (Fall 1972): 277-284.
The family's papers date from the late 1790s to the 1850s and document
the Spanish and Mexican periods of California. The originals are in the
Santa Barbara Mission archives with copies in the Huntington and

Bancroft Libraries.

2224. Gibbs, Donald L. "Little-Known Latin American Manuscripts at the University of Texas." *Latin American Research Review* 27 (1992): 146-164.

Gibbs has prepared a checklist of manuscript collections acquired by the Nettie Lee Benson Latin American Collection since 1940. Specific collection titles appear geographically under country headings. Each collection mentioned has a brief content summary.

2225. Gonzalo Patrizi, Luis. "Documentos relativos a Venezuela que se conservan en The National Archives de Washington, 1835-1906." *Boletín de la Academia Nacional de La Historia* 32 (enero/marzo 1949): 81-98.

This is a checklist of documents found in U.S. Department of State files in the National Archives. The presentation is by year with each entry including names of correspondents or authors and a content summary.

2226. Haigh, Roger M., and Frank J. Sanders. "A Report on Some Latin American Materials in the Genealogical Library of the Church of Jesus Christ of the Latter-day Saints at Salt Lake City, Utah." *Latin American Research Review* 10 (Summer 1975): 193-196.

The authors review microfilmed civil and church records from Argentina, Chile, Guatemala, and Mexico. They report 113,903 rolls of microfilmed records dating from the 16th century.

2227. Hammond, George P. "Manuscript Collections in the Spanish Archives in New Mexico." In *Archives and Libraries: Papers Presented at the 1939 Conference of the American Library Association*, edited by A. F. Kaufman. Chicago: American Library Association, 1939. 80-87.

While Hammond does describe some manuscript collections such as the Blackmore Collection, the Benjamin M. Read Collection, the L. Bradford Prince papers, and the Twitchell Collection, he also devotes nearly one-half of this essay to New Mexico's territorial and county records.

2228. Haring, Clarence. "The Pizarro--la Gasca Manuscript Collection in the Huntington Library." *Huntington Library Quarterly* 18 (August 1955): 409-414.

Haring describes the library's 3,000 pages of original letters and papers documenting Gonzalo Pizarro's rebellion against Pedro de la Gasca who represented Spanish authority in Peru. The documents date from 1544 to 1554.

2229. Hart, Francis R. "Spanish Documents Relating to the Scots Settlement at Darien." *Proceedings of the Massachusetts Historical Society* 63 (1931): 154-168.

The author lists, chronologically, ninety-one documents copied, mostly at the Archivo General de las Indias at Seville, Spain. Entries include date, place of origin, correspondents' names, and content summaries. The documents date from 1698 to 1700.

2230. Hébert, A. Otis, Jr. "Resources in Louisiana Depositories for the Study of Spanish Activities in Louisiana." In *The Spanish in the Mississippi Valley, 1762-1804*, edited by John F. McDermott. Urbana: University of Illinois Press, 1974. 26-37.

The author describes Spanish records at the Louisiana State Museum; the New Orleans notarial archives; Loyola University at New Orleans; the New Orleans Public Library; Tulane University; the state archives at Baton Rouge; Lousiana State University; and many other locations.

2231. Hoffman, Paul E. "New Numbers for the Stetson Collection." *Florida Historical Quarterly* 55 (January 1977): 347-351.

The author provides a conversion table for pre-1929 references to documents in the Stetson Collection of photostated Spanish records at the University of Florida to current archival citations for the original documents.

2232. Holmes, Oliver W. "Managing Our Spanish and Mexican Southwestern Archival Legacy." *Southwestern Historical Quarterly* 71 (April 1968): 527-541.

Holmes locates and comments on projects microfilming the key collections of Spanish and Mexican records in the U.S. He also cites many of the published guides that describe these records.

2233. Hussey, Roland D. "Manuscript Hispanic Americana in the Ayer Collection of the Newberry Library, Chicago." *Hispanic American Historical Review* 10 (February 1930): 113-118.

This is a checklist presented alphabetically by author and including title or type of document, the document's length, and dates. Some entries have brief content statements.

2234. Hussey, Roland D. "Manuscript Hispanic Americana in the Harvard College Library." *Hispanic American Historical Review* 17 (May 1937): 259-277.

A comprehensive list, at the time, of Hispanic manuscripts in the Widener Library at Harvard. Hussey subdivided the list under America; Spanish North America; Spanish South America; Brazil; the Antilles; and maps.

2235. "Index to the Spanish Judicial Records of Louisiana." *Louisiana Historical Quarterly* 6 (July 1923): 311-340.

This is more a guide than index. It begins in volume 6 and continues through volume 31 in 1949. Entries are detailed and include case titles or identifiers, abstracts of the cases, dates of documents, and extensive notes and comments.

2236. Liebman, Seymour B. "The Abecedario and a Checklist of Mexican Inquisition Documents at the Henry E. Huntington Library." *Hispanic American Historical Review* 44 (November 1964): 554-567.

The article describes a collection of forty-six volumes of Spanish-language documents relating to the Inquisition in Mexico, 1525-1811. The article concludes with a checklist noting the contents and dates of each volume.

2237. Lihani, John. "Spanish Archival Documents in Special Collections at the Margaret I. King Library." *Kentucky Review* 6 (Summer 1986): 74-88.

Lihani describes the topical nature, physical characteristics, and content of over 900 Spanish documents dating from the 12th to the 18th centuries.

2238. Lombardi, John. "Lost Records of the Surveyor-General in California." *Pacific Historical Review* 6 (December 1937): 361-371.

Lombardi reviews some Spanish land grant records relating to California, along with some early 19th-century San Diego municipal records. Most of the land grant records were destroyed in the 1906 San Francisco earthquake. These land records date from the 1850s.

2239. Love, Joseph. "Sources for the Latin American Student Movement, Archives of the U.S. National Student Association." *Journal of Developing Areas* 1 (January 1967): 215-226.

Love reviews the informational contents of the association's archives as it relates to Latin American countries. The archives are in Washington, D.C., and contain correspondence, reports, manifestos, and constitutions relating to student groups.

2240. Lyman, Susan E. "Latin Americana in the Society's Collections." *New York Historical Society Quarterly Bulletin* 28 (January 1944): 11-20.

The article describes both book and manuscript holdings. Lyman limits her description of manuscripts to collection and record series titles and inclusive dates. Most of the materials relate to Mexico with some Caribbean and Central American collections too.

2241. Manning, Mabel M. "East Florida Papers in the Library of Congress." *Hispanic American Historical Review* 10 (August 1930): 392-397.

Manning describes a collection of 65,000 documents relating to Spanish Florida during the period 1784 to 1821. She lists the more important archival subgroups and comments on key documents.

2242. Marks, Patricia H. "The Scholar as Sleuth: The Charles Carroll Marden Collection of Spanish Manuscripts." *Princeton University Library Chronicle* 46 (Spring 1985): 292-308.
    Marks discusses the provenance of some 15th-century Spanish legal documents and a group of 18th-century Spanish municipal documents collected by Marden and now at Princeton University.

2243. Martin, Lawrence. "South American Cartographic Treasures." *Quarterly Journal of Current Acquisitions* 1 (January 1944): 30-39.
    Martin describes twenty-two 18th-century Spanish manuscript maps along with a group of facsimile maps from Spanish archives dating from the 16th century.

2244. McClaskey, Josephine Y. "Inquisition Papers of Mexico. II. The Trial of Luis de la Cruz, 1656." *Research Studies* 15 (March 1947): 3-107.
    This is the second of a two-part series on Mexican Inquisition papers held by the Washington State University Library, Pullman, Washington. See entry 2250 below for part one.

2245. McLean, Malcolm D. "The Bexar Archives." *Southwestern Historical Quarterly* 50 (April 1947): 493-496.
    A brief account of the archives provenance and a summary of their content, along with a progress report on their processing and translation at the University of Texas at Austin.

2246. McWaters, D. Lorne, Bruce S. Chappell, and Michael Getzler-Eaton. "A New Guide to Sources of Spanish Florida History." *Florida Historical Quarterly* 56 (Spring 1978): 495-497.
    This article reports progress on a guide to Spanish records at the University of Florida. It also provides summaries of the East Florida papers, the Stetson Collection, and the Papeles Procedentes de Cuba, the three main collections of Spanish records about Florida.

2247. Merrill, William S. "Transcripts from the Spanish Archives at the Newberry Library, Chicago." *Illinois Catholic Historical Review* 2 (July 1919): 82-84.
    Most of the copied documents are from the mid- to late-18th century and relate to Spanish activities along the gulf coast and in Texas, New Mexico, and Arizona. Others are concerned with the Mississippi River valley, the West Indies, and the Philippine Islands.

2248. Munsterberg, Margaret. "Manuscripts on the West Indies." *More Books* 4 (October 1929): 313-321.

This article describes a few individual manuscripts from the West Indies Collection created by Benjamin P. Hunt. Most of the letters and documents mentioned relate to 17th- and 18th-century Haiti.

2249. Nachbin, Jac. "Descriptive Calendar of South American Manuscripts in the Northwestern University Library." *Hispanic American Historical Review* 12 (May 1932): 242-259; (August 1932): 376-386; (November 1932): 503-521; 13 (February 1933): 124-142; (May 1933): 267-280; (August 1933): 403-419; and (November 1933): 524-542.
   This serialized calendar was intended as a guide to the Donato Lanza y Lanza Collection of Bolivian papers at Northwestern. The coverage, however, is only for the colonial portion (1574-1799) of the collection.

2250. Nunemaker, J. Horace. "Inquisition Papers of Mexico. I. The Trial of Simón de León, 1647." *Research Studies* 14 (March 1946): 3-87.
   This is the first of a two-part series on Mexican Inquisition papers held by the Washington State University Library, Pullman, Washington. See entry 2244 above for part two.

2251. Patterson, Jerry E. "Manuscripts Relating to Peru in the Yale University Library." *Hispanic American Historical Review* 36 (May 1956): 243-262.
   This article is a checklist presented alphabetically by subjects, authors of documents, or collection titles. Entries also include dates, length, and location within the library. Patterson concludes the article with a name index.

2252. Patterson, Jerry E. "South America in the National Period: Manuscripts in the Yale Library." *Revista Interamericana de Bibliografía* 8 (April/June 1958): 135-140.
   A checklist of letters and documents authored by fifty-two 19th-century Latin Americans including Simón Bolívar, Juan José Flores, Antonio Nariño, Bernardo O'Higgins, José Antonio Páz, José Manuel Restrepo, Francisco de Paula Santander, Antonio José de Sucre, José Vargas, and others.

2253. Patterson, Jerry E. "Spanish and Spanish American Manuscripts in the Yale University Library." *Yale University Library Gazette* 31 (January 1957): 110-133.
   Patterson describes three key collections, those formed by Domingo del Monte, Hiram Bingham, and Henry Raup Wagner. The article concludes with a checklist of the manuscripts. Entries include author or title, dates, length or volume, and content notes.

2254. Platón, Jaime S. "The Spanish Archives of Laredo." *Texas Libraries* 22 (January/February 1960): 12-13.

Platón calls attention to a group of Spanish and Mexican records dating 1755-1846 transferred from Laredo, Texas, to the state archives in Austin. He limits description to record series titles.

2255. Pollak, Felix. "The Spanish American Collections at Northwestern University." *Hispanic American Historical Review* 35 (November 1955): 499-501.

Pollak briefly describes the Donato Lanza y Lanza Collection of Bolivian manuscripts accumulated by Nicolás Acosta.

2256. Proctor, Samuel. "Research Opportunities in the Spanish Borderlands: East Florida, 1763-1821." *Latin American Research Review* 7 (Summer 1972): 8-23.

A historiographical essay citing many published materials. The article closes with a listing of manuscript collections and Spanish records relating to Spanish Florida, mostly in the P. K. Yonge Library.

2257. Robertson, James A. "Spanish Manuscripts of the Florida State Historical Society." *Proceedings of the American Antiquarian Society* 39 (April 1929): 16-37.

Robertson describes Spanish records copied at the Archivo General at Seville, Spain. His description includes dates covered by the records, record series, information contained in the records, and their research values.

2258. Rogers, Paul Patrick. "The Spanish Civil War Collection." *Library Chronicle of the University of Texas at Austin* New Series 7 (Spring 1974): 87-101.

While mostly published materials, pages 95-97 list and briefly describe photographs, diaries, posters, and ephemera relating to the Spanish Civil War.

2259. Santos, Richard G. "An Annotated Survey of the Spanish Archives of Laredo at Saint Mary's University of Texas." *Texana* 4 (Spring 1966): 41-46.

Santos relates the provenance of these records and provides a general description of them. He follows this with a container list of the records and corresponding reel numbers of a microfilm set.

2260. Santos, Richard G. "Documentos para la historia de México en los archivos de San Antonio, Texas." *Revista de Historia de América* 63/64 (enero/diciembre 1967): 143-149.

The author provides a checklist of three archival groups, the Bexar Archives; the records of the Parish of San Fernando; and the records of San Agustín de Laredo. Entries include record series titles, volume statements, and inclusive dates.

2261. Schwaller, John Frederick. "A Catalogue of Pre-1840 Nahuatl Works Held by the Lilly Library." *Indiana University Bookman* 11 (November 1973): 69-88.

Most of the citations are published books. The article, however, concludes with a checklist of manuscripts written in Nahuatl.

2262. Spell, Lota M. "The Mier Archives." *Hispanic American Historical Review* 12 (August 1932): 359-375.

In the first part of this article, Spell reviews the career of José Servando Teresa de Mier Noriega y Guerra and discusses the research value of his papers. The article concludes with a calendar of the papers (1820-1822). Calendar entries include content notes.

2263. Strout, Clevy L. "Literary-Historical Treasures in the Thomas Gilcrease Institute of American History and Art." *Hispanic American Historical Review* 43 (May 1963): 267-270.

Strout identifies several manuscripts, most of which relate to colonial Mexico. The author includes dates, the names of authors or correspondents, and comments on the content and significance of the documents.

2264. Taylor, Virginia H. "Calendar of the Letters of Antonio Martínez, Last Spanish Governor of Texas, 1817-1822." *Southwestern Historical Quarterly* 59 (January 1956): 372-381; (April 1956): 473-486; 60 (July 1956: 80-99; (October 1956): 292-305; (January 1957): 387-400; (April 1957): 533-547; and 61 (July 1957): 125-146; (October 1957): 288-304.

This series lists 904 letters from Martínez to the viceroy of New Spain. The entries include place of origin and content notes. Generally, the letters document conditions in Texas during the period that Martínez was governor.

2265. Thompson, Nora. "Algunos manuscritos guatemaltecos en Filadelfia." *Anales de la Sociedad de Geografía e Historia* 23 (marzo/junio 1949): 3-10.

Thompson lists and describes manuscripts, mostly 17th-century, held by the American Philosophical Society. The manuscripts fall into two categories, religious or linguistic. Entries include title, author, date, and content notes.

2266. Tyler, Daniel. "The Carrizal Archives: A Source for the Mexican Period." *New Mexico Historical Review* 57 (July 1982): 257-267.

Described are municipal, state, and federal records dating from the 1820s to the 1930s from the town of Carrizal, Chihuahua. They include correspondence, court records, and military records. The University of

Texas, El Paso, has a microfilm set.

2267. Van den Eynde, Damian. "Calendar of Spanish Manuscripts in John Carter Brown Library." *Hispanic American Historical Review* 16 (November 1936): 564-607.

This is a detailed listing, with indexes, of individual documents bound into three volumes that were once part of the Sir Thomas Phillipps Collection. The papers are 18th-century documents relating to Spanish administration in the Americas.

2268. Van den Eynde, Damian. "The Franciscan Manuscripts in the John Carter Brown Library, Providence, R.I., U.S.A." *Archivum Franciscanum Historicum* 31 (January/April 1938): 219-222.

This article calls attention to four groups of manuscripts called the Pueblo de los Angeles papers; the Huexotzingo papers; the Tlaxcala documents; and the Temeluca papers. The author describes the contents of each and comments on their research values.

2269. Weber, David J. "The New Mexico Archives in 1827." *New Mexico Historical Review* 61 (January 1986): 53-61.

The article concludes with an inventory of the legajos in the archives. The information in the article is more useful in tracing the provenance of surviving New Mexican records than describing them.

2270. Whigham, Thomas L., and Jerry W. Cooney. "Paraguayan History: Manuscript Sources in the United States." *Latin American Research Review* 18 (Winter 1983): 104-117.

The authors cite and analyze the research potential of collections at the University of Texas, Austin; Miami University; University of California, Riverside; University of Louisville; the Library of Congress; the National Archives; University of Kansas; and others.

2271. Williams, Shafer. "The G.R.G. Conway Collection in the Library of Congress: A Checklist." *Hispanic American Historical Review* 35 (August 1955): 386-397.

George Robert Graham Conway was a British engineer who lived in Mexico and researched and collected Spanish colonial documents, especially those relating to the Inquisition. This article is a checklist of the materials he donated to the Library of Congress. See entries 2073, 2074, and 2208 also.

2272. Wright, J. Leitch, Jr. "Research Opportunities in the Spanish Borderlands: West Florida, 1781-1821." *Latin American Research Review* 7 (Summer 1972): 24-34.

Mostly a historiographical essay citing published materials, but Wright closes the article with a review of archives and libraries holding manuscripts and Spanish records concerning western Florida.

2273. Ynsfran, Pablo Max. "Catálogo del archivo de don Lucas Alamán que se conserva en la Universidad de Texas." *Historia Mexicana* 4 (octubre/diciembre 1954): 281-316; and 4 (enero/marzo 1955): 431-476.

A serialized catalog listing documents, writings, reports, and correspondence written by or collected by Lucas Alamán, one of Mexico's leading 19th-century statesmen. Entries include dates, names of correspondents or authors, and places of origin.

Index

Burr, Aaron:
  correspondence of, 23
  papers concerning, 1077
Burr, Nelson R.: 506, 1316
Burrus, Ernest J.: 2038
Burton, Clarence M.: 1555
Burton, Clarence M., Historical Collection
  (Detroit Public Library):
  Canadian papers in, 2183
  Dutilh family papers in, 176
  French records in, 2124
  holdings of, 1555, 1675, 1694
  Sanders, Robert, papers in, 177
  Seymour, Horatio, papers in, 1619
  Wayne County resources in, 1652
Burton, Shirley: 613-1
Bush, Robert D.: 1708, 2133
Business-related collections: 117-317, 1436,
  1534, 1547, 1548, 1610, 1629, 1669,
  1724, 1762, 1809, 1815, 1820, 1828,
  1843, 1844, 1864, 1876, 2056, 2061,
  2123
Butler, Pierce, papers of, relating to the
  U.S. Constitutional Convention: 1135
Butler, Stuart L.: 534
Butow, Robert J. C.: 1009
Butt, Marshall W.: 1323
Butterfield, Lyman H.: 1190
Butterfield, Margaret: 1161
Butterworth, Keen: 792
Byrd, Cecil K.: 793, 794
Byrd, William, songs of: 736
Byron, George Gordon, Baron, papers
  of: 940

Caddo Indians, papers of agents to: 390
Cadenhead, Evie E., Jr.: 2208
Cahn, Walter: 1452
Cahokia, Ill., records of: 1597, 1633, 1634,
  2123
Cahoon, Herbert: 795, 796
Cahoon, John M.: 1830
Cain, Melissa: 684
Cain, Robert II.: 482
Calderón Quijano, José: 2039

Caldwell, Erskine, papers of: 983
Caldwell, Norman W.: 1556, 1557
Calhoun, John C., correspondence of: 22,
  1181
California:
  art-related collections in, 651
  British-related collections in, 2190, 2192
  broadcasting collections in, 634-11
  court record collections in, 1326
  crime-related records in, 1833
  education-related collections in, 1408
  ethnic collections in, 326, 349, 400
  European sources for the history of, 2049
  federal records relating to, 545, 557, 598
  French-related collections in, 2190
  Italian-related collections in, 2139
  Jewish collections in, 435, 436
  legal collections in, 1330, 1338
  literary collections in, 771, 773, 786, 789,
    849, 937, 954, 959, 960, 1005
  medieval and renaissance manuscripts
    in, 2172
  Mexican records in, 2201, 2223, 2236
  Mexican sources for the history of, 2088
  motion picture-related collections
    in, 634-11, 681, 703, 719, 720, 726,
    729
  organized labor collections in, 256, 259,
    273-19, 266, 273-4, 273-7
  Paraguayan collections in, 2270
  performing arts collections in, 627
  photographs of, 1829
  political collections in, 1133, 1156
  Portuguese-related collections in, 2134
  religion-related collections in, 1893, 1898,
    1935, 1937, 1938, 1941, 1942, 1946,
    1961, 2018
  repositories, holdings described, 1815,
    1817, 1818, 1821, 1822, 1824, 1827,
    1829, 1830, 1831, 1832, 1833, 1834,
    1836, 1837, 1838, 1839, 1842, 1846,
    1848, 1849, 1853, 1854, 1855, 1857,
    1858, 1861, 1863, 1866, 1867, 1869,
    1870, 1871, 1874, 1877, 1880
  Russian sources for the history of, 2053

described: 94
Haverford College (Philadelphia, Pa.):
  Indian-related collections at, 410
  Quaker-related collections at, 1959,
    1969-3
Hawaii:
  Hawaii-related collections in, 1414,
    1416, 1417, 1422
  indexes to Hawaii-related collections,
    1421
  literary collections in, 774
  missionary collections in, 1420
  papers relating to shipping in, 254
Hawkins, Mary Ann: 556
Hawthorne, Julian, papers of: 780
Hawthorne, Nathaniel:
  letters of, 802
  manuscripts of, 796
  papers of, 797, 890
Hawthorne, Sophia Peabody,
  correspondence of: 461
Hayden, Carl T., papers of: 1235, 1236
Hayes, Benjamin, papers of: 1846
Hayes, Catherine: 1335
Hayes, John D.: 1062
Hayes, Rutherford B., papers of: 1208,
    1209, 1210, 1223
Hayes, Rutherford B., Presidential Center
    (Fremont, Ohio), holdings of: 1194,
    1208, 1209, 1210, 1223
Hayman, David: 854
Hayman, John G.: 2184
Haynes, F. Jay, photographs by: 81
Haynes family, papers of: 1876
Haynes, John E.: 273-13
Hayter, Early W., Regional History Center
    (Northern Illinois Univ.),
    holdings of: 1581
Haywood, Carl: 2103
Haywood, Dolores: 1945-8, 1945-9,
    1945-10
Head, Edwin L.: 1849
Health fields, collections and papers relating
    to: 1293-1309, 1548, 1768
Heaps, Jennifer D.: 529, 558

Heard family, papers of: 156
Heard, John P.: 557
Hearst, Charles, papers of: 936
Hearst, James, papers of: 936
Hébert, A. Otis, Jr.: 2230
Hébert, John R.: 56
Hebrew manuscripts: 441
Hecht, Arthur: 1109
Heckewelder, John, papers of: 414, 2025
Hedges, James B.: 141
Heffron, Paul T.: 269
Heiman, Monica: 855
Heindel, Richard H.: 1471
Heiss, Willard C.: 1970
Hellman, Lillian, papers of: 987
Helms, Douglas: 197
Hemingway, Ernest, letters and papers
    of: 818, 996
Hemlow, Joyce: 2185
Henderson, Cathy: 856, 857
Henderson, George: 628
Henderson, Thomas W.: 1746
Hendrick, George: 858, 859
Hendricks, William O.: 142, 143
Hendrickson, Gordon O.: 860
Henle, Fritz, photographs by: 52
Henshaw, William, orderly book of: 1018
Hensley, Glenn S.: 105
Hepburn, William M.: 861
Hergenhan, Laurie: 862
Hergesheimer, Joseph, papers of: 966
Herrick, Robert, papers of: 826
Herring, Jack W.: 863
Herron, George D., papers of: 1156
Hershey, Lewis B., papers of: 1027
Herzstein, Robert E.: 18
Heuser, Frederick: 1971
Hickerson, Joseph C.: 1589
Hicks, Muriel A.: 1972
Hidalgo del Parral, Chihuahua, microfilmed
    Spanish records from: 2197
Hiden, Martha W.: 1336, 1337
Hidy, Muriel E.: 144
Higbie, Charles: 1264
Higgins Library (Univ. of California-Davis),

Leland, Isabella G.: 1949

Leland, Waldo G.: 655

Lemke, W. J.: 151

Lemmon, Amos, farming journals, kept
by: 204

LeMoël, Michel: 2047

Lennes, Greg: 213

Lennox, Charlotte, correspondence of: 876

Lentz, Lamar: 1754

Lenzen, Connie: 1859

León, Simón de, Inquisition papers relating
to: 2250

Leonard, Kevin B.: 1612, 1980

Leonard, Levi O., railroad collection
of: 301

LeRoy, Bruce: 1042, 1860

Lesueur, Charles Alexandre, sketchbooks
of: 646, 655, 675

Leutze, Emanuel, papers of: 671

Levant, The, photographs of: 53

Leventhal, Herbert: 1089

Leveson-Grower, R. H. G.: 2071

Levitt, Stephan H.: 2107

Levy, Newman, theatre collection of: 713

Lewes, George Henry, Collection,
described: 846

Lewinson, Paul: 274

Lewis and Clark Expedition, papers relating
to: 1545

Lewis, Jim G.: 892

Lewis, Meriwether, papers of: 1441, 1545

Lewis, Sinclair:
correspondence of, 839
papers of, 808

Lewis, Tab: 273-16

Lewis, William B., correspondence of: 1191

Lewis, William D.: 74, 1482

Lewis, Wilmarth S.: 1483

Libby, Charles A., photographs by: 78

Liberia, Episcopal missionary papers
concerning: 1945-8, 1945-10

Librarianship and librarians, records relating
to: 1256, 1257, 1265, 1271, 1409

Library Company of Philadelphia (Pa.),
Indian-related collections at: 410

Library of Congress (Washington, D.C.):
Abbe, Cleveland, papers in, 1382
Africa-related sound recordings in, 2104
Afro-American collections in, 342, 350,
354
American Red Cross photograph collection
in, 1266
Andersen, Hans Christian, papers in, 838
architecture collections in, 1279
Archive of Hispanic Culture in, 670
Arnold, H. H., papers in, 1044
Arthur, Chester A., papers in, 1219
aviation collections in, 305, 306
Baker, Ray Stannard, papers in, 1315
Brady, Mathew B., photographs in, 1118
British foreign policy papers in, 33
cartoon collections in, 622
Cattell, James McKeen, papers in, 1393
Cleland, Thomas Maitland, papers in, 635
Conway, G. R. G., Collection in, 2271
copyright records in, 1351
CSA army muster rolls in, 1107
Daniels, Josephus, papers in, 1314
Eaker, Ira C., papers in, 1045
East Florida papers in, 2241
Edison, Thomas, motion pictures in, 721
Einstein, Albert, manuscripts in, 1363
Franklin, Benjamin, scientific manscripts
in, 1378
French-related collections in, 2132, 2161,
2165
Frewen, Moreton, papers in, 228
Gallaudet, Thomas and Edward, papers
in, 1282
German-related collections in, 2153
Gershwin, George, manuscripts in, 737,
739
Hale family papers in, 299
Harrison, Benjamin, papers in, 1230
history of science and technology
collections in, 1384
Housman, Alfred Edward, papers in, 816
Howard of Effingham, Baron, papers
in, 2188
Hughes, Charles Evans, papers in, 1353

records of: 344, 1784
Mason, Dorothy E.: 900
Mason, Glenn: 78
Mason, Jeremiah, papers of: 1241
Mason, Lowell, papers of: 749
Mason, Philip P.: 272-8, 273-20, 273-21, 277, 278
Mass Communications History Center (Madison, Wis.), holdings of: 1264
Mass media collections: 1260, 1264
Massachusetts:
  African-related collections in, 2097
  architecture collections in, 1479
  Brazilian-related collections in, 2234
  British-related collections in, 2181
  court records collections in, 1331, 1340, 1346, 1347
  ethnic collections in, 364
  federal customs records in, 497
  history of science collections in, 1370
  Japanese-related collections in, 2102
  Jewish collections in, 440
  legal collections in, 1325, 1328
  literary collections in, 784, 821, 822, 876, 890, 893, 903, 904, 909, 962, 973, 1004
  medical-related collections in, 1304
  military-related collections in, 1016, 1017, 1018
  music collections in, 732, 736, 768
  natural science collections in, 1377
  organized labor collections in, 273-10, 273-23, 273-26
  political collections in, 1129, 1159, 1177, 1188, 1195, 1206, 1216
  Portuguese-related collections in, 2129
  religion-related collections in, 1930, 1975, 1993, 1997, 2004, 2005, 2023, 2024
  repositories, holdings described, 1446, 1463, 1478, 1484, 1487, 1496, 1506, 1516, 1517, 1528, 1529
  scouting papers in, 1269
  shipping-related collections in, 254
  Spanish-related collections in, 2234
  state records of, 25

  theatre-related collections in, 688, 724
  whaling-related records in, 1472
  women-related collections in, 458
Massachusetts Anti-Slavery Society, papers related to: 364
Massachusetts Historical Society (Boston):
  China-related papers at, 247
  Howell, William Dean, papers at, 909
  Jefferson, Thomas papers at, 1188
  legal collections at, 1328
  manuscript collections at, 1506
  medical-related collections at, 1304
  playbill collection at, 688
  religious dissenters' papers at, 1997
  ships logs at, 246
Massie, Larry: 1341
Masters, Edgar Lee, papers of: 952
Masterson, James R.: 398
Mathematics, papers relating to: 1362, 1364, 1366, 1368, 1390
Mathes, W. Michael: 1863, 2088
Mathews, Thomas: 516
Mathis, Guy, photographs by: 88
Matson, Eric, photographs by: 57
Matthews, Linda M.: 161
Mattson, Francis O.: 658
Maury, Matthew Fontaine, records of: 544
Maxwell, Richard S.: 576
Maxwell, Robert S.: 215, 1762
May, Anne C.: 901
May, Lynn E., Jr.: 1988
May, Samuel, papers of: 364
Mayer, Dale C.: 453-1
Mayerson, Charlotte L.: 659
Maynard, Richard and Hannah, photographs by: 1829
Mayo, Peter, cartoons by: 667
Mazuzan, George T.: 162
McAdoo, William Gibbs, papers of: 1146
McAneny, Marguerite L.: 902
Mcaulay, Neill: 1063
McAvoy, Thomas T.: 1924, 1925
McCabe, James M.: 163
McCain, William D.: 577
McCall, Nancy: 1305

French-related collections in, 2124

lumbering collections in, 206, 229

Mexican-related collections in, 2199

military-related collections in, 1069, 1092

organized labor collections in, 272-8,
272-13, 273-21, 273-32

Polish immigrant records in, 425

political collections in, 1160, 1164

religion-related records in, 1899

repositories, holdings described, 1555,
1564, 1567, 1598, 1607, 1619, 1642,
1652, 1660, 1674, 1675, 1694

state records of, 25

Michigan State University (East Lansing):
folklore collections at, 1567, 1589

organized labor sound recordings at, 260

Michigan Technological University Library
(Houghton), archival holdings of: 1642

Middle East, photographs of: 52, 57

Middleton, Arthur P.: 29

Mier Noriega y Guerra, José Servando
Teresa de, papers of: 2262

Milhollen, Hirst: 1117, 1118, 1266

Military Government for Germany, records
of: 439

Military-related collections and papers:
1008-1068, 1654, 1672, 1681, 1768,
1786, 1812

Miller, David H.: 1245

Miller, Edwin H.: 461

Miller, Harold L.: 272-9, 273-8

Miller, J. G.: 279

Miller, J. Wesley: 630

Miller, James C.: 1019

Miller, James E.: 30

Miller, Paul, papers of: 1313

Miller, Samuel, papers of: 1896

Miller, William B.: 1990

Miller, William W., papers of: 140

Miller, Winlock W., Jr., papers of: 1178

Millie, Elena: 705

Mills and milling:
flour, papers relating to, 202

lumber, records of, 195

textile, records of, 238, 243, 244

Mills, Hazel: 1864

Mills, Todd: 1865

Milner Library (Illinois State Univ.), special
collections in: 1625

Milutinovic, Iris, papers of: 908

Miner, Dorothy E.: 1495

Ming, Virginia: 1765

Mining, gold, records relating to: 2209

Minnesota:
business collections in, 164

ethnic collections in, 404

federal land records in, 494

flour milling collections in, 202

microfilmed European collections
in, 2168, 2169, 2186, 2874

military-related collections in, 1052

organized labor collections in, 272-12,
273-35

Polish immigrant records in, 422, 432

political collections in, 1137, 1158

railroad-related collections in, 307

religon-related collections in, 1991

repositories, holdings described, 1591,
1603, 1604, 1605, 1606, 1641, 1689

women-related collections in, 455

Minnesota Eugenics Society, records
of: 1158

Minnesota Historical Society (St. Paul):
autograph collections at, 1603, 1604

business collections at, 152, 164

farmers' diaries at, 214

Lind, John, papers at, 1137

Stevens, John Harrington, papers at, 1605

women-related collections at, 455

Mirror Interviews, index to: 634-13

Mission records:
California, 1824, 1831

Texas, 1787

Missionaries, papers relating to: 1165, 1884,
1886, 1901, 1907, 1931, 1932, 1945,
1948, 1967, 1968, 1974, 1978, 1991,
2012, 2023, 2024, 2025, 2069, 2117

Missions:
China, records relating to, 2203

Spanish, records relating to, 2078, 2200

music collections at, 1533

Southern Labor Archives (Georgia State
Univ.), organized labor records
in: 272-2, 273-9

Southern Ute Agency, records of: 412

Southey, Robert, papers of: 910

Southwest Collection (El Paso, Texas Public
Library), holdings of: 1757, 1795

Southwest Collection (Texas Tech Univ.),
holdings of: 1731, 1761, 1809

Southwest Museum (Los Angeles, Calif.),
Maynard photograph collection at: 1829

Southwestern Missouri State University
(Springfield), organized labor records
at: 273-15

Soviet Union, WWII poster collection,
described: 1022

Spaatz, Carl, papers of: 1033, 1043

Space travel, papers relating to: 1365

Spain:
America-related manuscript maps in, 2046
civil war in, papers relating to, 2258
French maps of Mississippi in, 2076
Illinois-related records in, 1645, 1676
Louisiana-related records in, 1750, 2075,
2085
records and papers from,
in Arizona, 2197
California, 1842, 1869, 2172, 2201,
2218, 2223, 2228, 2236, 2238
Connecticut, 2251, 2252, 2253
Florida, 2198, 2211, 2222, 2231,
2246, 2256, 2257, 2272
Illinois, 2207, 2233, 2247
Indiana, 2202, 2203
Louisiana, 2127, 2130, 2140, 2211,
2214, 2230, 2235
Massachusetts, 2234
Mississippi, 2210, 2211
New Mexico, 2227, 2269
Oklahoma, 2208, 2263
Pennsylvania, 2265
Rhode Island, 2267, 2268
Texas, 2200, 2245, 2254, 2259,
2260, 2264

U.S., 2212, 2219, 2229, 2232, 2259
Washington (state), 2244, 2250
Washington, D.C., 2241
U.S.-related records in, 2082, 2083,
2084, 2086, 2087, 2092

Spanish Archives of Laredo (Tex.),
described: 2254, 2259, 2260

Spanish borderlands, papers relating to:
2036, 2038, 2077, 2079, 2081, 2082,
2083, 2087, 2088, 2090, 2091, 2092,
2094, 2207, 2210, 2211, 2212, 2219,
2247, 2256, 2272

Spanish maps in Washington, D.C.: 2243

Spanish mission records:
in California, 1824, 1831, 2223
Texas, 1787

Spanish Naval Museum (Madrid), Puerto
Rico maps in: 2050

Spanish-American War:
enemy records seized by U.S.
during, 2205
Illinois soldiers in, 1013

Spann, Marcella: 970

Sparks, Jared, Collection, manuscript maps
in: 1072

Speck, Frank G., papers of: 414

Spector, Ronald H.: 1023

Spehr, Paul C.: 721

Spell, Lota M.: 2262

Spence, Thomas H., Jr.: 1887-3

Spencer, Helen Foresman, Museum of Art
(Univ. of Kansas), photographs at: 106

Sperry-UNIVAC, records of: 167

Spijkerman, Henri: 2056

Spingarn, Arthur, papers of: 354

Spivacke, Harold: 758

Spofford, Ernest: 1518

Spokane, Portland, and Seattle Railway Co.,
records of: 308

Spokane, Wash.:
church records in, 1891
photographs of, 78

Springer, Nelson P.: 2014

Springfield, Ill., photographs of: 88

Spungen, Norma: 445

Williams, Elisha, papers of: 1286
Williams, G. Mennen, papers of: 1160
Williams, Harry: 1255
Williams, Jeanne, papers of: 811
Williams, Joan B.: 368
Williams, John: 1526
Williams, Lewis J., papers of: 1768
Williams, Marvin D., Jr.: 2031
Williams, Richmond D.: 190
Williams, Roger, papers of: 1520
Williams, Shafer: 2271
Williams, Stanley T.: 998, 999
Williams, William Carlos, papers of: 834, 835
Williamson, John G.: 2178
Wilson, Allison: 612
Wilson, Althea G.: 1000
Wilson, Angus, papers of: 906
Wilson, Don W.: 613
Wilson, J. Christy: 12-6
Wilson, Joan Hoff: 478
Wilson, Louis R.: 1811
Wilson, Steve: 1692
Wilson, William E., photographs by: 83
Wilson, Woodrow, papers of: 1184, 1185, 1192, 1228
Wiltsey, Thomas E.: 1356
Winans, W. Park, papers of: 1820
Winant, John G., papers of: 567
Winder, William H., papers of: 1029
Winfrey, Dorman H.: 764, 765, 1812, 1813, 2032
Wing, Donald G.: 1001
Wing, John D.: 191
Wing, John M., Foundation, records of: 1270
Winkler, Paul W.: 1178
Winschel, Terrence J.: 1123
Winterthur Collection, described: 190
Winther, Oscar O.: 1149, 1693
Winthrop College (Rock Hill, S.C.), women-related collections at: 449
Winthrop family, papers of: 1462
Wirt, William, papers of: 1193, 1784
Wisconsin:

ethnic collections in, 348, 413
literary collections in, 348
mass media collections in, 1264
medical-related collections in, 1307
natural science collections in, 1377
poster and propaganda collections in, 630
religion-related collections in, 1929
repositories, holdings described, 1539, 1576, 1577
state records of, 25
theatre collections in, 634-4, 679, 702
Wisconsin Center for Film and Theatre Research (Madison), holdings of: 634-4, 679, 702
Wisconsin State Historical Society (Madison):
business collections at, 184
Georgia-related collections at, 1539
Indian-related collections at, 413
map collection at, 55
McCormick, Cyrus Hall, Collection at, 208
organized labor records at, 268, 272-9, 273-8
Wise, Thomas J., correspondence of: 963
Wister, Owen, photographs by: 54
Witek, John W.: 2122
Witham, Barry B.: 634-13
Withington, Mary: 192
Witkowski, Mary K.: 273-34
Witten, Cora W.: 766
Witten, Laurence C., II: 27, 766, 767
Witthoft, Brucia: 676
Wittman, Elisabeth: 1309, 2033
Wolf, George D.: 1179
Wolfe, Richard J.: 1531
Wolfe, Thomas, papers of: 893
Woltz, L. O.: 1694
Women:
anthropologists, 1407
artists, 641
Catherine the Great, letters of, 1495
fine arts, 632, 639
literary collections, 778, 799, 809, 811, 813, 818, 829, 830, 843, 845, 846,

About the Compiler

DONALD L. DEWITT is Curator of the Western History Collections at the University of Oklahoma. He has been an archivist and manuscript curator for over twenty-five years and is the author of several articles on archival administration. He is the author of *Guides to Archives and Manuscript Collections in the United States: An Annotated Bibliography* (Greenwood, 1994), which complements this volume.

ISBN 0-313-29598-0

90000>

EAN

9 780313 295980

HARDCOVER BAR CODE